JEFF MILTON: A Good Man with a Gun

JEFF MILTON

A Good Man with a Gun

By J. EVETTS HALEY

with drawings by HAROLD D. BUGBEE

UNIVERSITY OF OKLAHOMA PRESS : NORMAN

By J. Evetts Haley

The XIT Ranch of Texas and the Early Days of the Llano Estacado
(Chicago, 1929)
Charles Goodnight: Cowman and Plainsman (Boston, 1936;
Norman, 1949)
George W. Littlefield, Texan (Norman, 1943)
*Charles Schreiner General Merchandise, The Story of a Country
Store* (Austin, 1944)
Jeff Milton: A Good Man with a Gun (Norman, 1948)
Life on the Texas Range (Austin, 1952)
Fort Concho and the Texas Frontier (San Angelo, Texas, 1952)

Dedicated to MILDRED TAITT MILTON
whose sparkling mind and warm devotion
brought utmost happiness to
this good man with a gun
and
whose deep regard for truth
promoted this book

Where Trails Begin

"I never killed a man that didn't need killing; I never shot an animal except for meat."

These words by Jeff Davis Milton, in modest answer to those who took him for a Western gunman, were apt and honest retort. And yet for almost seventy active and adventurous years his confident gamble with death against the most dangerous men in the West was his quick and sure grip on the handle of his gun. Upon the frontiers of Texas, Arizona, and Old and New Mexico, he had met the worst, from John Wesley Hardin to Bronco Bill Walters, and not a one had beat him.

More remarkable than that perfect physical combination of muscle, eye, and brain, which, coupled with courage, made great gunmen, however, was the civilized code of honor that sustained him through the worst that human design and depravity could conceive and offer. He came of a notable family. There had been a poet, who labored well in spite of infirmity, in England. There had been a long line of statesmen and warriors here. Gentility was implicit in his raising; vigor was bred in his blood.

Healthy danger always tilted her happy head in invitation to him. From his boyhood home in a governor's mansion in Florida to his death and reversion to the dust of the desert in Arizona, eighty-five years later, he looked straight down the gun barrels of life and never wavered. Long and honorable tradition stood as a staunch support behind him. What should happen to him was the last thing to fear.

As a cowboy on the rawest edge of the buffalo range, as a Ranger facing horizons that fade into infinity on the Staked Plains of Texas, as an adventurer among the lawful and the lawless from the dobe dust of the Río Grande to the sunny slopes of the Sierra Madre, and as a veteran officer in lone patrol on the Arizona desert border, strong zest for life always rode the roughest trails in the saddle with him.

He was a healthy-natured American. He never knew a hardship, though his grueling routine, to say nothing of his many gunshot wounds, would have killed any but the hardiest of men. A strong, sensitive, and imaginative man, nothing in life was ordinary or prosaic to him. Whatever he touched in his gay, generous, and courageous way turned to high adventure.

Milton was a marvelous storyteller. But since his conversational style was strictly anecdotal, this pattern of his life and character has been traced with difficulty. He wanted no book about himself. But he had gone the gentlemanly limit—from aiding in their escape from the law to killing a dangerous enemy—for his best friends. I was one of his friends.

I met him first at a Texas Ranger reunion in 1932, in the gracious shade of a pecan grove on the head of the South Concho River, in a land for which he had fought fifty years before. This story was started in 1937 at the suggestion of Harrison Leussler, of Palm Springs, and the late Ira Rich Kent, of Boston. It is the result of eleven years of fascinating work upon Jeff Milton's seemingly fantastic trail.

My obligations, which extend from the Canadian River to the Gulf of California, are indicated in the footnotes. Mainly I have made my own materials by seeking out the old-timers who knew Milton, his land and times, and by reducing their reminiscences to writing. To begin with, Brockman Horne and I set reams of material down. Then Hervey Chesley joined me in the quest, for the love of vicarious adventure, and recorded hundreds of pages of memoirs, while my own longhand notes, made during twenty-two years of research work on this, my home range, furnished the base and background upon which the story is really built.

With entirely too generous nature, Lena Chesley has copied my oft-rewritten and always mutilated script. Frank King, cowboy author and friend of Milton for over sixty years, has given me a lot of help. Mrs. Edith Kitt and the late Dr. Frank C. Lockwood, of the Arizona Pioneers Historical Society and the University of Arizona, were graciously at my call, while John and Helen Murphey, on the edge of the desert, tendered a retreat for writing. My friend, Earl Vandale, out of the virility of his classically trained and hence cultivated mind, out of the ample recesses of his remarkable memory and the store of his great library, has always been at hand to stimulate and suggest, to prod and produce.

The story could not have been written except for the abiding interest of Mrs. Milton. She realized that such a character as her husband would be seized upon by lurid writers who manage to profit from if not portray the West. Out of concern for the enduring qualities of character and culture, and out of deep devotion to truth, she has always stood ready to help and never to hinder the penetrating exploration of his nature and career.

Whatever merit this book may have as history is due in large part to my great mentor and generous friend, Dr. E. C. Barker, of the University of Texas, from whom, in one brief classroom course and through long association since, I find that human tolerance and critical historical appraisal can and should go together. The only hope I hazard is that this unadorned life of a stranger to fear may truthfully be in keeping with the temper of the times and the mettle of the man.

The Texas State Historical Association, the most outstanding combination of devotion to tradition and regard for scholarly ideals in the whole country, has promoted my pursuit by grants in aid.

And at last, while I have been happily ranging the high trails of history through these trying years for thousands of miles on end, my wife and little boy have kept camp and cared for our cows on the Canadian, far away and often alone, to feed themselves and finance my venture.

J. EVETTS HALEY

Canyon, Texas

The Chapters

The Illustrations

XIII

JEFF MILTON: A Good Man with a Gun

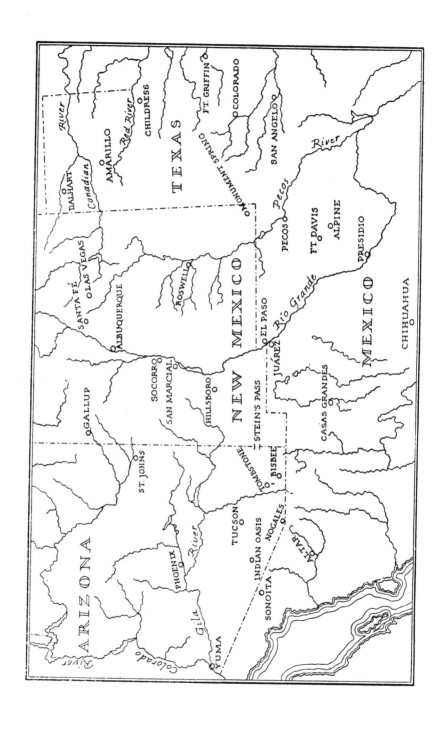

1

Jeff Davis in Florida

This story begins in Florida while the spirit of war was in the Southern air. The leisurely ways of life were disturbed by grave impending dangers. As if this were not enough, the spacious plantation home of Sylvania, near Marianna, was tense with domestic problems as well. Somehow word spread by the elusive grapevine that Jeff Davis "had arrived," and weighed and worried by the magnitude of the problems they faced, the local political leaders rushed to see him. And there Governor John Milton, of Florida, stepped across the colonnaded veranda to meet them, and, to their evident embarrassment and his obvious pride, admit that the report was true. Jeff Davis Milton, his youngest son and not the President of the Confederacy, "had arrived" at Sylvania.[1]

In this troubled world some fortunate few, with celestial detachment, claim to have been born under benign and lucky stars. Others stress subtle prenatal influence of environment as a potent factor in life. Still others point to strong bloodlines, to heredity, as the compelling force in shaping human destiny. All might claim proof of their convictions in the turbulent, the happy, the tempestuous life of Jeff Davis Milton. In a way he was lucky, if the happy laugh and lack of concern for danger and death that sustain the gallant and brave through hazardous adventure be luck. Again, the foreboding incidents preceding his birth could be taken to foreshadow the violence of the life that was to sweep around his rugged frame. And at last, no doubt, the strong blood that burned in his own virile veins had grown lusty and bold through long generations before him. As far back as their memory ran, the Miltons had been men of derring-do. Little Jeff would prove true to the tradition.

[1] This story was told by Mrs. Elise Gamble, Jeff Milton's oldest sister. Mrs. J. D. Milton to J. E. H., December 14, 1942.

At first it might be thought that he had little in common with that distinguished and distant relative, the great blind poet of England. Yet civilized taste and regard for the classics laid a strong hold on generations of Miltons. His great-great-grandfather, John Milton, had crossed from England about 1730 to locate in Halifax County, North Carolina, and other John Miltons had followed in due course and time. His great-grandfather —also John Milton—served as the first secretary of state in Georgia, saved the Georgia records from the hands of the British during the Revolution, and received the complimentary votes of the Georgia electors for the presidency in 1789. Statesmanship was traditional, while added regard for the culture of settled ways was found in the life of Homer Virgil Milton, Jeff's grandfather, a planter and an officer in the War of 1812.

His son, the future governor of Florida, was born on April 20, 1807, educated at Louisville, Georgia, and settled there to the practice of law. While living in Columbus, he "had to kill a man in a duel," according to a family story not often told; and from there he moved to Mobile, Alabama, and then to New Orleans, practicing law at both places. In 1845 he went to Florida and settled on a plantation some six miles out of Marianna, in Jackson County, which he named Sylvania,[2] where he gained the reputation of being "not only the most successful planter, but the most successful lawyer in this section of the state." In 1850 he entered the legislature, was proposed for the supreme court in his state, but shortly retired from politics until the vital issues of 1860 brought him out for the office of governor.

In spite of his devotion to law and politics, General John Milton, as he was generally known when elected governor of Florida, was a warrior at heart. His grandfather had been a captain in the Revolution, his father a colonel in the War of 1812, and in 1836 he had headed a company raised at Mobile called the "Alabama Artillery," which rendered distinctive service in the Seminole War, following which he had superintended the removal of some 2,500 Indians to Arkansas. Thus the Miltons

[2] From an undated Florida newspaper clipping detailing his career during the campaign for governor of Florida in 1861. J. D. Milton files.

4

were more than men of policy; they were men of action as well.

As governor, John Milton's ardor for the rights of the states was tempered by a judicious grasp of the problems of the entire South, so that he "gave the Confederacy a greater measure of co-operation than was usual among Southern Governors." He was vigorous and active in his defense of Florida and indicated he would much rather be fighting in the field than engaged in statecraft at home. No halfway measures were in his make-up. As the fortunes of the Confederacy ebbed, he "remained defiant, opposed to all peace proposals that left the independence of the Confederacy unrecognized, and, upon the collapse of the Southern cause . . . he destroyed his own life."[3]

He was married twice. Of his second marriage, to Caroline Howze, who was born in Lewisburg, North Carolina, March 20, 1825, ten children were born. The youngest of these, born on November 7, 1861, at the beginning of the Civil War, was named Jeff Davis. Hence it was not an implausible story, when the Governor was discovered missing from Tallahassee, that he had gone to Sylvania to meet the President of the Confederacy; and it was strictly in keeping with the political mind that there was an exodus from the capital to Sylvania to see him. Instead, they saw a day-old baby cuddled in the ample arms of his black mammy, Aunt Alice—the Jeff Davis who, in after years, recalled with a touch of precocious humor that "I had to laugh at their faces."

His only genuine recollection of his father, however, was the happy toss high into the air and the welcome landing in his resilient hands when the Governor happened to be with his family at the sunny plantation, and later the somber runner who caught up with his mother's carriage and bade her and little Jeff Davis hurry back to the shocked and saddened Sylvania. The incident was not without its sober symbolism. A long and virile line of leaders was passing, a cultivated way of life was changing, a gentle and gracious culture dying. Tragedy was written upon the docket of the times.

[3] Clipping, as quoted; *Dictionary of American Biography* (New York, 1934), XIII, 21; and "John Milton, Governor of Florida," by Daisy Parker, *Florida Historical Quarterly,* April, 1942, 346–61.

And yet out of the hopelessness and despair that seized those of age came the eager, ebullient, unconquerable spirit of a youth, who in the face of it all just "had to laugh." His sense of humor was simply a sense of perspective; his lust for dangerous living and high adventure a part of a strong tradition that would not die in spite of the wreck of his material world.

In the case of the landed Miltons the losses of war seemed irreparable. Sylvania was an extensive holding of more than 7,000 acres dependent upon the labor of many black hands, co-ordinated under the skilled management of one white man. The large, long, two-storied palatial home with the encircling veranda was approached through an avenue of shade, cast by magnificent water oaks. Acres of lawn lifted on a slight grade to the house; the grounds alive with "dogwood, several species of plum, sassafras, and many flowering trees and shrubs," and flowers too —"verbenas, oxalia, violets, white lilies, and azaleas."

The home was offset to the rear by other houses—the dwelling and office of the overseer. On a low hill about a half-mile behind was a row of two- and three-room houses where more than fifty slaves lived. There were barns, a blacksmith shop, and a big smokehouse to take care of the entire establishment's needs for meat. Beyond were large orchards of apple, peach, and pear. Still farther were the fields of corn, peanuts, cane, potatoes, and, most important of all, that fleecy crown of the Southern economy—cotton. Memory, substantiated by the record, paints the picture as a happy home.

Jeff Davis grew up under the indulgent care of his devoted mammy, Aunt Alice, and as the unappreciative recipient of the sympathy of seven older sisters who had "known better times." They had enjoyed the refinements of good education, travel, leisure, and comfort. Jeff Davis would never know what he had missed, and what they failed to realize was that Jeff Davis, in his happy zest for life, would never care.

On the whole, the Milton Negroes were a settled lot, who, for a while after "freedom came," continued in the service of the Milton family. Jeff's mother directed the plantation with the help of Overseer Whatley and when the big house that had graced the lush land with peaceful living burned to the ground, she moved the family into the near-by plantation schoolhouse and carried on her multiple duties from there. "We had the best bunch of niggers in the world," said Jeff, "and mother kept as many as she could feed. When I was twelve years old, I could plow a furrow as straight as anybody. We had to work." But the wild fire of a vigorous and prankish youth, of tempestuous fancy and an adventurous spirit, fitted Jeff Davis but poorly for the solid and settled life of a farmer. He remembered more of the pranks he played than the crops he raised.

Near by, Blue Springs boiled up out of the earth in a great, pellucid pool and flowed away more boldly than a Western river. When Jeff was about six years old, his brother John, some ten years older, threw him into the middle of this gushing flood, where he could hardly sink but where anyone might drown, and yelled at him to swim out. Finally the force of the water, after rolling him over and over, deposited him on the bank, and Jeff dragged himself away, even at that tender age "nursing his wrath to keep it warm."

The plantation was equipped with horse-powered cotton gins, and once when "Brother John" made him good and mad, Jeff vented upon him the choice language for which the Southern tongue and temper seem peculiarly fitted. John told his mother. She sent little Jeff Davis to the peach orchard for a sizable switch and administered that rigorous discipline that the proprieties demanded. But Jeff was still mad, and when he got back to the gin where "Brother John" was turning out the lint, he stirred up a nest of yellow jackets. The first thing John knew, "he was in the middle of them, and he was really a-moving! And so was I!" Jeff added.

Mrs. Milton supported a school on the plantation for her own and the neighboring children. Jeff attended, but on account of his irrepressible spirits he was what might have been termed a bad boy, or more lately "a harmful influence," while Mrs. Milton's Spartan rule, "Whipped at school; whipped at home," left a well-beaten trail to the peach orchard.

Communion at the Marianna Episcopal Church was calcu-

7

lated to assuage the tragedy and offset the violence of the times. Kneeling at the altar with his family for the first time to partake of "the Body and the Blood of Christ," little Jeff received the sacrament first. He grasped the sizable goblet of wine in a firm hand, but instead of taking his sip and passing it on, he drank it dry, to the consternation of his proper elders.

Meanwhile other influences had been brought to bear. The Southern life he knew was not measured and serene, but it was close to the soil. Men knew and mingled with the growth of the earth. Jeff liked to get out. He hauled the corn to Coker's mill to be ground into meal when flour was one hundred dollars a barrel and biscuits were a delicacy to be enjoyed once or twice a month. He always took his fishhooks along, and by the time the corn was ground, he was ready to start home with his meal and a mess of fish. He loved to fish, and once, when short of a catch, he substituted alligator, which, with flesh much like fish, Jeff claimed "is as fine as you ever ate." At home he turned the delicacy over to Mandy, their big, old Negro cook, saying, "Here, we cleaned this fish for you."

She took it a little suspiciously, commenting, "Yo ain't nevah done dat fo' me befo', Jeff Davis. Whut you do it dis time fo'?"

"Oh, I just thought it would be convenient for you," said Jeff, benignly.

When Mandy found no bones, she again voiced her doubts, but Jeff reassured her—he had cut them all out. So Mandy fried the "catfish" and found it delicious, until Jeff, the interested bystander, could withhold the joke no longer and told her it was alligator. Now to a Southern Negro an alligator was a horrible thing that would bob up in the swamps, mouth a-watering every time a dog would bark, and next to dogs was supposed to prefer a diet of pickaninnies. Jeff's mirth was quickly ended with an alligator strap across his back.

Besides small game, there were bear and deer back in the thickets; and when he was about twelve years old, he was taken on a hunt by his brother John and some friends. A few took stands at convenient clearings, while others, with dogs, beat the brush to stir up the game. That morning they put Jeff out just to fill up

8

space, at a stand where a deer "would never run." Boy-like, he, absorbed with dreams of Daniel Boone and big game, had slipped out his rod and rammed it down the barrel to measure the depth of his load. He was startled by the hounds rending the humid air at his very elbow. Out into the clearing came a splendid deer and Jeff shot him through and through, ramrod and all, his load proving heavy enough. The hunters came up to dress his prize, and before he knew it, they had slipped the emptied maw over his head, an olden ceremonial to initiate the novice into the ranks of seasoned hunters.

It cannot be forgotten that long wars are followed by spells of violent readjustment, and in the South this harsh period of some ten years' time is spoken of, simply but significantly, as the "Reconstruction." Even for the son of a governor, life was not all a serene round of farming and fishing, nor the diet always that of corn pone and catfish. Aunt Alice might rouse him from bed each morning to a bright new world by singing:

> *Get up Jacob*
> *Day is breaking;*
> *Peas in the pot,*
> *Hoe cake baking,*

but that sunny salutation from this old darky could not always dispel the somber realities of their bitter world.

Carpetbaggers, those political parasites of Reconstruction who contributed their opprobrious term to American idiom, were in control of the public offices. Out of ambition for power and perverted philanthropy, they incited the Negroes and intimidated the whites. The reaction was that famous extra-legal organization riding the black night in shining robes called the Ku Klux Klan. It spread throughout the South. Marianna had it, too. Jeff, burrowing in his brother's wardrobe in childish curiosity, discovered John's hidden habiliments of membership, but was afraid to disclose his find.

Jeff was still a little fellow dressed in an Ossenberg shirt when he, too, beheld the terror that the Klan struck into the simple souls of the credulous. Among the local leaders was a husky,

9

wild young veteran of the war, Sergeant Barnes, who, with two other masked and robed members, rode up to the Milton home one day. They caught little Jeff and old Uncle Wallace, one of the Milton Negroes, near the well. Both were too scared to move. The leader swung down with an ominous grace and asked Uncle Wallace to draw him a bucket of water. Taking the bucket from his shaking hands, the substantial specter in white deliberately emptied it without removing it from his lips, while Jeff and the darky gaped in amazement.

Then he held it out to the servant and said, "Uncle, I am very dry. Give me another bucket. I haven't had a drink of water since I was killed in the battle of Shiloh." The wooden bucket clattered at the Negro's heels as he fled in abject terror, and Jeff recalled that he was not far behind.[4]

Upon occasion the Klan broke up meetings of the Negroes and carpetbaggers, and when two of these hyphenated Yankees killed a Marianna man, the citizens marched into the court-house, carried some of them out, and hanged them in the gracious shade of the water oaks. Federal soldiers were sent, but they, as Jeff recalled, "were pretty decent men." Still it was not safe to sit before a lighted window at night. Heavy shades covered those in the Milton home, and the evenings were spent in darkness.

Once Jeff's brother placed a shotgun in his hand and told him to come along. Jeff took the gun and went. His brother stationed him in the yard in front of Judge Bush's home while he and his fellow Klansmen marched across the street and into the court-house to get a man. All Jeff was instructed to do was to shoot anybody who came through the gate. "Nobody came through," Jeff said. "I was glad, for they'd of got a load of buckshot for sure. That's what they told me to do; that's what I would have done."

Not always was he thus resolute and brave. Ghosts and graves bothered him for years. Once he was passing the Marianna graveyard at night, whistling to keep up his courage. It had

---

[4] Jeff guessed that Barnes had a pouch connected with his mask, into which the water poured. At any rate this trick was used by the Klan to impress the Negroes with their supernatural power, according to that late authority upon the South, C. W. Ramsdell.

been the habit of a woman who had lost her husband to make frequent trips to the cemetery, and just as Jeff was passing, she rose from kneeling at the grave. His keen black eyes saw that apparition in white rise from the ground, and of all unearthly things a voice called, "Jeff!" It was a good long heat from there to sister Elise's. Jeff made it in record time.

He toughened his system by chewing tobacco until his mother caught him. "Jeff Davis, come here a minute," she called, severely. As he started to stoop over and spit out the evidence, she checked him: "Don't you spit anything out." Jeff swallowed hard and obeyed. "Have you got tobacco in your mouth?" she asked. "No, Ma'm," said Jeff Davis. And when his open mouth supported his good word and the examination was closed, Jeff left posthaste for Sister Carrie's, but was vomiting violently before he reached that sanctuary of sympathy.

And yet out of that life of violence, in which, as a boy, he could take his part, there soaked into the fabric of his being the culture of the South epitomized by his own people. A genuine grace polished off the steely nature beneath; a grace suggested by his admiration for an old gentleman named Guyton—"the most polite man I ever knew," he said. As a boy he used to follow Guyton down the street, "and when he took off his hat to a lady, I tried to do just the way he did." Guyton would have been proud of his prodigy in good manners. This was no perfunctory gesture to the proprieties of the times. In gallant youth and in gracious age, Jeff Milton seemed to bestow the benediction of Southern gentility upon every lady he met.

He experienced additional schooling at Marianna. Algebra got under his skin instead of into his head, but he stayed with his studies until, as he put it, "the Latin ablative floored" him. When he outgrew school at home, he was sent to work for Lewis Gamble, who had married his oldest sister, Elise. Gamble had come to Florida with his father and with him owned and operated a store at Jackson's Landing, on the Chattahoochee River. And so at about fifteen years of age Jeff took his first job clerking in the store on the Chattahoochee.

Fishing was close at hand; and with his muzzle-loading rifle, longer than the hunter, and its sixty shots to the pound, he could knock a squirrel's head off every time. Meanwhile he had been reading, and the book he read most was the stirring story of Wallace and Bruce—*The Scottish Chiefs*. Over and over he read it until he cherished the virtues of Wallace, and really "burned to get hold of an Englishman." There were no English heads at hand, but the talk he heard was of the West—a far land of adventure, of daring and promise. That talk stirred afresh the fires set in his own heart by the bold exploits of Sir William Wallace. His youthful decision was made.

He would go to Texas and hunt outlaws; he would go to the frontier where the buffalo were. He would break with the settled Milton tradition; he would see the wild, unspoiled places; he would range afar. He would leave the land that his people had graced in cultured maturity, and had served so ably and well that their coat of arms was the mark and brand of civilized existence, of honored reputation, of patriotic service. With a vigorous independence bordering on irreverence, he later recalled, "The family had a coat of arms. I had it once but I throwed it away. Didn't need it. Had my own coat and my own arms."

That action was a portent of the future, and while the coat was rarely used, for he lived among men in shirt sleeves, his arms came into frequent play. And, thereby, at last, the escutcheon of the Milton warriors shone with a new luster, though he polished the shield in his own individualistic, unconventional way. After many battles that would happily have ranked him alongside Sir William Wallace and *The Scottish Chiefs*, he saw his own wild lands and times pass into a conventional mold that celebrated its Tombstone's Saturday nights with a contest in verse instead of in arms, and he registered his own lament:

Ah woe is me, that I should live this awful day to see,
When strong men fight with rhymes, not guns, ah woe is me.

12

2

To Texas

Jeff's mother managed their extensive plantation of Sylvania for years after the Southern tragedy symbolized by Appomattox and most intimately for the Milton family by the death of Governor John Milton. This period left little of the gracious way of life which the family had grown used to for several generations. Jeff's numerous, older sisters felt sorry for him. He had missed the bounteous board, the vivacious social life, the color and the charm that had been founded on impressed black labor and unrestricted acres of cotton.

Fortunately, however, healthy youth knows no problem except that imposed by its solicitous elders. Jeff was happy as a mud hen in the Florida Everglades. There was practically no "cash money," but there was plenty of simple food; there was the unfailing and refreshing fountain of youth in the wild life that flourished in the woods about him—where decrepit age had once sought rejuvenation; and there was deep passion in the changing times that reflected its somber shadows in the unlit windows at night.

For a boy who cherished the spirited exploits, the belegended chivalry, and the dauntless courage of Sir William Wallace, and dreamed wild dreams in the heavy air of Florida's woods, this was not enough. Western literature, travelers' tales, town talk, and youthful fancy turned him, heart and soul, toward that lodestar of excitement and adventure—the Lone Star State of Texas.

Texas, then half-settled, rough and ready and lusty and bold, was enough to fire the imagination of anyone who loved space above money, adventure above security, grass above crops! What these zestful youngsters who rode to do and dare failed to realize—and the semisophisticated age that followed seems incapable of comprehending—was that the frontiers, as Thoreau once intimated, are actually found in the minds and inhibitions of men. Adventure gravitates to men with great and courageous hearts, bold and inquisitive minds, vivid and creative imaginations. Life anywhere would have been adventure for Jeff Davis Milton. In the rugged hills, upon the sere plains, and in the frank and forthright cow towns of Texas, it could be nothing else. To Texas he must go.

That healthful process of "scatteration," the wide geographical dissemination of a large family in the ordinary process of marriage, helped him get started. His sister Mary had married "a little bitty man," as Jeff recalled, named Ed Everett, who "was a big bull among the Baptists." Everett, educated in law, had turned to teaching school in a place and at a time that called for robust discipline. He was a quiet but positive man from Florida who moved to Houston and took charge of a bunch of tough young men who habitually ran their teachers off. "Brother Ed" Everett, as Jeff always called him, simply took a six-shooter in one hand and a whip in the other, calmed the schoolhouse racket, and built a great reputation as a teacher in Texas. After thus distinguishing himself in frontier pedagogy, he turned to preaching and became a quite positive spiritual force among the Baptists, as Jeff has indicated.[1]

At one time Everett and his wife lived in that charming little town that sprawls among the scattered live oaks, on the bluebonneted prairies, above the murky waters of the Navasota. Jeff's sister Fannie came from Florida to stay with the Everetts and to teach school in Navasota. There she met Colonel James Quincy Yarborough, a native of Alabama, veteran of the Civil War, and a planter and merchant of Grimes County, Texas. He must have been a "typical Texan," for a contemporary account pictures him as "a man of strong likes and dislikes. There was not the slightest trace of the compromise element in his nature. He always took sides." He journeyed to Florida and asked Jeff's

[1] This Florida background was drawn from extensive notes made in conversation with Mr. Milton.

14

widowed mother for Fannie's hand, and upon their marriage he settled down to his mercantile business at Navasota.

He gave Jeff his first cigar. Notwithstanding that unfortunate adventure, Jeff adored this positive warrior from the rich plantation zone of Texas, and in the course of time his mother decided to let him live with Colonel Yarborough and Sister Fannie.[2]

Jeff was sixteen years old when, in 1877, he made the trip to Texas alone. He saw his first train at Eufaula, Alabama. The yellow fever plague had hit Memphis, as Jeff came west, through the town, but at its worst it hardly induced the temperature that he was running in his anxiety to reach Texas. At Navasota he settled dutifully to work at Yarborough's general mercantile, the largest store in town. But Navasota lay far from the frontiers of Texas, in a settled farming zone, and its adventurous living seemed salted away in the memories of the Texas Revolution and the War Between the States. Jeff stood the work for a year and then headed for the outside edge of Texas.

When his relative, Parham Yarborough, gave him a .44 Winchester, he and another boy named Allen Morrison bought a horse apiece and headed toward the frontier. In the Fort Griffin country they went to work for the "Sawed-Horn Cattle Company," an outfit owned by Billy Barry, nephew of old Buck Barry of Indian-fighting fame, by Captain Pete Hatchett, who was the boss, and by Ben Calhoun.

Calhoun and Barry had worked as bookkeepers for Colonel Yarborough, but had quit and joined Hatchett in establishing a ranch on the Clear Fork of the Brazos, some twenty miles above the abandoned ruins of Fort Phantom Hill, in what was then far West Texas. They bought longhorn cattle in Southwest Texas, sawed off their horns, and turned them loose on the wide-open Clear Fork ranges with plenty of room to spread into better beef.

[2] Jeff D. Milton to J. E. H., July 1, 1937; December 8, 1939; notes from John Quinn, December 11, 1943; and various MSS notes made by Mildred Taitt Milton.

Yarborough was born in Coosa County, Alabama, September 8, 1827, and died in Grimes County, December 23, 1890. At one time Wilson, Yarborough and Company had stores at Anderson, Yarborough, Navasota, and Tickle Foot, Texas. Earl Yarborough to J. E. H., June 30, 1945.

Hence the ranch came to be known as the "Sawed-Horn Cattle Company."

Now this was to Jeff's liking. With a horse between his knees, a Winchester on his saddle, and a six-shooter on his hip, he was at last out of the tall cotton and punching Texas cattle. Their headquarters was nothing but a dugout on the Clear Fork. When winter came in 1878, Captain Hatchett put him in a camp—a tiny tent—on California Creek, by himself, keeping horse camp. His *remuda*—the herd of saddle horses—ran to themselves out in the state of Texas. Everywhere, in that unsettled world, mustangs ran loose in wild, unbridled freedom. All Jeff had to do was to keep the gentle horses from being run off by the mustangs. But that was enough.

His work was made harder still by that peculiar quirk of nature which seems to make a wild animal want to lure the domesticated one away. Wild horses simply loved to fall in with the gentle ones. Then when a rider showed up, they threw up their heads, snorted, raised their tails, and took to the tules. "Shame on this tame life," they seemed to say to the gentlest horse. "Come with us. We will see the world. We will have some fun." And the most conservative old saddle horse would completely lose his head to this beguiling whinny, and set out as if he were determined to see the whole show in the next few minutes.

The horse wrangler rode a good fast mount, and when his *remuda* fell in with the mustangs, he rode to it, hell for leather, until the more conservative, gentle horses began to tire, and,

16

finally saying to themselves, "We are too old for this fast life," slowed down and let the seducers disappear in a cloud of wanton dust. Jeff daily circled his range, "cutting for sign," to see if mustangs had got into his herd. If they had, he repeated the chousing out process.

That broken, prairie country below the High Plains was still a part of the buffalo range. Fort Griffin had eclipsed Dodge City as the center of the buffalo trade, and Fort Griffin, down the river to their east, was likewise the trading headquarters of the Sawed-Horn Cattle Company. There Jeff saw buffalo hides piled like haystacks in Conrad and Rath's trading yards.

In that rough and ready town, greasy buffalo skinners bellied up to the bar alongside profane mule skinners; hide hunters checked in their bull, cow, and kip hides and took their lead, powder, supplies, and cash, in return; army scouts came and went on the trail of vagrant Indian bands, loose from the reservations, playing hide and seek around the cap rock of the Staked Plains; Texas Rangers broke the routine of weeks in camp farther west by leave in town; the vigilantes killed a few outlaws and put John Selman on the move; and Texas trail men and cowboys, high-hatted and high-hearted, tossed off the scanty pay and the superfluous energy of vigorous beefeaters at the saloons and in the dance halls. Here, to the most colorful and the toughest of the Texas cow towns, came eager-eyed Jeff Milton, fresh from the gentlest tradition of the Old South.

He joined "Cap" Hatchett in going to Griffin after supplies. Hatchett drove the wagon. Jeff, as befitted a proud young cowboy, rode a horse. They left town late, and Jeff rode ahead to kill their meat for supper. He got off the road and meandered farther ahead than he thought. At last he killed an antelope and tied its "saddle"—its hams and loins—against the cantle behind him. He turned back to the trail. Night came on, but not "Cap" Hatchett. Jeff, still just a lad of seventeen, was full of the tales of Indian fights. When the coyotes smelled his meat and began to howl, and were echoed in answer from every direction, he knew that they were Indians instead. Yet he made a fire, broiled a steak, and lay down on his saddle blanket with his old .44 rifle beside

17

him, prepared to die right there. At last the rumble of the wagon sounded the approach of Captain Hatchett, who was "kind of mad" because Jeff had wandered off so far, but sort of pleased that he had the meat.

Jeff was paid fifteen dollars a month. He furnished his own outfit, the tools of his trade—his saddle, bridle, bed, and guns—but the owners gave him a tent to sleep in and supplied him with flour, beans, coffee, soda, pepper, and salt. He killed his own meat. He did not have to hunt for it. He simply stepped out from his camp, drew a fine bead, dressed his kill, and threw a roast upon the coals. Deer grew fat in the shin oaks, usually known as the "shinnery," where the acorns could be garnered from the shin-high growth that partially anchors down the loose sand-country that lies along the Brazos west of Griffin. Turkeys by the thousands infested the stream beds. While back in the mesquite-grass flats, now largely covered with mesquite trees, were herds of antelope—the finest wild meat in the world.

Fort Griffin was still the bastion of a right sharply adulterated civilization on the outside fringe of Texas. Ranger Captain G. W. Arrington, from his base to the west in Blanco Canyon, scouted the country away into the New Mexico sand hills to the west. Cowmen were drifting toward the High Plains; Hank Smith was already at Mount Blanco; Pete Snyder had his trading camp on Deep Creek; and Teepe City, farther north, combined with them to describe a sort of a wavering arc of drifting but positive-natured humanity that pointed the way to the next bucolic settlement at Mobeetie, far up in the eastern Panhandle.

In between, except for the sheltered creek bottoms, was tree-less space. Beneath the rhythmic feet of their fox-trotting horses, the matted mesquite grass made a perfect carpet in the tight-land flats, sage and shinnery covered the sandy ridges, and buf-falo and grama grasses "haired over" the loamy soils that lay between the sand and the heavy land. Wire-stretchers were un-known, and posthole-diggers had not yet calloused and profaned the hands that rested lightly, with a sensitive touch, upon the bridle reins. The tensions of crowded and overwrought humanity were unknown, for people were scattered "some," and hence neighborly, friendly, and helpful to all who rode along.

As Jeff was coming out of the shin oaks one day in a snow-storm, he rode up to the hut of an old preacher, who, for some reason, had settled in that wild and apparently forsaken land. In the custom of the times he stopped for the night. At supper the hospitable host returned long and extreme thanks for their "bread and meat," but when Jeff looked down at the board, all he could see was corn-meal mush and mighty thin at that. Jeff thought of the generous blessing and the natural bounty of the land, and blurted forth, "Whut-uh-ye mean? All this game and no meat?"

The preacher replied that they had not had time to get any. This seemed strange, as turkeys were strutting at his back door. Next morning, Jeff, the generous provider, stayed over for a little while, went out and killed a couple of antelope and brought them in so that the old man's next blessing would be backed up with the substance of things thanked for.

Few men passed his way that winter, but those who did were remembered well. Frog Mouth, a Negro from Nick Eaton's ranch, rode by one evening, and as distances were long and the hour late, stopped to spend the night. It was too cold for him to sleep outside, so Jeff scrouged over to make room inside the tent on the ground for him. Ten days later Jeff was bothered with such a persistent itching that he was about to scratch himself "to pieces." He got out by the fire, pulled off his clothes, and found that he was infested with "gray-backs." Then he figured it out. Frog Mouth had sloughed off a few of the unwelcome guests for seed. Jeff had nothing in the way of camp equipment except a coffee pot and a Dutch oven. So for days he heated water in the coffee pot and scalded out his clothes, a patch at a time, which often froze while he was heating the next pot, until he had killed the last of the lice.

Once in a while, however, this simple routine of life was bro-ken by a trip to Griffin, and at least three men he came to know in the Clear Fork country as a boy were to cross his trail in later years. George W. Scarborough, blue-eyed, fair-faced, fighting

19

cowboy of the Clear Fork, was to join Jeff on many a man-hunt in later days. Together they were to meet the worst of bad men at El Paso in the time of John Selman, John Wesley Hardin, and others who took improper pride in their ability to kill; together they were to scour the Chiricahuas for Bronco Bill and Black Jack's band, together . . . but that is ahead of the story. Here Jeff met Gustave Peterson, a little South Texas Swede who became a soldier at Fort Griffin; a man as gentle natured and harmless as an honest old saddle horse. He was the antithesis of the fiery Scarborough but as deeply devoted to Jeff, and for a reason.

One night at Fort Griffin a rowdy was abusing the mild and unarmed Peterson. Jeff, strapping and idealistic youth, in the way of Sir William Wallace, came to Pete's protection. Pete was eternally grateful, and when, decades later and nearly a thousand miles farther west, that strange wild urge that sent the bold and rugged as well as the mild and diffident into the Arizona hills brought them together again, they met with genuine fraternal affection.

The last, and the most odorous, of all these individualistic men whose sign Jeff cut in the Fort Griffin country was old John Selman. He and John Larn ranched on the Clear Fork until Larn was killed by an outraged citizenry. Selman would have gone the same way, but Hurricane Minnie heard of the plans for their arrest, jumped on a horse bareback, and rode eight miles to Selman's ranch to warn him. Finally he reached El Paso and achieved further renown by shooting John Wesley Hardin. His dubious fame was short-lived, for George Scarborough presently did for him what many had previously prayed might be done for John Wesley.

At Fort Griffin, Jeff saw his first man killed when two buffalo hunters got into a fight. One had his gun out and the other was going for his, when someone yelled at Jeff to stop them. There was a shot, and blood and brains splattered all over Jeff, making him sick. He learned right there the importance of tending to his own business.

The bloodshed and violence of the little town were in strange contrast to the chastity and quiet of the open country. But together, they made up the frontier of Texas in the late seventies. And, as such, these were the times, and these the men, that made life on the Clear Fork interesting to Jeff Milton, and cast a portent of adventures to come.

He worked through with the general roundups in the spring, and then, with Allen Morrison, turned back toward the settlements of Texas. Like many other cowboys, they were broke before they got past Fort Griffin. They worked for a few days in an oat harvest near Brownwood, and at other places for their board as they headed southeast, toward the rich cotton lands of the Brazos Bottoms. At times they were downright hungry.

At last they passed Austin and laid out on the road to Manor, sleeping on their saddle blankets, pillowed on their saddles, on Walnut Creek. In the night Jeff felt a tarantula crawling on his neck. He brushed it off, but not before it had bitten him directly over the jugular vein. Soon the pain was almost unbearable, and he came near dying from the bite, at Manor, where a kindly village doctor treated him.

Soon afterward Jeff went to work for a farmer named Mooring, guarding Negro labor contracted from the penitentiary at near-by Huntsville. When he received his pay, he took it into Navasota and put it in the bank, just before it closed on Saturday. On Monday, thinking what a thrill it would be to draw a check against his first account, he struck out for the bank to experience it.

When he got there, he found the bank locked, with a notice on the door saying that it was closed for good. Jeff was disturbed. He talked with Dan Woods, the sheriff, to find out what the sign meant. Woods explained. Jeff said even if the bank was closed, *his* money must be there, for he had taken it in just before closing time on Saturday, and furthermore he intended to have it. Woods, a sympathetic Texan, showed Jeff an outside stairway against the building, suggested he hide under it until the bankers came down, follow close on their heels when they went inside, present his check, and demand his money. This sounded like proper business to Jeff. He did as suggested, but when he presented his check, the bankers told him they did not have the

21

money. Jeff pulled his gun and told them to hand it over, and as Woods sauntered in to witness the transaction, Jeff blandly said, "These fellows are cashing a check for me." And in spite of the condition of the bank, they found that his money was still there.

Thus he passed the time for a little while. Still Navasota and the Brazos Bottoms, interesting in their way, lovely as a location for a settled and sedate life, did not please the restless, imaginative, black-eyed Jeff Milton. He thought it over and decided that the life of a Texas Ranger was the stuff for him. Major John B. Jones had whipped that independent, individualistic group of frontiersmen into a model of deadly efficiency under a great aggregation of courageous captains. The time for his Frontier Battalion would soon run out, its noted leaders would soon be breaking away to take their individual trails, the frontier would soon be gone. But in that brief span of dauntless life and crimson glory that yet remained, Jeff still had time to test the tradition of the Milton warriors. He made up his mind and lit out at once.

3

"A-Ranging He Did Go"

On July 27, 1880, Jeff Davis Milton, sprouting a manly mustache designed in deception of his eighteen years, presented himself at the Adjutant General's office, at the Capitol, in Austin. He had come to join the Texas Rangers, and to Major John B. Jones, the meticulously exact, dynamic little man who dominated that office and the far-flung Frontier Battalion, he presented letters from leading citizens of Navasota—notably John Quincy Yarborough and H. H. Boone,[1] prominent lawyer, former attorney general of Texas, and one-armed war horse of the Civil War—attesting his manhood and character. This letter from Boone was enough, but the Texas law prescribed certain qualifications for a Ranger, among which was that of age.

"How old are you, sir?" asked Jones, after reading the letters.

"Twenty-one," answered Jeff, lying by a scant three years.

"You don't look it," said Jones, eyeing his mustache suspiciously, "but I think you'll make a Ranger."

"Orsay," he said, addressing his clerk, "swear this man in as a Ranger."[2] The clerk followed orders, and since Jeff did not have to swear to his age—which would have been too great a strain on his Southern honor—the ordeal was soon over and Jeff was definitely "in the service."

"Pretty young for a Ranger," he later admitted, "but boys were men before they were out of their teens in those days."

Jones immediately dispatched him to Swenson's Pasture on the edge of Austin, where the Rangers maintained a camp, and

---

[1] See N. G. Kittrell, *Governors Who Have Been and Other Public Men of Texas* (Houston, 1921), 69; E. L. Blair, *Early History of Grimes County* (Trinity, Texas, 1930), 137–38; Bentley and Pilgram, *The Texas Legal Directory for 1876–1877*, 42. He died May 23, 1897. Mrs. Susie Boone Wilson to J. E. H., June 30, 1945.

[2] Henry Orsay, clerk for General Jones.

23

where Jeff fell into the detail commanded by Sergeant Richard C. Ware, the man who had helped end the cyclonic career of that great Texas outlaw, Sam Bass,[3] just two years before. A felicitous fate had befallen Jeff. He found great and good men to emulate wherever he went. In Dick Ware he not only found an ideal of a resolute man of character but a worthy officer to follow, and Jeff must have basked a little proudly in the reflected glory of the man who had burned powder at the death of Sam Bass.

Up in Lampasas County, just above Austin, the Horrell and the Higgins factions had, during several years past, waged civil war from the courthouse square to the upper reaches of Sulphur Creek. The long-drawn feud had worn itself out with the shedding of considerable blood, but the passions that go with that gentle environment and its rangy Texan stock had not quite cooled. Four Horrell brothers had been killed besides a right smart sprinkling of men on the other side.[4] Sam Horrell, the least provocative and hence the last of as rugged a clan of fighters as ever looked down a gun barrel, was wanted in Lampasas County in 1880 on a charge of murder. He shook out his reins, and in company with Gus Stanley, charged with theft in the same county, and Tom Snow, an escaped convict, headed west toward New Mexico.

Out at Hackberry Springs, thirty miles southwest of where Colorado City now stands, was Company B, Frontier Battalion, of the Texas Rangers, under command of Captain Ira Long. Ware and Ranger Ed Hageman were in Fort Concho on July 5, 1880, and learned that Horrell and his party had passed through that day. They got word to Long on the seventh, and he left that evening with fifteen men for Camp Charlotte, on the head of the Main Concho, 115 miles south-southwest. Long spared neither time nor horseflesh, as he reached Camp Charlotte at three the next evening, took them all at once and sent them to Concho to await orders for their disposal. "What shall I do with them?" he wired by the post telegraph to Major Jones. "They

[3] Wayne Gard, in *Sam Bass* (New York, 1936); and Walter Prescott Webb, in *The Texas Rangers* (New York, 1935), 369 ff., have told the story well.
[4] James B. Gillett gives a good account of the feud in his book, *Six Years with the Texas Rangers* (Austin, Texas, 1921). See Webb, *The Texas Rangers*, 334 ff.

request to be taken to Austin as their lives would be in great danger in Lampasas County."

Sergeant Ware took them to Austin, conveyed Snow back to the stone walls at Huntsville, and returned to the Ranger camp at Swenson's Pasture, a mile and a half from town. There Jeff Milton joined him.[5]

Perhaps Horrell's fears of what might happen to him in jail at Lampasas were not quite groundless. Disregard for jails had almost become traditional in those stormy parts. The Horrells, themselves, had, in a pitched battle, delivered one of their brothers and a friend from the jail at Georgetown, where laws are traditionally observed and jails are designed to hold. That, however, was before two other Horrells were shot and killed in jail by a mob in Bosque County. Thus Sam Horrell's concern had precedent to sustain it. Anyway, the Rangers were sent to Lampasas to guard the jail while the captives came to trial.

They, too, understood that Horrell was to be mobbed and were ready for the show. Jeff conceived quite a liking for Horrell; and he told him that in case of a mob, he could take Jeff's extra gun "and step to them." At Lampasas a big crowd gathered at their camp in curiosity and stayed to watch them eat. "Give them room," Jim Swisher, one of the Rangers, ordered, "to watch the animals gormandize."

Soon John Bannister, another Ranger, was "shining up" to a local girl. Bannister got to meeting her at the well where the camp needs were supplied, until the boys decided that something stronger than thirst accounted for his interest in the sulphurous Lampasas water. Jeff caught on and picked up his Winchester one day when John left for the well. He waited in the brush near by until the tryst was done and John was headed for camp. As the young lady left, he stepped into the path ahead of her with his gun in the crook of his arm, greeted her, and cordially observed, "You're quite stuck on that convict, aren't you?"

[5] Ira Long to Jno. B. Jones, July 10, 1880; *ibid.*, July 12, 1880; "Monthly Return," Company B, August 31, 1880; Jno. B. Jones, Special Order No. 66, July 24, 1880—all in Adjutant General's Papers, Texas State Library, Austin. All contemporary references to MSS materials in this period are in the same papers unless otherwise noted.

"Why, sir, what do you mean," she exclaimed.
"That man's a convict," Jeff added, benignly. "Everywhere he goes we have to guard him."

Bannister could never understand why the romance that seemed to be flowering so nicely by the side of the well should wither so quickly, and Jeff was afraid to tell him. But soon the detail was on its way back to the camp of Company B, at Hackberry Springs, some 250 miles away, on the extreme frontier, leaving Horrell to the law and romance to those who did not "a-ranging go."

The last of the Horrells, however, made his escape from Lampasas. Years later Jeff rode up to a ranch in the Mogollons in western New Mexico and recognized Sam Horrell, who had settled there to live. He spent the night with him. While he knew that a big reward reposed on Horrell's head, he passed without sign of recognition. "Shuckin's," he said, "what was there to that?" Thus he proved again that the good peace officer tempered ruthless resolve with a measure of mercy, and rode the trails of danger and death for something besides money alone.

At the time he joined, the country the Rangers covered was "high and wide" if not "handsome." When they got back to Hackberry Springs, late in August, 1880, Sergeant Ware reported the "distance traveled 1,080 miles" on the Horrell, Stanley, and Snow detail alone. He might have added, except that it was then understood, one significant word—"horseback." Hence it is well to take a long look across those gentle undulations, the Staked Plains of 1880, and the life and the lack of life, that distinguished the seemingly endless terrain over which these young men ranged.

Almost through the center of Texas, to sketch their territory roughly, from just east of Wichita Falls down through the Breckenridge country and on through the Brady region, stretches a belt of sand that nourishes and delineates the western Cross Timbers of Texas. Beyond this growth of assorted oak lies what was then a gently broken grassland of little timber except along the water courses. Now, where this land "lies idle," which is an abominable designation for lovely grass, it is largely grown up in gnarled, twisted, and graceful mesquites. Sixty years ago every gentle slope between the streams was open country which unimaginative people have damned as "monotonous," but which stirred the spirits of real men with a feeling somewhat akin to that elation that seized upon Sir Walter Raleigh when he first gazed upon the marvelous grasslands along the Orinoco. If there be a direct relation between adventurers, freedom, and space, as has been claimed, no wonder then that these men who ranged this expansive land with boundless rims were ready to dare, to do and die.

Except for Tascosa in the western Panhandle, Mobeetie on its eastern edge, and a settlement of dry-land Quakers at Old Estacado in Crosby County, that doubtful aspect of civilization symbolized by the town still lay close to the Cross Timbers. Buffalo Gap was the picturesque seat of Taylor County, while the Texas and Pacific Railroad had just reached Weatherford on the first leg of its remarkable thrust across six hundred miles of unsettled land to El Paso, Texas. Near Fort Concho, the southern anchor of this semi-hemispheric band of ragged settlement, had grown the village of Benficklin, named for an old stage contractor, who, after braving the worst of Indians and highwaymen in the West, had died in the sedate East with a deadly fishbone in his throat. Benficklin washed away, and the settlement nearer the fort became San Angelo.

Athwart the southwestern arc of this frontier lay the Ranger camp of Hackberry Springs, a camp that came into being under that gentlemanly, diminutive but dynamic little captain from the Confederacy, June Peak. It was located upon some deep, catfish-filled holes in the southwest part of Mitchell County, tributary to the Colorado River and about thirty miles east of that truncated cone isolated from its parent Staked Plains called Signal Peak, near Big Spring. The buffalo were gone except for scattered bunches, but antelope covered the range in fleet-footed thousands, and turkeys were so thick around their camp that Jeff termed them a "nuisance." Deer were everywhere, and though it was "the most beautiful cow country in the world," only one ranch was then crowding upon them, an outfit owned by

27

Jim Lane and Tom Green, sons of two distinguished generals of Texas.[6] When the veterans discovered that a young and raw recruit had arrived with Dick Ware, Dave Ligon initiated him into the service. Dave was an educated man from Tennessee, and one of the best but undoubtedly the most profane man Milton ever knew. He was so terribly profane that the other Rangers would not sleep near him on stormy nights, when the lightning was bad, for fear that the Lord might strike Dave dead for the fearful maledictions he uttered, and that such heavenly intervention might take them in, too, by mistake. As soon as Jeff stepped off his horse at Hackberry Springs, Dave knelt down and uttered a long and eloquent prayer for the poor, ignorant recruit who had come to that wild land, and urgently implored the Lord to save him from ferocious Indians and fighting outlaws, in what Jeff said was the "damndest prayer I had ever heard."[7]

To say the least, it was a little disconcerting for the tenderfoot in camp, and not altogether reassuring about the future. But as

[6] Lane and Green were both from Austin. Tom Green had been a Ranger in Company A some years before, but quit the service and went to ranching. He later ranched in Mexico. W. H. Roberts to J. E. H., February 23, 1945; Sam Graham, "Reminiscences of . . . ," copy from Sam Graham, San Antonio (original in Texas State Library, Austin).

[7] Sam Graham, one-time Ranger with Jeff, told the story of one of his associates in Company A who got lost in the Nueces River bottom, in a thicket, one night. He was a very nervous man in the dark, and decided he'd pray, and the only prayer he could think of was "Now I lay me down to sleep"; but when he got that far, he stopped with the thought that that would never do, for it was surely no place to sleep. Sam Graham, "Reminiscences," 5.

28

for the fear of what Divine Providence might do to Dave, who defied the lightning, the Lord, and the angels, that fearsome faith of the young Rangers was later justified, even if in an inverse sort of way.

Oscar Oberwetter was a member of Company B who almost worshiped the eloquent and educated, if atheistic, Dave. Eventually they quit the Rangers and went up the cattle trail together. Oscar imitated Dave and tried to be just as tough as he was. In the midst of an electric storm a bolt stretched Oscar out on the ground, and all the water that fell in his face was not enough to revive him.

For the most part, however, they were of a reasonably reverent nature. Men who live close to the simple realities of life, to the wondrous processes of nature, and the sobering features of death, are usually so. And the life they lived was cut and fit to simple and strenuous lines.

Each man furnished his equipment—his saddle, ropes, guns, bedding, horses, and clothing. The broad-brimmed white hat upon his head, the heavy-buckled, cartridge-studded belt that carried the six-shooter on his hip, and the shop-made boots that encased his feet were the hallmarks of his trade. The Padgett Brothers, of Waco, were the biggest saddle makers in the state, and many a Ranger rode a "Padgett." Every little town had its bootmaker, and the best could be had for eighteen dollars, or less, a pair. The ornately stitched tops came with a later day. The Rangers rode with them high, almost to their knees, cut round at the top or dipped in a scallop like those of the present day. Not a man in Company B had chaps or leggin's, but everyone rode with his pants stuffed in the tops of his boots, and with "Mexican Chihuahua" or handmade Texas spurs eternally upon his heels. The pride in Texas spurs was Petmecky's, made in Austin, and from this pioneer shop came Jeff's first .44 pistol.

At that time the Ranger regulation for guns was the .44 Winchester carbine—the short-barreled "saddle gun," and the .45 Colt's six-shooter. Jeff happened upon this beautiful, silver-mounted .44 six-shooter at Petmecky's, the only one in town, and immediately bought it. "I thought I was just the king bee," he

29

said; ".44 pistol and .44 Winchester using the same shells. Some of the boys wanted to trade me out of it. I took it out to shoot, and at the first shot she hung tighter than Dick's hatband, and I had an awful time cocking it again. The next shot, the same way. The cap would come back and stop right against the firing pin, and you could not revolve the cylinder.

"I let all the boys know so they wouldn't buy any. At Fort Concho was a sort of an outlaw and gambler named Batty Carr, who used to rustle horses and mules from the government on the border. He had a beautiful .45 pistol. The handle of it was like a deck of cards—spades, hearts, diamonds, and clubs cut out of silver and inlaid in the handle. When I got back to Fort Concho, I kind of let it out that I had the .44. Batty Carr wanted it right now and wanted it bad. So I let him have it; traded it to him for his pistol."

Thus Jeff was armed. And the inlaid characters on his six-shooter were appropriate symbolism, even for a reverent man, for the steady grip of his hand on that six-shooter handle was his confident gamble for life through fifty long and venturesome years.

When the recruit joined, he was given a hundred shells, and the state furnished him twelve additional rifle and six pistol cartridges monthly. Like Jeff's old friend, Connally, who doled out the bullets to his boys in Florida and expected them to bring in a like number of squirrels "*shot through the head,*" Texas figured the Rangers could do the job with these. This may seem parsimonious in view of the later bounty of paternalistic states, but it is not in the record that the signboards and mailboxes of that day were riddled beyond recognition, though sometimes the culprits were. The Rangers were not armed for dramatic effect nor yet for sport. Bullets were for business.

The catalog of monthly rations, drawn for twenty men, suggests that neither were they there for the bounteous board that Texas spread, for, even with game, it was bound to have tested the ingenuity of the best camp cooks. It read:

243¾ lbs. bacon	25 lbs. salt
775 lbs. flour	11½ lbs. soda
71 lbs. beans	1¾ lbs. pepper
52¼ lbs. rice	180 lbs. potatoes
116¼ lbs. coffee	5¼ lbs. candles
116¼ lbs. sugar	
6 gal. vinegar	4,380 lbs. corn[8]

If his horse was killed in an Indian fight, by lightning, or by some other "act of God," the loss was strictly his own. There is a record of Jeff's being charged eighty cents for two pairs of horseshoes, all of which indicates that ranging, in the eighties, was not altogether a parade nor a picnic. But it surely was an experience in strenuous and dangerous living in a fresh and unspoiled land. That has always been inducement enough where the Anglo-Saxon blood runs strong.

Captain Ira B. Long, who succeeded Peak, was a quiet, large, heavy-set, active frontiersman of Young County. "I believe he was one of the most conscientious and fearless men I ever knew," said Jeff. "He wa'n't afraid of anybody. He could figure in his head faster than any man in the country, and he couldn't read or write."

He took the *Galveston News*, for years the leading paper of the state, which reached him by mail stage through Fort Concho, and then by Ranger post to Hackberry Springs. Jeff liked to read, and the Captain used to invite him down to his tent. Nobody knew that he could not read except his brother-in-law, Sergeant J. W. Adams, who wrote his reports. Jeff discovered the fact by chance. When he would come for the papers, Long would say, "Sit down here and read to me." If the story impressed him, he would add, "Now, Milton, read that over again. That is very interesting stuff."

"And after the second time I had read it to him," said Jeff, "for two or three months he could pick that paper up and recite the article verbatim, and I call that going some."

One day Jeff walked in and asked for a paper of a certain date. Long kept the papers stacked in his tent in order.

8 "Ration Return," Company E, July 31, 1881.

"Here it is," he said, picking one out of the pile.

"No, that ain't it," said Jeff. Long picked up another one and handed it over.

"No, that ain't it, either," said Jeff.

"Well, damn it, find it yourself," growled Long. Jeff did and started out.

"Come back here, Milton," he called. "You see I can't read?"

"Yes."

"I wish you wouldn't say anything about it," he asked, and Jeff observed his wishes.

"I never saw such a memory in my life," he recalled. "His first sergeant, Dick Ware, read his orders to him. Sergeant Adams wrote his reports. Nobody could beat him at figuring, but it was all in his head. I'm not saying he wa'n't an educated man. Truth was, he was."

Once a month a Ranger rode into Fort Concho and got the mail for the company, packing it back the eighty intervening miles in a tow sack. Jeff, prompted by a genuine interest in helping everyone out and spurred by boundless energy, wrote letters for one and all. Jim Swisher, of a pioneer Austin family, left many girls behind him, and Jim enlisted Jeff's romantic nature in correspondence. They framed missives in the gracious shelter of the whispering mesquites that would have melted hearts of stone, and generously scattered them to "only" girls back in the settlements. A month later, Jim, a rough, unprepossessing specimen of manhood who would "get red-headed" on provocation, called at the window of the grouchy postmaster at San Angelo and asked for his mail. From his looks nobody would have suspected that Jim got mail, and the postmaster barked, "No mail!"

"Damn you, I know it is here," swore Swisher with a mighty oath; "if you don't give me mail I'm coming in after you," and obviously he meant it. Hastily the official looked through his pack and shelled out a sheaf of fifteen to twenty letters.

From the Ranger service Swisher went north to become a sheriff in Wyoming. Years later Jeff was awakened at a hotel in San Antonio by an awful pounding on the door, and the imperious order to "open up or I'll break the door in."

32

"I'll cut you down, if you do," said Jeff, reaching under his pillow for his .45. When he opened up, there stood "an onery looking fellow with a game leg," and it was good old Jim Swisher.[9]

Among the men of Company B who interested Jeff most was a seasoned frontiersman from the Great Plains, and one of the oldest men of them all—"Buffalo Bill" Jenkins. N. L. Jenkins had scouted under Custer and Mackenzie. He was an immense, rawboned man of some forty years, and, no matter how cold the day, always wore his shirt open over his heavy chest of hair. He never wore undershirt, drawers, or socks, and the boys nicknamed him after his well-groomed counterpart from the Great Plains, "Buffalo Bill." He was a regular hulk of a man, and he covered the ground he stood on, which was a right smart space. Milton remembered him as one of the best shots, with the best wind, of any man he ever saw. He could run half a mile, stop, and draw as steady a bead with a rifle as if he had been standing still the while. He had a unique habit of orientation. He invariably lay down to sleep with his head to the north, even if he had to sleep downhill. In case of a surprise he rose to his feet from the deepest sleep with complete knowledge of where he was headed. Somewhere in Kansas he had some land, but he apparently favored fighting the Indians and outlaws of Texas instead of the grasshoppers of Kansas, for here he was, bigger than life, dangerous as a rattlesnake, and guileless as a child.

Jeff knew of his land because Bill could not write, and sometimes got Jeff to write his letters.

"Why in thunder don't you learn to read and write?" Jeff asked one day.

"I'm too old," said Bill with laconic finality.

"Shuckin's," thought Jeff.

On their next trip to Fort Concho, he bought a slate, a reader, and a Blue Back Speller. When idle in camps, he and "Buffalo Bill" would slip off into the mesquites and lie down on their stomachs in the grass, by the hour, while Jeff put his student

[9] Swisher enlisted along with D. L. Ligon, John H. Hoffar, and others, in June Peak's company, March 1, 1880. "Monthly Return," Company B, March, 1880.

through the elementary mysteries of "readin' and writin'," and, being an apt student, in three or four months he could sign his name. Eventually he could write a letter.

In the frayed and yellowed files of the Frontier Battalion, in the state library at Austin, rests an obscure letter of little moment in itself except that it touchingly illustrates the high purpose of a rough and rugged man. In struggling and erratic chirography it is signed: "N. L. Jenkins," and beneath, in clear-cut penmanship which might have been Jeff Milton's, this footnote to the Adjutant General: "This is N. L. Jenkins' signature."[10]

Anyone who wades through the mass of Southwestern frontier literature cannot but be impressed with the fact that there was more trailing and less killing of Indians than it takes to make volumes of books. Jeff almost got his first Indian. He and Bob Nevill were riding into camp one night, when Jeff, now well versed in Western stories, looked up a ridge and saw a chieftain's headdress, silhouetted in the moon.

"Bob, by Jacks, there's an Indian. I'll just slip up and kill that gentleman," whispered Jeff. Leaving Bob with the horses, Jeff, knowing the whole camp would be out at his shot and hence eager to have the scalp himself, crawled close. Just before he drew a bead, he discovered that instead of an Indian it was a Spanish dagger stalk, and he went back to Bob and the horses too disgusted for words.

When Long took charge of the company, a drought was on and the horses were in bad shape. He planned to strike northwest against the Indians and hoped to raise the company from twenty-six to thirty men. "I have promised to do all I can do with men and horses," he wrote to Major Jones. In the summer he laid

[10] These stories from Jeff D. Milton have, for the most part, been set down verbatim. They were elicited by the author during many visits with Mr. Milton, and faithfully set down, first by Brockman Horne, in stenotype, in the summer of 1937, and later by that tireless Texas interviewer, Hervey Chesley, in shorthand. They have been enlarged by copious longhand notes by the author, supplemented by letters and other earlier notes by Mr. Milton's wife, Mildred Taitt Milton. Quite often the stories are composites of several recountals, and hence detailed references to the Milton interviews are rarely given. The Horne and Chesley interviews, made in 1937, 1938, and 1939, number more than six hundred typewritten pages.
See N. L. Jenkins to Jno. B. Jones, September 2, 1880.

his plans for a scout across the southern segment of the Staked
Plains by Five Wells, Cedar Lake, Double Lakes, "and perhaps
to Monument Springs" in New Mexico. Already Captain G. W.
Arrington had crossed "the sands" west of the Yellowhouses,
and explored and named Ranger Lake and Four Lakes in the
same territory, farther north.[11]

Long took his men on various scouts across the plains, but in
that section the Indian menace was gone. In October, 1880, he
scouted to the Monument Spring, traveled 350 miles, and reported on his return: "no sign of Indians."[12] It was entirely too
quiet for a man of his temperament, and he tendered his resignation for mid-December. With genuine attachment for Jeff, he
called him into his tent, told him he was too young for that sort
of life, and advised him to resign and go back to the settlements.
They would get into business together, he said. With gratitude
Jeff declined.

Captain Bryan Marsh was sent to take Long's place. He was
a small man, never flustered, who preferred "Rock and Rye" to
alkali and gyp, and flourished more on war than on peace. In
fact, as Jeff said, "he would drink a right smart and scrap a right
smart. He was an old Confederate war colonel with one arm shot
off at the shoulder and the other hand almost gone. But he would
fight his shadow; wa'n't afraid of anything. Give him two drinks
and he would spit in a tiger's eye. Shore would!" And Marsh was
to prove it.

At the junction of the Conchos, the United States Army had
established a fort in 1867, which was one of an integrated system
designed to protect the Texas frontier from the Indians of the
High Plains, though the army was too unwieldly and static to
be effective in Indian warfare. Besides its recognized inefficiency
in the job at hand, the Fort Concho garrison was made up at this
time of colored troopers. On the whole Texas tolerated them—
that is, in the generous phrase of O'Henry, "they had nothing
against them; they let them live"—but nobody expected them

11 Ira Long to John B. Jones, April 17 and June 6, 1880; G. W. Arrington to
Jones, January 17 and 20 and February 9, 1880.
12 "Monthly Return," Company B, Frontier Battalion, October 31, 1880.

ever to set the woods afire, much less to be of any service. But at Fort Concho an unfortunate incident stirred up a racial riot.

Early in February, 1881, Tom McCarty, a ranchman, stopped in at a San Angelo saloon and killed a drunken Negro soldier. The local officers took McCarty in charge.

The soldiers made two attempts to raise a ruckus and avenge the death. First they tried to kill McCarty by shooting into the office of the Justice of the Peace, Billy Russell, who only escaped death himself because the bullet was stopped by a copy of *The Revised Statutes* that lay on his table. The codified statutes in Texas could really be useful. The soldiers printed circulars on a little press at the post "threatening the destruction of the town and all the inhabitants unless McCarty was surrendered to the Negroes." Women and children left town as colored soldiers walked the streets by day, muttering and threatening. That night they marched on the Nimitz Hotel, where they expected to find McCarty. Nimitz told them that he had gone. Sheriff Jim Spears remonstrated with the rioters who dispersed as the post patrol showed up.

The next night they were still after McCarty, who, meanwhile, had gone to the Tankersley Hotel. Mrs. Frank Tankersley heard them coming, got her guests out, and, according to one account, "outwitted the mob." According to Jeff's recollection, she took a shotgun, stepped out in front of the hotel, and said, "Cut it out. The first one that shoots a hole in my hotel, I'm going to kill him." And they shot no holes. "She was quite a lady," praised Jeff.

Next day the examining trial was concluded, and McCarty was bound over to the sheriff without bond. In appeasement, Colonel Benjamin H. Grierson, in charge of the post, ordered the company out on patrol along the bank of the North Concho, which formed the edge of the military reservation.[13] The civil authorities agreed to pass with the prisoner, the company was to fall in at a "respectful distance behind," and thus help escort him to the Benficklin jail, a dirt-covered structure of logs. This was

[13] For a sketch of Grierson, see Col. M. L. Crimmins, "The Border Command," in *The Army and Navy Courier*, November, 1928, 9.

done, the suspense was eased, and the women folks came back into town.

Then McCarty's brother, who resembled him, happened to ride into town and stopped at the Nimitz Hotel. A Negro saw him and spread the word: "Tom McCarty's out of jail!" And at last the fat was out of the skillet and in the fire. That night the Negro troops swarmed out of the fort and shot up the town. They wounded one man, terrorized the village, and completely riddled the Nimitz Hotel.

Meanwhile a runner was dispatched for the Rangers, carrying a petition from the district judge, the district attorney, and the sheriff of Tom Green County begging help in preserving "civil order, as the Federal soldiers had threatened to burn and pillage the town."

The runner reached Hackberry Springs on the evening of February 4, 1881, and immediately Marsh had the entire company of twenty-one men in the saddle, marching for Fort Concho. Jim Werner, the Negro cook and teamster, followed with their beds and six days' rations. Marsh reached San Angelo the next morning, making the eighty miles in record time, pitched camp in John Nasworthy's wagon yard, took two quick shots of liquor, and began thirsting for war.

Grierson had shown little judgment and no control of his troops. Apparently, in the midst of the trouble, he had not even canceled the leaves from post. Marsh sent J. M. Sedberry and a detail to guard the jail, and threw others out about town. Then with several men he headed impatiently for the office of the commandant of the post. After sending a guard to a roof to overlook the approaches, he took Milton, saying "Get your Winchester. Throw a shell in it. Kill the first man that bothers me."

A firm and eager hand pressed the lever down, a shell slid into the polished chamber, and with confident and expectant stride the last son of the Civil War governor of Florida crossed the reserved domain of the federal government to see this fire-eater from the Confederacy and the frontiers of Texas read the riot act to the commanding symbol of military power. As may be anticipated, much of Marsh's talk to Grierson is not "one for

37

the book." But properly expurgated his message was this: "I am going to kill the first man that comes across the river without a pass—nigger or anyone else. Keep these troops on this side of the river. If they cross, we'll kill every one of them."

"What do you mean," spluttered Grierson. "You have only a handful of men."

"Yes," said Marsh, "but enough to kill every one of these niggers if you don't obey my orders."

And when Marsh left, Grierson knew that, even with the power and prestige of the United States Army behind him, in this armless man with the mangled hand he had certainly met his match. Jeff admitted that he thought he was going to have to kill Grierson before the interview was done. When asked what would have happened if anyone had moved, he simply said, "Why, I'd a killed 'em, of course. Those were my orders. That's what I'd a done."

Things quieted down in a hurry. A few days later Sergeant John Hoffar was detailed to convey McCarty, under indictment for murder, to the settlements for safe-keeping. Ranger Charlie Trentham was sent off with Sheriff Spear to help arrest somebody else for murder, and Ranger Sedberry arrested several others for good measure. Marsh was matter of fact in his monthly report. "Soon after his arrival in town," that restrained and impersonal document reads, "Capt Marsh called on Col Grierson, Col commanding the Fort, for assistance to help preserve the peace, which was granted." The exciting news of the riot had crossed the state. Two days after he arrived, Marsh made his first laconic, reassuring report to Major John B. Jones: "Arrived here Saturday with company all quiet."

And that, for Jones and the state of Texas, was the official story. McCarty came to trial at Junction, and the jury was out just long enough to write the verdict on a piece of paper: "Not guilty."[14]

Though their main camp was at Hackberry Springs, much of

[14] Jeff D. Milton to J. E. H., December 15, 1942; B. Marsh to John B. Jones, February 7, 1881; "Monthly Return," Company B, February 28, 1881; *Dallas Herald*, February 6, 1881; *San Angelo Standard*, May 3, 1924.

the work of Company B revolved around the valleys of the Conchos. At San Angelo, Jeff helped take in Manning Clements, known unfavorably in Texas as a right good hand with a gun. Clements was placed under arrest by a Ranger, "Old man" Paugh, so-called by the boys because his forty-odd years made him the oldest man in the company. Clements resisted arrest when Paugh laid hands upon him, went after his gun, and was about to get the advantage. Jeff quickly poked his own gun in Clements' ribs and shouted, "Cut it out, or I'll kill you!" And Clements went peacefully along with Old Man Paugh.

It has been said by Jeff's Ranger associates that he was always comfortable company in a fight, but that in camp his effervescent spirits and puckish nature kept things in an uproar. One time on the Concho his practical joking backfired in his face. Major Jones was on one of his tours of inspection of the Frontier Battalion, and Jeff and Blub Thomas had been sent down to Austin from Company B to serve as escort. They were working west and had camped on the Concho. Jeff, who always loved to fish, had bought some hooks in Austin. After pitching camp for the Major that evening, he and Blub had gone off to fish. A ranchman who had settled near by rode up and said, "Boys, where did you get them hooks and lines? I have been wanting to catch some fish ever since I have been in this country."

With a sudden inspiration that bordered on suicide, Jeff pointed to the Adjutant General's tent, where sat the dark-complexioned, black-eyed, black-haired little Major, at his portable desk, and said, "I bought these from that little Jew up there in that tent."

The ranchman was elated. "You did? By Jacks, I'm sure going to buy some."

Blub Thomas looked at Jeff in dire alarm. But Jeff was spreading it on. "Well," he continued, "he's a Jew and he's a hard man to deal with. You'll have to pay a big price for them."

"I don't care if I have to pay him a dollar apiece," said the cowman, as he struck a trot for the tent.

"Jeff, you're a fool," wailed Blub. "That fellow will go up there and tell Major Jones, and he'll fire you sure."

"It's too late, now," added Jeff, a little soberly.

The cowman stepped down at the flap of the tent, and Jones greeted him cordially, "Good-day, sir. Is there something I can do for you?"

"I have come to buy some hooks and lines," said the stranger, proceeding directly to business, "and you needn't be stingy with your prices. I understand you hold a man up for them."

Jones indignantly wanted to know what he meant, and the man insisted that he need not demur—he was ready to pay the price. Jones was furious. He told the cowman that he was adjutant general of the state of Texas instead of a Jew peddler, and demanded to know who had sent him. But that gentleman had a healthy sense of humor, even if the joke was on him, and answered, "A fellow down the road told me."

Jones was a disciplinarian and a man of great pride in the service he commanded, and refused to take this for an answer. He made a formal roll call, lined the entire escort up, and said, "I know the man is here who told you."

The ranchman looked them over, soberly, for he was a dead-game sport who saw that the kid of the outfit was in a jam, and then replied, "He ain't there. It was some fellow down the road, horseback, that told me."

"If anything of the kind ever happens again," Jones warned his command, "I'll disband the whole company to get the right man." And, said Jeff, "he meant it too."

As soon as they were dismissed, Jeff slipped off to thank the stranger in private, and he said, "I gave him pretty near all the hooks I had."

4

Tough Towns of Texas

The Rangers of Company B turned from their duties along the Conchos and around the boisterous town of San Angelo to the Staked Plains of Texas. From their camp at Hackberry Springs in the breaks, they made frequent scouts across the wide plateau to the west and into the sand hills—one of the last resorts in Texas of the wild Indians. They cut for sign of raiding parties beyond Mustang Springs, and Five Wells, and even clear to Monument Spring in New Mexico. Their long, hard scouts on grass horses turned up no fights after Jeff joined, but they did prove that the Indian problem was almost settled.

Jeff recalled that his horse frequently refused to drink at the little creek formed by the Big Spring because of oil on the surface. He was not surprised that an oil field was later discovered near by, though his thoughts then were of more important things —the elemental problems of existence in that unfriendly terrain. A few amusing features of that life stayed with him in after years.

As lance corporal, he led a scouting expedition out on the Staked Plains in the winter of 1880–81. His party, caught in a bad blizzard, was about to freeze before it could reach the breaks. They carried a little pickaxe in their pack on the trailing mule for digging wood, as there were diminutive mesquites along the edge of the Plains with ponderous roots beneath. Until recent years cowmen hunted these mesquite "grubs" for branding and kitchen use, so called because they had to be grubbed or dug up, hence the expression "digging for wood." But now their pick was useless, as the baldies were covered with snow and roots could not be found.

Grading contractors for the Texas and Pacific Railroad, following the staked and surveyed course across the Plains, had cut and stacked the native hay for teamsters working west on

41

the dump. Jeff was delighted when they rode up to several of these stacks, saying to his men, "I'm going to have a fire."

Stud Robinson, one of his party, was disturbed. "Don't dare set that afire," he warned.

"I'm not going to freeze to death, hay or no hay," said Jeff, as he set fire to the stack. It burned all night and kept them warm. Back in camp he reported the incident to Captain Marsh who told him he had "done perfectly right."

Again, Jeff and J. M. Sedberry—a redheaded, brown-eyed man, six feet, one inch in height and a regular bear in a fight— were caught on the Plains in a heavy fog and got "completely turned around." They had no food, which was usually not a serious thing for the Plains were alive with antelope, and when these were missed, they could always fall back on a diet of prairie dogs. But the fog which hung on for two full days was too heavy even for that.

"The only thing we struck was a coyote," said Jeff. "We was hungry and he was good. But it was a funny thing—as soon as the fog raised, there was thousands of antelope right on top of us."

A few years after the railroad was built and the town of Big Spring was started, Jeff stopped off at John Birdwell's railroad eating house for dinner. "Rabbit stew" was the dish of the day. Jeff took one look and declined. The waitress, however, was insistent that he have "rabbit stew," as it was "very nice rabbit stew," and kept on until his outraged sense of honesty overcame his Southern breeding and he settled the hash by blurting, "Take it away. I've boiled too many prairie dogs in my time. Their bones are too red for me to eat. Any fool knows that rabbit bones ain't red."

With a delicate sense of the proprieties the waitress took it away, though Jeff was repentant when he noticed that an old lady near by no longer relished her meal.

The Texas and Pacific was building west at a phenomenal pace in view of the fact that there was no dirt-moving machinery for the building of grades other than scrapers and mule teams. It had reached Dallas in 1873; Fort Worth, three years later. Not until the summer of 1880 were its promoters ready to attempt the

600-mile stretch between there and El Paso. In June they reached Weatherford; by March 1881, they were at Sweetwater; and in April they reached the Colorado River, where Jeff saw the first piling driven. In December of the same year they joined tracks with the Southern Pacific at Sierra Blanca about 120 miles southeast of El Paso.[1]

Plodding men bent over scraper handles piled up that long grade behind the incessant circling of patient teams, stormed at by profane and impatient mule skinners. The hours were from daylight until dark—until men and teams gave out. Jeff saw the contractors place barrels one-third full of uncooked oatmeal along the right-of-way and fill them with salted water. Then these sweating and swarming men dipped and drank the gruel in passing to keep their energy up and the work a-going. Competition compelled the T. and P. to hurry.

It was racing with the Southern Pacific, then building west from San Antonio to connect with its east-bound grade that snaked its way through the sand dunes of the Río Grande, east of El Paso, to meet it. There was a rush and a fever of activity along the right-of-way, and an expectant, exciting air pervaded West Texas much like that quiet but uncertain prelude to one of its violent summer electric storms. No one was quite sure what the change would be, but all knew that life would not be the same after construction passed—after the "coming of the cars."

Soon Fort Griffin and Fort Concho, as the toughest towns of the border, began to feel their prestige wane. For the construction crews of the railroads were a lusty breed with money in their jeans. Those who cast their fortune on the turn of a card, who looked upon the liquor when the liquor was really red, who disdained not their women with the same unnatural flush upon their pallid faces—these and nondescript others flocked west along the grade to "the end of the line."

Things got rough and at such times conservative people always thought of the Rangers. In May, 1881, M. S. Coleman, contractor for the dump and line, wrote to Ranger Captain D. W. Roberts "for protection to our camps."

[1] S. G. Reed, A History of the Texas Railroads (Houston, 1941), 364–66.

43

"A very rough element numbering sometimes one or two hundred is following at our heels," he wrote, "and as we are now getting into the wild portion of the state we feel insecure without some protection." He suggested that Roberts lay the matter before the Adjutant General, and if he thought proper, "we would be glad to have a detail of a dozen men or so to accompany our outfit through to the Río Grande. We would cheerfully furnish wagons for moving the camp of the Co as the track laying progresses, and in case of disturbances in the new towns springing up in our rear, our locomotives will be at the service of the Co. when required."

The sore spots were continually shifting from one shortly-settled location to another—to "the end of the line." It was a simple matter to move, for, as Captain S. A. McMurray later reported, these camp followers use tents, "pull up" stakes, and move as the railroad progresses.[2]

The Rangers of Company B, still camped at Hackberry Springs about thirty miles south and west of where the grade cut across the red clay flats to the murky waters of the Colorado, had for some time been giving their attention to that infant prodigy in hard drinking and high playing, reckless spending and generous shooting, called Colorado City. Officially, the railroad reached there on April 16, 1881, but nobody in those rough parts, with the red dust in his bleary eyes and red liquor and gritty "sand in his craw," waited on anything "official."

With healthy and independent American enterprise, these disciples of easy money and easy virtue freighted their tents, their meager luggage, and the tricks of their trade in by mule team. They quietly slipped out of the settlements to this wide-open spot in an open land, and they pitched their tents and plied their wiles with such brazen abandon that the fine red dust that they stirred with their wanton feet, and that floated in whirlwind streamers into the chaste, ethereal blue, was an appropriately tinted symbol of their trade.

For profitable years past, some writers have sketched the

[2] M. S. Coleman to D. W. Roberts, May 30, 1881; S. A. McMurray to W. H. King, September 3, 1881.

44

chronicles of Tombstone, Arizona—where Jeff Milton lived for many years—as the reckless apogee of crimson crime, as the "town too tough to die," and other doubtful marks of fame that genuine bravery would blush to own. It was tough, but much of its character was the assumed bravado of wayward men who felt the cool shiver of crawling flesh along their flexible spines when they met men of real steel.

But on the frontiers of Texas, according to Jeff, the situation was different. Here the tempo was not set by fugitives from conscience and crime, though they mingled unnoticed among a more vigorous breed. Here the scene was not dominated by pimps, prostitutes, outlaws, and hangers-on, but by legitimate cowmen who had played their part in pioneer Texas. For generations they and their fathers had battled the enemies of Texas— Mexicans, Indians, outlaws, Yankees, and a perverse but not unyielding nature. From long experience they knew they could face the music. They moved with courage and confidence. They would drink, gamble, work, play, fight, and die—all with the reckless abandon of men who needed neither air conditioning to make life tolerable nor vitamins to make blood red.

"They would fight anybody and anything," Jeff recalled. "They were good men, but if you monkeyed with them, they'd kill you, certain."

Colorado City sprang up as a tent town late in 1880. The Rangers reported being there in November. Saloons, dance halls, stores, and dwellings—all were tents. The Nip and Tuck Saloon was the biggest in town.[3] Life started off with such a riotous rush that a detail of Rangers was kept there, rather steadily, from the first, Jeff along with the others.

They issued an order for all cowboys to shed their six-shooters upon coming into town, and were forced to take the guns off some who resented this outrageous infringement of human rights. But on the whole the cowboys submitted to authority. Yet one day as Jeff and Ranger Williams were passing John Birdwell's Saloon, a man came out, ·saying, "No damned Ranger could take a pistol off so-and-so in that saloon."

[3] "Monthly Return," Company B, November 30, 1880.

45

Another came out, met them at the door, and stopped to say, "That man is in there with a six-shooter on. Don't go in! Any man that tries to take his six-shooter is going to get killed. There are fifteen or twenty of them in there together."

"By Jacks, if we don't get that six-shooter, we just as well quit the service," Jeff said to Williams, and stepped inside.

At the bar, with his back to the door, stood a man whose coat bulged high over what was obviously the handle of a .45, and from him they could hear a belligerent roar, "By God, I'd like to see the man that can take a pistol off of me."

Jeff jerked his six-shooter, poked it into the gentleman's ribs, and saying quite crisply, "I'll take it," whipped up the man's coattails and pulled out the deadly weapon—an old, sawed-off plow handle. The bunch had bought a plow and had cut off the handle for the purpose. The roar that rent the air almost raised the roof.

Jeff looked at the plow handle in his hand, smiled at Birdwell behind the bar, and said, "Set 'em up, John, dad-blame it. The drinks are on me." And while it cost him nearly twenty dollars— for the house was full and the drinks were ample—he always declared that the fun was worth it.

Birdwell, an old Ranger and frontier marshal, had come in and set up a saloon. When a titled Englishman, the Earl of Aylesford, came west to see what the land and the life were like, and to hunt to his heart's content, he was greatly impressed with old John Birdwell. At times they got drunk together, in a gentlemanly sort of way, and once were seen sitting in the shallow Colorado River, sobering up—with a bottle between them.

The Earl kept after John to take him on a hunt. He wanted to kill buffalo, antelope, and bear—there were then some bear in the canyons and breaks at the foot of the Plains. John always thought of his saloon and pleaded the press of his business. One day the Earl asked him what it was worth, and when John named the price, he at once bought him out, put some extra hands behind the bar, and gave the stock away, an early civic philanthropy of which the populace approved. Then John had plenty of time to hunt.[4]

46

In addition to the money brought by construction of the railroad, the cattle industry was booming and everybody was flush. The stakes in the halls were high, but life was cheap. Here Jeff saw a young cowman sitting cross-legged on the edge of a monte table gambling his life away with Clay Mann backing him, his herd as security. At last, when he had lost twenty thousand dollars, Mann told him that was as far as he could go.

"You can't let me have any more?" inquired the venturesome soul.

"That's all your cattle are worth," said Mann.

The young cowman pulled his gun, shot himself through the head, fell dead off the table on the floor, and the game went on.

In February, 1881, Colorado City was assuming the appearance of a town. It had four hotels and restaurants, a wagon yard, feed, grocery, and general merchandise stores, a beef market, two law offices, a doctor, five saloons, "several carpenters, one printing office and any quantity of bummers. Most of the buildings," read an item in the *Fort Griffin Echo* "are the portable kind, built in sections." The largest "frame building" in town, to distinguish it from the original tents, was that of Dunn, Coleman and Company, devoted to general merchandise and ranch supplies.[5]

The meat markets and the restaurants banked heavily on game. The Rangers used dried buffalo meat at camp, while local hunters brought venison and antelope saddles in for those who wished them. Jeff recalled seeing a man drive in with a wagon bed full of dressed turkeys, which he could not sell for twenty-five cents apiece, and which he unhappily dumped into the Colorado. Everybody lived on heavy baits of good red meat, and suffered not from anemia as he went his own vital and rambunctious way.

---

[4] The Earl of Aylesford acquired a ranch in the Colorado country. He died in West Texas in January, 1885. See *Fort Worth Gazette*, September 2, 1884, and January 29, 1885.

For a while he was a distinguished citizen of the village of Big Spring, where he built "The Cosmopolitan Hotel." See John R. Hutto, "Big Spring and Vicinity," *West Texas Historical Association Year Book*, VIII (Abilene, Texas, 1932), 85.

[5] *Fort Griffin Echo*, February 19, 1881.

47

Much of the trouble in the little town centered around John Good, whose heavy, gold watch chain—ostentatiously drooped across his ample chest in his present prosperity—could hardly span a career that had been "too checkered for anything." Good was born in the Lockhart country and was now a "sure 'nough cowman." He was of arrogant spirit and designing nature and had already left a devious trail behind him. From South Texas he had moved into the Coleman country, and Jeff first saw him in San Angelo doping a foot-peddler's drink with croton oil.[6]

Good's specialty was in raising hell, and when the proposal was made to organize Mitchell County and a settled Texas Ranger, Dick Ware, was mentioned for sheriff, Good found himself on fertile ground. He became a leader of the cowmen and champion of the rougher elements.[7]

Mitchell County, the subdivision on the new Texas maps that lay athwart the Colorado River at this point, was proposed for organization. By the laws of Texas, certain qualifications regarding the number of legal voters were prescribed, but since nobody outside the county itself was concerned, and since such laws—like many since—were interpreted with an independent convenience bordering at times on chaos, they hardly formed a barrier to legitimate business. And so the county was organized on January 10, 1881, though its total population in 1880 was only 117 people.

The filling of the offices stirred the greatest interest, and the race that raised everybody's blood pressure was that for sheriff. The Texas Rangers symbolized a rugged and impartial regard for the law. Dark-eyed, quiet, sober, businesslike Dick Ware decided to run. His part at the killing of Sam Bass had given him a wide reputation without going to his head. Jeff thought him a fine man and a splendid officer. To elect Dick Ware sheriff was

[6] W. H. Roberts to J. E. H., December 4, 1943; Joe McKinney to J. E. H., February 27, 1945.

[7] It is said that Good's brother, Isom Good, with a reputation in his own right, was the father of Milt Good, who, with Tom Ross, killed Robertson and Allison, inspectors for The Texas and Southwestern Cattle Raisers Association, in Seminole, Texas. Roberts to J. E. H., December 4, 1943.

48

to write the community's insurance for a quiet and sedate birth, and a vigorous shove down the road toward decent life.

For those who were wed to riotous living, the idea was simply too much. John Good rallied the rougher elements in town around the standard of another cowman named W. P. Patterson. The Rangers stood together as a man. They talked about running Jeff for judge, for they knew he could read and write and that he came of illustrious ancestry. The thought was enough to kill him, and was abandoned when they found him standing on the legal barrier of age. By law a judge had to be twenty-one. So did a Ranger. But they were not given to splitting legal hairs and after all Jeff was right: "What fun was there in being a county judge?" Therefore, they went down the line for Dick Ware and elected him sheriff. His discharge from the Rangers followed on February 1, 1881.[8]

Upon the same date John N. Hoffar was promoted to sergeant, in his place; J. M. Sedberry to first corporal; and a new Ranger, L. B. Wells, was enlisted. Ware moved from Hackberry Springs into town and took up his duties, while the tense feeling engendered by the hot election, instead of cooling, gradually simmered to a deadly heat. Patterson was a prominent cowman. Good, and his following of all sorts bad, had pushed him hard in the race; and in the idiom of the range the defeat was galling to his old sore back. Ranger Bill Roberts said that he was not a bad man "except when drunk." He got drunk often and stayed drunk long. On occasion he shot up the town, while a detail of Rangers, camped at a dugout near the river, was kept there even after the election.

There was no jail, and when Patterson was arrested for disturbing the peace, the Rangers simply chained him to a big mesquite until he sobered up and simmered down. He was arrested three times within a few days. For an independent cowman to be chained to a mesquite in town was a humiliating ex-

---

[8] Roberts, as cited; Jeff D. Milton to J. E. H., December 8, 1938, and June 11, 1939; "Monthly Return," Company B, February 28, 1881. Judge R. H. Looney wrote "A History of Colorado," published in *The Colorado Weekly Record*, August 8, 1930, to February 13, 1931, Colorado, Texas.

perience and Patterson did not forget it. On the night of May 16, 1881, he was in town again, and again on a tear.[9]

Sedberry, Milton, and Wells were on duty when, sometime after midnight, they heard shooting near the Nip and Tuck Saloon. They ran down the street to the place. Just as they got there, they met Patterson and his friend, Ab Adair,[10] coming down the street. When they inquired who did the shooting, Patterson answered that he did not know. Sedberry told him he would have to examine his gun, and Patterson swore, "Damn you, you will have to go examine somebody else's pistol."

Sedberry and Wells grabbed his arms, but Patterson, a muscular man, jerked loose, pulled his gun, and shot at Sedberry, who escaped with powder burns. He did not have time for another shot as Milton cut him down with his .45. Unfortunately, the inexperienced Wells shot him after he had fallen. Under the best of circumstances, the feeling was bound to be intense; but after this action, it came near getting completely out of hand.

An angry mob gathered at once, and there were threats to hang Milton, as the argument and feeling flowed hot and high in the Nip and Tuck Saloon. A near riot was on when Good mounted a poker table further to stir the outraged citizenry to action. At that moment Jeff, himself, stepped in with Winchester in hand and threatened to kill Good at once, and he not only got down but also got better.

Sedberry, Milton, and Wells gave themselves up to Dick Ware and were technically placed under arrest. But they kept their guns and went on about their business, while a runner notified Captain Marsh, at Hackberry Springs, and that old one-armed warrior came in at a high lope, lusting for trouble. With him was Charlie Trentham, devoted friend of Jeff's and always ready for the worst that local war could offer. To make things worse, the general roundup was camped near by, and cowboys and cowmen swarmed into town, mainly to dilute the brackish

[9] Lee Rice, pioneer cowboy of the Concho country and early settler in the Mogollons of New Mexico, came through Colorado City while Patterson was chained to the tree, and stopped over at the Ranger camp. Lee Rice to Jeff Milton, January 31, 1942.

[10] Ab Adair was John Good's son-in-law.

Colorado River water with a generous potion of whiskey, and to fight for their rights in the current uprising, whatever they might be.

On the eighteenth the examining trial was held before Justice Smith in a clapboard hall that served as courthouse. Sedberry, Milton, and Wells went downtown armed with their Winchesters and six-shooters. Everything quieted down except the agitation to disarm the Rangers under arrest.

"I've got mine on and I'm going to keep it on," said Jeff.

At the appointed hour they were arraigned in court. The place was crowded with high-tempered, armed men fretting for a fight. Both Rangers and officials feared a riot, but to conform to the legal conventions and to pay proper respect to the "Judge," the three under arrest agreed to be disarmed after Jeff had suggested a safe alternative to his companions. Marsh's Rangers were to escort the "prisoners" into court and stand behind, "guarding them." Thus they marched in and faced the hot-blooded audience in the courtroom, but according to Ranger Charlie Robinson, one of the escort:

"The three prisoners stood, backs to a solid wall, facing the judge and spectators. Jeff Milton stood at the extreme left, and he wore no gun. But I stood next to him. At my right hip I had my own gun. On my left hip, within an inch of Jeff's right hand, I wore Jeff's gun in an open holster, as handy to his trigger finger as if it had been slung from his own belt. At my right was Sedberry, also unarmed, but with a ranger next to him wearing Sedberry's gun on his left hip; then Wells and the third ranger likewise. Patterson's killers took one good look and left the room."[11]

The examining trial was not without its amusing frontier features as Justice Smith left his livery stable to open court. The Rangers employed as lawyers young R. H. Looney and C. C. McGinnis and Son, to represent them at the examining trial. The Judge was apparently deficient in law as well as practice, for

---

11 "Monthly Return," Company B, May 31, 1881; Jeff Milton to J. E. H., July 1, 1937, March, 1938, February 13, 1943; "Captain James B. Gillett, a Great Texas Ranger," by Frank M. King, *Western Livestock Journal* (Los Angeles), January, 1942, 49–50; "Brush Poppers," by Stuart N. Lake, *The Saturday Evening Post*, April 11, 1931, 20 ff.; and W. H. Roberts, as cited.

when he transgressed former Ranger John Birdwell's partisan sense of justice in some forgotten ruling, Birdwell rose in wrath from the audience and shouted, "Judge, you're full of prune juice."

Smith wanted to bind the boys over to Ware to be held without bond, since the trial had to go into another day, but old Captain Marsh protested this affront to the service and told the court, "The boys are going to camp with me tonight whether you make their bonds or not, and they will be in court tomorrow."

Smith insisted they would have to go to jail.

"Hell, I'm not going to jail," Jeff retorted, and when Smith saw that Marsh and his Rangers were there to back up this decision, he compromised and set their bond at $1,500 each.

J. M. Culp, a merchant, and John Shaughnessy, a gambler who later moved to Yuma, Arizona and became mayor there, rushed to sign Jeff's bond. Shaughnessy had been running a faro game at Abilene. Jeff first saw him when he walked into his gambling hall and pulled out a dollar. Shaughnessy, a hair-lipped Irishman, asked where he wanted to play it.

"I don't know," said Jeff.

Seeing that he was a boy who had never played before, Shaughnessy gently but firmly said," Well, you can't play at my game."

Thus they were bound over to await the action of the grand jury, and Jeff and his fellow Rangers went back with Marsh to camp.

The news of the killing and the threatened clash went out over the state, and General John B. Jones sent that veteran Ranger, D. W. Roberts, from his camp in the country below to investigate the affair. Apparently the state was concerned lest the fiery Marsh do something to fan the resentment to the sort of showdown that he best knew how to meet. Roberts is said to have come incognito and made his investigation before disclosing himself to Marsh.

Late in May he reported to the Adjutant General that Patterson "was a drinking man and very troublesome while under the influence of liquor. Considered a dangerous man, under those circumstances." He found that the cattlemen had "made a good deal of sensational talk, and some threats," but that the general roundup had moved on, and that the ranchmen had taken the cowboys back to their cows, "which virtually quells the disturbance, so far as any general riot is concerned."

"As to any *feud* existing between the Rangers and the 'cowboys,'" he continued, rather ingenuously, "I think it is a mistake as *Rangers* are not supposed to be any party to a feud. I can see nothing ominous of any further serious trouble here."[12]

That summer, W. H. King, a former legislator considered unfriendly to the Texas Rangers, was appointed Adjutant General, and thus became the commanding officer of the force. He reported to Governor O. M. Roberts that he "was met . . . by complaints of bad management, drunkenness and other improper conduct" on the part of Company B. Captain Neal Caldwell had investigated the charges and found them "largely true." This, General King felt, had bred "among the people where it was stationed a strong feeling of hostility." And so he determined to disband the company.[13]

Meanwhile, Jeff and the others were under indictment for the killing of Patterson—an indictment, King felt, "to be largely the result of the prejudice and antipathy against this company, as it is thought by some of the best citizens of Colorado City that the killing was unavoidable." Still the burden of their defense fell upon the boys alone, for, as King observed, "the State makes no provision for the legal defense of her soldiery, even though prosecuted for an act done in the performance of duty imposed upon them by the authority of the State itself."[14]

Jeff and his friends, like most youths of their time, had no money. But Jeff enlisted the help of his responsible relatives in the lower part of the state, and Spoonts and Liggett, of Abilene, were employed as counsel. Company B shifted its base to the Big Spring, and as serious trouble was brewing at Graham, Jeff and "Buffalo Bill" Jenkins were dispatched to that quiet but

[12] D. W. Roberts to J. B. Jones, May 27 and June 1, 1881.
[13] Report of the Adjutant General, 1881, 23.
[14] *Ibid.*, 24.

53

dangerous community in the Cross Timbers, "in complyance with & order from Gov. Robards," the records quaintly recall, to guard the jail.

They went by rail to Weatherford and, after stopping over for the night, shifted to stage. They got a nice room at the hotel, and Jeff went out to see the town while "Buffalo Bill," who never slept except with his head to the north, decided he would go to bed. When Jeff came in, there lay Bill, properly oriented, but on the floor, head pillowed on his boots and coat. Jeff waked him with the obvious question.

"Why ain't you sleeping in bed?" he asked, pointing to the pillows and the clean sheets.

"Oh, Jeff," said Bill, "it's just all so nice and clean that I can't stand to muss it up." And Bill stayed on the floor.

Next morning they had to help hold the mules while they were being hooked to the stage. When all was in readiness, they turned them loose, grabbed the stage, and were merrily off at a run along the winding road that led northwest, over the hills and through the Palo Pinto woods, to Graham. The three dangerous and desperate McDonald brothers[15] were being held in jail and a break was expected. The first night that they were on guard, Jeff saw a man coming over the walls in the darkness, but when he hit the ground, Jeff's six-shooter was poking in his ribs. They put him back and never let anyone enter, thereafter, unless one of them was inside, too.

After things quieted down, Jeff left for a visit with his brother-in-law Ed Everett and his sister Mary at Terrell. He extended the trip to visit with Colonel Yarborough and his other Texas sister at Navasota, and arranged additional counsel for his approaching trial, retaining former Attorney General H. H. Boone and the distinguished T. D. Cobbs.

While he was away from Graham, another jail break was made, and the prisoner was almost into the woods that surrounded that little town before he fell a dead and riddled carcass. "Several were shooting at him," said Jeff, "but Buffalo Bill Jenkins

[15] See Carrie J. Crouch's *Young County* (Dallas, 1937), 158–60.
[16] This was probably a prisoner named Dozier. *Ibid.*, 158.

54

was bound to have killed him," for Bill could run half a mile at
full speed and still draw a true and steady bead.[16]

Jim Melton, and a very fine man as Jeff remembered him,
was the Graham sheriff. Jeff and Bill understood that the county
was to pay their board and keep, but when the month of July
was up and the commissioners refused to pay the bill, Jeff, then
a corporal in the Texas Rangers where a corporal was really
something, told Bill they were pulling out. When it was obvious
that he meant it, the commissioners reluctantly agreed to meet
the bill, but Jeff waved them a jovial good-bye: "Too late, boys,"
he said, "we're gone!" and gone they were.

The action of the county was a niggardly one that brought
tragic results. Shortly after they left, the sheriff's brother, Dave
Melton, and another deputy, named Sam Murphee, entered the
jail. By a ruse Melton was thrown off guard, and one of the
prisoners grabbed his gun. Murphee, who had stepped outside
the cell, rushed in to his aid and was killed in his tracks. Then,
with Melton as a shield, the McDonalds retreated from the town
with an outraged posse in pursuit. In the fight that followed, two
townsmen were wounded and the three outlaws killed. Four
men dead and two wounded; "if they had only paid our board,"
said Jeff, "this would never have happened."[17]

Jeff and Bill went back to Company B, now camped at Big
Spring, which the railhead did not reach until April 28, 1881,
but which, in February consisted of nine tents, one of which was
John Birdwell's store. "The principal stock in the store, we mean
tent," wrote an observer, "is 'red liquor,' and a few cigars. . . .
Buffalo hunters, railroad graders and bone gatherers, with now
and then a cowboy, are the principal patrons of those having
anything to sell." The place had taken its name from a near-by
spring that belched out from "under a huge mass of overhanging
rock,"[18] and here Jeff saw buffalo bones piled in immense and
grotesque ricks along the right-of-way, awaiting transport to an
eastern market.

[17] Crouch, *Young County*; "Monthly Return," Company B, August 31, 1881;
Dallas Herald, January 5, 1882; *Fort Griffin Echo*, January 7, 1882.
[18] *Fort Griffin Echo*, February 19, 1881. See *Dallas Herald*, December 15,
1881.

The movement west followed a definite pattern in keeping with the pace of the railroad. These drifting dregs of humanity, leavened with rugged enterprisers in trade, kept moving with the "end of the line." By the late summer of 1881 the rails were pushing down the alkali slopes to the abrupt rim of the Pecos, and, as Captain Dan Roberts observed some months before, those toughs with temperaments too salty for a settled land had gone west with them—to settle for a troubled moment on the salty slopes of the devious Pecos. The Rangers of Company B were close behind.

5

Rangers and Railroads

As the Texas and Pacific Railroad built west during the summer of 1881, Captain Bryan Marsh moved camp from Hackberry Springs, farther west, to Big Spring. Business and devilment, one and the same for the Texas Rangers, now followed the rails.

Corporal Jeff Milton was dispatched from there on July 1, after one "Colonel Pool, wanted in Mitchell Co. for theft." He traveled sixty-five miles west by rail to the end of the line and struck out, horseback, to capture his man near Monahan's Wells —two natural holes of milky but splendid water in the sands—in that then forbidding belt of land that separated the cap rock of the Staked Plains from the alkali flats along the Pecos. On the way back he served attachments upon "a bunch of witnesses," as Marsh said, and lodged his prisoner with Dick Ware, sheriff at Colorado City.[1]

Again Jeff recovered some stolen stock at Monahan's Wells, and, as he returned, met the railroad construction crews just below the cap rock, about twenty miles west of where Odessa stands. When he and his men rode out of the sand on tired and thirsty horses, they found the water troughs at the camp with covers, locked down. Jeff told the construction men that he had to water his horses, as it was a waterless land and they were a long way from the next natural supply—some fifty miles from Mustang Springs.

"You can't get it here," came the dry response.

"That's just what you think," flared Jeff, getting hotter than a sand lizard and picking up a near-by axe. "I'm going to show you something," he said, as he swung on the trough cover with the axe while the construction boss "hollered like hell." "Further-

---

1 "Monthly Return," July 31, 1881.

more," said Jeff, as he held the man with his black and burning eyes, "we're going to eat supper with you." And they did.

Jeff dutifully reported the incident to Captain Marsh, and that amused old warrior of the same Southern strain looked at his nineteen-year-old protégé in passion and arms and simply said, "You wanted water for your horses, did you, Jeff?"

"Yes sir," came the answer, "and I got it."

All that year the T. and P. was industriously pushing west. It reached Big Spring in April, 1881; it had crossed the Pecos to reach Toyah on September 12; and it joined tracks with the Southern Pacific near Sierra Blanca, in December—a real accomplishment in construction. But because of the rivalry between the roads about which would be completed first, everybody was in a swivet and a sweat; the mule skinners were dipping their oatmeal water with a ready will, and, in the inelegant but expressive term of the times, were "tapping 'em on the tails."[2]

By virtue of joint use of the Southern Pacific tracks from Sierra Blanca west, the T. and P. gave transcontinental service first. The Southern Pacific diverged from this common course to strike southeast through the Big Bend of Texas, and the lines co-operated to open the Trans-Pecos to settlement. It was a tough land that they could settle but could not change; a land that for three years was to beckon and hold Jeff Milton with the firm hand that it fastens on vigorous men. This great area that protrudes like a hitchhiker's thumb on the map of Texas was Ranger jurisdiction. It may be well to note what first brought the Rangers there.

The backwash from the frontiers of Texas was already lapping along the west banks of the Pecos, and while Jeff's company was following the T. and P. and scouting on the Plains, another company of Rangers had been sent to Fort Davis, a post established in the Davis Mountains in 1854, abandoned during the Civil War, reinvested during Reconstruction, and now the prin-

[2] For the story of the building of the T. and P., see S. B. McAllister, "The Building of the Texas and Pacific Railway," 123 ff., thesis, University of Texas; and S. G. Reed, *A History of the Texas Railroads*. For something of the beginnings of Big Spring, see the *Dallas Herald*, December 15, 1881, and John R. Hutto, in *West Texas Historical Association Year Book*, VIII, 75-96.

cipal settlement in that entire region between El Paso and Del
Río by the projected route of the Southern Pacific.[3]

Company E was located at the post which nestled below the
jutting and forbidding brow of adjacent peaks of the Davis
Mountains, brown, bare, and sheer. The little town about it lay
open to an eastern and southern sun, in a valley that was lush, for
that lank land, with black grama flags waving merrily in the
eternal wind—grass that put firm fat on a horse's ribs like a steady
feed of corn.

To the north, at the base of the Davis Mountains, great
springs break out to flow across "the flat," as we still call that
great, gray, and alkaline plain that fans out for fifty miles and
more to the east and northeast to where the Pecos draws off its
bitter drainage, apparently writhing and twisting in cramps,
itself.

To the northwest, the rolling lands rise by easy stages into
the Delaware Mountains. Where they leave off, El Capitán, of
the Guadalupe Range, raises its head as if in abrupt and high
concern over the salty and repellent world that lies below it.
From three principal points of the compass up to a hundred miles
away, it seems to hang from the skies in inviting and pellucid

[3] Alice V. Cain has given an outline of the life of Fort Davis in her thesis, "A
History of Brewster County," 183–96, West Texas Historical and Scientific Society, Alpine, Texas.

blue on the borders of Texas. But at close view, it looks down with inscrutable austerity upon the hard land that stretches in glittering miles through the Salt Flats to the south, and upon the foreboding route of the Butterfield Trail by which early travelers, even thirty years before these Rangers came, crossed the high and still lonely land between there and the settlements around El Paso.

West and south of Fort Davis, the Río Grande, that perverse and individualistic stream which gives character to the border of Texas, loops leisurely through this desert land, impudently cutting its toughest terrain in two, and then bending back in a neighborly gesture to join the Pecos, before ambling off again to the southeast, eventually to reach the Gulf. The land which lies below the Davis Mountains within the loop is known as the Big Bend, a vast and stubborn and hence challenging and interesting world in itself.

In this land there were no railroads and few people, but much space and many hazards. Besides those severe and inescapable ones imposed by nature, were others generated by Indians and outlaws. The Mexican border, with no established patrol but with inviting refuge and even sanctuary for hard-pressed people from either side, was a problem in itself. By 1880 the Indians were in the nature of a passing and transient worry, but with outlaws it was different. No positive catharsis had yet been applied to rid this lusty region of them. Moreover, as is often the case with vigorous bodies, the ailment was tolerated until it threatened the life that sustained it.

When the Lincoln County War ended, Billy the Kid's fighting men drifted away in all directions—some south into Texas. For a year or more these outlaws operated across the Trans-Pecos and down into Mexico. In the spring of 1880, John M. Dean, county attorney at Fort Davis,[4] wrote Governor O. M. Roberts in transmittal of a petition from the citizens, pointing

[4] Fort Davis was the county seat of Presidio County, which was organized May 12, 1871. In 1885 the county seat was removed to the railroad at Marfa.
Pecos County, with Fort Stockton as the county seat, was organized in 1875. See Clifford B. Casey, "The Trans-Pecos in Texas History," West Texas Historical and Scientific Society *Publications* (Alpine, Texas), V, 17.

out that "many lawless men congregate around the cattle camps in New Mexico and from there they come in large parties to depredate upon the peaceable and law-abiding citizens of this state."

"They are well aware of the fact that the United States troops will not stir to protect the citizens from such attacks as theirs," he continued. He spoke of their bold daylight robberies for twelve months past, and felt sure that "the presence of a few Rangers would undoubtedly have a good effect."

Already a band had come into Fort Davis and robbed Sender's and Seibenborn's Store. They drifted down through the Fort Stockton country, where one of the outlaws, Bud Graham, was taken by the citizens, and from where the county judge wired Austin for help. Lieutenant Charles L. Nevill, operating in the Hill Country of Texas with Company E, sent a detachment under Sergeant L. B. Carruthers to Fort Davis.[5] About the same time Sergeant E. A. Sieker of Company D was sent to the Fort Stockton country.

Sieker had to guard the Fort Stockton jail to prevent Graham's delivery by the outlaws still at large. Carruthers found that Jesse Evans, of Lincoln County War fame, was the leader of the band that had escaped. The forts, he reported, "seemed to be the rendevous [sic] for the gentry, who come in to get supplies, lay their plans and gamble, also lay over places for them on their way in and out of Mexico. . . . the merchants here expect to be attacked daily."[6]

"I find that the band numbered some twenty men last year," he continued, "and that they have their agents here and in Stockton. Their agent here is Capt Tyson, his real name is John Selman, who I find is Ind[icted]. in Shackelford Co. I think from what I can learn that he is Chief of the gang and as he was getting very scarey I had him appointed Dept. Sheriff and Jailor." It all came very handy, as the jailer, fearing that the prisoner would be transferred from Stockton and a jail delivery would follow,

[5] John M. Dean to Governor O. M. Roberts, May 21, 1880; G. M. Frazier to Roberts, May 24, 1880; L. B. Carruthers to C. L. Nevill, June 8, 1880.

[6] E. A. Sieker to John B. Jones, June 15, 1880; Frazier and others to Roberts, June 15, 1880. Carruthers to Nevill, June 8, 1880.

61

had resigned, and the outlaws had so "threatened the life of the Sheriff . . . [that] he is afraid to do his duty."[7]

From Fort Stockton, Sieker took the trail of the four who had escaped after the Fort Davis robbery, overtook them near Presidio, chased them to a mountain top, put them at bay behind huge boulders, charged right in, and fought it out at close six-shooter range. Both sides lost a man before Evans' band gave up.[8]

Still apprehension prevailed, and Major John B. Jones ordered Company E, under Nevill, to Fort Davis. Meanwhile, the Rangers attempted the disposition of old John Selman, alias Captain Tyson. Already Jeff had crossed his trail at Fort Griffin, where he had been ranching in partnership with John Larn, but had left between suns. He crossed the unsettled Staked Plains on a good fast horse, with a delegation of leading citizens close behind who were going to insist that he stay. From the Pecos he drifted into the mountains toward Lincoln, stole some horses from Billy the Kid's band, burned some haystacks on the Ruidoso for good measure, and then showed up as Captain Tyson at Davis.[9]

Late in June, 1880, Carruthers arrested Selman, his jailer, and Major Jones advised Sheriff W. R. "Bill" Cruger, of Fort Griffin, an old buffalo hunter commemorated in a frontier ballad, who wired back:

" . . . cannot bring Selman here alive   charges cannot be sustained in law   nine chances to one that the mob will hang him   will you have him brought here or shall I go after him.
"W. R. Cruger
"Sheriff"[10]

"Old John" admitted that he would "be killed, as his business

[7] Carruthers to Jones, June 14, 1880.
[8] E. A. Sieker to John B. Jones, July 12, 1880.
[9] The checkered career of this old renegade can only be suggested here. My interviews with Frank Coe, of San Patricio, and John Meadow, Tularosa, New Mexico, in 1926 and later, contain much information about him. Meadows worked for him and Larn at Fort Griffin. Coe was ranching on the Ruidoso and fighting alongside Billy the Kid. A portion of the losses to Selman were his.
[10] Cruger to Jones, June 30, 1880.

partner J. M. Larn was in 1878," and by the same "mob."[11] But we must leave "Old John" and his troubled trail until Jeff Milton again cut his sign in El Paso, for Nevill arrived with Company E in August, 1880, and took over the prisoners and the guarding of the jail at Fort Davis from Sieker, who left at once for Fort McKavett, in Menard County, taking Selman with him.[12]

Nevill camped at the jail and posted a guard. Then he took to the field with the federal troops against the Indians under Victorio. At the end of the first month, he reported that the prisoners were getting restless. Fort Davis, having Negro troops, had a Negro deputy, and the prisoners had offered him one thousand dollars to release them. Nevill threw the Negro in, too. Then the whole bunch tried to dig out of the jail with a spoon, as the colored deputy knew the weak spots because he had helped to build it.

Then one of the prisoners, August Groos, alias John Gunter, played paralyzed in the arms and legs and swore "he would die if he did not get to stay out in the air." Nevill set him outside in the rarified air with a guard near by. But when somebody who had hit up a tune on a fiddle suddenly changed from a waltz to a jig and Groos went to patting his paralyzed foot "pretty lively," Nevill locked him up and wrote Major Jones, "He is not dead yet but getting well very fast."

Nevill found one of the candidates for sheriff in close cahoots with the outlaws. They were an ingenious bunch, as successful outlaws always are, and next he intercepted a letter that Jesse Evans had written to one "Billy Antraum" in New Mexico, telling Billy that he was "in a damned tight place." He wrote that if Billy would come, he could deliver them from the jail dead easy, but delay would see him on the road to Huntsville.[13]

[11] Selman said that W. C. Gilson, then of Fort Elliott, in the Texas Panhandle, would give the names of "the mob," which he forthwith did himself, naming Gilson, Deputy Sheriff James Draper, Judge W. H. Ledbetter, buffalo hunters John Poe and John Jacobs, ranchman George Matthews, and others. Carruthers to Jones, June 28, 1880.

[12] Nevill to Jones, August 8, 1880; D. W. Roberts to Jones, August 26, 1880. Nevill had been appointed second lieutenant, September 1, 1879, when he took command of Company E. Special Order 27.

[13] Huntsville, Texas, is the penitentiary town.

63

"If he comes," Nevill wrote to Major Jones, "I will enlist him for awhile and put him in the same mess with Evans & Co." A week later he wrote that "Billy Antrim, alias Billie the Kid," who, he understood, "is a fugitive from somewhere and a noted desperado," had organized a party and "may be here in a day or so." But Billy the Kid thought better of tackling the Texas Rangers, and Jesse Evans, of a prominent Lampasas County family, came to trial and got ten years for robbing the store and another ten for killing the Ranger, George Bingham. The others were admitted to bond just as a detail of Rangers brought in some wounded fugitives taken near the New Mexico line. As the Fort Stockton doctor had refused to treat them, they were brought to Fort Davis and turned over to the hospital steward there, who, Nevill happily observed, "can kill as quick as any of the profession."[14]

Nevill was too isolated—"too far from fruit and society," as the Rangers used to say—to keep the men he needed, and wrote Major Jones for more. Then he moved six miles down the government road south of Fort Davis and set up camp at the ruins of an abandoned Mexican ranch in Musquiz Canyon, where there was "a good corral seven feet high" built of adobe. He left five men to guard the jail, took three to Musquiz to "guard the hay" and look after the horses, and had the balance for scouting service.

The Musquiz camp was near a hole of fine spring-fed water in the bottom of the canyon. The ranch is supposed to have been founded in the middle fifties by Manuel Musquiz, who came as a refugee from Mexico and took advantage of the protection of newly founded Fort Davis. Though the Musquiz Ranch was quite an establishment and the fort was right at hand, the Apaches swept in and killed three of its inhabitants, and went south with their cattle. It was then abandoned, though parties

[14] Nevill to Jones, August 28, September 1 and 5, October 16, 1880; "Reminiscences of Sam Graham"; and W. H. Roberts to J. E. H., December 4, 1943.

One unusual aspect of this situation was the fact that Billy the Kid and Jesse Evans were on opposite sides during the Lincoln County War. Evans had helped in the murder of Tunstall, the act that set off the conflict, and for a long time was hunted by the Kid. Perhaps the fact that both were now outlaws had appeased their antipathies.

from Fort Davis raised a garden there for a while.[15] Nevill re-occupied it on September 15, 1880.

It consisted of the large corral with three inside rooms in front of an arched entrance. Nevill's men built stables across one end of the corral and halfway across another side, and stretched their tents in the middle. They replaced the fallen-in roof with live-oak pole framework, and thatched it over with palmilla grass, which is "very tough and lasting."

The winter of 1880 was a bad one, but there was plenty of grama-grass hay. The commissary was housed in a tent. Nevill took one room for his mess, and as there were too many men to make mess comfortably in the other two rooms, they built a third of palmilla, and so passed the winter—scouting for Indians, guarding the jail, and ranging in routine.[16] Prior to this, however, the problems of railroad construction engaged Nevill's attention.

The grading of the right-of-way was far in advance of the rails, and Nevill expected trouble in the summer of 1880 as the crews converged on the Pecos. He scouted northwest toward the river to investigate reports that Billy the Kid with some twenty men was there. Instead of the Kid, he found, at "the crossing of the Texas and Pacific Railroad on the Pecos River . . . a small town of about 200 persons." Everybody seemed glad to see him, for, as he reported, "there had been a great deal of reckless shooting in the place, bullets going through tents and in every direction."

He spent the night and arrested a man for shooting up the tent town. But he had to turn him loose because there were no civil officers and the proper jurisdiction was San Angelo, 230 miles away. Nevill decided that that sort of shooting was not worth the trouble of taking him there.[17]

[15] C. G. Raht, *The Romance of the Davis Mountains and Big Bend Country* (El Paso, Texas, 1919), 136, 146; Crimmins, "The Border Command," *The Army and Navy Courier,* November, 1928, 13. Nevill to Jones, September 17 and 28, 1880. The present highway crosses the camp.

[16] Graham, "Reminiscences of . . . ," 18; Graham to J. E. H., April 30, 1944; Nevill to Jones, September 17 and 28, 1880.

[17] Nevill to Jones, June 27 and July 10, 1880. At this time Pecos City was on the east side of the river, and in the San Angelo, or Tom Green, instead of the Fort Stockton District.

A year later Captain Marsh's company, as already observed, was giving its attention primarily to "the end of the line." Late in July, 1881, Company B moved camp from Big Spring, where water was selling at twenty-five cents a barrel and "the population . . . [was] composed largely of fast men and women living in tents" and seemingly taking "life easy," to the end of the track, twenty-five miles east of the Pecos. They scouted to Pecos City, and though they were hunting horses "stolen by the Indians," Corporal Robinson was left there with a detail "at request of citizens."

On the eighteenth of August, Jeff and Bill Jenkins came in from Graham "where they had been stationed guarding the jail." Robinson and another struck out toward New Mexico—mecca for troubled and embattled souls—to capture Joe Smith, wanted in Texas for murder. They came back by the Hashknives, the only ranch in that section beyond the Pecos, and carried their captive on to San Angelo—230 miles from camp to jail. By the twenty-third the track, and the Rangers with it, were within five miles of the river.[18]

Then Major John B. Jones died, and W. H. King was appointed adjutant general by Governor O. M. Roberts on July 25, 1881. King, quite critical of Marsh's administration of Company B, reorganized it with S. A. McMurray as captain, September 1, 1881, authorizing him "to secure such men of the disbanded company as were suitable and might be willing to re-enlist."[19] Sedberry, Wells, and Trentham were among them.

On August 30, 1881, McMurray took Jeff and the others to Pecos City, still a tent town and still on the east bank of the river.

[18] "Monthly Return," Company B, August 31, 1881. Couts and Simpson moved the Hashknife cattle from Taylor County to the Pecos in 1880. Colonel W. E. Hughes, of St. Louis, bought Couts' interest in 1881, when they had 15,000 cattle. By that fall they were said to have had 20,000 head on the west bank of the Pecos. Down the river from the Rangers, on the east bank, was the Carter Ranch, established by J. W. Carter in 1879 and enlarged in 1880. From there to the New Mexico line, on that side, the world was open and unoccupied. *Fort Griffin Echo*, October 23, 1880, and January 29, 1881; *Dallas Weekly Herald*, October 13, 1881; Mrs. J. W. Carter to J. E. H., October 31, 1927. Trav Windham, veteran of the Hashknives, says the ranch was established in 1879, though contemporary papers say 1880. A. T. Windham to J. E. H., January 10, 1927.

[19] Report of the Adjutant General, 1881, 23.

He "found all quiet . . . except for the drunkenness & roudyism that usually attends a frontier R.R. town." The Rangers were hard put for a place to camp. There was no wood, no grass, and nothing to drink except the Pecos whiskey and the Pecos water—a toss-up as to which was the worst, except that they operated adversely on opposite extremes of the body.

The railroad quickly spanned the river and pushed west across the alkali flats. McMurray wrote that within a few days it would reach Toyah Springs, where he thought it best to locate his camp, "as there will be nothing worth looking after here, in fact there is nothing here now except saloons, restaurants & gambling houses, they all use tents & 'pull up' and move as the R.R. progresses. The rough element of course keep with the whiskey & the crowd." He observed that the only two ranches within twenty miles, were Hughes and Simpson's Hashknives, up the river, and Carter brothers', down, and they needed no help.

As usual, the railroads were having trouble with the whiskey men. They claimed they owned the land and wanted McMurray to keep the undesirables off. But that official, with a proper regard for the limits of his authority, wrote King that "I consider it something for the courts to decide. . . . The nearest Justice of the Peace," he continued, "is at Ft. Stockton & by the time they could get suit instituted for trespass etc the R. R. & saloons would have moved probably into another county."[20]

Thus the summer wore off, and with the change of the seasons came a change of life for the Staked Plains of Texas. Never again would they be the same. Instinctively the Rangers knew it, and many of the noted captains of the Frontier Battalion were quitting the service. McMurray followed the track to its junction with the Southern Pacific, and then shifted camp back to the settlements—to Colorado City.[21]

But the move was not for the wildest spirits. Their faces were set toward the evening sun and they were bound to keep on until

[20] McMurray to General W. H. King, September 3, 1881. For a description of Toyah, the tent town, see *Dallas Weekly Herald*, November 3, 1881.

[21] Report of the Adjutant General, 1881, 23.

the frontier was gone. "Buffalo Bill" Jenkins headed west on his own. Jeff, Sedberry, Trentham, Robinson, and Wells went down to throw in their happy and high-hearted lot with that hearty and humorous leader, Charlie Nevill, who had been promoted to captain. In September, they joined him at Musquiz. Jeff was delighted with him and the country, though that genial man never quite warmed the cockles of his heart like the one-armed Confederate who had left them.

With the T. and P. more or less out of the way, their problems now lay mainly to the south and southeast. The Galveston, Harrisburg and San Antonio Railway, usually called the G.H.&S.A., had planned to build west from San Antonio. C. P. Huntington intruded when he was needed, the Southern Pacific acquired the assets of the G.H.&S.A., and construction of the line had started from both ends—El Paso and San Antonio—in the summer of 1881. The road reached Del Río about a year later, on June 22, 1882, but work in the west moved at a better pace. By December 6, 1881, the rails had encircled the sunny side of the Sierra Blanca and reached the village of the same name. They were at the site where a boxcar, left on a siding by a hole of water, became the original Marfa, on January 16, at Sanderson late in May, and approached the Pecos in the early summer of 1882.[22]

But the work of the Rangers was still by horseback, and remarkably they covered that vast, rough, and sometimes repellent land and got the job done. Almost any of Nevill's reports indicates how they fanned out from camp in the Davis Mountains in every direction to do it. In laconic style he observed:

Sedberry and two others were in from Fort Concho—"distance marched 582 miles"; Privates Irving and Nevill were back from New Mexico—"distance marched 500 miles"; Captain Nevill chased a man as far as Sierra Blanca—"distance marched 208 miles"; Corporal Gourley after horse thieves—"distance marched 110 miles"; Sergeant Gillespie scouted down the S. P. as far as Eagle Nest and Vinegaroon—"distance marched 450 miles"; Privates Sheffield and Carruthers returned "from the Guadalupes

---

[22] Reed, *Texas Railroads*, 197–98; McAllister thesis, "Texas and Pacific Railway," 126–27. Graham to J. E. H., April 30, 1944.

Mts. where they had been to escort W. J. Glenn (of Gano's party) on a surveying expedition, distance marched 320 miles"; Sedberry and Wells back from Colorado City attending court with Milton—"distance marched 400 miles"—all horseback.[23]

For some time trouble had been crystallizing on the lower end of the gyppy Pecos. Early in June, James Converse, chief engineer and superintendent of construction for the Sunset line, wrote to Adjutant General King that "Our contractors on the Pecos are daily annoyed by a lot of hard cases, and the only way we can maintain order will be to have 8 or 10 of your men at the Pecos or some of the R. R. camps."

Whereupon Lieutenant L. P. Sieker, commanding Company D, scouted west from Uvalde to investigate. He left Sergeant D. T. Carson and six men at Connell's Camp, five miles west of the Pecos, and reported that he "found the country sadly in need of some restraining force as there was but one Dept. Sheriff and no Justice of the Peace."[24] At the same time, Nevill was headed east, and Captain T. L. Oglesby, of Company F, of the lower border, was headed west. They reached Eagle's Nest, an eerie and unholy holdout on the Río Grande, about twenty miles west of where the road crossed the Pecos, the same day.[25]

Oglesby reported that Sieker's men had "done excellent work, putting things to wright and keeping the roughfs strait—." There were 8,000 workmen, he continued, swarming over a stretch of seventy miles—"the worst lot of roughfs, gamblers, robbers and pickpockets collected I ever saw. . . . There is nothing for Rangers to do but hold this rough element in subjection and controll them." Three days later, as he prepared to leave for Cotulla, he reported that disturbances were incessant, and "it is the hardest element I have ever had to deal with."[26]

In September, 1882, Sieker placed Corporal Lindsey at Vinegaroon, a tough village at the mouth of the Pecos, with

23 Nevill, "Monthly Return," September 30 and October 31, 1882.
24 Sieker to King, June 19, 1882.
25 The railroad originally crossed at the mouth of the Pecos and "rimmed out" to the higher country. The Pecos High Bridge was not built until 1891. See Reed, *Texas Railroads*, 198. Nevill to King, July 5, 1882. Eagle's Nest became Langtry.
26 T. L. Oglesby to W. H. King, July 5 and 8, 1882.

orders to stay there, because, as he put it, "that is the place where gamblers and saloons most do congregate."[27]

Oglesby's observation that there was no justice of the peace and hence no civil jurisdiction closer than Fort Stockton, two hundred miles away, raises the interesting question, where was Roy Bean, "The law west of the Pecos?" He was there.[28] Oglesby apparently did not recognize his jurisdiction, and another Ranger has, perhaps, indicated why. According to Bill Roberts, of Sieker's company, Bean raised the racket that brought the Rangers out. He had gone down to Chatfield and Connell's camp, made up of Canadians, and shot up the works. He shot holes in their pots, pans, and kettles, and ran the entire crew off from supper. Then he came back to his tent saloon and laughed about it.

"When we got there," Roberts said, "Roy Bean welcomed us and wanted us to make his place our headquarters—an old 'A' tent with a pine board out in front for a bar." Carson said, " 'Let me tell you something. We're out here because of you. If you do anything like that again you'll go to Stockton in chains.' Old Roy was good after that."[29]

But Roy Bean, self-styled Law West of the Pecos, did get court going in his own individualistic way. Details from Nevill's company, Jeff Milton among them, were frequently at Vinegaroon. Jeff came to know him well, and never considered him all bluff, bluster, and fraud. Jeff was in and out of his court and knew his constable, a slim, bleary-eyed old cowpuncher whose lids turned wrong side out from wind and glare.

It was he who gave sweep to Bean's almost unlimited jurisdiction in time and space. Jeff recalls the trial of a man for horse theft in Bean's justice court. Roy was about to send the culprit to the penitentiary when the defense attorney vigorously objected that he lacked jurisdiction in the case. The stocky bundle

[27] L. P. Sieker to King, September 20, 1882.

[28] C. L. Sonnichsen, in *Roy Bean, Law West of the Pecos* (New York, 1943), says (p. 80) that though Bean did not qualify in the Fort Stockton District until December, 1882, he was appointed the August before, and "long before bond was filed . . . was in active operation."

[29] W. H. Roberts to J. E. H., December 4, 1943.

70

of beef and arrogance stopped him with a roar and addressed his droop-eyed confederate.

"Constable, do I run this court?"

"Yes, your honor."

"If I told you to take this man out and shoot him, what would you do?"

"Why, I'd take him out and shoot him, your honor," came the unpretentious answer.

Bean turned to the lawyer and said, "Now, young man, do you think I have jurisdiction in this case?" And it turned out that he had.[30]

But later, Jeff recalls, District Judge T. A. Falvey, of El Paso, in whose jurisdiction Bean's court really did lay, called in the old reprobate when he could never get a report from him.

"Where's your docket?" asked Judge Falvey, a little severely.

"Docket," echoed Bean in bewilderment. "Your honor, what's that?" Falvey explained that this meant his record of cases and accounts.

"Why, Judge," said Bean, somewhat relieved, "I've never kept one. MY court is self-sustaining."

Some years after he left the Ranger service, Jeff was on his way west from San Antonio, riding the S. P., and found Joaquin Miller on the same train, big hat, buckskins, and all. It is a long ride and congenial Jeff engaged him in conversation, finding him a "nice old chap, though kind o' windy." As the train neared Langtry, talk turned to Roy Bean; and Miller, with an appreciation of the picturesque, expressed a desire to meet him.

"That will be easy," said Jeff. "He comes down to the train every day to get his paper and we'll meet him." Sure enough, when the train pulled in, there stood the bearded and portly Bean at the platform, waiting to get his paper from the butcher boy.

Jeff stepped off and greeted him, saying, "Judge, there's a man here who wants to meet you."

"Who is he?" asked Bean.

[30] Mr. Sonnichsen, in *Roy Bean,* gives a version of the same story, crediting the Rangers in attendance (pp. 86–87).

"Joaquin Miller, 'the poet of the Sierras,' " said Jeff.

'Good," roared Bean, "I'll just keep him here and make him write some poetry about me."

Jeff turned to present Miller, who had followed him out, but he was beating a hasty retreat back up the steps, passed out of the car on the other side, and struck a trot for the back end of the train. After all, there is a limit to adventure as well as art.

But to revert to the railroad-construction days, it simply remains to be said that at last, in January, 1883, the Southern Pacific tracks were joined, the floating population floated off elsewhere, and the scattered ranches and the far-riding Rangers settled down to the job of keeping the native "roughfs strait."

6

Down in the Big Bend

With the railroads more or less out of their way, the principal work for the Rangers lay down in the Big Bend. Little except their Indian scouting now took them in other directions, though a little of that should be noted.

Some of Nevill's men were with George W. Baylor, January 29, 1881, and helped get the upper hand of the Indians in the Diablo Mountains north of present Van Horn.[1] But at that time Jeff Milton was still at Hackberry Springs.

When a band of Indians stole the horses of P. H. Pruitt,[2] a ranchman below Fort Davis, Nevill and his men made chase. They followed the trail northwest through the Davis Mountains, up the gradual ascent of the Delawares toward the point of the Guadalupes and the Mescalero Apache reservation.

It was a long trail. When a horse gave out, the Indians stopped, killed him, and packed the meat. The Indian horses were all barefooted, but the Rangers found, from the tracks and feet they left from the dead ones, that they had shod them with rawhide.[3] Besides horse meat, for food they began eating the seed pods of the Spanish daggers. "I've eaten them," said Jeff, "and they're not bad—pretty good food. We followed them to the

[1] John Waller has given a good account of this fight in "George Wythe Baylor," *Southwestern Social Science Quarterly*, June, 1943, 31–33; "Reminiscences of Sam Graham," 20–21; W. H. Roberts to J. E. H., March 29, 1946.

[2] P. H. Pruitt moved down the Musquiz about ten miles from Fort Davis. He and Jim Dawson settled on range first used by Haley and Crosson and vacated by them when they moved south in 1881. Pruitt came from Arkansas to Fort Concho, and then to the Limpia, three or four miles above Fort Davis. The Indians stole him out so often that he moved down near the Rangers. J. J. Dawson to J. E. H., January 2, 1928; Jim P. Wilson to J. E. H., January 1, 1928; Nick Mersfelder to J. E. H., January 2, 1928.

[3] This was a not uncommon practice. They cut pieces of hide large enough to cover their horses' feet, and tied them with a rawhide string around their legs, just below the fetlocks. When the hide wore away, the process was repeated.

spring down in the hills below the foot of the Guadalupes. There they had come in from every direction and left their signs telling one another that they had gone on."

Nevill records that they were very close on September 18, that they camped without fires and prepared to attack next morning, first sending a scout to a high peak to locate the Indians. But those wily Apaches had been there ahead of him, had discovered the Rangers, and had scattered to the four vagrant and elusive winds, mainly "on foot" and hence leaving no trail for a horsebacker to follow. The Rangers turned back toward Fort Davis.[4]

Just before they got back, Jeff learned all he wanted to know about buckskin breeches. He had made a beautiful pair which he proudly wore on this trip. The party was caught in a hard rain, and Jeff rode into Fort Davis with his breeches clinging to him tighter than a wet chamois to a windshield and stretched down about a foot below the bottom of his boots. Once he was disillusioned, however, his break with tradition was drastic and complete. Even if Big Foot Wallace had worn them, they were not the proper garb for him. He stepped off his horse at Keesey's store[5]—before the sunshine had a chance to exercise its extreme reversal effect—and bought a pair of "duckin's." He unsheathed his bowie knife, slit the pants down either side from belt to boot and beyond, and let them fall off on the floor. That, he said, "was my last experience with buckskin pants." And that, too, was about the last of their Indian troubles.

When Jeff arrived in the early fall of 1881, the country was unused and unclaimed. The most noted ranchman in the Big Bend proper was Milton Faver, who had settled on the outside edge of that little wave of Mexican settlement that washed up from Chihuahua and played out on the north bank of the Río Grande. He was located in the canyon of Cibolo Creek some eighty miles west of south of their camp.

There has been much conjecture as to when he came, but he

[4] Nevill to King, September 25, 1881; "Reminiscences of Sam Graham," 15; J. D. Milton to J. E. H., July 1, 1937, and November 3, 1939.

[5] For information on Whitaker Keesey, see Raht, *Romance of the Davis Mountains and Big Bend Country*, 158, 202.

apparently reached that region about 1852. Back of that he is supposed to have contracted tuberculosis in New York City, and his doctors advised him to go West to die. Since he had considerable life insurance, the companies, confident they would soon have to pay it all, settled on a liberal basis and felt lucky at that. Faver took his money and somehow found his way up through Mexico to the Big Bend of Texas, where there were few Mexicans, fewer Americans, and only passing Indians to bother him.

But he did not die until age took him. He settled on the Cibolo, married a Mexican woman, raised some half-breed children and a lot more cattle in the F brand, and left his legend if not his mark upon the land that renewed his life. He was there and prospering in the memory of the oldest settler, though at times his trail was rocky. Once the Indians stole all the stock he had except sixty calves. But even recalcitrant nature rewards those who eternally endure. He stayed with that rugged land and in the progression of a generation of seasons had, by the early eighties, built that milk-pen bunch into a herd of 15,000 head.[6]

6 Raht, *Romance of Davis Mountains,* 136, 139, 144, 162, 225; W. B. Hancock to J. E. H., January 1, 1928. The best account of Faver is found in *Voice of the Mexican Border,* Marfa, September, 1933, 22–24.

He spread out and established another ranch on the Ciénega. His adobe headquarters was characteristic of the cattle frontiers of Mexico—sprawling and buttressed against a hot and hostile world, sufficient to all the needs of that simple and isolated life. In passing there early of a morning with the Rangers, Jeff recalls seeing a bevy of children, each with a cup in his hand, bearing down upon the gentled but none too generous cows in the milk-pen, each after his own breakfast.[7]

After the Sunset Railroad got into service, this hoary veteran of the Big Bend came out to take a trip. When the train started, he was terrified by the swaying motion, and the conductor found him lying in the aisle. In benign and bearded appearance he might have passed for one of the saints, only saints were not raised on the waters of the Río Grande. He carried his gun in his shirt, where it was covered by his flowing beard. Jeff recalls that once when a desperado jumped on him thinking him unarmed, he stuck his hand under his beard in an obeisant gesture, pulled out an old hog-leg, and sent the discourteous one to the promised land.[8]

But even legendary men, who deserve to live always to enrich anecdote and flavor life, have to die—even those who simply dry up in the rarified air along the Río Grande. His battered ranch house still stands, and those who wish the last tangible evidence of this unusual man can climb the mountain behind it, peer through the hand-cut grill of cottonwood poles that admits the perpetual sunshine to his dobe-closed grave, and read the silent requiem:

En Memoria a
Meliton Faver
Quien Murio el dia 23 Deciembre del ano 1889 a la
una de la tarde
Si tuvo faltas que sean olvidadas, y solo tenga
presente sus buenas acciones[9]

[7] A similar practice is suggested in that delightful story of life in Baja California, Fierro Blanco's *Journey of the Flame* (New York, 1933), though there they had no cups.
[8] J. D. Milton to J. E. H., July 1, 1937.
[9] Copied from his tombstone, October 20, 1932.

76

Over on the Alameda in the same section was old man John Davis, who came soon after Faver and who likewise married a Mexican and went to running cattle. There was nothing but space between them and the welcome waters of Limpia Creek at Fort Davis. Then two sheepmen came to the mouth of Musquiz Canyon below the Ranger camp. One was Lawrence Haley, a rugged and individualistic Irishman. The other was George Crosson.

Haley drifted up from the lower end of Texas with the backing of old man John Twohig, pioneer San Antonio banker. No trace of timidity inhibited his movement despite his profession.[10] He leisurely tromped out the turf as he mosied west from the county distinguished as the "Free State of Duval." In 1881, after two or three years of impudent trespass upon those who claimed the intervening grass, he reached Fort Davis and turned down to the mouth of Musquiz to be under the protection of the Rangers. There he and Crosson threw in together, and when the danger of Indians had subsided a few months later, they scouted south with Ranger escort and picked out their new and permanent locations below the site of Alpine. Even then one of Haley's herders was killed by the Indians, but it was beautiful country which he said must have been Milton's "Paradise Lost" until he found it.[11]

"It was a great country," agreed Jeff, sixty years later. "And just to think what a man of my age could have done if he had had the sense of a louse. But I was a young buck who didn't give a damn whether school kept or not. I had a good time and I always kept one hundred dollars to bury myself if I should die." After all, what boy of twenty, with the spirit of Sir William Wallace in his blood would want to settle down on rocky range with placid sheep as neighbors?

With him were kindred spirits to make life a vivid experience in that gray and grass-grown land. Nevill was a big, sturdy, un-

[10] John Twohig and Company, banking firm, opened in 1869. Twohig died on October 14, 1891. Frederick C. Chabot, *With the Makers of San Antonio* (San Antonio, 1937), 348-49.

[11] Hancock and Wilson, as cited; J. J. Dawson to J. E. H., January 2, 1928; "Reminiscences of Sam Graham"; Milton to J. E. H., June 11, 1939; W. H. Roberts to J. E. H., December 4, 1943.

forgettable man. He had a healthy sense of humor and was possessed of tolerance. A "perpetual smile" played upon his sandy face and shone from his brown eyes. He was continually telling yarns. While his sociability mixed too easily with whiskey in later years to do him the most good, yet at this time he was a broad-shouldered six-footer, weighing about two hundred pounds, and a natural leader of men.[12]

Among his men was George W. Simonds, more generally known to his fellow Rangers as "Old Wizard Oil." He showed up at Fort Davis in a fancy buggy drawn by a six-horse team, selling that marvelous balm that was good for all ailments. When he drifted down the canyon into the Rangers' camp and found them possessed of none, he, being enterprising and imaginative, decided he had better quit peddling for ranging, and joined to prove that he was right.

And though he was a rawhide sort of a fellow from Pennsylvania who would fight, he never lived down the name of "Wizard Oil." He would bet a month's wages that anyone could tie him hand and foot, throw him in the Río Grande, and he could swim out. His accommodating associates did, confident they would have to pull him out or see him drown. Nevertheless, though he was trussed up in a riata like a strait jacket, he was so limber that he swam like a wiggle-tail and slid out on the bank like an eel. Immediately these Texans put him down as a man of accomplishment, and thereafter, despite his unfortunate geographical origin, he commanded plenty of respect.

In camp he was always writing something down, in an untutored land a sort of suspicious pursuit which the Rangers dismissed as correspondence. After all, a man might write a letter once in a while. But when he showed up one day with a copy of *Leslie's* magazine containing an article that he had written, called "Mad Milton, Red Rover of the Río Grande," all of them knew that "Old Wizard Oil" was a man of the world.[13] Jeff,

[12] His people are said to have come up from Galveston to Austin, where his father ran a hardware store. He and "Mage" Reynolds, another noted Ranger leader, were brothers-in-law. W. H. Roberts to J. E. H., December 4, 1943.

[13] There has been some debate about the publication; if not *Leslie's*, then it may have been the *Detroit Free Press*. J. D. M.

moderately pleased with this renown, gave him an old "wore-out" silver-plated six-shooter, with a deck of cards inlaid on the handle. And the last that he heard of this versatile Ranger was that he had gone home, married, caught a man kissing his wife, cut him in two with the old .45—much to Jeff's approval, and was languishing in jail. That seemed terribly unjust to those tolerant Texans.

Then there was Buck Guyse, from down in Texas, who made a pretty good Ranger except that "he kind of wanted to be tough." At Fort Davis, in October, 1881, Buck and Jeff got on a glorious drunk, shot up the town, and took a pot shot at Deputy Sheriff Fairchild, all in good clean fun, of course. They were having a mighty fine time until Jeff remembered that they were Rangers and started back to camp. On the way he got off his horse to see if the earth was still firmly fixed, and old man Pruitt came by, picked him up in his wagon, and carried him to camp, where Jeff jumped into the cold and deep spring hole to sober up. The Sheriff, who really liked Jeff, came out to say that the boys had done no harm, and Jeff got off with thirty extra days on horse herd.

Buck, instead of coming in, passed through the Ranger camp at Musquiz and went down to where Joe Nations kept a cow camp. Nevill was away, but Sergeant J. T. Gillespie sent Julius Bird, Joe Irving, Nick Brown, and a Ranger named Anderson to get him. They met Buck on the road, but instead of coming straight up, as common sense would dictate, Buck ran into the rocks—there are always rocks in the Davis Mountains—and opened fire on them. Julius Bird charged right up on him and shot him through the shoulder, which, as Bill Roberts said, "kind of relaxed him." Gillespie sent him on to Davis for medical treatment, from where, a little later, Buck lit a shuck for New Mexico on the doctor's horse. But he sent the horse back, for while shooting up the town and deserting from the Rangers might be bad, horse-stealing in Texas was downright serious business.

When Nevill got back, he told them all, by special order, that in case of violations of the law "their treatment . . . must be no different from that of any other criminal.

79

"The men are reminded that the State pays men to suppress lawlessness enforce the laws and not violate them . . . and that the Battalion is not and will not be an asylum for any class of offenders."[14]

Jeff missed objectionable mention in the official dispatches—perhaps on account of his age, for he had just turned twenty—but he had plenty of time to mull over the matter on horse herd. Meanwhile Buck was disturbed from peaceful courtship of the Widow Corn's daughter on the upper Pecos in New Mexico, was taken into custody, and brought back to Nevill, at El Paso, by one "Patsy" Garrett, recently elected sheriff of Lincoln County.[15] Buck later returned to marry Molly Corn, fell into trouble along the Hondo, and was killed in that troublesome spot.

Though Musquiz Canyon seemed a perfect place to camp, the entire company was plagued with sickness in the spring of 1882—they suspected in part from pollution of their hole of water. Gillespie was down and out at Fort Davis with pneumonia, Pace was taken with the same trouble while on a scout to Toyah, some men had been down with mumps, and others were bothered with something that bordered on malaria. Nevill decided to move to a new location twelve miles below, at a good spring near the foot of that sharp peak, which, on account of its singular appearance, was called Bishop's Mitre. By the first of April they were through moving, and called the place Camp King.[16]

Scouting went on through the Big Bend while another little incident broke the even internal tenor of their ways. They supplied their own horses and guns, but the state furnished horse rations of corn, or was supposed to. After absence on extended scouts, the Rangers, coming in on "ganted" horses, starved and drawn, could draw horse rations for the period of their absence and thus recruit their mounts. After one long trip Nevill announced that, by orders from Austin, there would be no more back rations. Jeff, always harboring a tender regard for animals,

---

[14] J. T. Gillespie to W. H. King, October 31, 1881; Nevill, Special Order No. 12, November 5, 1881; J. D. Milton to J. E. H., January 28, 1945; W. H. Roberts to J. E. H., February 23, 1945.

[15] "Monthly Return," Company E, July 31, 1882.

[16] Nevill to King, April 2, 1882.

dearly loved his horses. He looked at his mount and was out-raged. "The very idea of the state of Texas being so damned chinchy that it would shut off corn from a horse," he fumed. "It's plumb reedic'lous."

That night he and Charlie Trentham slipped into the com-missary, where corn and bean coffee were kept in great tow sacks. They dragged one sack out, packed it a hundred yards and more up a canyon, cached it away, and prepared to fill the morrals for their expectant mounts. They cut it open to find that it contained coffee. They were too disgusted for words, though they said a few.

Next morning the cooks were furious. The coffee was missing. Nevill called everybody in, but nobody, not even the guard, knew a thing about it. Now a camp without coffee is a camp in trouble, and in four or five days he again called the company to account.

"Men, I know for certain that some of you got that coffee," he began. "You got it for corn. Whoever has got it can bring it back, and from now on corn will be issued as back rations." Still nobody knew a thing, but next morning the missing sack was in the commissary, green coffee was roasting in the pans, and every-body, in a decidedly better humor, was going on about his busi-ness.

After all, horses were their chief pride and joy in life, their partners in adventure, and their eternally faithful allies that daily carried them past death and danger. Why shouldn't they love them? Besides, their horses gave them diversion, and they liked to remember the race horse they discovered by chance. T. P. Pace, whom they called "Trot" Pace, had a sway-backed bay that ran out to meet them one day as they rode into camp. Pace step-ped on the gentle old fellow bareback, and as they headed for home, the old bay burned the breeze. The squad gave chase, but nobody could catch him. He flew up to the corral, bogged all fours, and piled Pace off on the ground. That looked like busi-ness to them.

Dock Gourley and others tried him out, trained him awhile, took him up to Davis, and matched him against a horse owned by a saloon man named Fletcher. The Rangers bet all they had, old sway-back came through as winner, and the money they wasted in town that night was at least double their scanty wages.[17]

After they were well settled at Camp King, or Bishop's Mitre, Nevill sent Jeff over to the mouth of Musquiz where a ranchman named Joe Dorsey from South Texas had just located above Cal Nations. Perhaps Nevill meant the mission as a sort of added rebuke to Jeff, for he was to arrest and bring Dorsey in under a charge of "shooting in a public place," the polite language of legality for shooting up the town.

Jeff found him at his ranch and said, "Dorsey, I've got a warrant for you. Come on."

"I won't go," said Dorsey, bowing up at being arrested by a youngster of twenty.

"Let me tell you something, Dorsey," said Jeff. "You either go or get killed, and I'll pull you in, just as you damned please."

"Well, if I've got to go . . ."

"You're going, shore," Jeff interrupted. So Dorsey caught a horse, saddled up, and Jeff took him to jail at Davis.[18]

To the south of the Rangers, Presidio was the only town in the Big Bend. It perched on the edge of the river adjacent to Presidio del Norte, on the other side, and there much of their business came to a focus. When it was not business, it was pleasant to sit and play poker with Bill Russell, brother of a sheriff under whom Jeff was later to serve in New Mexico. Bill had a store, and being on the Texas border, Bill likewise had time for poker and conversation and those leisurely arts that have sometimes suffered from civilization. Russell, Nevill, Jeff, and the local priest often sat down to a good game there. Then it was Jeff's delight to skin the priest, not out of pure perversity, of course, but simply because priests were supposed to be very good.[19]

[17] Pace went to El Paso years later as deputy United States marshal, fell into unhappy straits, walked down to a secondhand store "to buy" a gun, asked for a shell, and blew his brains out.
[18] The official return spells the name incorrectly, as "Dossy." "Monthly Return," Company E, September 30, 1882.

82

Always some harried soul was leaving posthaste for Presidio, and not for poker or piety, but usually because the Rangers were not far behind. If the fugitive crossed the river, they crossed, too, and often brought him back. As a rule the Mexican officials co-operated, though co-operation was not deemed essential, and extradition was hardly known. At one time Jeff and Doc Gourley took a man from the Mexican officials only after argumentation and dispute. Everybody, including the fugitive, was sitting on his horse. Simply as precaution, Jeff had dropped the loop of his riata around the culprit's head. When it looked as if the Mexican officials were going to decide to keep the unwilling repatriate, Jeff, with riata dallied around the horn of his saddle, hit a lope for the Texas side in spite of their yelling, and the prisoner followed the rope.

Once when the company was camped near by, Jeff and Trentham crossed the river to have a good time. Trentham dropped into a barbershop and Jeff went off to buck a game of monte. Trentham was a quiet man with no monkey business about him. Of spare and slender build, he was broad shouldered, with long arms and big hands like hams that hung almost to his knees, and, as Jeff said, "My, how he could use them!" He was devoted to his friends and death to others. All through the Patterson trouble at Colorado City, he had stood by Jeff as solid as a river rock.[20]

After Jeff had finished with the monte dealer, he looked around for Charlie. A Mexican told him that he had got into a fight with a soldier in the barbershop and "had laid him out." Two more tackled him, and he "knocked them cold." Five or six jumped on him, and Charlie's long arms and hamlike hands were bowling them about until one cracked him over the head with a

[19] Presidio, Texas, seems to have started after 1848, through interest in the Chihuahua–San Antonio trade on the part of John W. Spencer, John D. Burgess, Ben Leaton, and others. They had come into Presidio del Norte, Mexico, about 1848, and moved to the Texas side later to be under United States jurisdiction. E. E. Townsend to J. E. H., October 19, 1945; Alice V. Cain, thesis, "A History of Brewster County," 181; Raht, *Romance of Davis Mountains*, 84–85; Henry T. Fletcher in *The Southwestern Historical Quarterly*, October, 1944, 295–96.

[20] Trentham, a Texan, enlisted in Company B, under Captain Long, October 29, 1880.

saber, and the squad piled in and overpowered him. They had taken him to the *juzgado,* and they made Jeff think he was to be taken out and shot. Men have been shot for less on both sides of the Río Grande. Jeff fogged it for the Ranger camp, and Nevill and his command of some fifteen men almost knocked the river dry getting across to where about two hundred soldiers held Trentham on the other side.

"Boys, this may be business. We may have to kill the whole outfit," said Nevill to his men, as they headed for the jail. Those who were there leave the rest to imagination. Jeff dismissed the incident simply by saying, "We rode up to the jail and told the commanding officer that we had come for that man. And we got him. And that's all there was to that."

But at times they had more serious business than barbershop brawls and breaking the dealers at monte. They assisted ranchmen in scouting for ranges, escorted legitimate wayfarers through that thirsty land, and spent much time as guards for the Gano surveying parties in 1881 and 1882.

Texas, as possessor of the public domain, had issued scrip as bounty for service in her cause. This scrip, calling for lands to be located on the public domain, was trafficked about by veterans of her wars and by others to whom issued, and at times was located in great blocks by land agents, surveyors, and people of industry and means, among whom were the Ganos, of Dallas.

General R. M. Gano, Kentuckian, Texas legislator, veteran of the Confederacy, and now, with his two sons, resident of Dallas, had, by the late seventies, come into possession of some 100,000 acres of land in West and Northwest Texas. By April, 1881, the Ganos were extending their interests to the Big Bend country. Late that month Charlie Nevill reported leaving Camp Musquiz,[21] "with five men and 30 days rations to escort Gen. Gano and his party of surveyors through the section of country between here and the Rio Grande." They went out by an army outpost, Peña Colorado, below present Marathon, south to Cot-

---

[21] See William S. Speer and John Henry Brown, *Encyclopedia of the New West* (Marshall, Texas, 1881), 176–77, and "Monthly Return," Company E, December 31, 1881.

84

tonwood Springs on Maravillas Creek, and down it to the river. Out of this work of the Ganos came one of the first trips through the canyons of the Río Grande. In December, 1881, "Powell, Gage & Gano, Surveyors" were back again, wanting the Rangers "to accompany them while meandering the Rio Grande river from near Presidio, Texas to south east corner of Presidio Co." The party, anticipating six weeks for the trip, had boats for five Rangers and five surveyors. It wished an escort on account of the Indians. And Nevill stated in his report that since "the country bordering on the river is so rough it is impossible to meander it and carry our horses, as the trip is very risky. . . . I have concluded to lead it myself."[22]

They left Camp Musquiz December 13, and on the eighteenth, together with the surveyors, pulled out from Presidio down the river.[23] They drifted down through Santa Helena, the Mariscal, and what became the Dead Horse Canyons. The incidents of that still hazardous and rarely attempted voyage are left largely to the imagination, though Nevill reported that on December 23 a boat turned over, and a week later "my boat ran against a snag in a very swift riffle. I barely escaped drowning as I had on my pistol and belts, coats and boots. I lost my Field Glass and 300 rounds of ammunition besides considerable rations lost in the first upset and Trentham of my company came near drowning and Mr. Gano."

Sergeant Gillespie and nine men, Jeff among them, left Musquiz in mid-January to join the party at the mouth of Maravillas

[22] Nevill to W. H. King, December 9, 1881. E. E. Townsend, veteran of the Rangers and the Big Bend, refers to this expedition as the first to navigate the canyon. In 1850, Captain Love made his way up the Río Grande, 1,014 miles from Ringgold Barracks, near its mouth, to within 25 miles of Presidio del Norte. He was stopped by falls in the stream. Gano's party was apparently the first from Presidio down to this point. Reports on Love's trip with explanatory note by M. L. Crimmins are in West Texas Historical and Scientific Society Publications, V, 44–52. See also Townsend, "Rangers and Indians in the Big Bend Region," ibid., VI, 43 ff.

Henry Fletcher, of Marfa, says that Dr. Udden, the geologist, told of meeting a northern Swede who had been in the gold rush, and who, with his brother, returning from California soon after, heard the Indians were bad, got a boat, and came down the river from El Paso to Matamoros. Townsend to J. E. H., October 19, 1945.

[23] Ibid., and "Monthly Return," Company E, December 31, 1881.

Creek, 140 miles away.[24] Two days before the parties joined,
Nevill observed a bunch of Indians on the Texas side, put into
the bank, and in the skirmish that followed killed and captured
nine of their horses but none of the Indians. It was really a "hell
of a country" on horses.[25] He jumped another bunch that had
just crossed into Mexico, "but they fled as soon as we pulled into
shore," he said, and were too far off "to waste ammunition shooting with Winchesters." Next day he found another trail of fifty
horses going into Mexico, which he believed to have been made
by the Indians "that have raided Pena Colorado so often the last
year." Eventually, according to Sam Graham, who was with
Gillespie's party, the navigators lost all their boats but one. But
they had surveyed the canyons of the Río Grande, and they took
their horses and turned back up San Francisco Creek to their
permanent camp.[26]

The escorting of Gano's surveyors continued into the summer
of 1882, and Jeff came to know the Big Bend country like a well-
read book. There was no more interesting territory for them to
scout then, as there is no more fascinating land for the lover of
nature now, than that strange life zone of growth and that wrath-
ful display of geology found in the Chisos Mountains and the
lower Big Bend. It is still a world apart, unchanged by the puny
hand of man. And the men who lived in it then seemed strangely
in keeping with its perverse and enduring surface. It never encouraged ease and comfort, but continually warned the wayfarer to be on his guard. Even yet it never warms and beckons,
but it somehow holds those who are its own with a hard and un-

[24] Stud Robinson, one of the party and a Ranger who kept putting on pants
as winter progressed instead of changing to clean ones, enlivened camp one night
by getting his breeches on fire. He peeled off a pair to find the next on fire, and so
on, until three pairs were off before the fire was out.
[25] E. E. Townsend points out that this incident provoked the naming of
Dead Horse Canyon and occurred near present Boquillas, and that, unfortunately,
"the mighty rift through the mountains . . . is now sometimes called Boquillas
Canyon." See Townsend, as cited, 46.
Rangers with the surveyors were Nevill, J. M. Sedberry, C. T. Trentham, Joe
Irving, and Charlie Eans. Townsend, as cited, 45; J. D. Milton Notes, by Mrs.
J. D. M.
[26] Nevill to King, February 4, 1882; "Monthly Return," Company E, January
31, 1882; "Reminiscences of Sam Graham"; Milton to J. E. H. in various interviews.

breakable grip, while provoking awe in the heart of the irreverent. Nothing about it cultivates flippancy or familiarity, but there hangs over the land like the purple haze of distance a pervasive inducement to diffidence and even austerity.

Thus two old prospectors whom the Rangers found eternally rustling stubborn burros and hunting elusive gold down in the canyons of the Maravillas seemed to belong there and nowhere else. Jeff and the boys called them "Spike" and "Juggie." They had grown old at their fruitless but optimistic quest, though hardly mellow and tolerant with years. They were prowling that wild land in spite of Indians and outlaws, desert and sand, and hell, but not high water. They camped together of a night, but each with his own outfit. No matter which built the fire first, the other never infringed upon it with his can of coffee or bait or bear meat, but built another near by and cooked his scanty meal to himself. When Spike went after the burros, he brought his into camp and left Juggie's jackasses strictly alone. Juggie could rustle his own, himself. They impressed the Rangers as being rather rugged individualists, and seemed completely happy and at home down by the Río Grande.

Jeff found the ravens of the Chisos country much more sociable. Two of these fellows with the raucus voices and voracious appetites sailed down on the fringes of their camp one day near Presidio to gather scraps from their mess. Next day the Rangers broke camp and moved down the river, and when they stopped that night, those ravens were right there. So day after day these camp followers kept their trail and grew fat and sassier still.

Even though the going was rough, the land gave meat to those who could take it: mountain sheep on the rimrocks, bears in the manzanita thickets in the Chisos, javalinas in the hills, deer in the scattered canebrakes along the banks of the river, and fine catfish in its holes. Jeff always liked to fish, and as the Rangers made camp one evening, he " 'lowed" he would have some. But as he had no hooks, the boys knew he was simply talking. They reckoned not his ingenuity as he took some horseshoe nails from the pack, bent them into hooks, cut a cane pole from a near-by thicket, flailed a few grasshoppers from erratic flight,

87

and dropped his line into the stream with a six-shooter bullet for a sinker. Soon the air was fragrant with supper as catfish simmered and swam in the grease of their frying pans.

Yet through the months there was more serious business for Jeff, Sedberry, and Wells. The impending trial for the killing of Patterson at Colorado City had, by successive continuances and legal mutations, been postponed for more than two years. Semi-annually, however, they had to go back from Fort Davis for each session of court. In advance of their first trip, Nevill reported to Adjutant General King, in September, 1881, that the boys would have to be in Colorado City for the October term, that feeling was still high, and that the Rangers "think the cowboys will try to avenge Patterson's death . . . it was attempted on Wells once and but for the timely arrival of two other rangers he thinks they might have killed him. . . . the cowboys were trying to provoke a quarrel every time they met."

Hence Nevill sent an escort under Corporal Sam Graham with them. They camped one night on the Pecos at Horsehead Crossing, where Jeff stood second guard. The river was alive with ducks, which, in wildest sort of flight during the night, were swooping and cutting over their camp until Jeff thought they were going to fly into the fire.

From Horsehead Crossing they rode east along the old trail, by Sterrett and Sherwood's ranch on the Middle Concho, in sight of the military outpost of Camp Charlotte, by Tom Green's ranch near Hackberry Springs, and across familiar ground to Colorado City. Court convened and the case was continued. The boys, again released on bail, returned to the Ranger camp at Musquiz. Again in March, 1882, they returned to court. Corporal Gourley and three other men met them with horses at Toyah on their return by rail. In October, they went again, and so on through change of venue to Buffalo Gap, the seat of Taylor County. At last, in the fall of 1883, after the county seat had been moved to Abilene, the case came to trial. Nevill, in his monthly reports noting their trips "to stand trial for killing of one Patterson," always faithfully and loyally added "while in discharge of their duty."[27]

The memory of the long-drawn-out case for the killing of a man who was about to kill them must have been bitter for them all, and especially for young Jeff Milton. Yet he never alluded to it in later years unless he was pressed, and then only in laconic and unfeeling phrases. He never harbored resentment.

Charlie Trentham and Stud Robinson were witnesses, and the loyalty of Trentham was one of the compensations of the tragedy compounded by the apparent ingratitude of the state they were serving. The case was moved from Colorado City on account of the difficulty of securing a jury. At Buffalo Gap in April, 1883, the state had trouble rounding up its witnesses. The defense was ready for trial. Judge T. B. Wheeler granted continuance, but to assure the appearance of the principal witness for the state—Ab J. Adair, who was with Patterson at the time of the shooting—put him under bond. In November, 1883, the trial was held at the new town of Abilene, on the Texas and Pacific Railroad, where Spoontz and Liggett represented the Rangers.

But Jeff's family, in keeping with the mission of his furloughs back to the settlements, had arranged for more distinguished defense. H. H. Boone and his partner, T. D. Cobbs, of Navasota, were on hand.[28] Boone had written to Adjutant General King that "the most important question of law" in the case was whether the defendants, who were simply privates in the service, "were lawfully authorized to arrest Patterson?" They had found that the Act of 1874 creating the Frontier Battalion made "only the commissioned officers thereof 'Peace Officers,'" he continued. "We find no statute that makes the privates of the Batt'n 'peace officers.'" For Milton, Sedberry, and Wells, it was a most important point of law; for the Frontier Battalion and a continuance of its effective work, it was equally important.

Without question, as Walter Prescott Webb has pointed out in *The Texas Rangers*, "the intent of the framers of the law was that every Ranger in the Frontier Battalion was an officer, and

[27] Nevill to King, September 11, 1881; "Monthly Return," Company E, October 31, 1881; *ibid.*, March 31 and October 31, 1882; "Reminiscences of Sam Graham," 26–27; Sam Graham to J. E. H., April 30, 1944.

[28] For sketch of Cobbs, see L. E. Daniell, *Texas, The Country and Its Men* (n. p., n. d.), 298–303.

that as such he had all the powers of a peace officer." In fact, he ranged the entire state of Texas with the general understanding that he had the right to apprehend any lawbreaker at any place at any time. It is an ironical quirk of history that this point of law, raised by a former attorney general of Texas in defense of the son of a governor of Florida for the fearless prosecution of duty, should eventually be ruled adversely to the rights of the Rangers, and, according to Webb, "in reality destroyed the Frontier Battalion."[29]

In November, the Rangers were on hand, and the case was called. According to Jeff, there was ample reason for Ab Adair's reluctance to appear in court. Under pressure of the ubiquitous Good and other friends of Patterson's, he had perjured himself in the Colorado City examining trial. Jeff fell in with Adair on the train as they journeyed to Abilene, and that unwilling and unhappy witness made a clean breast of the whole thing. But he told Jeff that he was going to tell the truth this time—"they will never force me to it again." He tried to give him a splendid watch, but Jeff fortunately refused the proffered gift.

They got off the train at Abilene but returned to Colorado City that night, leaving Adair drinking and gambling at one of the saloons. Next morning he was found along the railroad tracks between two boxcars, dead from a gunshot wound. Nobody had seen him die. The coroner found it to be suicide. Jeff thought how close to tragedy the fates had tempted him; had he accepted that watch on the train, the finger of suspicion would have been on him, and there might have been another trial. Throughout life he was notably loath to oblige himself to any man.[30]

Yet even the seriousness of the trial was broken by levity. Over a Sunday, Jeff passed the evening in conversation with other guests on the front gallery of his boardinghouse. A man about thirty-five, who appeared to be "all stomach," kept hurrahing him until he finally said, "My parents taught me not to an-

[29] H. H. Boone to W. H. King, October 18, 1882; Webb, *The Texas Rangers*, 453.

[30] Jeff D. Milton to J. E. H., December 15, 1942.

swer back to old men, but if you don't quit joking me I'm going to roll you over on your stomach and sit on you."

"Why," said the man of immense girth, "I'll tell you what I'll do, young fellow. I'll bet you, by Jacks, that I can take you by the seat of the pants and hold you out by one hand." Jeff, big and husky himself, "just had to laugh."

"I'll bet the drinks for the crowd that you can jump a-straddle of my arm, and I can take a pencil in my hand and write your name on the wall as good as your own hand," added the jovial one.

"I'll just take them," said Jeff, jumping up. And the man with the enormous belly just slipped his right arm through Jeff's crotch, and holding him out at arm's length wrote his name on the wall. So they all crossed the street to the saloon and had their drink on Jeff.

Then the stranger asked, "Are there any big men in town?" Jeff knew of two; one as big as a Jersey steer, and another that broke the beam at around three hundred pounds. "I can pick them up the same way," the fat man said. "I'm pretty near broke. Let's win a little money."

Jeff let the other Rangers in on the deal, and they pooled their cash. They all went back into the saloon where the big man turned to hurrahing Jeff again. "Say, kid," he boomed so all might hear, "I'll bet you a hundred dollars that I can take the two biggest men in town, one on each arm, and hold them out and walk to the back of the saloon and back here before setting them down." The bartender knew these two local mountains of flesh and fat, and at once called the stranger's pile, which was all he and the Rangers had. Then he sent out and waddled his prizes in. Nothing fazed, the stranger gathered one on either arm and performed his stunt, saying, "Gentlemen, if that ain't satisfactory, I'll take 'em out and set 'em down in the street."

He confided to Jeff that he was "the strongest man in the United States." He had been a butcher in Chicago, and had no idea how strong he was until a boisterous celebrant rode into his shop, which made him so mad that he picked up the horse and man, he said, and threw them both out. But Jeff did not see that.

91

After all there are things that must be taken on faith. Thus Sunday wore off at pioneer Abilene, and during the week the long-drawn case came to trial.

A prominent cowman, whom Jeff gratefully recalled but would never name, before the jury retired, came to him to say, "Son, if it don't come out right, remember: I've got the fastest horse in the country tied out there with a Winchester on the saddle. I'll hold 'em back long enough for you to get a head start."

And so late in 1883 the jury brought in a verdict finding the Rangers not guilty;[31] and Jeff, Sedberry, and Wells were again free to adventure, untrammeled and unafraid, on that shifting frontier of Texas that lay west of the Pecos and down in the Big Bend.

[31] Minute Book, District Court, Vol. B, 104, Abilene, Texas.

7

The Birth of Murphyville

When Jeff joined the Rangers, the usual period of enlistment was a year. Those who lusted for the meager fare but vigorous life usually stayed longer. Jeff stayed three years. But that restless nature that lays an irresistible hand upon many strong spirits was inclined, on occasion, to manhandle him. Anyway, times were changing; and he was ready for a change, too. Already the boldest leaders who had lent luster to the force had hung up their guns and quit the service.

The list was formidable and not without significance. Old Confederate fire-eaters like Marsh and Long, and the diminutive and genteel Peak, had left the frontier and gone back to the settlements. Men like Reynolds, Nevill, Ware, Oglesby, and Arrington had quit to become sheriffs of counties they had helped to conquer and settle. Young Jeff, while still lacking their renown at mature twenty-one, followed them out of the service, on May 10, 1883.[1]

Yet he liked the country and two days later took a job at Dan Murphy's general store, in the town of Fort Davis, selling dry goods. His bosom friends—the sandy-complexioned warrior, Sedberry, and the quiet and dangerous Trentham—must have blushed in their beards over this prosaic fall of "Mad Milton, Red Rover of the Río Grande."

But Jeff would have "just had to laugh" had the incongruity occurred to him as he went on about his business. And going "on about my business" with Jeff was simply zestful living from day to day; living tempered by an individualistic philosophy of life that seemed to have scant concern for ordinary business, and none whatever for the future.

[1] Memo. from Joseph Johnson to J. D. Milton, Adjutant General Department of Texas, notes the day of his discharge. Copy in Jeff Milton files.

Yet he was a good dry-goods clerk. Ready retort, good humor, good looks, and genuine Southern conviviality made him good company in that robust age. Men then traded with people they liked rather than with those who shaved the margins and split the pennies. Jeff sold on commission in such overhanded fashion that Murphy thought he was making too much and put him on a salary instead.

Selling dry goods is essentially a dry pursuit, but Jeff's friend Joe McKinney, a husky cowpuncher from Uvalde, turned his deft fingers from the dealing of monte to the tending of bar on the other side of Murphy's store, and of an evening Jeff knew the difference between a counter and a polished bar. Good company means good times.

The chronicles of high-hearted men throughout the ages have recorded the fact that excitement cannot be channeled to chosen pursuits, but that adventure is essentially for the adventurous. At the dance halls and about the saloons at night Jeff soon saw that Murphy's bookkeeper, a man named Hughes, was flying a lot higher than their small salaries would warrant. Jeff eyed him and the money drawer with suspicion. A few days later he stopped Dan Murphy, the owner, an Irishman direct from Erin, in the presence of Hughes, and said, "Mr. Murphy, I'm quitting." Murphy wondered why. Leveling an ominous finger like a gun barrel at Hughes, Jeff replied, "Because that man is a damned thief. He's stealing from you. I won't work with him. I'm going to quit."

Hughes spluttered his indignant denial. However, Jeff had marked a bill in the till the day before, had retrieved it after Hughes spent it in the evening at the fancy houses of Fort Davis, and now presented the marked note to Murphy. Hughes continued his denials; but the next morning, between two and three hundred dollars two cowboys had deposited with the store was gone, and so was Hughes.

At this time Fort Davis was the hub of that wide and isolated range marked on the maps as Presidio County. A move to organize it had been made in 1858, but the Civil War had intervened, and it was not until 1875 that organization was effected.

94

In November, 1882, Nevill quit the Rangers to become sheriff.[2] John M. Dean, a hot-hearted Southerner who was rumored to have killed a Negro and who came west as a stage driver, had taken the job as district attorney. The Rangers were still camped at Bishop's Mitre Peak, the country was settling with cowmen, the Negro soldiers with their monthly pay were still at the post to bolster business, and everything seemed well in hand.

Joe McKinney took time from tending bar to deal a little monte to the Mexicans and the Negroes. Both races were given to gambling. Ordinarily the Negroes were the best sports of all when it came to losing. One night, however, a veteran colored sergeant "as striped as a zebra" got into Joe's game. Joe could not keep him from winning, and soon the sergeant was feeling his importance. At last Joe got his deal under control and was taking him in when the Negro lost his temper and said, "I think you s——o——b——s are crooking me." Joe quietly gathered up his winnings, straightened his immense frame from the chair, and hit him.

The Negro got up and struck a trot for the District Attorney's office, where he circumspectly approached Dean to inquire, "Mistah, is dey any law 'ginst calling anybuddy uh black son-uv-a-bitch?"

Dean looked up from his desk and said, "Well, aincha?"

The frontier had made Fort Davis an important swing station on the long trail that looped across Texas from San Antonio to the West Coast. By the same token, the passing of the frontier destroyed its importance. The railroads that displaced the overland trail, independent of water and grass, split the Big Bend in two by easier grades some twenty miles to the south. There a siding was built on Dan Murphy's land near Burgess' Spring in an oval and open valley heavily seeded by nature with grama grass. Murphy dedicated the land to the town, and in December, 1883, the faint stirrings of settlement that were to become the village of Alpine were officially recognized with the postoffice of Murphyville.[3]

2 Alice V. Cain, thesis, "A History of Brewster County," 191–96.
3 In 1882 the railroad was built across the spot where Alpine stands. Through

Frontier settlements then first stood for something to settle a man's thirst. And the consuming thirst characteristic of that dry land, when nurtured on long and dusty rides, and then washed down with rivers of red whiskey, boiled back in an effervescence of Western spirit that shot holes in the roofs and the lights out of the saloons. The passing of time simmered the reaction. Growing age in a settlement, like the passing years in a man, seemed to induce a sort of intolerance for the bucolic ways of boisterous youth, and even put men out on patrol to preserve the peace. As Murphyville threatened to become a civilized town, Sheriff Charlie Nevill called Jeff from behind the dry-goods counter, where genius with guns was going to pot, and sent him saddling away to the south.

So Jeff as a deputy, properly mounted and armed and again on the trail of bold and desperate men, was in a fair way of restoring himself to decency in the eyes of his friends.

When Jeff went to work, Murphyville was still just a mote on the railroad map and an ambitious stirring in the hearts and heads of some men. Yet it is an old story in the growth of the West. The mark on the map was casual; the conception in the minds of vigorous men was the vital substance that insured its growth. At first these villages were as rambunctious as a five-year bronc, but respectability reached them with a violent rush. Jeff gathered the disturbers of the peace of the town-to-be with a generous will, and in place of a jail locked them in a boxcar on the siding of the Southern Pacific. When he went to give them some air next day, his jail was gone.

---

trains began running the next year. Alice V. Cain notes the beginning of the town as a boxcar telegraph and post office combined. The name was changed to Alpine in 1888. See Cain, thesis, "A History of Brewster County," 66, 68.

Daniel Murphy, owner of the land and merchant at Fort Davis, was born in Cork County, Ireland, February 5, 1830. In 1873 he bought a portion of the town of Fort Davis from Pedro Guarro, who had filed on it in 1855. He dedicated his land on the railroad to the town of Murphyville in 1883. He saw its name changed in 1888. He died November 15, 1902, and slept undisturbed until February, 1946, when progressive citizens dug up his dust to make room for a new street that was hardly needed. From Epitaph at Fort Davis; Transcript of Patent Record, Jeff Davis County, Vol. IV, 36; *San Angelo Standard Times*, February 21, 1946. See also Henry T. Fletcher in *The Southwestern Historical Quarterly*, October, 1944, 296; and West Texas Historical and Scientific Society *Publications*, V, 17.

Jeff's friend Reeves, the railroad agent, wired up and down the line. At last they found that an enterprising crew had taken the car in tow, Jeff's prisoners were rolling toward Del Río, and when the door was opened, there was no charge of demurrage due to delay in unloading.

The first report upon his arrival was that the celebrating cowboys—and cowboys in town at that time were always celebrating, either their early arrival or late departure—were going to run him out of town. Jeff stepped into House Brothers' store, as he recalls the first one there, bought a shotgun he saw on the counter, and hunted up the saloon where whiskey and talk flowed most freely. With the ten-gauge in the crook of his arm, he stepped in at the back door.

"I thought I just as well stop it," he said. "I covered them and made them all strip off and back off from the bar. 'Boys, every one of you get your six-shooters off as fast as you can or I'll kill every damned one of you right here.' And believe me, they shucked them, too. I made quite a talk to them, like a man would talk to men. I told them they all wanted to be gentlemen when they came to town, to pull their six-shooters off and leave them behind the bar, and it had quite an effect on them. Never had no more trouble—not a word." After that they heaped their Colts on the counter with pleasure.

But they took to warting him with their practical jokes. Once in a while at one end of the little town they'd let loose a volley of six-shooter shots. Jeff would break down the street at a run and be searching for them in the dark. Meanwhile they would circle behind the buildings and open up again at the other end of town. Jeff got the smallest shot he could buy, some number ten, and called on a friend for help. The next time the shooting started he sent his friend running like a dray horse up the Murphyville street and lay low in the grass at the other end. Shortly he could hear the men coming, laughing at the ribbing they were giving the deputy. Again they cut loose, and so did "the law," and the stinging number tens ended the rare good sport of shooting up the town.

The Ranger camp had again been moved from Bishop's Mitre Peak, about twelve miles northwest, and located at a spring at the base of the mountain just west of town. Jeff often visited with the boys there, and especially with that sandy-hided, redheaded Ranger friend, Sedberry. When Christmas of 1883 came, Jeff made an early-morning round and rode out to the Ranger camp. Sedberry, who never drank, had bet Jeff a Stetson hat that he was going to get drunk on Christmas day. Sedberry was a great officer, and Jeff just knew he would not do it. So he went out to collect. When he rode up and caught the gleam in Sedberry's eye, he kissed the bet good-bye.

"Old Sed" was already raring to go, and to Murphyville they went. After his first drink there, he put his well-filled wallet— for he saved his money—and his six-shooter in Jeff's hands and went on a regular tear. In one saloon a great big bully, so mad he was crying, "had a little bitty man hemmed up in a corner where he was going to whip him."

"Let me have him," shouted Old Sed, as he made for the fray, grabbed the fighter by the shoulder and spun him around, saying, "I'll put him to laughing in no time." "And believe me," recalled Jeff with admiration that outlasted the years, "he shore did."

Then the daily passenger train came through. For fifty years

98

the chief diversion in many West Texas villages was the arrival of the train. Crowded people can hardly conceive its significance. It roared into town trembling the place with a sort of a tidal wave of expectancy. After depositing its meager sacks of mail and its chance drummer, it puffed away into the distance charged with a suggestion of exotic romance that these stranded souls in that spacious world sometime hoped to sample. Everybody met the train. Of course, "Old Sed," all sheets in the wind, was there. He mounted it with the uncertain step but the confident air of a Southern gentleman. From one end to another with hat in hand, he bowed his auburn head to every lady in abject apology for his drunken condition. Jeff trailed dutifully behind. The conductor was forced out of schedule until he was through, for J. M. Sedberry, Texas Ranger, was nothing if not a thorough gentleman.

It was a perfect Christmas day for Jeff, the Rangers, and the balance of Murphyville who held the law and the proprieties of decent living in high regard.

"Goddamn you," said Sed to Jeff; "you owe me that Stetson."

Murphyville grew like the grama grass after the July rains. The railroad built a freight station, House Brothers put up a big store, and saloons sprang up in square-fronted structures, with hooker houses behind. Joe McKinney came down from Fort Davis with Murphy's backing and opened a saloon with his monte game on the side.[4] Jeff, still something of a novice at piking, walked in and laid a dollar down on the card that a crowd of Mexicans were playing. Now Joe was a loyal friend with pride in an honest game, but his nimble fingers, in spite of "the cut," kept touch with what was turning up. Stepping away from the dealer's chair for a moment and motioning Jeff to one side, he circumspectly advised, "Jeff, when you see all those Mexicans bet on one card, put your money on another one."

With John Slaughter, a distant relative of the John Slaughter of Arizona, a man with the blackest eyes, mustache, and hair he had ever seen, with him as a partner, Jeff went into the saloon business. Jeff was to run the joint, which they set up in a railroad warehouse. Three posts supported their bar. On each post Jeff

[4] Joe McKinney to J. E. H., February 2, 1945, and April 14, 1946.

99

tied a scabbard, and in each scabbard a six-shooter stuck out within easy range of his hand. When he opened for business, John Kokernot and some cowpunchers came stomping in. Jeff set out the whiskey and glasses. One picked up a glass and broke it on the bar. Jeff quietly reminded his initial customers that glasses were hard to get.

"Hell, I'll just break 'em all," the rowdy answered, and raised his arm to sweep them off on the floor.

But faster than the fall of his hand was Jeff's draw from the post beneath the bar, and the flash of his hot black eyes above the barrel of the gun as he warned, "If you do, you're a dead 'un."

Then he shooed his erstwhile customers out the door despite their desire for further trade, and was locking up as his hunting friend, Tom Hands, came along to buy a drink.

"Nuthin' doing," said Jeff. "We're closed." And "closed" they were. No need, he said, "to be in a business where you got to kill a man for nothing." When Hands saw that Jeff was really in earnest, he offered to buy him out. Thus, in a scant two hours, Jeff began and ended his only venture in the liquor business.

After all, ordinary business was not for him. It was more pleasant to rent Preacher Nations' pack mules and head over the ridges with Hands on a hunt than to be trying to make money. When they returned with venison hams, one-half for Nations, who ran a hotel, in return for his mules, Jeff walking alongside his saddle horse loaded down with what the mules could not carry, neither cared whether he had anything else or not. For occupation, there was still the job with Nevill, full of opportunity for shooting and fighting, but "not for nothing." To discriminating men like Jeff, there was a decided difference.

Once in a great while some untoward incident reminded them that they were a part of the state of Texas. Murphyville had a barber, and Jeff slid into his chair one day for a shave. With what to him seemed alarming abandon, the barber took one swipe with the razor all the way across his face.

"Hold on, here, barber," complained Jeff, "you're liable to cut me."

"He laid his razor right across my Adam's apple," recalled

100

Jeff, "caught me by the arm, leaned over, and looked me right in the eye. I'll never forget it. His eyes looked like the ends of two black pins. Rubbing his razor up and down on my Adam's apple, he said, 'What's the matter? Don't you like the way I'm shaving you?'

"I saw he was as crazy as a loon. 'Yes sir,' I said, without moving a hair. 'You're the best damned barber I ever saw.'

" 'Well I'm going to give you a shave like you've never had before,' he said, reaching down to get his strap. When he drew his razor back to strap it, I bounced out of that chair like I'd been stuck. He grabbed me, but I had my six-shooter out and let a shot or two go right between his legs. He jumped back, and I went out of there in a hurry. He slammed and locked the door. I got some help and came back. We broke it in and roped him, and finally got him down after he had cut the rope four or five times. Then we sent him to the asylum at Austin. If I'd said a word or moved, he'd 'a cut my throat, certain."

And so they went the uneven tenor of their individual ways until Jeff took down, bad, with pneumonia. At the time he was staying with Reeves, the Southern Pacific agent, in the railroad freight house. Reeves called in the local doctor, who gave up the case and said he was bound to die. The philosophy of futility had no place with them, and Reeves was so furious that he kicked the doctor down the station stairs and sent for the post surgeon at Fort Davis. At last Jeff was up, weak but well. Then that strange and vital spark that drove men West demanded another change. He headed for New Mexico.

8

From the San Mateos to the Mogollons

Early in 1884, Jeff Milton left El Paso with a chance and friendly suggestion that he stop off at the village of San Marcial, up the Río Grande in New Mexico, and get acquainted with two Texans, Charles and Billy Featherstone, general merchants there. The suggestion sounded interesting, for the heavy hand of radical change rested on that region, too.

The railroad had just been built down the river to El Paso from Aubuquerque, bringing ambition and dislocation to the dobe-like delta that had slept for inert centuries in the lap of a lazy sun. Except for a three-dollar gold piece and a little loose change, Jeff got there flat broke, else he might have gone on to Socorro, which was his original destination. He stepped off the train where lately cowboys had taken in and shot up the old Mexican town, and where a man named Zimmerman, owning a site on the railroad, was promoting a new town.[1]

Jeff deposited his saddle and little trunk at the San Marcial Hotel, and wandered into a pool hall for acquaintance and a friendly game. He was full faced and youthful in appearance, and, having shaved his mustache off, might have been taken for a boy of sixteen. He started a game with what he called a "one-horse bad man" who was blowing real loud all over the place. The bartender warned him against it because the man was "a bad one," and as Jeff took the lead in the game he got much worse. At last he left a perfect setup for Jeff's winning shot, and was so furious that he walked around the table to him and began cursing him, saying, "Don't you knock that ball in."

"Why, I don't see how I can help it," said Jeff.

"I'm going to give you the damndest thrashing you ever got, if you do," said the "one-horse bad man."

[1] *Albuquerque Journal*, February 13 and April 12, 1883.

"I'm very sorry, sir," Jeff answered, in his most genteel Southern manner, "I can't help but knock it in."

"You heard what I said," roared his companion.

Jeff tapped the ball lightly and then swung with his cue, and the ball and the bad man went down together. Jeff stomped him a little, took his gun, and walked out.

"No trouble a-tall," said Jeff, as he went on about his business.

San Marcial was then a railroad division. Now the upper waters of Elephant Butte Lake lap against its abandoned location, but the summer Jeff got there it claimed a population of one thousand. Jeff took the first work that turned up, which was at a dollar a day with an Irish section gang. When he needed a job, any sort of honest work was always good work for him.

Since Jeff had his saddle, Winchester, and six-shooter—standard cowboy equipment—stored in town, Billy Featherstone kept his weather eye open for a better job as people drifted in and out of his store. When John W. Virgin, manager and part-owner of the Illinois Cattle Company came in, Jeff got it. He loaded his gear in the ranch wagon, and he and the driver headed for the ICC headquarters twenty-eight miles to the west, in Red Canyon, on the eastern slope of the San Mateo Mountains.

Cattle ranching in western New Mexico was just getting into good swing. But for years grizzled and leg-weary men, with strange tales on their lips and wild hope in their hearts, had wandered in and out of that jumbled mass of mountains reaching from the San Mateos, by the Río Grande, to where the crags of the Mogollons break off in the upper reaches of the Gila River. Even possession of the substantial riches in silver that poured out of these hills could not appease the lust for the fabulous, belegended gold of the Lost Adams Diggings. Men still suffered and slaved, thirsted and starved, and fought and died in that rough region for the gold they hoped to get.

Although it was wild and largely unsettled, there were still a great many people in that immense land that rose and fell and twisted and turned in rugged and wanton confusion from Gallup and Grants, on the Santa Fé Railway to the north, down to where the Southern Pacific snaked its way through Stein's Pass and

103

across the playas to the village of Deming, on the south. For the next two years this angry hump of the continental divide was to be home, and its danger and violence the breath of life for Jeff. He seemed to sniff its adventure from afar.

It was a good day's ride from San Marcial up the river to Socorro, the county seat, then waxing fat on the mining business. Albuquerque, seventy-five miles farther north, was the principal town of the state. Down the river, Hot Springs was then simply an abandoned adobe near some holes of hot water, but Las Palomas, a short way farther, was a lively and promising village on the banks of the river. To the southwest, Hillsboro was sharing its deep and inviting cottonwood shade with cowboy, miner, and political official as the incipient seat of Sierra County. In the adjacent hills above, Kingston was a roaring mass of temporarily prosperous humanity in the middle of its mining boom, and farther west, Silver City was digging into Chloride Flat with a more lasting, tenacious hold on life.

Around the base of the Mogollons to the northwest, up the valley of the San Francisco, a tributary of the Gila, the village of Alma had started. Still farther up the "Frisco" were three tough little Mexican settlements, the Lower, the Middle and the Upper Plazas, the last of which became the town of Reserve. Back through the 120-odd miles of mountains between there and the Río Grande were such mining camps as Fairview, Cooney, and Chloride. Nevertheless, the country was still suffering the ravages of the Apaches.[2]

Grass covered its hills like a washed and well-worn saddle blanket. A man on foot could be trailed across its grama carpet like a percheron in a wheat field. Montague Stevens, an English ranchman who came in 1881, says grass-fat cattle then dressed out like beef on corn.[3] At this very time two other dynamic de-

---

[2] The Chloride Flat and Silver City discoveries were in 1871. Gold was found at Hillsboro in 1877, and the town started in August. The Kingston silver discovery was in October, 1880. F. A. Jones, *New Mexico Mines and Minerals* (Santa Fé, 1904), 53, 81, 99; H. H. Bancroft, *History of Arizona and New Mexico* (San Francisco, 1889), XVII. O. W. Williams, *In Old New Mexico, 1879–1880* (n. p., n. d.), 18, tells something of pioneer Silver City. See also *Albuquerque Journal,* January 24, 1883, for Kingston.

velopments in business and industry were combining with grass to settle this region with ranchmen.

One was the keen financial interest of Eastern and English capital in the Western range. The other was the invention of barbed wire and its current and widespread use in Texas. The parent state of the longhorn business was fencing its grass with wire. Men either leased or bought their ranges, and fenced, or they got out. Many who moved loaded their wagons, called their dogs, rounded up their herds, and headed for New Mexico and Arizona.

The great open grasslands of the Pecos had been taken, and these grizzled men with guns on their hips and the fires of desire in their eyes trailed west in easy stages to take the ranges still reserved by danger and distance. Western New Mexico, in rugged isolation and with lurking hazard and hardship, looked good to them. Both in peace and in violence they took it by infiltration of their trailing herds. Many of these Texans—as might be suspected of a rural people who had never attached themselves to the soil—were wayward and "little men." Others might now be considered great buccaneers, and at least extensive operators and enterprisers—bold in imagination and vigorous in execution. Almost all were short on cash. Their principal capital was hearts of courage and heads full of cow sense.

At the same time the lure that led the Eastern man with money attracted others with more capital than experience from Colorado on the north to California on the Coast to venture there in the cow business, too. Thus Jeff came with the boom in beef. Out of this general movement sprang the Illinois Cattle Company—the ICC ranch—in the San Mateo Range, to which Jeff that expectant day in 1884 was making his way in the ranch wagon.[4]

John W. Virgin and O. H. Simms, both of Leadville, Colorado, bought out several San Marcial and Socorro ranchmen in

[3] Mr. Stevens notes that yearlings dressing 400 and big steers 700 pounds were not uncommon. Stevens to J. E. H., April 11, 1946.

[4] Stevens, as cited; and Bancroft, *Arizona and New Mexico*, XVII, 797, notes that the cattle in Socorro County increased from 9,000 to 70,000 between 1882 and 1884. Sheep decreased from 300,000 to 100,000.

the spring of 1883. In the fall of 1884 they put their holdings into a New Mexico corporation called the Illinois Cattle Company in return for $15,000 in stock.[5] John Virgin and his wife lived at the ranch, and other stockholders, Simonds and Johns, were there at times during Jeff's employment.

There was the usual ranch work to do. The boss put Jeff and another hand called "Old Chip" to digging a well in Red Canyon, just below their headquarters. He gave them a coil of fuse and the first dynamite Jeff had seen and left them to finish the job.

"Chip, they say this will go off," mused Jeff, as he shaved a sliver from a stick with his knife at the blacksmith shop. "Let's try it," he added, as he laid the shaving on the anvil and picked up the shop hammer. He hit it a heavy blow. The report was right. Jeff was jarred to his toes as the hammer went out through the roof. Then with proper respect they drilled a hole in the bottom of the well, tamped it full of dynamite and attached the fuse.

"They hadn't told us how much to use," said Jeff, "and instead of a piece about two feet long, I tied on the entire coil. Chip was to pull me out by the windlass. I lit it, but the fuse had a flaw about two inches from the end, and when the fire hit the flaw, it shot out at the side and went 'p-s-s-s-s-' and I never waited for Chip. I skinned up that rope like a cat. Instead of trying to help, Chip was running for the ranch like a scared coyote and I took after him. We waited and waited, but it didn't go off. About the time we were sure the fuse had gone out, it went off and tore the bottom out of the well and all the rope off our windlass. But we got the water."

As Montague Stevens has said, "There was a craze for cattle." The various stockholders of the Illinois, one of whom was named Doc Simonds, felt it, too, and came prowling around the range in the San Mateos. One day Simonds came rushing in from a walk in the mountains to tell Jeff and Julius Estes, another hand, to hurry and bring a pack horse, as he had killed a grizzly bear.

---

[5] Besides Virgin and Simms, Thomas M. Swain, George M. Virgin, and Samuel P. Johns, of Lake County, Colorado, were interested in the company. Socorro County Deed Records, VIII, 278, and XII, 278 and 356.

He had no gun of any kind, and when they inquired he said he had killed it with a rock.

"He's crazy as a loon," said Jeff. But Simonds insisted, and they saddled up and followed him off.

"The old man's lost his mind," Jeff said again. "We'll tie him up when we see for shore, and send him back to town."

They found the joke on themselves. While Simonds was out on his walk, he had looked over the rim of a deep canyon and directly beneath him, near the bottom, was a grizzly lying on a ledge. Simonds got a big boulder in both hands, braced himself at the edge against a leaning juniper, dropped the rock several hundred feet, and actually hit the bear in the top of the head, crushing his skull. And there the boys found him almost as big as a steer and dead as a door nail. They dressed him and packed the meat to the ranch, wondering what might happen to a tenderfoot next.[6]

From their range on the eastern slope of the San Mateos, they could look down into the Río Grande, the stream that cuts New Mexico almost in half and gives character and a distinctive culture to the land it divides and drains. The interests and activities of the region drew to a focus on the banks above its shallow and uncertain current. Old-timers claim a peculiar potency in the extended use of its waters—that the men who live on them long enough are liable for anything. And the history turned up by the stream, to say nothing of that washed away, seems to substantiate their claim.

Three cowboys quit the ICC and neighboring ranches, rustled up some counterfeit plates, and began making money down the river from San Marcial. It seemed a profitable pursuit, and they wanted Jeff in the business. They were "nice" boys, well liked by Jeff, but he wanted none of it, and warned them they had better beware. Suspicion leaked out with their leaden dollars, and soon a federal agent showed up from El Paso and asked to see Jeff. Jeff agreed to meet him later in a back room of a saloon, and then got word to the counterfeiting cowboys to be

---

[6] Montague Stevens has told his hunting experiences in this region in a delightful volume, *Meet Mr. Grizzly* (Albuquerque, 1943).

hidden in an adjoining one, with ears cocked against the thin and resonant walls. The agent made known his business and the boys lost no time hitting a high lope for a thicket down the valley, from which they threw their dies and all of their money into the river.

Jeff went back to the ICC's, where the boss was a cowpuncher by the name of Barney Hankins. He and Jeff were hardly on the best of terms, especially after Hankins told the men at the corrals how he used to run a big outfit in Wyoming and whipped these tough Texans who came up the trail into submission with a quirt. One evening Doctor Edwards' wife and Mrs. Billy Featherstone were guests from San Marcial. After supper they sat in the living room, one end of which was cut off by a curtain. Behind it were Hankins' and the boys' beds. Mrs. Virgin proposed a game of cards, but Hankins, who was lying clothed on his bed behind the curtain, stepped out to growl, "I don't allow any card playing on this ranch."

"What do you mean?" said Jeff. "I've got a deck in my trunk." He got up and went behind the curtain to get it. When he opened the lid of his trunk, there lay his six-shooter. "I had to put it somewhere," he said, "so I just stuck it in my waistband and went back in the room."

Mrs. Virgin, an educated and cultured lady, obviously embarrassed, spoke up to say, "Well, I guess we can't play."

"Chipman," said Jeff to the other hand present, "we'll play a game of seven-up."

"No, I won't permit *any* playing," insisted Barney, and so Chipman declined. Now the quirting story had always been a bitter dose for Jeff's sensitive stomach, and the more he thought about that game the worse he wanted to play.

"Well," he jauntily announced, "I'll just play a little game of solitaire." As he seated himself at the table and laid out the cards, the ladies all laughed, the tension was eased, and they agreed to join him. Jeff dealt a hand while keeping one eye cocked on Hankins, who sat armed on the other side of the room, and who was now so mad that his breathing was audible. After what Jeff said was "a very nice game," the ladies retired to their rooms in another part of the big log house, and Jeff went behind the curtain where Hankins had lain down, still fully dressed and armed.

Jeff took him by the shoulder, and, not wishing to disturb the ladies, told him he wanted to see him outside. When he tried to shake Jeff off, he punched him in the ribs with his gun, commanding, "Get up from there, you son-of-a-bitch, or I'll kill you, shore." He got up.

Jeff followed him outside and cordially advised, "Now, you've been telling about quirting those Texas cowboys, old stud. Let's see you step to it."

"We had quite a talk," recalled Jeff, "and I told him all about it. Then I told him never to give me another order. After that we went back to bed, but in three or four days he left the ranch for good. He wa'n't no cowpuncher a-tall; nothing to him! And the idea of him quirting those Texas cowboys! Why, it's plumb reedic'lous."

Jeff and a tall, slender, brown-eyed Texas cowpuncher of about 150 pounds named Jim Hammil decided to see the country. With a pack outfit they left the San Mateos and headed toward the Mogollons. On Diamond Creek, a tributary of the Gila in the Black Range, Jeff got out his fishhooks, cut a willow pole, and caught his first mountain trout. To insure the safety and success of their trip, they carried two gallon jugs of whiskey in the pack. While there in camp, they opened the second for a chance traveler who quit traveling then and there, and who stayed on with a sense of contentment that grew in inverse ratio to the level of the jug.

"I'm gonna bust that jug," Jeff confided to Jim. But first he slipped the empty one out of the pack, poured most of what was left into it, hid it in the brush, drank part of that left, and rapped the jug against a rock as he set it down.

"By Jacks," he shouted, "if I didn't bust that jug!"

So they lost congenial company. But with ample time and by easy rides, fishing when appetite prompted and killing a buck when they needed meat, they moved over the Mogollons and turned up the valley of the Frisco—that long upper tributary of the Gila in extreme western New Mexico. All went peacefully

109

and well until they reached the tough little Mexican settlements on that stream. A few isolated Mexican settlers, suspicious of these brash Texans who were taking the country, lived there herding small bunches of sheep, raising a little frijoles and corn, and, where possible, robbing the scattered Americans who passed that way.[7]

The Upper Plaza had already been the scene of battle between the Mexicans and the Texans in the fall of 1884, when six or seven cowboys from the WS, Spur, and Slaughter ranches rode in for a few drinks, and one named Charlie McCarty got drunk, hollered, and shot up the vacant village. Elfrego Baca, a Socorro deputy passing through, put him in Montague Stevens' buggy and took him before the alcalde at the Middle Plaza. The balance of the boys went down to the house where he was held to go his bond. Baca, who had gone into an adjoining jacal, poked the dirt from between the picket walls and shot without warning into the riders, killing Bert Herne, a Spur cowboy. The others, all in the open, whirled their horses for shelter, and as they did so, Baca killed the horse under Young Parham, boss for John Slaughter.

The falling horse caught and crushed Parham to death. The others took refuge and opened fire on Baca's jacal, where he stayed at bay, flat on the floor, exchanging shots for some thirty hours. Word of the trouble flew out through the ranch country like a blue-darter hawk on the wing. Jeff and others heard about it over toward the Río Grande, and struck out to help. But before they got there, Baca had given up and been taken to Socorro.[8]

[7] Stevens, as cited; Evans Coleman, Arizona Pioneers Historical Society, Tucson, Chapter IV, n. p.; Evans Coleman to J. E. H. and Hervey Chesley, February 27, 1945.

[8] Montague Stevens, one of the founders of the WS Ranch, near Alma, experienced English ranchman of western New Mexico, gives this account, abbreviated by the author. His associates, James H. Cook, *Fifty Years on the Frontier* (New Haven, 1923), 255–61, and William French, *Some Recollections of a Western Ranchman* (New York, n. d.), 44–55, tell the story in some detail. A thoroughly inflated and unreliable account is to be found in Kyle S. Crichton's *Law and Order Ltd., The Rousing Life of Elfrego Baca* (Santa Fé, 1928), 31–48.

Parham and McCarty had come with the Slaughters from Texas. Stevens to J. E. H., April 11, 1946; Henry Martin to J. E. H., March 5, 1944; George Cook to J. E. H., March 6, 1944.

This was the nature of the neighborhood Jeff and Jim approached as they rode into the Lower—sometimes called Baca—Plaza and drew rein in front of a little store run by a Mexican by the name of Saraceno. Just as they stopped, Saraceno ran out and grabbed Jeff's mount, a small roan mare, by the bridle reins. Jeff had bought her on the Río Grande for a pack horse and, as his regular mount had gone lame, had saddled her that morning for the day's ride.

Now to monkey with any man's horse without permission in the West is a dangerous pursuit; to grab his bridle is an insult and an invitation to battle.

"Get off that horse," the Mexican shouted.

"Whut uh yuh mean?" snapped Jeff, whipping his gun out and dropping it in Saraceno's face, adding, "Turn those reins loose or I'll shoot you loose."

Saraceno jumped back and apologized that he did not mean anything.

"Yes, you did," said Jeff, hotly. "Do you think this mare is yours? If you do, I'll give her to you."

"And from what came out, I guess she had belonged to him," recalled Jeff. "Perhaps somebody stole her, but it wa'n't me." Saraceno, however, continued to protest his mistake as Jeff stepped down and pulled his Winchester from its boot. Saraceno in-

111

vited them inside for a drink. Jim, of a less suspicious nature, left his short saddle-gun in its scabbard on his big bay horse, Old Mike, that stood dozing with drooping lids and drooping reins in the sun in front of the store.

Inside, the boys broke the ice with a little liquor and a little trade. Saraceno broke out all over with Latin grace and friendship and invited them to dinner. They accepted, following him out at the back door into the living quarters, attached at the rear, and sat down at the table with the family. Jeff carried his rifle with him, laying it across his lap as he ate with a sort of uneasy feeling that was not due to the nature of the food.

The meal ended in a cordial vein. The boys rose to go, passed through the cool darkness of the store, stepped out into the glare of the afternoon sun, and blinked their eyes at the trap that was laid.

Banked about in front were heavy sacks of wool that had been hurriedly rolled into place, and from behind them protruded several guns in the hands of hostile Mexicans. Jeff's quick eye caught it all in a flash, as well as the fact that a man stood close against the wall at the door, six-shooter in hand, to disarm them. He beat them to it as he poked his cocked rifle in the belly of the Mexican by the door, and backed off against a big clay oven alongside the house, taking the unwilling hostage with him, telling him at once that if a shot were fired "he'd go to hell, for certain."

The Mexican kept "hollering" to his *compadres* behind the sacks not to shoot. Then Jeff felt something against his own back in spite of the protection of the oven. Jim called to him that another Mexican had a gun in his back. He never looked around but repeated his warning that if a shot were fired there would be at least two *hombres* headed for hell. Thus they fell into a parley, and at last Jeff and Jim agreed to surrender, be taken before the alcalde at the next plaza, and have the case heard there.

Six or seven Mexicans took their guns and triumphantly marched them up the valley to see the "judge." Those early trials were a travesty on justice, and Jeff began to get worried. In the excitement, their captors had overlooked Jim's rifle which was still on Mike in the scabbard under the skirts of his saddle. Jeff asked to go outside on the legitimate excuse that a well-ordered nature has provided. He circled behind the horses to attend to his business, while his guard stopped to wait until he was through. On Mike's off-side he slipped out the gun, took his guard unawares, disarmed him, stepped back into the room, and told the alcalde and guards in profane and certain terms that the business was up. Jim gathered the guards' guns from where they had clattered to the floor, piled them in an adjoining room, and advised them that court was adjourned. After marching them off some two hundred yards from the arsenal, they turned them loose.

Leisurely they rode up the Frisco, turned up the tributary Tularosa, and in a few miles came to John Slaughter's ranch, settled by that noted cowman a short time before.[9] There they got another horse, and Jeff sent the mare back to Saraceno. Months later he found her again on the Río Grande range where he had bought her, and where, in spite of the proprietary claims of men, the more impelling urge of a homing instinct had sent and kept her.

And while horses are stolen and sold, and horses grow old and die, the passions of the men who love them live on. In time, Jeff had become a Socorro deputy himself, when again he and Jim were riding up the Gila. Although Jeff would not tell the story, its essential features have been pieced together through the years. A sudden volley from the brush dropped his horse dead in its tracks. The same bullet that killed his horse went in above his knee and ranged down and out through the calf of his leg. He tugged hard at his Winchester pinned with him beneath his horse. "Then," he said, "there was a lot of shooting." After it was over, he plugged the hole with a rag, and he and Jim struck out, Jeff on the pack horse, for the two days' ride to the ranch he had homesteaded at Crow Springs, adjacent to the ICC's in the San Mateos. He poured some turpentine through the wound,

[9] John and Will B. Slaughter moved from Blanco Canyon, at the foot of the Staked Plains, into Socorro County, in 1882. Will settled the WIL S Ranch, in the American Valley, near Quemada, some thirty-five miles east of Springerville. W. B. Slaughter to J. E. H., October 9, 1926; Coleman to J. E. H., as cited.

and the long and jagged hole soon got well. Sometime later he rode into Socorro, and Charlie Russell, the sheriff, suggested he investigate the reported deaths of three Mexicans down on the Gila. But Jeff demurred. "They wouldn't bother anybody," he countered, "and besides, they's nothin' to it."

At times it was not uncommon practice for cowboys to file on desirable locations while working for a ranch on the public domain, and then deed the land to the owner of the ranch when they had proven up on the claims. Six or seven miles from the ICC headquarters, on Red Canyon, was a fine spring on tributary North Canyon that Jeff pre-empted. Then, as was the custom, too, he turned in to meet the requirements of title while holding down his regular job.

He camped at the spot and began to cut logs for a cabin. Of a morning the wild turkeys, having never seen a man, would wake him from his suggans by gathering around to "put-put-put" at the strange animal that had moved into their range. He looked up one morning to see a big grizzly testing his reach and his claws on a naked white aspen in a grove near by. Before he thought, he grabbed his gun and shot him; and before he could think again, the grizzly was coming for him. He vaulted through the window and up on the roof, and shot again, breaking old bruin's neck.

After he had proven up on the claim, Virgin came by to demand it.

"Nothing doing," said Jeff. "I filed on it, built a cabin on it, lived on it, and proved up on it. It's mine."

"I've been paying you thirty dollars a month," argued Virgin.

"Yes, for doing sixty dollars' work," added Jeff. And so they more or less fell out over the claim, though Virgin wound up by buying it.

Jeff saddled up and rode down to San Marcial. There, as his horse's hoofs stirred the dust of its arid and alkaline street, of a sudden the thought of home—of a governor's estate in the humid woods of Florida, with the fragrance of flowers, the deference of good and loyal servants, the grace of genteel living, genuine conviviality, and lively conversation—hit him with a bang. He put up his horse at the livery stable, stored his saddle, cleaned and dressed up—for he always liked to dress the part of a gentleman—bought a ticket, pushed his .45 inside the waistband of his civilized suit, and mounted the train for home.

He took the Santa Fé line, a long and roundabout journey, happily playing the role of a green country boy as they rolled along. At Kansas City, where he changed trains, he stopped off long enough to see the lights, and the lights were those in a good saloon, which were light enough until some doubting soul bet him he could not shoot them out. Now for a cowpuncher of Jeff's rollicky temperament that was temptation compounded with challenge. The lights went out in a hurry and so did Jeff.

After he had spent all his money on his visit in Florida, he borrowed enough from his brother to get back to the West. He took the southern route through Texas, stopping off in Austin to see his friends. There he called on Senator Temple Houston, who had been asked to pilot a bill through the legislature to reimburse him some $3,000 for the costs of the Patterson trial. But the senator seemed more interested in the personal cup that cheered than in the restitution of the honor of the state in the eyes of a youthful Ranger, and Jeff again set out.

He left by the Sunset line and sped west past Langtry and Roy Bean, past Murphyville and Marfa, and at last into El Paso for a reunion with Sedberry and "Buffalo Bill" Jenkins. He took a room in the Grand Central Hotel, and Bill—with a heart as true as steel and an exterior as hard as a malpais rock—rose to the special occasion, saying, "We'll drink some of that stuff they call sham-pain."

So far as they could later recall, the rough features of life faded out, and before morning the whole world looked level. Bill soon felt the overwhelming harmony of a peaceful and well-spent life surging in his soul like a bull in a china shop, and broke forth in song that shook the walls and reverberated from the heights of Mount Franklin with old Ranger sentiments never designed for decent surroundings. The landlord called, but "the law" did not. It was a superb celebration.

Next day, however, in the sober reflection that follows the

115

spiritual elation of high-hearted souls, Jeff realized that the only bright lights for him were the blistering shafts of an arid sun on the mountains of western New Mexico. He stuck his .45 in his waistband, checked out of the Grand Central, and headed toward the black malpais mesa that frowned down on the glaring dobes of San Marcial.

9

Usually in the Name of the Law

Like almost everyone else in those days, Jeff, too, became affected by the craze for cattle. He had in mind a likely location which he hoped to homestead. He went to the federal land office at Las Cruces, found that the water—Crow Springs, northwest of Nogal Canyon in the San Mateos—was vacant, and did the necessary filing. The nearest neighbor to Crow Springs was an extremely positive but fine old Texan, bear hunter, and cowman by the name of Steele.[1]

Jeff began cutting junipers for a picket house, built it and covered it with a roof of dirt, and improved it with a Pueblo-style fireplace in a corner inside. Outside, no better game country could be found. Turkeys were next to a nuisance, deer were everywhere, and bear were thick enough for an inveterate hunter.

When he hungered for meat and thirsted for adventure, he and Dick Steele, the old man's son, took an ancient Indian trail across the San Mateos and had a look at the land on the other side. Jeff had got a Marlin rifle to try for a change, and when they ran on to a grizzly, Jeff knocked him down. He leaned his rifle against a tree, pulled his butcher knife, and started to stick the bear. When he pricked the animal with the knife, the bear sprang up and swiped all the clothing off Jeff's abdomen with one swing of his awful paw. Dick dropped his rifle and skinned up a tree. Jeff broke to run. As the bear was at his heels, he jerked his six-shooter and whirled, and just happened to stick the gun in its gaping mouth as he pulled the trigger. It was a lucky shot

[1] The place he homesteaded is now called the Steele Tank, and is about twenty miles above Rube Pankey's ranch along the Hot Springs–Socorro road. Pankey to J. E. H., February 3, 1945.

117

that pierced the brain, and the bear fell dead. Dick slid down the tree.

Jeff exclaimed, "What's the matter, man? You're as white as a sheet."

"You ought to see yourself, fellow," said Dick.

Along this Indian trail, strewn with human skeletons, far up in the San Mateos they came to an old and fallen-down cabin. Prying around the ruins, Jeff turned up a gallon can, half full of sirup, which they took along and found "very delicious." One day, however, the sirup failed to pour, and Jeff pried the obstruction out with a knife—a dead mouse, wonderfully preserved if not completely candied.

At Crow Springs he lost two of his "very best friends." One day he killed a grizzly and found to his sorrow that she had two cubs. He took them home, and in time they came to sleep on one side of his cabin while he slept on the other. "We got to be just as good friends as if they'd been two men," he recalled. But when work took him away upon an extended trip, some passer-by shot and killed one of his friends, and the other, tired of the tragedies that plague the human race, took to the tall uncut and the wild bunch.

Jeff worked in and out of his camp at Crow Springs though the claim fell into dispute. One day three men rode up from Nogal Canyon to tell him that the location and the land belonged to them. He met them at the door, impatiently heard their tale, and then reached behind the facing for his rifle, saying, "If you want this land, I'll give you just six feet apiece. If you don't want it, then get a-moving," and get they did, a whole lot faster than they had got, in coming. "No monkey business about it in those days," explained Jeff in retrospection.

Yet eventually those men acquired the land. Jeff suspected manipulation in the federal office, and though he hired a lawyer, he lost the claim. For a short time he ran a ranch near by, on Nogal Canyon; long enough, at least, to put a splendid and strapping cowboy named Dan Walker in charge. Then he turned again to his individual campaign toward inducement to decency, which, in a voluntary way, had kept him stirring around right sharply ever since he had been there. At last the pervasive and usually civilizing element of legality was upon the land, and since at that time and place the assertion of law was the height of adventure, Jeff was ready to lend a vigorous hand.

When he first came, Socorro County seemed to cover the whole country. It did reach from the Río Grande to the Arizona line. But in April, 1884, Sierra was cut off with Hillsboro as the county seat. Jeff was there for its organization.[2]

Socorro had been a settled if not entirely peaceful community for time out of hand. Jeff soon got acquainted there, at the principal store of Sperling Brothers, at the Windsor and Grand Central hotels, and with the people whose business it was to look after the law. In the past, Socorro County had been predominantly a range for sheep, but now the cowmen were pushing to the lead. Along the Frisco, on the western fringe of the county, English capital had taken a hold with characteristic enterprise and ready will. Farther north, Texans were sprinkling and peppering that land with their herds, and making it a salty range with their hands: the Hall brothers with the Spurs in the Luna Valley; Bill Slaughter and his WIL S in the American Valley, near present Quemado; his brother, John, down on the Tularosa above the Upper Plaza; Jim Reed·and Wes Bruton, who had just bought out Joe Fowler, between there and Socorro; and a few scattered more.

Besides, there were others, resolute men not altogether to the cattle-manor born: English gentlemen Wilson and Stevens with the WS brand near Alma, and Stevens and Upshur with the SU, northeast of present Reserve; quixotic Patterson, out of the army and building a surface tank with a wheelbarrow at Horse Springs; Baldwin with his road-ranch at the Datils; Solomon Luna, with 40,000 sheep all over the place; his brother, Tranquilino, with a deft forefinger in New Mexico politics; and a number more.

On the whole they were vigorous and relatively law-abiding

[2] On account of the mineral development, Grant County, with Silver City as the seat, was cut off and organized in 1868. See F. A. Jones, *New Mexico Mines and Minerals*, 82, and Bancroft, *Arizona and New Mexico*, XVII, 797–98.

men, direct in speech and action, lusty in their appetites, elemental in diversion, and Rabelaisian in their humor. Socorro was a lively place when they hit the town in unison, and the timid folks beat a hot trail home and barred the doors.[3]

Then practical jokes grew in severity with the drinking, and the black glass globe that touched off the top of the Windsor's flagpole in a sort of sober, ornate glory disappeared in a flash of crystalline dust when some rash individual bet Jeff a hundred dollars he could not hit it with his six-shooter.

They were just as strong in their antipathies as in their loyalties, and diminutive Bill Slaughter detested the very tracks that one of his neighbors made. Everyone knew how he felt, for they were not the sort to cover their emotions with poker faces or inhibit themselves to the point of perversion. One night when Bill got thoroughly drunk, they put him to bed, pulled up his undershirt, and painted his enemy's brand in ink across his abdomen.

"In those days a man didn't look at his damned belly the first thing of a morning," said Jeff, "but got up, took a drink, and went to work." Bill paced off in the early sun for the nearest bar. Everybody was in on the secret, and at once the unusually early crowd began rawhiding him about his pet peeve. He hardly felt jovial at the best and when somebody said, "Why, you actually belong to that man," Bill denied it in language they understood best. Another said, "Of course you do; he's even got his brand on you." They bet good money that he did, as Bill's color mounted with his blood pressure. Then somebody slipped his shirt up, exposing the brand, and he was mad enough for murder.

When they could not think of anything else to do, they put body lice on a bridegroom to give him the proper start in that brave new world. It was kind of rough in a way, but on the other hand they "would have gone to hell for him in a minute."

[3] In 1880, Socorro had a population of 1,272 people. Bancroft, *Arizona and New Mexico*, XVII, 978.

Besides the Jeff Milton notes: Montague Stevens to J. E. H., April 11, 1946; W. B. Slaughter to J. E. H., October 9, 1926; Evans Coleman to J. E. H., February 27, 1945; Jim Wilson to J. E. H., January 1, 1928; and for Tranquilino Luna, see sketch in [George B. Anderson,] *Illustrated History of New Mexico* (Chicago, 1907), II, 417; *Albuquerque Journal*, December 16, 1885.

In their own social relations, however, the amenities bore down on them until they hurt. When Jeff walked into an eating house in Rincon in his shirt sleeves one day, the manager told him that "gentlemen must be dressed in coats." He retired, pulled his Fish-brand slicker from behind the cantle, and came rustling back in it.

When Jeff reached western New Mexico, it was a noticeable fact that the temper of the land was changing with the character of the men. Joe Fowler was a case in point. He was an Austin gambler who came with a consort called Belle, began dealing monte in Socorro, and put the first ranch in the Burro Mountains west and north of there. He was a killer by nature, who had gone the tough rounds of the trail from Texas to Dodge in 1878, had dealt from there to White Oaks, back to Dodge, and on to Socorro.

"One-Armed" Jim Reed, from deep in Texas, bought the Fowler ranch out. At the Grand Central bar Fowler got on a tear and was making a tenderfoot dance. By the ruse of a drink, a drummer helped the bartender get his guns, and in rage Fowler stabbed the drummer to death. Now that seemed a little raw. An outraged citizenry took him to jail, gave him a decent trial, deduced his killing of twenty-three men, and sentenced him to die. He made an attempt to escape, and a mob gathered and dragged him from his cell, abject, blubbering, and craven.

They carried him down to a cottonwood—Socorro is full of convenient, sturdy, and noble cottonwoods—and a great crowd gathered as a willing volunteer climbed up to tie the rope. They slipped a noose around his neck and drove a wagon from under him, but by a crude oversight they had given him too much rope and his feet touched the ground. Those below yelled at the man in the tree to untie the rope and take up the slack. But Fowler's weight had drawn the knot too tight and the man on the limb called back, "I can't untie it."

"Never mind," answered an ingenious and helpful hand near by, as he jumped on Fowler and clasped him with legs and arms to add his weight to that unlucky wight. Others caught the idea and followed suit from all sides. As the crowd broke up, someone

121

close to the scene was explaining the hanging to that English gentleman, Montague Stevens, out on the fringe of the mob. When he came to the details of the crowd's swarming over Fowler at the end of the rope, he added, "It looked like bees a-hiving," which struck the man from Cambridge as the "strangest simile" he had ever heard.[4]

Whatever the question of its rhetorical nature, however, there was none whatever about its human value. The next election emphasized the trend. It "didn't make a damn" if Cleveland was elected president; what was important to them was the race for sheriff. Charlie Russell, a rangy Texan from the Spicewood community of Blanco County and a former sheriff there, was elected over the incumbent, who immediately left for parts unknown, allegedly far in the hole. Russell took over in January, 1885, "like an old hand at the business."[5]

Nearly two years before, another independent movement had been initiated that set the lawless by their ears. There was need for action.

That noted character, Colonel A. J. Fountain, major of the New Mexico Volunteer Militia, had reported that "high-handed depredations were being carried on by rustlers in Socorro and Dona Ana counties . . . ," that some thirty to forty men, stealing stock there, were extending their operations clear into Chihuahua, Mexico, and that some relief was necessary. The Governor, too, expressed concern. On March 1, 1883, a month after Fountain's report, a Central New Mexico Stock Growers Association was organized at Albuquerque, with W. C. Moore as chairman and E. Louis Kohns as secretary. While Moore[6] moved on, the

[4] Jim Wilson, of Alpine, worked for Fowler. Wilson to J. E. H., January 1, 1938; Montague Stevens, *Meet Mr. Grizzly;* William French, *Recollections of a Western Ranchman,* 26 ff.

[5] *Albuquerque Journal,* January 14, 1885; W. H. Roberts to J. E. H., December 4, 1943; R. H. Crosby to J. E. H., August 4, 1937.

[6] *Albuquerque Journal,* February 13 and March 2, 1883. This must have been the same Moore who left the LX Ranch, in the Panhandle of Texas, because things were getting too hot for him. The fantastic mutations of the struggle for law on the part of these men is an intriguing subject that can only be indicated here. For Moore's background, see "Jim East—Trail Hand and Cowboy," by J. Evetts Haley, in the *Panhandle-Plains Historical Review,* 1931, 46–48.

association stayed, and joined with Russell in an attempt to suppress the stealing of cattle.

Jeff had been in two or three fights already. Russell had heard of them. Besides that, he was the brother of Bill Russell, Jeff's old merchant friend at Presidio, and that helped draw them together. Russell offered him a job as deputy, and Jeff accepted. The Stock Growers Association hired him, too, as a detective; and Edmund G. Ross, appointed that summer as territorial governor, gave him a special commission. Jeff still had his place at Crow Springs, and from there and Socorro he prowled central and western New Mexico in all directions.

During all this time the Apaches were troublesome, for the red deeds of Mangas Coloradas and Victorio were re-enacted in the raids of the renegade Geronimo. Through the early eighties, he and his warriors were scourging the San Mateos and the Mogollons, while such noted army men as Crook, Chaffee, and Van Horn floundered in the field against them. Fountain was out, too, with the New Mexico militia. Nevertheless, by the end of 1885, a citizen of Grant County reported at least a hundred settlers killed, and General Crook and Sheridan were being denounced in the papers as "frauds."

Then the frontiersmen of Socorro, impatient with the slow movement of the regular army, organized on their own, were sworn in, elected Sheriff Charlie Russell as their captain, and set off to tend to Geronimo and Victorio's warriors by themselves. Of course Jeff joined, overtaking "Russell's Army," as they called the squad of forty to fifty men, in the Elk Mountains. They wanted to elect him lieutenant, but as a handy man after game he preferred to be grub rustler, instead. Moccasin Forbes, an old Indian fighter, drifted in from nowhere to join them on the march. He, Jeff, and another frontiersman named George Wandlous were put out as scouts. When Jeff walked slap-dab upon a cinnamon bear in the brush, he shot the animal before he had time to think, others opened fire in excitement, and a "bad man" whom they had elected lieutenant beat it to the rear to "see that nobody escaped," much to the amusement of the "army."

The usual lack of discipline delayed their movement. A

preacher named Bush, "a little, dark, gray-eyed man—a dandy, and not afraid of nobody," went along with a gun that Jeff had lent him. Another "bad man" in the crowd with a six-shooter in his belt tormented Bush almost to distraction.

"Next time he opens up," Jeff finally said in brotherly advice, "box the bully's ears and try to do it while I'm around." When the tormentor started again, Bush did as advised; and the bad man, faced with a short cut to "kingdom come," left off the hurrahing at once. Russell had trouble with another sassy insubordinate and told Jeff that he might have to place him under arrest. "Next time he says a word, just knock him down," said Jeff, "and if that don't quiet him, I will." The medicine fit the case.

Thus with minor distractions they scouted through the Elk Mountains and rimmed-out the Mogollons, finding where the Indians had camped, where they had eaten horses in droves, and then moved on. At last, out of salt, hungry, and discouraged, they turned back, scattered to their camps and ranches and straggled into Socorro, while the regular army, with discipline and organization, eventually corralled Geronimo. The citizens took back what they had said about the soldiers, and General Nelson A. Miles, then in command, was wined and dined at Albuquerque as the man of the hour while "Russell's Army" was forgotten.[7]

About twenty-five miles west of Socorro, a railroad was building in to tap the old lodes of lead and the new ones of silver, and a booming village was now shattering that "beautiful legend . . . that no murder has ever been, or could ever be committed under the compassionate gaze of that contrite countenance" of Our Lady Magdalene, a great image formed by the growth on the side of a mountain. Jeff passed through as the first houses of Magdalena were being built,[8] and at the mining camp of Kelly, near by, saw the corpse of a cowboy that violently assailed the verity of the legend.

[7] The *Albuquerque Journal* of the period contains many references to these Indian troubles. See issues of June 2, 3, 5, and 9, and December 27, 1885. There is, besides, a voluminous Apache literature on the period, of which Dr. Frank C. Lockwood's *The Apache Indians* (New York, 1938) is noteworthy.

[8] See Jones, *New Mexico Mines and Minerals*, 119–22, for the discoveries around Magdalena and the legend of the place.

The boy had raised a row with the village butcher, beat him up, and vowed to return. The man crammed his muzzle-loading single-barreled, eight-gauge duck gun half-full of buckshot, and when the belligerent came back, dropped the gun across his butcher's block and cut him half in two. There was a nice distinction between this and murder, and such simple shootings bothered them but little. Jeff, who was after outlaws and thieves, rendered judgment: "It was perfectly proper. Of course he ought to a-killed him. And I went on about my business."[9]

Jeff's first serious business as an officer was the roundup of the Johnson gang, in the Black Range far to the southwest of Socorro. In the early eighties a great cow outfit came to life with headquarters on the Río Grande, the Vega Blanca ranch at Las Palomas, a village a few miles downstream from present Hot Springs. It was principally financed by a Californian named George W. Grayson and managed by an English stockholder named Willard S. Hopewell. They were doing business in Socorro County in 1883 as "Grayson and Company."

They are said to have bought out about two hundred individual ranchmen in consolidation of their vast holdings as they spread their outfit, the J Half-Circle Cross, into the biggest ranch in that part of New Mexico. In a peculiar perversion of its brand, it came to be called the "John Cross" outfit, a term so tenacious and persistent that many New Mexicans still think it was owned by a man of that name. Their country ran from the river at Hot Springs west for many miles to the crest of the Black Range, from Fairview to Hillsboro, and back through the broken lands between there and the Río Grande. Eventually they claimed 50,000 head before drought and short grass brought ruin and dissolution. But now they were riding high and handsome.[10]

Jeff came to know the outfit well in its early development. In prowling the country soon after he came, he met Grayson under

[9] It was at Magdalena, too, that Scott Reed, "One-Armed" Jim's boy, died in a double killing. Cole Railston to J. E. H. and Hervey Chesley, February 26, 1945.
[10] Henry Martin to J. E. H., March 5, 1944; Rube Pankey to J. E. H., February 3, 1945; W. H. Roberts to J. E. H., February 23, 1945; B. C. Mossman to J. E. H. and Hervey Chesley, February 24, 1945; Cole Railston and Montague

amusing circumstances. Some sloughs along the river had been
filled by an overflow, and as Jeff jogged down the trail toward
Las Palomas, he saw a man wading around in their shallow water
and deep mud, at intervals swinging hard into the murky mess
with a club that he carried in his hand.

"That man has lost his mind, shore," mused Jeff, as he turned
off to investigate. Instead of a madman, he found old Grayson,
killing catfish. He was stirring up the mud by wading through it.
When a big catfish came gaping to the surface for air, he tapped
him on the head with the stick, picked him out of the water with
his hand, and dropped him in a tow sack.

As may be imagined, Grayson was not only a man with a
genuine zest for life but one with a hard head for business. And
when a regular band of Black Range cattle rustlers, spurred by
that familiar envy incited by size and success, fell upon the "John
Cross" brand, he and Hopewell wanted to do something vigorous
about it. They enlisted the help of Jeff, who was always "raring"
to go.

Jeff and Grayson arranged a roundup secretly designed to
concentrate on thieves instead of cattle, and with a crew of cowboys and cowmen swung up the Animas Creek and combed the
canyons and ridges of the Black Range. They came into Hillsboro with a dozen or more men as captives, lodged them in a
dobe building that served as the Sierra jail, and went into camp
themselves at a lovely spot on Las Animas creek near the pleasant town of Hillsboro, leisurely to await the flow of legality that
passed in New Mexico for justice.

Donaldson, secretary for the "John Cross" outfit, came up
the ridge from Las Palomas with plenty of whiskey, which he
passed around right freely while Jeff was amusing himself at
target practice by riddling, with rifle, dirt-filled tobacco sacks
and tin cans that others were throwing in the air. At length when

Stevens, as cited; Sierra County Deed Records, Vol. A, 44, 139–42; Socorro County Deed Records, Vol. X, 279, 301; Record of Mining Claims, Socorro County,
Vol. G, 527.
Another great ranch at this time was that owned by Head and Hearst, also
of California, said to be twenty-five miles wide by eighty miles long, extending
from Warm Springs south into Mexico. *Albuquerque Journal,* May 13, 1883.

the liquor had induced that tolerance for disorder generally associated with its indiscriminate use, the bookkeeper made bold to suggest that courts were slow and judges reactionary, and that the shortest cut to conviction was to go down and kill the captives then and there.

"We had a bunch of pretty wild boys," said Jeff, "and a lot of them roared out that they were ready to go."

"It struck me kind of sudden-like," he later recalled. Perhaps the shudder of revulsion that passed through his heart came in part from an outraged and civilized tradition that had flowed strong through unbroken generations behind him, and in part from an elemental sense of fair play that seems to temper the souls of brave and reckless men. At any rate, he stepped out from the crowd with the warm barrel of his gun swinging free in the crook of his arm, faced them all, and said, "Nothing doing, boys! I'm not in that kind of business."

"What's that?" called Donaldson.

"That's what I said," snapped Jeff, throwing a shell into his gun, "and that's what I mean."

Another big, square-shouldered, straight-shooting cowman from down on the river stepped out with him, saying, "By God, I'm with you, Milt!"

Then others came to their side, and the hanging died a-borning. "It would have been murder," he recalled. "After all they wa'n't bad men—just cowthieves."

Toppy Johnson was the recognized leader of the captives. Jim, one of his boys, likewise a captive, was riding a fine gray mount that, Jeff said, "was one of the most beautiful horses I ever saw." As there was no plumbing in the jails then, a guard always followed the captives when they had to take to the brush. Jim Johnson made an excuse to step out with Jeff and then proposed that he had a thousand dollars in cash which he would give him, along with a bill of sale to the horse, if Jeff would let him get ten steps head start in the brush.

"Nothing doing," said Jeff. "One jump, and I'll kill you."

From Hillsboro, Jeff and his posse took the captives before a justice court at Las Palomas, where they lodged them in a big dobe room with a standing guard. But the chicanery that attends impatience with the orderly measures of the law had not ended at Hillsboro, and one night as he passed the guards in the dark he heard someone whispering, "When they make the break, let the first one go and then kill every man."

Jeff just stepped in where the captives were and brought them upright, saying, "Listen men! There's some son-of-a-bitch in here who is putting up a job on you; who is planning to lead you in a break and get all of you killed." Then he told them what he had overheard, and the outraged captives rushed for the conspirator, who, himself, barely escaped with his life, as Jeff regretfully recalled. At length some twelve of them were indicted and properly tried in Sierra County. Toppy and others went off to the pen at Santa Fé, and Jeff drifted back into the San Mateos.[11]

Thus his work went on, usually in long and wild rides through the jumbled mixture of canyons and mountains that make up western New Mexico. It was a congenial pursuit for a young man without physical fear who loved to tackle the trails alone. One trip carried him far from Socorro to Cooney Camp,[12] as he had got wind that a man named Williams, wanted for murder in Texas, was there. Though a dead hard man, he proved to be the "nicest" murderer Jeff ever saw. Jeff went by rail to Lordsburg, took the narrow gauge across to Duncan, Arizona, bought a horse, and doubled back into the Mogollons.

At Cooney Camp, Jeff located Williams' cabin, waited until he showed up, quietly approached, and stepped inside, six-shooter in hand. Williams was standing at the stove with his back to the door, holding a frying pan.

"Don't turn around and don't drop the pan," commanded Jeff, quietly, "or I'll have to kill you. Just set the grease on the stove, unbuckle your gun, and let it drop to the floor."

"Don't shoot me," Williams said, looking back.

---

[11] Sierra County Court Record, Vol. A, 46–51, 131–34, 143.

[12] James C. Cooney was a quartermaster's sergeant stationed at Fort Bayard who discovered silver and copper in the Mogollon Mountains in 1875, located his find in 1876, and saw his mines become an active camp in spite of the Apaches. Victorio attacked the camp in April, 1880, and killed several miners, Cooney among them. See Jones, *New Mexico Mines and Minerals*, 129–32.

"I won't," returned Jeff, "if you do what I say."

Williams did, and then Jeff told him to turn around and kick the gun over to him. Jeff picked it up and told him his business. He took him down to the camp, bought another horse, and with a small supply of grub and blankets they set out on a four to five days' ride that would place them at Socorro. When night came, they cooked supper and spread their blankets. Jeff shackled himself to the prisoner with a pair of leg irons and pitched his six-shooter and rifle off to one side. Then they lay down and slept together. After the second night he dispensed with the shackling, as they had become good friends, and after all Williams was one of "the nicest fellows I ever saw," said Jeff. "A lot of nice men have had to kill people, you know."

Like all good Western officers of that day, his captures were often matters of negotiation with brave and desperate men whose sense of pride and fair play could more easily be considered than ignored or defied. Russell told him of another man wanted for murder in Texas who he thought was hiding near the Arizona line, in the Springerville country, but advised him not to go alone for fear he would be killed.

"I'll go," said Jeff, and he went. As he passed through the Escondido Mountains, walking and leading his horse through the snow to keep warm, Winchester in hand, he came near killing a man in a bearskin coat before he realized that he was a man, a ranchman mounted on the first pair of snowshoes Jeff had ever seen. He invited Jeff to his camp, where he had just killed a beef and where he filled him up on the best son-of-a-gun stew Jeff had ever eaten. On the same trip he spent a night with an old-timer named Johnson near Springerville, whose outlaw son he later ran down and killed in Arizona. At last he got directions to the fugitive's camp, with a warning that it rested on a little bench, and he might ride up on it before he was aware.

That was exactly what happened. With a sawed-off shotgun across the fork of his saddle and his six-shooter on his hip, he topped a little rise and the cabin was right before him. The occupants had discovered his coming. In the door stood the man

129

he wanted with a rifle in his hand and a six-shooter on his hip. Sitting on either side of the door were two other men similarly armed, Winchesters across their laps. Jeff rode right up to the door, bade them good day, called the fugitive by name, and told him he had a warrant for him.

"Are you going to serve it?" asked the man in the door.

"By Jacks, it don't look like it; not under these circumstances," he replied, while all roared with laughter in appreciation of the humor of the situation.

"I'd better take that shotgun," said the one in the door, reaching for it. Jeff handed it down, as he saw they had him and there was nothing else to do.

"Get down," invited the outlaw, with the usual drawl. "I'd like to read that warrant."

"Certainly, sir," said Jeff, forking it over. They didn't bother to take his six-shooter or the rifle off his saddle. The fugitive read the warrant, folded it carefully and deliberately, and handed it back. Then they visited throughout the afternoon.

At last the man said, "It will take me from two weeks to a month to get my business in Texas in shape so I can stand trial. When I get it in shape, I'll quietly drop you a letter, Milt, and you can come and get me." They were decent men whose words were honor, and Jeff knew he meant it.

Night came and they invited him to sleep inside. "I'm very fond of this horse," Jeff said, nodding toward his mount staked on grass, near by. "If you don't mind I'll just sleep out with him."

"Your horse will be perfectly safe," said the outlaw. "I'll guarantee that." So Jeff slept inside.

Next day he mounted his horse, took a short cut through the mountains that the outlaw pointed out, and reported to Russell that he did not find his man. Within a month the letter came, Jeff made the return trip to the cabin on the shelf, and this fugitive from Texas came back with him to the toils of the law at Socorro. He, too, slept like the gentleman he was at the hotel with Jeff, instead of in jail, to await the coming of another sheriff from Texas. Jeff put the $500 reward in his pocket and went on about his business, happy to learn later that the man came clear at his trial. After all, he was wont to observe, a lot of decent men have been provoked to murder in Texas.

And though others were to die in front of Jeff's guns and many wounds were to tear at his own sturdy frame, his pursuits of the lawless at the time, and its memories in age, were remarkably free of animus and hatred. This was high and hearty adventure for him; living between danger and death was a fascinating game. And when he tired of the chase, he went back to Crow Springs to hear the wild turkeys "put-put-put" about his cabin of an early morning, and watch the bears flex their claws in telltale hieroglyphics high as they could reach on the quaking aspens, high in the San Mateos.

From his camp there, he drifted down the slope at times into the nearest town. One night he was asleep in the San Marcial Hotel when the booted steps of a man in the hall awoke him. As they beat a firm and familiar tattoo, he sat bolt upright in bed and shouted in the dark, "Sed!"

And Sed it was. His old Ranger friend, J. M. Sedberry, had hunted him down. Sed had been having a time of his own. After taking that first drink with Jeff at Murphyville when he was twenty-eight years of age, he had quit the Rangers and had driven the Western Trail to Dodge City. There he had got on a terrible tear and when the officers tried to take him, he had stood them off and got out of town on a borrowed and bareback horse, with nothing on him but a rope and a half-hitch around the animal's nose, and headed for Texas. Sed never did things by halves. He quit drinking just as he started, all of a sudden, but with less warfare and noise.

Jeff joyfully got him a horse, and they talked of a thousand things dear to warm-hearted young men as they jogged across the thirty short miles to Jeff's claim in North Canyon. The world was still theirs if they wanted it, and they decided to take what they needed for a cow range. Friends in Texas would furnish the stock and put up the money. They prospected the left-hand prong of North Canyon, pitched camp, and spread their bed in a low-roofed cave. From there they rode the country by day, keeping an eye open for hostile Indians, while at night a friend-

131

ly skunk kept plundering their scanty provisions. Jeff had picked up an old .40–.90 Ballard rifle equipped with a set or hair trigger, which he decided to use on the skunk. He fastened it firmly to a tree at the mouth of the cave and baited its muzzle with a piece of meat tied by a string to the trigger.

Along in the night, both Jeff and Sed were awakened by the roar of the gun. Thinking that the Indians had them, Jeff bolted from bed to knock himself down against the overhanging rock. Then, by the time he recovered, the pungent odor had reached them, and rubbing his head, he rolled over saying, "Shuckin's, Sed, that's only that skunk."

They did start a little herd, but the insistent demands of the law, speaking through warm personal friends like Charlie Russell, and it always spoke louder in that way then, kept Jeff pretty well on the move. One day in the fall of 1885, he walked into Russell's office. The sheriff looked up from his desk and handed him a warrant and a telegram. They were from Captain Jim Gillespie, in charge of his old company in the Big Bend, in Texas, and called for the arrest of Ranger Charlie Trentham, wanted for the murder of Mac Leakey, following a row at Marfa. He had escaped bareback, on a Ranger pack mule, and was thought to be headed that way.[13]

"Cap, I've done resigned," said Jeff. "I ain't a deputy no more."

"What-a you mean, Milt?" said the astonished Russell.

"That man's a friend of mine. For three years, spring and fall, he rode three to four hundred miles with me to court, and he rode it back, standing by me when I was in trouble. I'll help him anyway I can, as sure as shooting."

"Is that true, Jeff?" queried the sober Russell, who too had tasted some of the bitters of life in Texas.

"Every word true!" said the somber young man before him.

---

[13] N. M. C. Leakey was apparently the son of John Leakey, the first settler in Frio Canyon, for whom the town of Leakey was named. He had bought property in Marfa and was killed there by Trentham in the late fall of 1885. See District Court Minutes, Presidio County, Marfa, Vol. III, 523–34, and, for the family, A. J. Sowell, *Early Settlers and Indian Fighters of Southwest Texas* (Austin, 1900), 612.

Neither spoke as Russell's rough fingers twisted warrant and message to bits and let them roll off his hand into the wastebasket. Then he looked up and said, "Jeff, go on about your business."

He caught a train for San Marcial and hit a high lope up the ridges toward Crow Springs. Leaving Sed in camp, he took his two very best horses, tied some food on his saddle, and headed southeast—for Trentham and Texas.

The country he covered was—and still is—a vast, wild land where rugged ranges seem to rise on the rim of the earth, and the deserts between dance and shimmer in the heat waves to swallow and obliterate those who venture upon them. To ride them alone without water or trail in the whirring silences and the blighting glare of day, and the brilliant starlight of their nights, is to grasp the infinitesimal nature of man and experience the complete humility of spirit with which he looks upon the face of God.

How then, encompassed by this awesome nature, and lost in a vastness that seemed to border on infinity, could one man on a horse with nothing to guide him hope to go straight to another who was an elusive fugitive?

It is an uncanny thing, but it is a fact that in that *jornada del muerto* of desert sand, to the east of the Organ Mountains, some twenty-five miles from Las Cruces by a course he figured a fugitive from Marfa might follow, a bobbing blur miles before him took shape in the heat as a gangling man on "a gant and give-out horse." On closer range he started to turn and run, but Jeff stopped him with a yell. Warily and dangerously he rode on up. Not much was said.

"Hello, Charlie. Turn yours loose and saddle this horse." Charlie did. Then heading his abandoned mount toward the river, they pushed along Jeff's back trail to the sheltering woods and the friendly waters at Crow Springs. Charlie spent the winter and then decided to move on. Jeff gave him a splendid horse, wished him well, shook his weathered and powerful paw, and, aware of the dangers of the federal mail, said, "Goodbye Charlie! And remember, don't ever write."

133

And out into the wild country that lay to their north, out of the jurisdiction of the Texans with whom he had served long and well, out of touch with his friends, and out of the reach of the law, rode Charlie Trentham—a decided comfort to the few he loved, but a potential barrel of trouble for others. He was never heard of again.

10

Between Cowboys and Bad Men

Life for Jeff in western New Mexico was largely a matter of living either with or between cowboys and bad men. Nothing could have been more interesting. It was something just to know that unspoiled range inhabited by wild animals and willful men. Just to be living there was in itself great fun.

For a man of Jeff's breeding and taste, with pride enhanced by generations of genteel living and patriotic service, and high personal honor whetted on the stories of Sir William Wallace, any adventure at that time and place was possible.

Some experiences were provoked by that peculiar psychology of the Western gunmen, who fell into two distinct types. The most familiar type, from the standpoint of attempted literary analysis, was that skillful hand with a gun, possessing a perverse nature if not perverted conscience, who came to enjoy the craven deference that the "rag, tag, and bobtail" of creation pay to the killers. Pride too, of its kind, played a part with them. They were proud of their marksmanship and their speed with a gun. They confused killing with courage and basked in the transient power that came with the name of being "bad," while living under the secret apprehension of meeting someone who was really worse. Therein they were usually right, as their paths of glory often led, but prematurely, "to the grave."

There was another type of gunman that might better be called a "good man with a gun." Skill with weapons was likewise his. But no perverted pride in being bad pushed him out to war, though a sense of honor was right-hand bower to his courage. He lived on familiar terms with life and death and was not afraid to die. He looked with contempt upon the professional bad man, and was really dangerous to cross, for he lusted at times for the exhilirating stimulus of battle as a thoroughbred lusts for a race.

135

In a strongly impersonal way he could look upon death without wavering, and draw his gun and squeeze the trigger without remorse. Out of this group came the great peace officers of the West.

Jeff's adventures were enhanced by his reputation as a Texas Ranger that came west with him. Once he pulled out secretly from the ICC ranch for a few weeks, to western New Mexico and northern Arizona on detective work, and an associate at the ranch, Martin by name, bruited it about the country that he had run the Ranger off. The story came to Jeff upon his return. It met him all over Socorro, and at San Marcial his good friend from Austin, Howell Cobb Brown, who was staying at his ranch in the San Mateos, told him about it, too.

"Where is he?" asked Jeff.

"He's over at the San Marcial Hotel eating dinner with the Virgins and some others," replied Brown.

"That's just where I want him," said Jeff, as he headed for the hotel. When he stepped into the dining room, he saw Martin "whiten up" a little where he sat at a table.

"Hello, fellows," greeted Jeff; and then turning to Martin, he quietly added, "Howdy-do, Martin? I understand you ran me out of the country. I thought I'd come back and talk it over."

"Who told you that?" countered Martin.

"Everybody," said Jeff.

"By God, I didn't say it, but what if I did?"

"Well, by God," said Jeff "you're a so-and-so, and I'm going to give you the damndest thrashing you ever had in your life. Pull your gun!" he commanded, while Virgin and the others started to jump up. "John, you and the rest just set still," he snapped. "I'm going to teach this fellow something."

"And I taught him something!" Jeff would conclude.

Jeff's work as a cowboy detective for the Central New Mexico Stock Association took him all over the country. When he was not out for the sheriff's office, he was out for the cowmen, trying to move with the news behind him, incognito if possible. He would drop into a ranch as a drifting cowboy and take a job as a hand. Thus he worked from Hulvey's 7HL outfit, near the Arizona line, through the intervening country between there and the Río Grande; from Joe Hampson's Double Circles, in the White Mountains, back through Bush Valley, that became Alpine, and the Spur range; back through the WIL S and John Slaughter country; across the San Augustine Plains; and down into the Mogollons.

He bought a remnant of cattle in the Flying A brand that Jim Hall had in the Luna country, some of which were so wild they had to be roped and necked to gentle steers to be taken out of the mountains. He gathered about a hundred more than Hall expected and made good money on the deal. He held his claim in the San Mateos during most of this time, and when he was gone from there, his cowboy friends on neighboring ranches branded mavericks for him faster than his own small bunch could possibly produce them, just because they liked him.

G. L. Brooks, then secretary of the stock association for which Jeff was working, suggested he go up near Grants after some men who were thought to be stealing cattle from the Ácoma Land and Cattle Company—the ALC's. This outfit had been organized in 1884 by Joe E. Saint, one-time grocery drummer, with Eastern backing. Saint had acquired a lease on the Ácoma Indian Reservation, set up headquarters near Grants, and, with commendable enterprise but woeful lack of cow sense, spread out all over the country.[1]

Some miles to his south a man named Thompson, who had married a Mexican widow, had located at some splendid springs called the Cibolleta. There he ranched with two grown stepsons, two attractive stepdaughters, and a little bunch of cattle. He was under suspicion. Jeff was sent to catch him in the act of rustling cattle. Posing as a cowboy in search of work, he dropped in at the Thompson ranch and was given a job. Then Brooks wrote

[1] The Ácoma Company was chartered in New Mexico, June 25, 1884. Saint acquired a lease on 100,000 acres of reservation land for a period of thirty years. He served as general manager of the company, which had $300,000 in paid-up capital. It was the largest outfit in that section, claiming 18,000 cattle at one time. Records, State Corporation Commission, Santa Fé; R. E. Twitchell, *Leading Facts of New Mexican History* (Cedar Rapids, Iowa, 1911), III, 34; Joe McKinney to J. E. H., April 14, 1946; Tom Rainy to J. E. H., February 27, 1945.

Saint that Jeff was in that section at work, and Saint, not suspecting Thompson, let the news out to him.

That evening Jeff came in from his ride and threw his saddle off on the ground a few steps from the room where he slept, left his rifle in the scabbard, and, to keep down suspicion, dropped his six-shooter and belt on top of it. Thompson was unaware of his return. Jeff could hear him in another part of the house telling the two boys who and what Jeff was, and making plans to kill him. Jeff stepped back outside just as they did, reaching inside his shirt for a special-made, short-barreled Colt .45 that he carried out of sight, in a holster under his arm, and drew it, saying, "Hold on here, fellers, let's talk this over."

He walked over and picked up his rifle, sent one of the boys out to rustle his horse, and, aware that his detective business was up, saddled and rode away from Cibolleta Springs.

Then in the late fall of 1885 he got the job for his old Texas friend, Joe McKinney, who had been in trouble at Fort Davis and was ready for a fresh range. Joe casually rode in through the malpais and drew rein at the Thompson ranch, addressing the Mexican wife and her two grown daughters in jolly and musical Spanish, for Joe was from South Texas and spoke the language like a native. He was taken in at once, beloved by the old lady and charmed by her Mexican daughters. He admitted that they may have been killing some beeves, but they treated him so well that he felt it would be base ingratitude to catch them. Besides, he did not like Saint. Therefore, he threw up the job, crossed to the Navajo Springs, and began punching cows legitimately.[2]

As Jeff rode east from the Ácoma after his untimely discovery, a cinder blew in his eye, and by the time he reached Belen he was practically blind. He went into the store of two German Jews, fine men, whom he knew there, and they treated him for several days—until his eye was well.

Back in San Marcial, in 1886, he found that Kim Ki Rogers had sold his ranch at Engle and was looking for someone to gather and deliver his cattle. Jeff took the contract on the basis

[2] Joe McKinney to J. E. H. and Hervey Chesley, February 27, 1945.

of a dollar a head. He hired two Texas cowpunchers, Jack Hutchinson and Dan Walker, finished up an outfit with others, hired a cook, took a wagon, crossed the river, and swung down the *Jornada*—that great dry segment of range that lay between San Marcial and Engle.

Kim Ki Rogers and a Boston doctor named Daley had come to the country and started the outfit that became the Bar N Cross Ranch. Kim Ki was a colorful character. The *Albuquerque Journal* called him "the heavy weight cattleman from Engle" when he was found "cavorting" around Socorro. He had been a rail road conductor. He now owned the general store at Engle, held the seventy-mile-long *Jornada* black grama range, and was cutting a wide swath through the *tornillo* thickets, especially when bellying up to the friendly Socorro bars.

By report, he had gone into ranching when he was caught by a railroad spotter confusing company change with his own but, when fired, he pulled out his fine gold watch, sported his diamond rings, and remonstrated, "You shouldn't fire me. I'm now well-to-do. The next man you hire may have some incentive to steal."

Whatever the legend of the man, however, it is a fact that he and Doc Daley came to own the cattle and control the country that lay east of the river from Doña Ana almost to San Marcial— the country now bordered by the eastern waters of the Caballo and Elephant Butte lakes. Their headquarters, the village of Engle, had a hotel with the high-sounding name of the Humboldt House, managed by Colonel David Branson, of the Humboldt Mining Company, and likewise headquarters for the Southwestern Stage Company, with a tri-weekly coach into the mountainous regions to the west.[3] Now, in 1886, Rogers and Daley were selling out to the Detroit and Río Grande Cattle Company, of which Colonel Phillips Mothersill—who "didn't know a bull from a cow"—was general manager. Jeff and his outfit were to make delivery.

The new owners were Northern men. General Russell A. Alger, of the Union Army, governor of Michigan and later secre-

[3] *Albuquerque Journal,* April 24, 1883, and December 27, 1885.

139

tary of war under McKinley, was the principal in the firm, while two other Michigan men, Plumber and Heard, were stockholders. They sent Mothersill down to manage the outfit. Jeff gathered his first herd, threw it into the company corrals near Engle, and asked the manager what he wished to use as a tally brand.

"Just turn them loose," said the Colonel. "They're all branded; no need to brand them again."

"Why, man," said Jeff, as he thought of the mix-up that would follow with the untallied stuff on the open range, "we'll be gathering cattle for the next hundred years!" Then he explained the absolute necessity of a tally brand. One was chosen and the work proceeded, though when he mentioned the incident to Kim Ki, that businesslike ranchman reproached him for not following Mothersill's suggestion, as it would have enhanced, indefinitely, Kim Ki's count.[4]

As was usual in open-range work, they held their cattle in day herd as they gathered them, and posted a night guard when the sun went down. One night the stuff stampeded, and Jeff, riding hard on the flank, had his horse fall in a narrow gully and pin him underneath. The herd went on while Jeff's horse, back down in the narrow ditch with all four feet uphill, could not get up. Jeff grabbed his bridle and held up the horse's head to stop his floundering, finally worked his leg from under the animal, and then pulled him around to where he could get up. But the herd had already gone south and scattered to the winds.

Thus their work went on. They gathered herds along the water, trailed them to the pens near Engle, branded them out, threw them south, and worked back along the waters toward the north—toward where Mount Fra Cristoval severely scanned the upper end of the *Jornada* range. Jeff sent a man to kill a beef while they were camped at a roundup ground on the river just north of Elephant Butte. A poor old Mexican had a half-dozen cattle on the range near by. When they got in from the drive that day, the beef was hanging from the wagon spokes. It is always

[4] The Bar N Cross came to run 15,000 head of cattle. B. C. Mossman to J. E. H. and Hervey Chesley, February 24, 1945; Cole Railston to the same, February 25, 1945.

good Western ethics to hang your beef hides up in plain view, to prove, by the brands, that you eat your own. Jeff did not see the hide. Turning to the cook, he asked, "Where in the devil is that hide?"

"He threw the hide and head in the river," answered the cook.

"What did he do that for?"

"Why, he didn't want anyone to find it," confided the cook. "He killed a beef belonging to that old Mexican that he don't like."

"Hell he did," said Jeff, hotter than the barrel of a .45 as he headed for the offending hand. "You ride in that river and drag that hide out. I'm a good notion to pen you," he stormed.

"I made him drag the hide out and stretch it, and then pay the poor old Mexican. And then I fired him—yes, I did."

At times they all took off to ride into San Marcial, and one incident alone—albeit an international incident—disturbed the roundup and held up the work.

A striking feature of that day and place was the militant patriotism and national pride that burned in these isolated Western hearts. An affront to the national dignity or lack of deference to the nation's power and honor became a personal matter that

141

should be rectified at once with their own arms and blood. Hence it was not surprising that the "Cutting incident" stirred the cowpunchers at the village of San Marcial to the boiling point of war. Down the river at El Paso, on June 18, 1886, A. K. Cutting printed a piece in the paper about a Mexican citizen with whom he was in controversy. A few days later, when caught over the river in Juarez, he was thrown in jail, refused bail, and held *incomunicado*. Then there arose a tense diplomatic problem, with officials of state in Washington protesting to the national government of Mexico, denying her jurisdiction in the case, and demanding Cutting's release and indemnity. Texas was rearing to charge, too, in the usual Texas way.

Diplomacy takes time. Meanwhile Cutting was lying in a "loathsome and filthy" cell, which was simply not to be endured by Western men. The boys got to talking about it in the comfortable surroundings of the San Marcial Hotel. They took a drink or two and talked some more, and the more they talked the hotter they got. They immediately organized to march down the river, whip the Mexican officials, tear the jail down, take Cutting home to Texas, and reinstate the honor of the United States.

Just then, Jesse James, the noted outlaw guerilla, was reported to be still alive and at refuge in New Mexico. Jeff proposed that they commandeer him.[5]

"We can get him, shore," said Jeff. "We'll make him leader and go take Cutting from Mexico, certain." But an old cowman with handle-bar mustaches vigorously dissented.

"To hell with Jesse James," he shouted. "I move we make this feller, Milton, captain." This they did. Then they sent the word out to the warlike men who inhabited the camps and ranches to report at once at San Marcial. However, before they could get started, Mexico turned Cutting loose.[6] Of course she did. She was bound to have heard they were coming. It was disappointing to them all in a way, but certainly the national honor was somewhat

[5] Jesse had, in fact, been dead for over four years. See J. A. Dacus, *Lives and Adventures of Frank and Jesse James* (St. Louis, 1882), 439–41.
[6] J. B. Moore, *A Digest of International Law* (Washington, 1906), II, 228–42, and *Report on Extraterritorial Crime* (Washington, 1887) set forth the facts and the diplomatic procedure in the Cutting case.

142

restored in the desert cow camps of New Mexico, and proud, free men could again admit their nativity without apology.

Jeff went back to Kim Ki's cows. He gathered the last snaky stuff, tallied them out to Colonel Mothersill's satisfaction, picked the *tornillo* thorns out of his knees, peeled the riggin' off his horse at the livery stable, and cleaned up at the San Marcial Hotel. After paying his bills, he found that he had made considerable money.

Dan Walker, "a pippin of a cowboy and a dream of a man," rode off into oblivion as good cowboys do, while Jeff and Jack Hutchinson drifted upstream to take in the New Mexico Fair and cowboy tournament at Albuquerque.

Joe Hampson, the railroad contractor who had founded the Double Circles, was entertaining with a full purse and a lavish hand. "7HL" Hulvey, from west of Grants, Jim Hall, the little Texan from the Luna Valley, Nat Greer from St. Johns and the Little Colorado, Jeff, and all the others were there.

They threw a big banquet at the Old Armijo Hotel, where, as Jeff said, "Wine, champagne, and everything else flowed freely." Hampson beat on the bar with a "California fifty-dollar slug," the first gold piece of that denomination the bartender had seen, and he turned it down as spurious. The hotel brought memories to Jeff, for there at its colonnaded entrance some time before, he had been forced, for the first and only time in his life, to throw up his hands.

He had ridden in from the west just after the report had come down from near the Colorado line of a murder by a man somewhat fitting his description. He had put his horse in the livery stable and with gun still on strode across to the hotel. Four men jumped out from behind the columns with their guns thrown down on him. One was greatly excited and kept jamming him with a cocked shotgun.

"Say," Jeff soothed, keeping his composure, "put that gun down before you kill a man accidentally. What the devil's the matter with you fellows, anyway?" They were very much on the prod as they unbuckled his gun and kept him covered.

"Do you fellows know Governor Ross?" Jeff continued. They

143

did—one saying that the Governor was over at the Commercial Club right then. Jeff induced them to take him by to establish his identity, for he had a special commission from the Governor. When they stepped in at the door, Ross happened to see Jeff and walked right up and shook his hand. That ended his capture. But Jeff, to give the incident a light touch, pulled his .45 from his shoulder holster, as he had not been searched, saying, "Governor, they got my six-shooter, but I've got another one right here."

So, with soberer memories of the Armijo Hotel to keep him company but never to dampen his spirits, Jeff joined the others that night in painting Albuquerque a bright and brilliant red. It was apparently the first big cowboy tournament, roundup, or rodeo in the entire country, for the *Albuquerque Journal* boasted that "in no other city in the United States can this novel, exciting feature be witnessed in public." There was plenty of racing, roping, and riding. Jeff put his money on his fine friend, Jack Hutchinson, who had stage fright so badly that he missed his steer by twenty feet. But Nat Greer, whose roots likewise ran back to Texas, joined others in herding a bunch of wild broncs in front of the grandstand where each man roped one for himself, saddled him without help, mounted by himself, and rode him until the bronc stopped pitching or he "got throwed." Nat Greer took the championship saddle.[7] As they headed back home, they admitted to themselves, as the dobe dust fogged about their hazy heads, that it had been a genuine "blowout."

Winter was at hand, and Jeff, with money in pocket and the homing instinct of a wild goose in his heart, thought again of the gracious sun of Florida. He mounted a train and took a round-about rail for home.

After a good long visit he returned to San Marcial. Things had changed. Charlie Russell was gone from the sheriff's office at Socorro. Joe McKinney had quit the Wabash Cattle Company, on the Zuñi River, and had gone into St. Johns, Arizona, to serve as a deputy under its notorious long-haired sheriff, Commodore Owens. Commodore had built a reputation as a killer of men,

[7] *Albuquerque Journal*, September 29 and October 1, 1886.

144

along with its concomitant trouble, and when Joe told him of Jeff, he wired at once offering him a job as deputy also. The message was waiting at San Marcial.

Jeff caught the train through Albuquerque to Navajo Springs, and went from there by stage to St. Johns. As he was getting acquainted around that delightful Mormon village that industriously tends its poplars, hollyhocks, and hay fields high on its volcanic slopes, a rough "old boy" named J. V. Brighton came sidling up to him one day to say, "Let's have a drink."

They went in and had two. Then Brighton broke out all over in talk. He was hipped on the topic of being a detective. He had taken a correspondence course and ordered a badge, of which he was very proud. He showed the badge to Jeff and suggested he ought to have one; it could be ordered by mail at a nominal cost.

"They've got some of these bad men around here," Brighton continued. "I'm going out and get 'em." Now he was dead right about the first. But Jeff, as he looked at the badge on the correspondence-school detective through the tolerance induced by drink, put the rest of it down as idle talk.

Down in the mountains south of St. Johns, Ike Clanton and some of his bad-men friends were still at large. Commodore Owens decided to send Jeff after him. However, before he got off on the trip, a telegram came from Joseph Magoffin, collector of customs at El Paso, offering Jeff a job as mounted inspector on the Arizona-Mexico border. He decided at once to take it.

He and the long-haired sheriff "didn't hit it off together," anyway, according to Joe McKinney. And for that matter neither did the Commodore and Joe. Jeff was off again in about a week after his arrival.

But what of Brighton? He did go after Ike Clanton, found him on Bonita Creek, below the Double Circles, and shot and killed him. Then he heard of some bad men in California, went out there, and killed two or three of them. Then he drifted into Tucson after Jeff entered the customs service, rounded up another bad one at Silver Lake, and killed him; then went from there—but there must be an end.

145

"It was all business with him," recalled Jeff with proper respect. "When he heard of a bad one, he wanted him, and I think he got about eight in all."

All of which may prove but little about bad men, though it does illustrate the fact that nobody can tell what's coming out of a correspondence school until he has opened and examined the package.

Wilson, Yarborough & Company
Anderson, Texas, 1868

JEFF MILTON
at the time he joined the Texas Rangers

CAPTAIN BRYAN MARSH

Courtesy Miss Lucy Marsh

Camp of Company E, Texas Rangers
near Bishop's Mitre Peak

Courtesy E. E. Townsend

Texas Rangers at Musquiz

Standing, left to right: "Boggs" Davis, Nick Brown, Geo. W. Simonds, Jeff D.
Milton, J. M. Sedberry, W. H. C. Carruthers, unknown, Ike Lee, Bill Sheffield;
seated, left to right: Haskell (?), L. B. Wells, Capt. J. B. Gillespie, "Doc" Gourley,
Ed Sheffield, Honest John Brockmar, Bob Neville

C. T. RUSSELL
Sheriff, Socorro County, New Mexico, 1885

JEFF MILTON at twenty-six

Jeff Milton and George Scarborough

MARTIN M'ROSE AND TOM FINNESSY

Courtesy Mrs. J. E. Dunaway

$500 Reward!

OFFICE OF THE SHERIFF,

COUNTY OF PIMA, TERRITORY OF ARIZONA.

By virtue of an Order of the Board of Supervisors of
Pima County, Territory of Arizona, made
This 30th day of December, 1890,
Empowering me so to do, I hereby
Offer a Reward of $500 for the body
Dead or alive of

Manuel Verdugo,

Who was under Sentence of Death and who
escaped from the County Jail of Pima County
aforesaid,

December 29th, 1890.

Description:

Manuel Verdugo is about 5 feet, 6 inches
tall and weighes about 150 pounds.
Has no beard but a very thin, dark
mustache. Has a black Scar on side of Left
Eye, about the size of a half dollar; aged
23 years; has a very round head and
a smiling countenance·

The above is a Good Picture of him.

M. F. SHAW, Sheriff.

One bad man Jeff Milton chased

Colonel Emilio Kosterlitzky

BURT ALVORD

JEFF MILTON
in determined mien

Photograph by Esther Henderson

Border *rurales*

MILDRED TAITT MILTON

JEFF MILTON
a characteristic pose

Photograph by Esther Henderson

Back to the dust of the desert

The site, about fifteen miles southwest of Tucson, where Milton's ashes were scattered as he had wished

11

To Tucson

J eff left St. Johns by way of stage to Navajo Springs and by rail to El Paso. There his Austin friend, Howell Cobb Brown, had interceded with the Collector of Customs, Joseph Magoffin, to get him a job, telling him that Jeff was the sort of a man he needed on the Arizona border.[1] Magoffin advised Jeff of his duties and sent him on his way. Apparently he was formally enlisted in the service on March 11, 1887.

He stepped off the train at Tucson, an ancient Mexican town that now spread beyond its once protective walls. In spite of the coming of the railroad and the recent shot of American enterprise, it still slept within the recesses of its cool adobes through the heat and glare of the noonday sun and sprawled somnolent in its scanty shade the rest of the time.

An old Texas frontiersman, W. S. Oury, was in charge of the Tucson office of the Collector of Customs. His job was to watch the dribble of exports and imports that moved, spasmodically and sometimes surreptitiously, across the Mexican line.

Jeff had orders to report to him. In the matter of blood and iron, what a fabulous character he was. He was born a Virginian but grew to a full-fledged warrior in Texas. He served with the ill-fated Travis, though reported carrying messages and hence absent from the Alamo. He drew a white bean with the men who survived the massacre after Mier, fought with Taylor in the Mexican War, took part in the California gold rush, and reached Tucson by the back track in the eighteen fifties. At times he was rough, and he was always ready. Now, grizzled with the riotous adventure of all but seventy years, he took young Milton, who

[1] Magoffin, son of the original James, was appointed collector by President Cleveland in 1886 and served until October, 1889. Lee A. Riggs, MS, "A Short History of the District of El Paso" (copy in files of the author); Frank W. Johnson, *A History of Texas and Texans* (Chicago and New York, 1914), III, 1405.

147

was likewise from a Southern and hence proper state, straight to his heart at once.[2]

Jeff's arrival was expected. He stepped off the Southern Pacific and registered at the old San Xavier Hotel. What struck him as an odd frontier character noted his name and made himself known as Morgan R. Wise, the official in the customs service whom Jeff was coming to relieve. In personal appearance he was unkempt and unkept, from his dirty celluloid collar to his sockless feet, and Jeff eyed him with disdain as Wise transgressed Western custom by asking him where he was from.

"Alabama," said Jeff.

"If I were you, young man, I'd take the next train home. They'll kill you out here for three dollars and a half."

Jeff "just had to laugh" as he headed for Oury's dobe office. Wise followed him in and Oury turned to acquaint them: "Mr. Wise, this is Mr. Milton, an old Texas Ranger."

"Why, I thought you said you were from Alabama."

"I was in Eufaula once," Milton added, dryly.

Oury gave Jeff the lay of the land. He was to be stationed in Tucson. His domain was the Arizona-Mexico border, especially that portion that lay west of the red ridges of Nogales, clear to the indigo waters of the Gulf of California. He was to be furnished nothing. He must equip himself and buy his horses, but he would be paid one hundred dollars a month. He was to ride the line by himself and was expected to do the job alone.

His predecessor, a native of Pennsylvania and a former member of Congress, had come west after the crash of 1873 to recoup his health and fortune. He was a frugal man who would not buy a mount, but went his self-appointed rounds of duty afoot, armed with nothing worse than a pitchfork.[3] That looked like poor business to Jeff, who immediately hunted a horse. A one-eyed well-driller named Morgan, working for Maish and Driscoll, took him to one of their ranches up the Santa Cruz to show him some that they had for sale. They made the twenty-mile drive in a buck-

[2] Dr. Frank C. Lockwood, in *Life in Old Tucson, 1854–1864* (Tucson, 1943), 92 ff., gives a vivid sketch of this remarkable character.

[3] For a sketch of Morgan R. Wise, see the *Biographical Directory of the American Congress, 1774–1927* (Washington, 1928), 1720.

board up that valiant trickle that defied the dryness of the desert to water the little town of Tucson.

Morgan likewise figured that Jeff was a tenderfoot. As they meandered the trail toward San Xavier, five Papago Indians approached them. Morgan, thinking he would have some fun, shouted in feigned alarm, "Oh my Lord, look at the Indians! We'll be killed sure."

"Killed, nothin'," said Jeff, jumping from the buckboard and drawing his rifle from its scabbard, "I'll get every one of them!"

"My God, don't shoot, they're friendly Indians," shouted Morgan, in dire and downright alarm, and again Jeff "just had to laugh."

He bought his horses and returned to town. While fitting up a camp outfit for his first trip to the desert, he began to get acquainted with Tucson. The old town stood—or rather squatted—along the Santa Cruz, a little stream that came north from the borders of Mexico giving water and life to the locality and furnishing the most practicable trail for the men who first trudged that way from down in the valley of the Montezumas. Its dark, dobe shelters had repelled the light and the heat for many generations, but had never pushed back the hard, hot, and hostile frontiers that hemmed it in. And although the land had been held by the United States for years, it was still, in tradition and culture, distinctly Mexican. The physical climate and the human temperament went well together.

Its inhabitants rose late. Nobody killed himself with work that would obviously wait until tomorrow. The siesta or afternoon nap was a wise and rejuvenating custom where the heat sapped the vitality of those whose nervous energy inclined them to burn the breeze. The sun would attend to that. As Jeff wandered past "Chris" Christensen's wagon yard, he noted that the horses hunted the shade. In Charlie Brown's L-shaped Congress Bar, men lounged lazily over its polished rail, or were draped, dozing, in its scattered chairs, but with an unconscious ease not due to climate alone.

Both here and at Billy Reed's saloon—the biggest gambling house in Tucson—keno, poker, and roulette were not uncommon.

149

The Mexicans favored monte, and the Chinese flocked to faro. Every man could make his choice, while the only sure winner was the house. Sometimes a kitchen was kept going at the rear to feed those whose purses, hopes, or turns of fortune kept them at the tables late. The fare at the Congress Hall was under the questionable skill of Charles Alzamora, who, likely as not, in the midst of frying some eggs would rush from the stove, smoking pan in hand, to lay a bet on the turn of a card in the main saloon. His antics in search of fortune instead of his ability as a cook won him the nickname of "Frying Pan."[4]

The owner of The Congress was Charles O. Brown, a man of fifty-six when Jeff came—a man who did not drink or gamble and who had married a native—a "Mexican shawl woman." All Mexican women then wore shawls about their heads except the aristocratic ones—"*las mujeres de sombreros*"—"the women with hats." Josie Brown, a daughter by an earlier marriage, was to become one of Jeff's friends.

Francis Heney and Judge Richard E. Sloan were among the prominent lawyers, but neither was constitutionally immune to Jeff's temper and tongue, those complementary features of his

[4] Harry Drachman to J. E. H., January 28, 1945; Joe Wiley to J. E. H., April 18, 1946.

150

dynamic nature that often went off together, as Tucson was soon to discover. Dr. Henry E. Crepin was the official guardian of the health, while Dr. John C. Handy, who was later killed in a fight with Heney, though perhaps by another man, was decidedly the doctor about the town. George J. Roskruge was busy mapping the diverse features of Pima County, that stretched, as a mighty wedge, 180 miles from east to west, beveled on its lower edge by the Mexican boundary that bent back on the bias from the 111th meridian, just west of Nogales, for almost 230 miles to where it cut the lower delta of that notorious stream, the Colorado of the West.[5]

The biggest ranchmen in the Territory were Fred Maish and Thomas Driscoll, who had drifted down from the Black Hills in 1869 and within twenty years had four big ranches and eight or ten smaller ones, principally along the Santa Cruz between Tucson and the Mexican line. They claimed 25,000 to 30,000 cattle when Jeff came and were among the most enterprising men in town. In a land where conversation was vibrant with stories of adventure, the latest on Fred Maish was going the rounds.

After delivering a herd of beef cattle up about Fort Grant, he was paid off with several thousand dollars in gold which he tied to his person. On his return, the Gila was in flood. When he started across, his horse went under and the gold weighted Maish down. He could not swim with the gold. He could not afford to lose it. He simply hung to it, held his breath, and walked out on the bottom.

In Tucson, he and Driscoll were owners of the Palace Hotel, where was kept hefty Mexican Mary, a common-law wife, who, as Jeff recalls, "was as big as a horse but not bad to look at." The situation was not altogether out of place in the social customs of the times until the Edmunds Act was passed by Congress in 1887, designed to put a stop to such practices by forcing the men to

[5] Roskruge, born in England in 1845, came to the United States in 1870 and to Arizona in 1872. He joined a surveying party as cook and packer but was soon chief draftsman in the Surveyor General's office, then deputy surveyor of Arizona and New Mexico, and at this time county surveyor of Pima. See Bancroft, *Arizona and New Mexico*, XVII, 620. His map of Pima County is a historical collector's gem.

marry the girls.[6] One noted Papago squaw man conveniently pitched his camp down near the Mexican line. But for some less fortunately situated, this sort of shot-gun legislation on the part of a pious and paternalistic government was simply intolerable. Though Maish was nearly fifty, he had a lot to say.

"Why Jeff," he hotly complained, "we ought to form a posse, go back there, hunt that son-of-a-bitch up, and take him out and hang him." It was just as well for Mr. Edmunds that he legislated on an uncontrollable legal problem back on the quiet Potomac instead of attempting to enforce his moral philosophy along the holy waters of the Santa Cruz.

Just three years earlier the local enforcement of law had been wrested from Bob Paul, and what some said was the domination of the Southern Pacific Railway, by a North Carolinian seasoned in Texas, Eugene O. Shaw. He died in October after Jeff's arrival, and his brother, Fasion, was appointed to his unexpired term.[7] Young Allen Bernard was his deputy, and Bill Moore was undersheriff.

Phil Drachman, a native of Poland, was running a herdic, hauling people about the place. Sam Drachman had put in a cigar store to meet the smoker's needs, advertised by a life-sized wooden Indian out in front that was the pride of Tucson. The long and bloody Apache warfare was fresh in everybody's mind, and when a drunk cowboy unexpectedly met Sam's Indian face to face one day, he pulled his gun and filled him full of lead, much to Sam's disgust but to the undisguised delight of the town. It was dangerous then and there to be any kind of an Indian.

In the way of outfitting for the camp and trail, L. Zeckendorf's store was a popular place. Then for social diversion there was Levine's Park or Carillo's Gardens. The most noted of them was owned by Leopoldo Carillo, a Mexican born in Ures, Sonora. He had crossed the Plains from Missouri before the Civil War,

[6] Richard E. Sloan, *Memories of an Arizona Judge* (Palo Alto, 1932), comments on the application of the Act to Arizona, 116–20. George Franklin Edmunds was senator from Vermont. *Biographical Directory of the American Congress*, 934; Edmunds Act, March 22, 1882, *U. S. Code*, Title 28.

[7] Harry A. Drachman to J. E. H., January 28, 1945; *Sunshine and Silver* (Tucson), November 2, 1884; *Arizona Daily Citizen*, January 1, 1890.

contracted grain and cattle with the government posts around Tucson, ranched on an extensive scale, and established an amusement park in the lower edge of town. There, about a lake fed by springs, in the gentle shade cast by palm, fig, and lemon trees, Carillo set up a sort of a frontier forerunner of the modern carnival. In exotic style, romantic couples could boat on the lake or conventionally dance in the hall. Men could drink at the bar or try their marksmanship in the shooting gallery.

It was there that Harry Arizona Drachman recalls seeing Jeff flipping half-dollars in the air, and then drawing his six-shooter and hitting them on the fly. He and the other admiring town boys were to get all that Jeff missed, but the boys got little to spend. There, too, instead of shooting it away, Jeff could pitch his silver to the modest orchestra and in fancy be swept away from that arid land to the strains of *"Sobre las Olas"*—"Over the Waves."

Leopoldo, the owner, had been caught near Altar a few years before and held for a heavy ransom. But now, in the peaceful retreat of his Gardens, Carillo could be seen sitting on a table top in his gambling hall, his thin legs crossed under him for days on end, eight decks of cards before him as he played the apparently complicated game of *panguingui*.[8]

Jeff's work, however, was not in the welcome shade of Carillo's Gardens, but in the great stretch of desert that lay between there and the Gulf of California. He packed his horse and pushed into it. He observed it carefully and well as he rode along.

Three considerable and distinctive ranges of mountains—the Catalinas, the Rincons, and the Santa Ritas—curved in a slightly distorted horseshoe about the town of Tucson. They flanked it in a rugged barrier from the north to the southeast, and seemed to orient the movement of men who desired the open world toward the west—out over the Tucson hills into a land of incessant thirst and sun. The blessed waters of the Santa Cruz crept off to the north and lost themselves in the thirsty air and the avaricious sand. Farther north, the Gila struggled through a torrid world

[8] Leopoldo Carillo to J. E. H. and Hervey Chesley, March 3, 1945; Harry A. Drachman to J. E. H., as cited.

of its own clear across Arizona to throw its colorful and gritty detritus, a little wearily after its long western journey, into the bold and brazen arms of the Colorado. The desert, west of the Santa Cruz and south of the Gila, was to be home and place of work for Jeff.

Three old and important trails practically bounded the land he was to patrol. One came down the Santa Cruz from Mexico. Another, followed in part by those significant movements of Anglo-American history—the Mormon Battalion, the Boundary surveys, and the Butterfield Trail—approached by way of the springs and streams east of Tucson, turned down the Santa Cruz and the Gila, and across the desert to California. But the last, and most tragic, was the devil's own road, *El Camino Diablo,* which more or less bounded Jeff's jurisdiction on the south and pointed the hazardous way for the hardy souls who took the direct course from Mexico to the West Coast. It was likewise tackled by gold-seekers from the States whom neither heat nor hell could deter in their thirst for fortune.

Jeff found it a strange land with a peculiar contradiction in its perverse and forbidding nature. The worse it grew, the more appealing it became; the worse its hazard, the stronger the desire of healthy blood to possess it. More than two hundred years before he rode into it on a well-shod horse, swarthy men scorched swarthier still, with the fervor of the Cross burning in their hearts hotter than the sands beneath their sandaled feet, had laid out this trail for that greater glory of God that seems to come from the self-denial and suffering of men. Kino first, in the sixteen nineties, and Anza in the seventeen seventies, had passed this way.

Into the land between these trails—a great and arid plain serrated by red lava and granite ranges passing from north to south, and apparently rising straight from the floor of the earth—the Papagoes, a gentle and honorable native race, had retreated from the violent Apaches that inhabited the riotous ranges to the north and east, and insinuated themselves so gradually and naturally into the desert life that they were a part of it. But when the white men made their rash inroads with greater demands on

154

its economy than its frugal nature would consistently furnish or bear, the desert dried up its scanty food and water and in sullen, implacable wrath became again the waste that its name implied.

Jeff came to the desert in its transition years. As he rode south to the border, he found the splendid mission church of San Xavier deserted. As he passed up the Santa Cruz River, the storied, granitic monolith of Baboquivari rose high to orient him on the west. The missions were in decay and disuse, and the popular expression of the day emphasized the south-bound rider's unhappy progression into that inhospitable land; "Tucson, Tubac, Tumacacori, to hell."

Tubac was a tiny Mexican town. Nobody lived about the mission of Tumacacori. Jeff found the chapel a good place to camp and shelter his horse in times of storm. And if there can be any sacrilege in the proper care of a good horse, perhaps he expiated the offense by stopping a souvenir hunter from cutting a toe off the recumbent figure of Christ at San Xavier. And so with ebullient spirits at peace, but with an eager eye for that fresh yet ancient world, Jeff pushed on to Calabasas. This forlorn settlement had recently been boomed at a distance by that perennial bane of orderly growth—the high-powered promoter of American real estate. However, instead of a thriving city shipping cotton from its river piers by steamboat—as its imaginative promotion literature had shown—it was a decadent settlement on a dribble of a stream, with a little hotel and one saloon.

From Nogales, Jeff headed west. His first stop, thirty miles out and an easy day's ride, was at Oro Blanco—the white gold mine, directly on the border. But in Bear Valley, about halfway between, he passed the ranch of "Hank 'n Yank." Hank Hewett and Yank Bartlett were two noted army packers who had ranged against the Apaches with General George Crook in the seventies.[9]

Into the same valley after they left came Johnnie Bogan and Nona Bernard, other friends of Jeff's, to start a horse ranch. They

[9] John G. Bourke, On the Border with Crook (New York, 1891), 155; Martin F. Schmitt, "Frontier Mule Power," The Cattleman, October, 1946, 48. James H. Hewett, born in Tennessee in 1828, was a forty-niner. Arizona Pioneers Historical Society, Tucson.

did right well until the mountain lions took after their colts, as mountain lions have a habit of doing. Bogan began belling his horses to frighten the varmints away. The lions behaved until they found that the bells were harmless. Then they got just as bad as ever, if not worse, for Jeff suspected that they hunted by the sound of the bells. Anyway, Bogan and Bernard were completely cleaned out.

From the Oro Blanco, Jeff's trail led west by the village of Arivaca, situated on a creek of the same name that ran out and dried up in the Altar Valley. Next he reached the settlement at Sasabe. Then, by a long ride of more than a hundred miles that approximated the boundary line, he came to Sonoita, on the river of that name, which was originally an Indian village discovered by Father Kino in 1699. Sonoita was the jump-off into the desert for those who ventured past Altar from Mexico; and, for Kino, bent on Christianizing the desert Indians, it was, as Bolton has written, "the very hub of the Papago wheel."

So Sonoita became a Spanish and Mexican town, which Lieutenant N. Micheler, of the Boundary Survey, described in 1855 as "the door of the State of Sonora, from the California side," though "a miserable, poverty-stricken place" contrasting "strangely with the comparative comfort of an Indian village of Papagos within sight."[10]

Now, a third of a century later, it looked all right to Jeff. He found it "the principal town west of Nogales," in a thriving and industrious mood under the feudal dominion of Cipriano Ortega. Water was still diverted from the Sonoita River to its thirsty fields of corn, beans, and melons and its vineyards and orchards of giant fig, pomegranate, and other fruits. The stream flowed west. Some eight miles lower down, Don Cipriano owned the town of Santo Domingo, where the Mexicans kept a customs house. In the ranges about these happily isolated communities, gold mining was still carried on in primitive fashion, and burros turned the old arrastras of two millstones that reduced the ore for the owners.

[10] W. H. Emory, *Report on the United States and Mexican Boundary Survey* (Washington, 1857), I, 123.

It is unfortunate that more is not known of Cipriano Ortega. He was an imaginative and enterprising Mexican whom Jeff described as "an all-around business man and organizer." He mined, he milled the ore, he raised the necessities of life, and he dug wells throughout the desert on both sides of the line for the tenuous connection of his colony with the salt deposits of the Gulf, and the outside world in the United States. According to tradition among the natives today, he came into prominence first as a fighting man who subdued the Sand Papagoes, or the Areñenos, an unruly tribe that once inhabited the sandy stretches from the head of the Gulf clear over to the region of Santo Domingo.[11] He became a warm and helpful friend to Jeff.

Cervantes was another old-timer at Sonoita who owned a store and whose boys dug the hot well near the boundary line twenty-five miles southwest of Indian Oasis. When Jeff expressed a wish to get some nuggets to send East to his friends, Cervantes took him behind his counter, pulled out a half-bushel measure that held "the most gold" that Jeff ever saw, and told him to pick the specimens he wanted. Now Sonoita looked like the proper place for a man of peace and Jeff happily left on the trail.

The old trace which he had traversed from the east and another which led up from Mexico joined at Sonoita to continue west past some springs and a lake right on the line called Quitobaquito, an unusual oasis with an unusual name, apparently of Spanish origin and possibly meaning, "look out, little cow."[12] From here the old trail followed down the stream to *Agua Dulce*

[11] Nacho Quiroz to J. E. H., March 7, 1945; Carl Lumholtz, *New Trails in Mexico* (New York, 1912), 394ff.; W. J. McGee, "The Old Yuma Trail," *The National Geographic Magazine*, April, 1901, 129–30.

[12] Or "get away, little cow." Nacho Quiroz, an intelligent observer of modern Sonoita, attributes the name to Papago origin indicating a "place by the lake where the crow-foot grama grass grows." Quiroz, as cited; Tom Childs, of Ajo, favors the Spanish explanation. Childs to J. E. H., March 6, 1945. Quiroz says that the place names are mainly Spanish corruptions of Papago names. See Mrs. Jeff D. Milton, "Days among the Craters," *Ajo Copper News*, August 10, 1933.

The legend of the ogress of the Papagoes, recorded by Father Kino's *compadre*, Manje, in 1699, is still told by the natives in slightly altered form with its location at Quitobaquito. Quiroz, as cited. For the original, see Herbert Eugene Bolton's *The Rim of Christendom* (New York, 1936), 408–409.

157

or Sweet Water. But the next watering to the west, showing the effects of progressive evaporation and concentration of the mineral salts, was called *Agua Salado*, or Salty Water. There, at times, water was to be had only by digging in the sands of the Sonoita.

From here on, water and fortitude were the only things in the world to count. The trail bent north of west across the Tule Desert, leaving the Pinta Range on the right, and coming to water, after a heart-breaking grind, at Tule Well, which, Jeff thought, was likewise dug by Cipriano Ortega.[13] Even for a water-starved man it was a bitter dose. In 1901, W. J. McGee, in writing for the *National Geographic*, found it "a caving pit in rocky detritus with a barrel of liquid at the bottom—liquid even more saline than the Gulf, in addition to its overpowering flavor of copper salts and strong tinctures of sodden insects and drowned rodents, from which even the thirstiest horses turn in wry aversion."[14] But rats or not, it was wet, and Jeff bailed it out with his bucket and rope.

Cipriano dug another well about six miles northwest of Quitobaquito, a hole about thirty feet deep excavated by hand. Once when Jeff got there, his pack mule was so dry that she threatened to jump into the well. Then all native buckets were of rawhide, and Jeff drew the one at the well full of water. Even if well cured, rawhide, when wet, has a peculiar odor, and his mule, dying for water, still wouldn't drink from the bucket. So Jeff made a hollow in the sand, mashed his slicker into it for an improvised trough, drew water in the little pail he carried on the pack, and she drank to satisfaction.

Upon another occasion he was pushing back to Tucson and

[13] The well had not been dug when Raphael Pumpelly made his retreat from Arizona at the outbreak of the Civil War in 1861. See his book, *My Reminiscences* (New York, 1918), I, Chapter XX. Kirk Bryan, *The Papago Country, Arizona* (Washington, 1925), gives something of its history. The Boundary Survey of 1893 drew its water from the Tule Well when in this vicinity, and its chronicler indicates that it was dug during the Gila gold rush, in the late fifties, but Pumpelly would certainly have noted it. *Report of the International Boundary Commission, 1891–1896* (Washington, 1898), Part I, 24. Access to the well was by steps at first.

[14] McGee, as cited, 137. Kino came over this route in 1699; Anza in 1774. See Bolton, *The Rim of Christendom*, 408–12.

came to Maish's Well, northeast of the Baboquivaris, hot, tired, and dry. This time when he drew the water and poured it into his slicker, his horse refused to touch it. He drew another bucket, and there, clinging to its rim, was a lock of Papago hair. To a man of the land, the tragedy was plain. Someone had killed an Indian and chunked him in the well. Decomposition had at last caused the hair to slip. Though it was still fourteen miles to the next water at Robles' Well, on the trail to Tucson, both Jeff and his horse put off drinking until they got there.

To revert to Jeff's progress along the Devil's Road is to carry him on a few miles west of Tule Well to the original watering of Tule Viejo—some tanks formed in a canyon at the base of the mountains.

In this section of the desert, "sign" seemed to last always. From here the wagon tracks of the forty-niners stretched west toward Tinajas Altas before Jeff's dark eyes, squinted close to keep out the glare. The desert floor lay level as a plain. Along this segment an estimated four hundred people had lost their lives in only eight years of the gold-rush period, and their scattered skeletons seemed to gloat with ghastly grins of death at the probable fate to which he was riding. Here, a few years later, Captain Galliard, of the Boundary Survey of 1893, "counted sixty-five graves in a single day's ride of a little over thirty miles." And farther west at Tinajas Altas, the high tanks in the Gila Range, the wayfarer looked "down on three-score cross-marked graves,"[15] and how many more only "Goodness knows."

Dread death by thirst hung over the land with an eternal malevolency. Galliard pictured a characteristic scene on the trail. Eight miles west of the Tule Pass where "the ancient trail was a thread of yellow in a field of black" malpais, he found a thirty-foot "circle of pebbles with a great pebble cross in the center recording the thirst-death of a family of seven who staked life on a demijohn of water which was accidentally broken. . . . The wagon tracks made when the poor Mexican drove his exhausted team to one side of the road were plainly visible, thirty years afterward, and at the very spot," he wrote, "still remain pieces of

15 McGee, as cited, 106 and 138; *Boundary Survey*, Part II, 25–26.

glass and wicker-work from the broken demijohn, and the skulls of the twc horses."[16]

This retention of sign almost indefinitely is all the more remarkable because the desert sometimes has its sandstorms. Jeff, in later years, was apt to say, "I passed that point twenty years ago" and ride by to show his horse's tracks in proof.

Down near the line, below here, was a camel skeleton, which must have come from Jefferson Davis's experiment in transportation back before "the War." It was the delight of the guide for the Boundary Survey to guess that the animal had died of thirst,[17] and he may have been right. But Jeff was a conservative, careful man with abundant respect, even reverence, for the infinite forces of nature. He carried a gallon canteen in his pack and a smaller one on the fork of his saddle. In later years he had three gallon canteens made especially to fit his pack and the mule's back. He made some of his rides in the cool of the night and never really suffered.

The heat, of course, was intense. It sometimes reached 120 degrees in the shade. In June, 1893, the Boundary party just west of Sonoita found it regularly registering 130 to 140 degrees in the sun at mid-morning, and estimated it at 150 degrees during the "heat of the day," though this too "was hotter than usual."[18] The temperature of the water varied from 80 degrees at Quitobaquito, to "boiling hot" water out of Cervantes' Well.

Those who knew the desert, when deprived of water, fell back on the bisnaga or nigger-head cactus. They pounded it to a pulp and extracted the juice for drinking. Antelope, deer, mountain sheep, and even cattle lived for months without drinking, without water at all except for what they got from eating cholla.[19]

But all across this desert were dim trails pointing the way to the capricious springs and water holes, from the Papago tanks in the malpais of the Pinacates, to the Tinajas Altas in the Gilas, to Heart Tank in the Pintas, and back to the more abundantly

[16] McGee, as cited, 137, purported to quote Galliard. The *Boundary Survey* records the incident but not in these exact words.
[17] *Ibid.*, II, 24.
[18] *Ibid.*
[19] Lumholtz, *New Trails in Mexico*, 152-53.

watered range around the Baboquivaris. Jeff came to know them all.

Jeff's next water west from Tule Viejo came from those historic potholes of Tinajas Altas, where eight holes in the enduring granite held the annual precipitation of some three inches in precious storage against the ravages of an annual evaporation of seventy-five inches. The thirsty air literally lapped up the water.

When the lower holes here were emptied, the traveler climbed the slick granite to the higher holes and bailed the water down the channel into the lower ones, while his gaunt mount sniffed the air, expectantly, below. Forty-five miles farther west along the boundary, through the almost impassably heavy sand of the Yuma Desert, was the next water, in the Colorado.[20] But that was not the way of the trail.

From Tinajas Altas, Jeff usually rode north to the railroad, at Wellton, by the right-hand fork of the old trail. Sometimes he retraced his course the way he had come, or cut straight for Tucson by Heart Tank, where he packed the water from the heart-shaped potholes down to his horse, and by the other waterings widely scattered between. He could always water out at Ajo, next at Redondo's Well, an easy stage to the east, and then take the trail by the Gunsight Mine, Covered Well, Maish's and Robles' wells, and thence to Tucson.

At this time the desert was being assailed by Maish and Driscoll, who were running 25,000 cattle on their great ranches up the Santa Cruz from Tucson. Drought and decimated ranges were forcing them into the desert, where Morgan, their driller, was at work. Already one imaginative ranchman had been there and failed. His permanent water—the only thing that eternally counts in the desert—now alone perpetuates his name.

Maish and Driscoll might have taken their lesson from him, for Jesús Redondo, born and bred to the desert, had already been there and gone. His brother, José, came out of Mexico in the gold

[20] Anza described Heart Tank, away to the east, and the Tinajas Altas, in 1774. Herbert Eugene Bolton, *Anza's California Expeditions* (Berkeley, 1930), II, 28–29. For Kino's trip, see Bolton's *Rim of Christendom*, 408 ff. Kirk Bryan, *The Papago Country, Arizona*, 132 and 422, describes these tanks in detail.

rush to the Gila in 1859, and settled at the site of Arizona City or present Yuma. Jesús, the cowman, followed from Altar, apparently because of political trouble, and began farming on the Gila. Then he flourished in the cow business and spread out over the open range. He moved a herd to the desert, east of the crude mining works of Ajo, to what is still called Redondo's Well.

He owned several great ranches in Sonora, among which were *La Cucha* and *Maculara*—the last famous for its riders and ropers. He did well at first, as his cattle ranged on fresh grass from the Gila Bend to Yuma, and from the river to the Gulf. He moved 2,000 head to Poso Redondo, where he elevated the water with a steam pump, fired with mesquite chunks snaked up to the boiler by the horn of the saddle. He built no storage but pumped the water direct into redwood troughs a hundred yards long, and worked his herds in a spacious corral of mesquite logs a city-block square.

For a while he was the only cowman in the western part of the desert, and prospered well until he overtaxed the patience of the land and its native men. Then the Papagoes drove his cattle away in bunches. The tall grama grass, nature's careful accumulation of time, disappeared with heavy grazing And at last Jesús Redondo pattered back to Yuma in his *guaraches* to plead poverty through his declining years.[21]

But it is the spirit of adventurous men to try where others have failed, and Jeff saw Maish and Driscoll moving thousands of cattle into the desert west of the Baboquivaris. At La Ventana, water was pumped from two wells between eight and nine hundred feet deep. La Lesna, a spring then, dried up but perennially dug out by the Papagoes, became a well ten feet deep. Indian Oasis was also a spring in a splendid hunting range, surrounded at this time by the greatest pile of deer heads Jeff had ever seen. Here Maish and Driscoll drilled another well, built an earthen reservoir, and located a herd of cattle.

[21] John Cameron to J. E. H., January 29, 1945; Tom Childs, as cited; Father Paul Figueroa, MS, "Yuma and Vicinity before the Railroads," 1, 14, 22, 52, in Arizona Pioneers Historical Society; *Arizona Sentinel,* January 26, 1878. John Cameron says Redondo could always go out in his back yard and dig up a little money.

At Fresnal, nine miles northeast of Indian Oasis, they drilled another, where, on an extensive range, they advertised 5,000 big steers for sale in 1891. They employed from seventy-five to one hundred hands and with scrapers and teams built great reservoirs, tanks, or *charcos*, for the conservation of the runoff water of the hard and infrequent rains that dashed off the granite ranges round about. They kept their driller punching down holes at Robles' ranch, at Arivaca Junction, at Indian Oasis, and elsewhere. They were, admittedly, boring with a big auger to show these backward natives how it was done. But to no avail. They demanded too much of a frugal, hard, and exacting Nature. They, too, were bound to fail.[22]

Thus Fred Maish, once owner of the Palace Hotel, mayor of the expanding town of Tucson, and proud possessor of cattle on a thousand hills, died in poverty. Meanwhile Jeff Milton, seeking only enough grass for a horse and pack mule, enough meat for his skillet, and the simple necessities that a hundred dollars a month would buy for him and his mount, was satisfied with that and demanded no more. Hence he lived on in comfort and contentment. It is idle but human to reiterate the moral. There is not only an inescapable relativity in this matter of want and wealth, but an inexorable desert reminder that there is no evasion of the laws of Nature. How comforting and well that it is so.

But what of the happy, industrious life that flourished on the Sonoita River when Jeff Milton first saw it, sixty years ago? It is a tragic, ironic quirk of history that the "march of progress"— the impact of a highly mechanized civilization—that brought fantastic comforts and ease of living to some lush lands, should

[22] This comment on waterings is based primarily on Jeff Milton's recollections, supplemented with notes from John Cameron to J. E. H., January 29, 1945; *Boundary Commission*, Part II, 21; *Arizona Enterprise*, August 29, 1891; Lumholtz, *New Trails in Mexico;* and best of all printed records, Kirk Bryan's *The Papago Country.* Louis Menager says the well at Fresnal was drilled as an oil prospect.

For additional material on these noted ranchmen, Maish and Driscoll, I have consulted Cameron, Tom Childs, and such printed sources as *The Arizona Enterprise,* February 7, 1891, and March 10, 1892; *The Courier,* November 25, 1882; *Arizona Weekly Star,* February 19, 1880; *Tucson Directory,* 1881, 69; Deed Records, Pima County, II, 110–16; and Grover C. Maish to Mrs. Edith Kitt, Arizona Pioneers Historical Society, Tucson.

utterly destroy the civilization that flourished here. As long as the land was completely isolated, and as long as its people were absolutely alone, they prospered beyond their needs. But easy contact with the outside world enlarged their desires beyond their natural means and lured their youth away from the most alluring of lands, to bring desolation to a graceful culture and a gentle way of life.

Now, Sonoita, instead of being Kino's hopeful "hub of the Papago wheel" on the *Rim of Christendom,* or the "gateway to Sonora" of the pioneer Anglo-Saxon days, is little more than a drab gasoline way station for careless fishermen hurrying to the teeming waters of the Gulf of California. While the flourishing San Domingo of Cipriano Ortega is dead, gone, and forgotten.

But all this was still in the hands of the gods of the desert when Jeff turned back from that first long ride in the pursuit of his customs patrol in 1887. He had no smugglers in tow and no contraband or revenue to report. But he did nourish an under-standable thirst as his horse stirred the dust on that dry and ancient trail that rounded the point of the Baboquivari Range and pointed straight to Tucson.

164

12

Customs and Otherwise

The boundary line west of El Paso is approximately seven hundred miles of almost altogether arid country. In that entire distance only five running streams—barely running at that—cross the line in spite of the fact that the boundary cuts through the numerous mountain ranges at right angles.

When Jeff Milton entered the service, for nine hundred miles —from Presidio, Texas to the Gulf of California—the border was patrolled, the duties collected, and the office work done by a total force of only twenty-five men.

Collector of Customs Joseph Magoffin was in charge of the entire district. Between his headquarters at El Paso and the Gulf of California, deputy collectors were maintained in offices at Deming, Tombstone, Nogales, and Tucson. Eleven mounted inspectors patrolled the entire line.[1]

At that time there was less pious talk of international good will but more unostentatious practice of it than is evident in late years. On both sides, Americans and Mexicans battled the same problems of environment and human nature. It took no fuss in an international conference to impress them that this was so. But they did get together out on the ground. Tucson was a long way from smuggler's taw for Jeff. So at first he just moved his headquarters away down below the line to Altar, in Mexico, and worked out across the desert from there.

Then he moved back to Pedro Aguirre's ranch, where the runoff from the Baboquivari Range formed a fresh-water lake close to the Mexican line. Ben Hamilton was placed in camp with him. They rented a house from Aguirre, took their meals at his ranch, and drew on the village of Sasabe, six miles away, for their

[1] Lee A. Riggs, "A Short History of the District of El Paso," MS, copy in the files of the author, p. 6.

165

meager supplies. From this position they were able to patrol the border with less cost in horseflesh.

Hamilton had been in the service before. In fact, when Jeff arrived at Tucson, he was in jail and standing trial for the killing of a man at Nogales. With the help of friends from El Paso he won an acquittal. He was then placed on the border with Jeff. But he was a touchy, nervous sort, and they got along poorly together.[2]

Fortunately they could do their riding alone. Once on the old Ajo road, Jeff met three suspicious-looking Mexicans, with twenty horses and mules, who he decided were smugglers. He indicated that he was a prospector, pushed rapidly on to cut a circle through the mountains, and, by riding hard, came back in the lead and took them with his shotgun. He disarmed them and guarded them night and day on the road to Tucson. White-wing doves were in flight, and to impress his captives with the fact that they were his, he shot a mess of the birds whizzing in flight over his head as he jogged along on his mule. The meat was delicious and the lesson was sound. He landed them in jail at Tucson and saw them sentenced to the penitentiary at Yuma.

The temper of the service changed for Jeff when the pioneer deputy collector, William S. Oury, died. At that time Jeff was still stationed at Tucson and was in the office on the morning of March 31, 1887, when Oury walked in complaining of a pain in

[2] Hamilton's case went to the jury on April 23, 1887. George Hand, "Diary," of that date, Arizona Pioneers Historical Society.

his side. Jeff suggested a call at the doctor's. Protesting that it would do no good, Oury walked behind his desk, suddenly caught his side, and collapsed in Jeff's arms. Jeff gently laid him down, and then ran down the street for the doctor. When he got back, the old man whom the *Tombstone Daily Prospector* lauded as being "of brave and generous impulses, ever ready to fight an enemy or succor a friend," was dead.[3]

Jeff stayed on for a short while in Tucson and was again in the office when the earthquake of May 3, 1887, shook the town. Suddenly there was the sound as of heavy cannonade. The cornices and parapets came tumbling off the adobe buildings, and Jeff went out the nearest window. He ran down the street calling to the women and children to get outside. Buildings fell in, but the San Xavier Church, where a lot of terrified Mexicans took refuge in spite of the frantic attempts of the clergy to get them outside, stood safe and sound. In places the earth breached in wide crevices, and water burst high in geyser-like sheets sometimes a hundred feet long. Springs dried up in the general derangement of structure, and below John Slaughter's San Bernardino ranch, in Mexico, Dr. G. E. Goodfellow, of Tombstone, reported a great fault in the earth's crust that extended for thirty miles. Jeff rode down to look at it and found it so wide he could not jump it with his horse. Dr. Goodfellow was "engaged" as United States commissioner "to report on earthquakes in Southern Arizona," while Jeff went back to riding the line.[4]

Upon hearing that another Texas Ranger, Vernon C. Wilson, was in charge of the office at Tombstone, Jeff asked for transfer there. The request was approved, and he packed his gear, saddled his horse, and headed east by north for the mining town that was the turbulent county seat of Cochise. "Vic" Wilson, as he was called, was a nephew of Governor Coke of Texas, and as a Ranger had killed his horse in the wild ride from Austin to Lampasas carrying the orders that brought the Texas Rangers together in

---

[3] April 1, 1887; memo. in Oury file, Arizona Pioneers Historical Society; Lockwood, *Life in Old Tucson*, 42 ff.; Hand, "Diary," March 31, 1887.

[4] *Tombstone Epitaph*, March 15, 1889; *Tombstone Daily Prospector*, May 3, and 5, 1887.

JEFF MILTON

time to get Sam Bass, at Round Rock, ten years before.[5] He had
been at Tombstone for several years.

Here C. B. Kelton, mounted inspector, was put to riding with
Jeff. Captain Kelton was another Southerner with a decided impatience with monkey business. When it came to an issue of
honor and arms, he was always rarin' to go. According to one
account he had gained the title while crossing the Plains with a
wagon train in 1868, though Jeff thought he had earned it as one
of Morgan's men during the Civil War, which he had entered at
fourteen. He weighed about 180 pounds and a heavy saber scar
across his face was no detriment to his warlike looks. He was
strictly of Southern traditions. He walked the floor in passion
when he thought of politics. "If you breathed like you were a
Republican," said Jeff, "he went out of his head. But he was a
very fine man."

He was a deputy United States marshal under W. K. Mead
from 1884 to 1889, deputy collector at Lochiel, later sheriff of
Cochise County, and eventually a member of the Territorial
Legislature. It was a land with little reverence for titles and
everybody called him "Cap," even if he was an unregenerate
Confederate and a fighting fool. He and Jeff became warm
friends at once.[6]

There were others of the same breed who had drifted west
after "the War" and "*the War*" was invariably the Civil War.
Mostly they were from south of Mason and Dixon's line and
enough of them from Texas. Little John Slaughter was the peer
of them all. "Buffalo Bill" Jenkins was a one-man labor board
up at the Clifton mines, and Tom Green, another Texas Ranger
—big, burly, and bold—had just preceded Jeff along the line. He
was the son of General Tom Green, and fabulous, too, in his own
way. Jeff had known him well in Texas.

On the border he had ridden the line alone. Once he cap-

[5] This story is told in James B. Gillett's *Six Years with the Texas Rangers*,
171 ff.

[6] Kelton, who never married, died at Greenville, Alabama, October 8, 1925,
when nearly ninety. He was then owner of the Windsor Hotel at Tucson. Biogra-
phies File, Arizona Pioneers Historical Society; *Tombstone Prospector*, November
26, 1923; *Tombstone Epitaph*, October 16, 1925.

168

tured a pack-train load of mescal. He took the band of smugglers and mescal into camp and sat down to sample a keg. After all, these mounted inspectors were more or less judge, jury, and sometimes executioner. Tom Green wanted to see if it was really contraband. It was! When he woke up, the smugglers and all the mescal, except his keg, were gone, and so was part of it.

Jeff and Cap Kelton were scouting the same sector of the Arizona border. Their territory ran from the southeastern corner of Arizona, below the rough and ragged range of the Chiricahuas, back through the San Bernardino Grant that Slaughter acquired, through what is now the Douglas and Naco country, across the San Pedro and San Rafael Valleys, and over the mountains to Nogales. It was a big country and rougher in places than a curry-comb. But that was the way they liked it.

The best of it had already been taken for cattle. In 1882, over the mountains east of Nogales, some Pennsylvania Scotchmen by the name of Cameron had acquired the San Rafael Grant. They were distinguished people, twice represented in the United States Senate and twice holding the cabinet post of secretary of war.[7] Colin Cameron, the nephew of United States Senator James D. Cameron, came to southern Arizona to develop the grant into a great ranch. He built his headquarters on the line south of the Huachucas and called it "Lochiel."[8]

But when Cameron came to use his land, he found that men had squatted all over it, and for years the boundaries of the San Rafael Grant and the rights of the squatters were fought in the courts. When Jeff first rode over the long grassy ridges that reach down from the timbered body of the Huachuca Range to finger gently with the northern fringe of Mexico, and looked across Cameron's storied domain, he was riding not on the Arizona border, but bold and fancy free with *The Scottish Chiefs*. And from boyhood memory Thomas Campbell's verse burst aloud on his lips:

[7] Simon Cameron and his son, James Donald, held these offices at various times. See *Biographical Directory of the American Congress*, 780, for their records.

[8] Later a customs house, opened near by, took the name of Lochiel. For a brief statement of the San Rafael del Valle and the Mexican grants, see James H. McClintock, *Arizona*, II, 530, and H. H. Bancroft, *Arizona and New Mexico*, 600 ff.

Lochiel, Lochiel, beware of the day
When the Lowlands shall meet thee in battle array
For a field of the dead rushes red on my sight
And the bands of Culloden are scattered in flight;
They rally, they bleed, for their kingdom and crown,
Woe, woe, to the riders that trample them down.

His pack mule, following dutifully behind, raised not one long ear in concern but continued to dream of corn. Yet it was symbolic sentiment. Cameron was cautious because his range was spotted with "little men." By what right did they hold it? A fighting old-timer, Billy Fourr, in the Dragoons, to the north, was once asked the same impertinent question about his land in an Arizona court.

"Why," he slowly said with utter incomprehension of the complication of title but complete mastery of elemental possession, "why, I took it away from the Indians."

And so with these squatters on the San Rafael; they had taken it by right of priority, fortitude, and blood. When Cameron came, it did not matter to them if he had bought it on national guaranty going back to the Treaty of Guadalupe Hidalgo, nor less still that two of his folks had held the post of secretary of war. They knew something about war themselves. Cameron was now in trouble and "Lochiel's Warning" sounded somewhat proper as Jeff bore down on these feudal headquarters in an inhospitable land late in the eighties.

Meanwhile Cameron was taking his squatters to the courthouse instead of to personal task. Everybody was hot and bothered, but for personal protection he never carried a gun. It may have been a hard land, but decent men did not kill people then unless they were armed.[9]

At the mouth of a canyon on the south side of the Huachucas,

[9] Cameron was born at Danville, Pennsylvania, December 10, 1849, and died March 6, 1911. His home at Tucson was called "Lochaber." He imported the first good Hereford cattle to southern Arizona, kept good horses, favored the line riders—especially Jeff—and ran a good outfit. See James H. McClintock, *Arizona* (Chicago, 1916), III, 804–805, and Sloan, *Memories of an Arizona Judge*, for something more about the man.

northeast of Lochiel, some religious enthusiasts had formed a little settlement and called it "Sunnyside." Though they were referred to as "the holiness band," they are known to old-timers of the region as the Donnellyites, after their dominant leader, a water-front tough from Los Angeles who at last got religion and got it bad. He came in to take over the settlement, to open mines, to determine their morals, and to make them prosper. He did. Everything they made went into a communal pot, and Brother Samuel Donnelly not only ran the roost but extended his philanthropies to scholarships in the university, at Tucson.[10]

It was an "interesting" departure from democracy, and the colony was a commercial success until Samuel Donnelly lay down and died, as dictators have a habit of doing. With the credulity of those who are bred to follow a leader, his faithful, however, kept vigil for the re-enactment of a miracle. He had said that on the third day he would rise again, but the weather was warm, and at last they despaired, packed him off, and planted him, properly, in the ground. In a land where just anything could happen, Jeff watched them go their free and diverse ways.

There were other settlers in the same region when Jeff first came that way. John Hand lived at a spring in the Huachucas. An Italian named Campini, said to be a smuggler, owned the first place east of Lochiel. He had ingeniously built a false bottom in his wagon which he filled with liquor with a string attached to the neck of every bottle. He would drive into Fort Huachuca on the northern flank of the mountains, find a prospective customer among the regular troopers—and all the Regulars then were prospects—and tug innocently at a piece of string hanging out of the bed of his empty wagon. It was an engaging and profitable sport that always fished up a bottle of mescal smuggled from Mexico.

Ten miles or more east of Lochiel, a ranchman named Jim Parker was holding down Parker Canyon, and at the bottom of the long eastward slope that ended at the San Pedro River, old

[10] *Tombstone Daily Prospector*, March 24, 1887; J. A. Rockefellow, *Log of an Arizona Trail Blazer* (Tucson, 1933), 149-51.

171

JEFF MILTON

Bill Plaster had come in from Grimes County, Texas, to be "a particular friend" of Jeff's and to cover all the ground he stood on, as well as a right smart more. Bill Greene had not then dreamed of his fantastic fortune at Cananea, but was running a butcher shop at the fort, and working as a hand in the mines. Farther east, across the lower end of the Sulphur Springs Valley, on the San Bernardino Grant, was a little man with a burning eye, a steady hand, and a heart of steel, who was making his mark on that wild land—John H. Slaughter, from southern Texas.[11]

Away back to the north of the line, Fairbank and Charleston were beginning to lose some of their lusty spirit as the mining business waned, and the fact that the fighting Texan was about to civilize Cochise County was ominously implicit in a story in the local paper that a man named Slaughter had defeated Major Blood and Captain Cutts in the race for sheriff, and the news could be read in Tombstone's *Epitaph*.[12]

Meanwhile Jeff and Cap Kelton, working under Vernon Wilson at Tombstone, were busy along the border. At this time, boundary markers indicated the border at distant intervals, but no barbed-wire fence retarded the fugitive in flight. Men drifted back and forth across the line more or less of their own free will. Jeff and Cap caught a number of Mexicans in what is now the Naco region, convicted them of smuggling, and sent them to the penitentiary from Tombstone. "At least we thought they were smugglers," Jeff said, although he discovered later that they had made the capture in Mexico and actually abducted the unfortunates from their native land. Still they had "lots of fun."

In May, 1889, Jeff and Cap struck south through the Bisbee Mountains. Down the canyon below Bisbee the road forked. One prong led off to the left; the other to bisect the border a few miles south. "We'll just camp here and catch a smuggler, tonight, shore!" said Jeff. They camped on a trail near the road about three hundred yards above a set of corrals. They unrolled their

[11] See Bernice Cosulich's article in *The Arizona Daily Star*, February 19, 1938, and Frederick R. Bechdolt, *When the West Was Young* (New York, 1922), 160 ff., for something of the career of this remarkable man.
[12] *Tombstone Epitaph*, March 28, 1889.

beds and were ready to turn in when they heard a racket—a wagon coming up the road. Cap went down to investigate. Jeff, who had pulled off his clothes and lain down on his blankets, heard something coming up the trail on which they were camped. Six burros, each balanced off with two kegs of mescal, with a smuggler behind them, filed up the trail. It was a bright moonlight night, but he did not see the camp until he was almost upon it, and Jeff, from his pallet, took him with ease.

He made the Mexican unpack the burros and hobble them out and then let him lie down on his blankets six or eight feet from his own bed. Cap was still down towards the corral where a herd of four or five hundred cattle had been penned, and Jeff went back to bed. Then, just for the hell of it, he began to snore. In a few moments the Mexican rose up and looked at him, while Jeff, lying on his side, squinted out with an amused eye and snored all the louder. Then all of a sudden the smuggler jumped up and tore off down the moonlit mountain at a dead run.

Instantly Jeff was on his feet with his six-shooter in hand. "It was a beautiful night to have killed him," he recalled. As he flagged it down the slope, Jeff could plainly see the spot where his galluses crossed on his back and "I could have hit it, certain. I started to kill him. Then I realized it wouldn't be right, as it was my fault. But I started shooting. I shot four times. But he drifted down that slope, jumping through bushes as high as my head. He was going so fast he couldn't stop, and he went over the fence into that corral. The cattle stampeded, tore it all to pieces, and scattered all over the country." And the Mexican smuggler went with them.

In a few moments Cap Kelton came puffing up the trail, looked around with pleased expectancy, and said, "Where's the body?"

"Cap, I missed him," answered Jeff.

"Missed him, hell!" Kelton bawled impatiently to the man who he knew could flip coins in the air and hit them on the fly. "Where is he?"

"He got away," Jeff soothed. Cap was furious. Jeff at last admitted, "Of course I could have broken his neck in this bright moonlight, but he was running straight from me and I just couldn't shoot him." Cap was so mad he would not speak.

"Everybody's smuggling in this country," reasoned Jeff, as the hours wore on. "Why should I murder him?"

Along late next day Cap's gentle Southern heart began to melt with like compassion and at last he loosened up, saying, "I don't blame you, Jeff, for letting that fellow get away."

In a better mood they packed their prizes and headed back up the trail over the site of Warren and up the gulch that contains the precariously perched town of Bisbee. In the edge of town the burros turned off the trail, and Cap hurried to head them.

"Just let them go," said Jeff, suspiciously. They turned up a hill, circled behind some houses, and trotted into a tunnel in the side of the mountain. It is impossible to fool a burro. They were definitely at home. Jeff poked around in the tunnel and turned up some fifty gallons more of mescal. And from there, high over the pass and down to Tombstone, both he and Cap talked happily and freely, "for certain." The *Epitaph* observed their arrival with the stock and liquor, but nobody except Jeff mentioned the Mexican who got away.[13] And that was a long time later.

"I was kind of sorry I didn't kill him," he then recalled, "for afterwards he almost killed Cap, and somebody else had to kill him." If the break had been a legitimate one instead of the result of his own prankish nature, Jeff could have saved the others the danger and trouble. It was not only "a beautiful night to have killed him," but he could easily have hit that cross on his galluses at a hundred feet in the moonlight, and hit it, "certain"!

In the fall of 1889, the complexion of the Customs Service changed. Cap Kelton could pace the floor of their quarters, where Jeff and Vernon Wilson had set up camp at the old stage stand, at the site of Hereford, in voluble fury without altering the facts of politics. Cleveland had been beaten the year before. Magoffin was replaced by a Republican in October, 1889, and the entire force went out. It was not the loss of a job but the principle of the thing that counted. Men born to battle don't bother about jobs. Life is adventure instead of work for them.

[13] *Tombstone Epitaph,* May 31, 1889.

174

Jeff went out at the end of October. He packed his mule, saddled his horse, and headed toward Tucson.[14]

Vic Wilson wound up in California, when, on the trail of Sontag and Evans, notorious train robbers, he walked up alone to the door of a cabin in which they had taken refuge and was riddled with bullets.[15] Cap Kelton, with Southern appreciation of the vital value of politics, devoted himself to the struggle with his usual ardor. Jeff fell back into the frontier life that was burning itself out with colorful zest on the Santa Cruz.

He became an unpaid deputy under Fasion Shaw, he traded in horses awhile, and he and Jim Blades, a son of a preacher from near Dallas, prospected and hunted in the Santa Ritas together. Jim had likewise been a customs inspector out of Nogales, and they had worked together there, where Jim hated George Christ, the deputy collector of the Nogales district, for something he had done to a friend of his. The two met Christ on the edge of town once when Jim would have killed him except for Jeff.

"No, you can't do it here," said Jeff. "They'll pull us both for murder. But if you want to kill him, wait 'til he gets downtown, and then just walk up and do it."[16] Jim later fell on unfortunate days, in utter despondency went down in the Blue Nose Mine, near Patagonia, and when the first shell snapped, resolutely cocked his gun again and blew his brains out. But at this time he was in the healthy spirits of a man of thirty-five, and he and Jeff joyously prowled around the mountains together.

Once while they were sitting on the ground near the fire, eating dinner in camp, a big, black tarantula came teetering by. Jeff mashed him and caught him up by one of his long, angular legs, held him a moment as he pawed the air, and asked, "What shall I do with him?"

"Drop him in the coffeepot," said Jim—who "had had a few drinks," according to Jeff, "while I wa'n't exactly sober."

[14] Riggs MS, as cited, 1; Milton memo. from Customs Office.

[15] See Opie L. Warner's *A Pardoned Lifer, Life of George Santag* (San Bernardino, 1909), for something of the activities of the Santag-Evans gang. It does not record, however, the story of Wilson's death.

[16] George Christ became the first collector of customs at Nogales. Harry Saxon to J. E. H., February 27, 1945.

Jeff tilted back the lid and dropped him in. Jim got "madder'n a hornet," for it is hardly of record yet that stewed tarantula is the proper brew for a second cup of coffee. They rode for miles that day while Jim, silent and ominous as a sphinx, knitted his brows "like a gathering storm" on the crags of the Chiricahuas and plainly "nursed his wrath to keep it warm." Jeff was a jovial creature addicted to the art of lively conversation, and Jim's refusal to say a word got under his hide. Jim started to break up the camp, but Jeff told him he wouldn't stand for it. Then he sort of apologized in a way.

"Jim, I oughtn't to have done it, but I was just obeying orders. That's what you told me to do and that's what I done." At last Jeff's sunny disposition thawed Jim out a little, and the crisis posed by the coffeepot passed in absorption with work, just as later crises have done.

In passing Tubac, they stopped and slept in a little, vacant house. They made quite a round to the east and camped at a spring in the Patagonia Mountains, before starting to see a horse race at Lochiel. While Jim pottered about camp, Jeff eased off to kill a deer. He shot and dressed a small buck and started in with the venison saddle. Suddenly he got too weak to carry it. He made his way to camp, told Jim he was sick, and sent him for the meat. While Jim was gone, Jeff noticed that his hands were broken out. He pulled up his shirt and found he was broken out all over. When Jim came in, he told him he had the smallpox.

Now for lovers of good horses a race is a vital thing; smallpox in the nature of an irritant. They saddled up and headed for Lochiel. When they rode into Washington Camp—a mine on their trail—and stopped with an old friend, he exclaimed in concern, "My God, Jeff, you've got the smallpox," and insisted that he go to bed. Jeff refused. Instead, he would go on to the horse race, as a lot of his old friends would be there, and be glad to see him. At last they prevailed on him, however, that he must go back, and Jeff turned his roan toward Tubac. When he was almost there, he rode up on old Doctor Rogers, of Tubac, out on a bird hunt.

"Jeff," he greeted, "you've got the smallpox. Come down to

the house and go to bed." Jeff insisted he was going on to Tucson.

"Tucson nothing," said Rogers. "You won't know anything in a few hours. You're going to bed." Rogers managed to get him down, gave him a dose of medicine, and in two hours he was completely out of his head. Rogers got an old Mexican woman to nurse him and rub him with ointment, and inside three days he was up again, against the doctor's wishes, and on his horse, saddling toward Tucson.

An old Confederate named Sanders, badly shot up at Chickamauga, then owned a bathhouse at the springs in Tucson, the only place to get a bath. Jeff, cleanly by nature and meticulous about his personal appearance, headed for the springs. Sanders met him and in alarm tried to shoo him away. Then Dr. Spencer heard of his foolish notion and rushed out to see him.

"My Lord, Jeff, you have as pretty a case of smallpox as I ever saw. What're you gonna do?"

"I'm gonna take a bath," said Jeff with finality.

"Why, that cold water will kill you," said Spencer.

"Better dead than dirty," rejoined Jeff, as he slid into the springs.

Before general immunity by vaccination, smallpox was the dreaded scourge of the Mexican border. Dr. George Crepin, the city health officer, came by when he heard of Jeff's case and remanded him to the public pesthouse for isolation.

"Nuthin' doin'," said Jeff, as he mounted his horse and struck for a vacant house on the edge of town, where he went into camp for several days, alone. News reached Josie Brown that he was there. Regularly she and her little brother drove out with fresh fruits and other delicacies, and sped the hours in lively conversation until the scabs were gone. Then for a brief spell he settled into the interesting life that stirred the light and volatile dusts of Tucson.

13

Adventures in Arizona

Jeff found life in Tucson much as when he first came. Making a living was not an easy matter, but within the modest limits of his needs it was never anything to worry about, and he would not have worried if it had been extremely hard. He liked people and they liked him, and it was easy enough to trade in horses and cattle, live in a simple adobe house, and get along in the world. Although it was a drinking world and he was by nature a sociable soul, he never mixed with the crowd promiscuously, but always stressed the fact that "I did just what I wanted to do" and then "went on about my business."

He could handle his own in the roughest place but had no part in common company. He never forgot that he had been born and bred an aristocratic gentleman. He found the flippancy and familiarity that go with boorish manners and vulgar tastes intolerable. The Southern code of self-esteem and personal honor were the enduring values of life with him. Loyalty to land and friends was as invariable in his little world as the trusted course of the stars. "Real men," in his own emphasis, deported themselves with natural dignity; and women were always ladies, who moved in his handsome presence with the grace and the veneration that a wise God intended and noble gallantry insured. Not death but dishonor was the only thing in the world to fear. Woe betide the rash man who bothered a friend, or crossed his own trail forgetful of the civilities of decent living. On the frontiers that he knew and relished, Jeff Milton was simply Sir William Wallace on a cow horse. This, his code and cultural background, were the keys to his adventure.

A sustaining feature of good living anywhere is the fact that those who thirst for heartening evidence of high character can always find it. Jeff found it even in the desert. He liked that land.

178

Intriguing, apparently anachronistic growth and valiantly adapt-able animal life made it fascinating to him. Besides, its native people, the Papago Indians, whom he greatly admired, were his friends.

Their women held to a rigid code of chastity. Their regard for property rights was high. Jeff's property, consisting of his packs, was sometimes left for days on the desert as he hunted and prospected, but was never disturbed by these Indians, although some had other tales to tell. As guides, the Papagoes were good in camp and perfect on the trail. They were tough and apparent-ly tireless; some could run a deer down.[1]

Jeff and Juan the Coyote, such a runner, prospected as far south as St. George's Bay, on the Gulf of California, in Mexico. One night they camped at Libertad, seven miles from some grass called Indian wheat, the only feed for their horses. Juan took the animals back to it and returned to camp. Next morning, bare-footed, he trotted out and brought them in before breakfast.

Another Papago friend of Jeff's was old Quelélé, named for a northern Sonora carrion hawk. About four years before Jeff met him, a Mexican officer had captured this old Indian for some offense and ordered him shot. Then he asked his name.

"Quelélé," answered the Papago with manful scorn.

"What do you mean?" roared the officer as he sensed the im-plication.

"Quelélé," the Papago repeated, disdainful of the fact that he was about to die. "I'm a Mexican buzzard. I eat dead Mexicans."

"Turn him loose," said the officer, in admiration. "Whoever talks to me like that deserves to live."

"He wa'n't afraid of nothin'," admired Jeff. And, as for dura-bility, "He walked all over the desert when he was ninety-four, and lived to be nearly a hundred."[2]

Within their own customs the Papagoes imposed a rigid dis-cipline upon their fellow tribesmen. When an Indian murdered

[1] See Lumholtz, *New Trails in Mexico*, for one named Santiago who could do the same.
[2] Lumholtz speaks of him on page 193, *New Trails in Mexico*; Tom Childs to J. E. H., March 4, 1945.

a German merchant at Sonoita, the Papagoes themselves brought him there to trial, found him guilty, and took him out and killed him, for, as Jeff appraised in admiration, "there was no monkey business about them."

In the most inhospitable part of the United States these Indians made their own living without bounty from anyone, much less from Washington. Jeff used to stop on his rides at the mining camp of Quijotoa. There was no feed near by, but the squaws cut the grama ten to twelve miles away in the desert and packed it in on their heads, selling it to him at fifty cents a bale. And when short of meat, he could buy a mountain sheep for $1.50 at any time.

At least four white men had married into the tribe. Over at Ajo, Tom Childs left his father's mining business, drew his patrimony of $83,000 when their mines were sold, it is said, and married a Papago. South of Ajo, he built a notable ranch, where his Indian friends came in on him in bunches and ate his beef until his mining fortune was gone. Beef was good for desert men, but they never ate pork. There is not a hog on the whole reservation, because, in 1857, when Crabb's filibusters gave up after a fight at Caborca and were stood up against an adobe wall,[3] their bodies were left where they fell to be eaten by the hogs. So, with a native sense of the fitness of things, the Papagoes never eat hogs.[4]

The most noted killing by an Indian, in Jeff's early days on the desert, was that of a prospector named Howard, who was shot off his mule as he paced through the brush close to Indian Oasis by a young Papago who sat on a near-by hill.

Charlie Shibell, the marshal, Fasion Shaw, the sheriff, and a posse of about thirty men put out from Tucson to run him down. They took the trail up a canyon in the Coyote Range, to find themselves, of a sudden, waylaid by a heavy force of Papagoes in ambush. The Indian chief granted a truce, and they told him what they wanted. He dressed them down because they were on

[3] See H. H. Bancroft, *North Mexican States and Texas* (San Francisco, 1889), II, 694 ff.

[4] Carson Morrow to J. E. H., January 28, 1945.

the reservation, out of their jurisdiction, but let them go back, telling them that the Indian who had done the shooting would be sent in on a certain day. The posse pulled out of the pocket it was in and gladly backtracked to town.

When Shaw came to his office that morning, a Papago pony was tied to a near-by tree and the culprit sat on the courthouse steps. He was there because the chief had said he would be; he was there because he was wanted. Shaw took him in and he came to trial. A lawyer, assigned to defend him, explained his constitutional immunities to him through an interpreter. Then he was put on the stand and the vital question was asked: "Are you guilty or not guilty?"

"I'm guilty," he said. But the judge interposed to explain again that he did not have to plead guilty.

"I killed him," he said. "Why lie about it?"

"What did you kill him for?" asked the prosecuting attorney.

"I don't know why I killed him. I shot him to see him fall off his jackass."

"So of course they had to hang him," said Jeff.

His dying request was a pair of red-topped boots. Jeff and others went down to L. Zeckendorf's store and found him a beautiful pair with a white star in each top, and he put them on and marched up to the gallows the proudest man in Tucson. He waved aside the blindfold, and when Shaw fumbled nervously with the noose, he reached up to help him adjust it. Then, with Jeff and other deputies gathered around, Shaw, with averted eyes, swung his hatchet and cut the rope. It sprung the trap and as his red boots flashed down in the desert sun, his simple soul sped out to Montezuma. Even juvenile pride can be a sustaining thing.

"He was the only man there who wasn't scared to death," said Jeff. It is no wonder that he admired the Papago discipline and character.[5]

Jeff served as a deputy under Shaw, but it was a job without pay. Once in a while there was an opportunity for reward, and

[5] Mrs. M. F. Shaw to J. E. H., January 28, 1945. Jack Weadock, in *Dust of the Desert* (New York, 1936), 25 ff., has a chapter on this incident.

181

while he captured hundreds of men in his life, he found that rewards usually went to others. Still it was good sport to take the trail of the Mexican murderer, Manuel Verdugo, when he escaped the jail at Tucson and went west, directly over the A Mountain, into the desert. And though Jeff helped retake him and return him for execution, "some slick," he recalled, got the $500 reward that Sheriff Shaw had posted.[6]

Thus Jeff did not make his living by capturing criminals, but acquired a little pasture west of town and began trading in horses. When a homesick cowpuncher or a disappointed miner rode in with an empty purse and a hankering for a visit home, Jeff bought his mount and pack mule and dropped them into his horse trap. Then, when a pilgrim arrived from the East with the dream of a mountain of gold in his head and a little minted metal in his pocket, Jeff would sell him a rested-up horse and mule to help convince him that he could not find it. Business wasn't bad.

Besides, to a man of Jeff's nature at that time and place—to a man of his nature at any time and place—life was bound to be intriguing. To this sort of man "something is always happening." For one thing it snowed in Tucson while he was there. That sort of weather was quite unusual, and as he had his personal mount in a corral and stable back of the house in which he lived, he went to see how they fared. When he got there, he found a little local Jew named Max Zier, from whom he rented the stable, turning his horses out in the snow and putting his own inside. Zier was too small for a big burly man with a conscience to whip, but to show him how his horses must have felt, Jeff "just rolled him over and crammed his collar full of snow." When Zier got up, he cursed Jeff and ran.

Next day, Zier filed complaint, and Jeff was arrested for assault and brought into court, where Zier charged he had stomped him in the face. Jeff was wearing heavy Arizona boots with hobnails, specially made for use in the desert. Before the court and the bland and unbruised countenance of Zier, he raised his boots

[6] M. F. Shaw broadside offering the reward, December 30, 1890, in files of the author.

for the jury to see and said, "Why, gentlemen, look at him. The idea is plumb reedic'lous. I'll just show you what I did to him," he added, reaching a powerful hand for Zier's collar. But Zier was gone, to the vast amusement of court and jury, and the charge went with him.

Jeff was in court more than once. At this time the famed and tragic feud between Dr. Handy and the Lawyer Heney was being brewed. Handy, who was a good friend of Jeff's, was having family trouble, and in the suit for separation, Francis Heney was representing Handy's wife. Feeling was high, and Handy tried to run over Heney with his horse and buggy when he happened to catch him in the street. As Jeff was seen in company with the Doctor, he, too, drew the dislike of Heney.

Once, when driving, Dr. Handy left Jeff sitting in his buggy in front of his home. Shortly he came back out carrying his child, in spite of the protests of his wife. Jeff put his foot down hard.

"Doc, you can't do it," he said. "I'm not going to see any man abduct a child." And although Dr. Handy was angry over this intrusion, he reluctantly handed the child back to its mother.

Out of this situation, however, Heney indulged in gossip about Jeff. One day Judge Satterwhite walked out of the courthouse to tell Jeff of an insulting remark Heney had just made about him before Judge Richard E. Sloan's court.

Jeff barged inside ready for action, though Sloan was still on the bench, and verbally tore into Heney. Sloan tried to quiet him, but Jeff "told him to shut up," or he would "take him on." And he did. Brewster Cameron, the clerk, "went under a desk," and Jeff added, "I told Heney what kind of a so-and-so he was. If anybody had raised a finger, I'd'a killed him. When a man gets worked up like that he's ready to stop it. And I did."

Court broke up in great confusion, with Sloan calling to Shaw for Jeff's arrest. The news was all over town in a few minutes, and his friends rushed to make his bond—there were always friends to make a fighting man's bond in those days. But Judge Sloan quashed the case.[7]

[7] Sloan wrote his life as *Memories of an Arizona Judge*, but he did not tell about Jeff Milton's day in court.

Jeff had little patience with gossip about anyone, and none whatever about himself. His discipline of the Tucson saddle maker was another case in point. He had no "steady" girls in Tucson but "went with all of them that were nice." Miss Levine, a daughter of the owner of Levine's Park, was happily in this category. One day when he met her on the street, she said, "I'm surprised at you, Mr. Milton, for what you said about me." Then she related an indecent remark about her and some other young Jewish ladies that the saddle maker had attributed to Jeff.

"Did he tell you that, Miss Levine?"

"Mr. Milton, he certainly did."

"Can you wait at home for the next twenty minutes?"

"Yes, sir, I can," she answered.

"Well, he'll be right there and tell you on his knees that he's a damned liar, certain," said Jeff, as he set off for the saddle shop down by the Palace Hotel.

"I never fooled with him, but walked right in, grabbed him by the throat, stuck him with my six-shooter, and drug him outside," said Jeff. "He began to yell, and I asked him what he meant by telling those lies. He said he hadn't."

" 'Yes, you did,' " I said, " 'and you're going up there and tell her you're a goddamned lying son-of-a-bitch, or I'm going to kill you.'

" 'Let me get my hat,' he said.

" 'You're not going to get anything. You're coming with me.' I took him up the street. Miss Levine smiled when she saw us at the door.

" 'Now, tell her.'

"And he got down on his knees and said, 'Miss Levine, I'm a goddamned lying son-of-a-bitch,' and he was, sure."

"Now is that satisfactory, Miss Levine?" asked Jeff in his most gracious manner. She admitted that it was, while the saddle maker started off crying, "I'll git my gun."

"Hurry up and get it," said Jeff. "I'll be up there in a few minutes; soon as you can get it. I'll be a-passing right by in front of your door, and if you've got anything to do business with, then step to it."

"But I never had no more trouble with him," he reflected.

It might be supposed that the amenities of life were neglected. Undoubtedly they were not. The preachers were there and always welcome. The pastor of the little church standing at the location of the Pioneer Hotel, in present Tucson, knew his way around a frontier town.

Sheriff Shaw, who was not then married, lived just behind the church. At times he, Jeff, Lee Faison, and Bill Moore, his deputies, would gather there for a quiet game of poker. The preacher had an uncanny way of getting wind of the game and drifting over to watch it. When a good-sized jack pot was on the table, he would reach over after it, saying, "Boys, I'll take it," and they would always agree, for faith not only moved mountains but convinced them that the best pots were meant for the Lord.

This preacher's church had a beautiful choir, and at times Jeff strode in for services, to admire the ladies as well as to revere the Lord. One day he and a cowpuncher by the name of Nick Wilcox were taking in church when the preacher shouted in the manner of vigorous advocates, "Everybody that wants to go to Heaven, stand up!"

Except for Jeff and Nick, the congregation rose in mass. But Jeff was against mass movements, even those headed for Heaven; and when Nick started to rise, he caught him by the coattail, saying, "Sit still."

The preacher saw them and shouted even louder, "Everybody that wants to go to Heaven, stand up!"

Jeff took a firmer hold on Nick's coat, but, Nick, who "wanted to go to Heaven, shore, skinned out of it" and came up in his shirt sleeves.

The preacher looked at Jeff with a baleful eye and said with pious irritation, "Don't you want to go to Heaven, sir?"

"Yes, sir, I do," answered Jeff quietly, "but your trail may not be mine,"—"just like that." The preacher said no more, but a day or two later he was back at the sheriff's poker game, levying on the best jack pots and still in the name of the Lord.

Open-handed generosity and loyalty to friends seemed like religion enough to them, and they had plenty of opportunity to practice it. Among Jeff's close friends was Major Fred Smith, who held an office similar to the present collector of internal revenue, but was usually known as the "receiver of public funds." While he had killed a man in Tombstone before moving to Tucson, things now seemed to be coming his way. He was a genial Virginian with a good job and a beautiful and socially popular wife.

However, the loose financial habits of that time and place brought tragedy to the Smith home, the gala social spot of the day in Tucson. Smith came to tell Jeff that he had lent several thousands of dollars of government funds to a man in Phoenix who he thought was his friend. Now the borrower would not or could not pay it back, and as it was about time for the audit of his accounts, he knew the deficit must be made good.

"They'll send me to the pen if I don't get that money," he added, as he implored Jeff to help him out.

"Yes," said Jeff, readily, "I'll go with you to Phoenix if you'll kill him if he won't pay you." Smith agreed and off they went. They called at his house and Jeff sat in the hall while the two talked it over in a back room. After a while Smith came out, smiling.

"Did you get the money?" asked Jeff.

"No," Fred answered, "but he's going to send it to me tomorrow."

"You'll never get it," fumed Jeff, pulling his gun and pushing it toward Smith. "Go back in there and kill him."

"Oh, yes," said Fred with the easy faith that was his undoing, "he'll send it." They returned to Tucson. A few days later Fred called to say that the auditor was coming, the money had never been sent, and he would have to go to the pen unless something was done.

Jeff knew what to do. That night he saddled two horses, and he and Smith rode out seven miles beyond Tucson, to where the tracks of the Southern Pacific climbed to the crest of a long grade. Jeff knew the crew, and when the westbound train reached there that night, he flagged it down and pushed an unhappy man aboard with this parting advice, that he took:

186

"Fred, don't ever write to anyone—not even your wife."

"And that was the last I saw of Fred Smith," he said—"a fine man."

But he had not seen the last of Ben Hamilton, the bad man of the Customs Service who stayed at the Smith home and made a loose remark to Jeff one day about the handsome woman. Things came to a sudden showdown, and Hamilton took back-water at once.

The bad blood between them, however, was further stirred by the small talk of Charlie Winston—Shaw's jailer—and a smuggler named Charlie Hood, who was later killed at Empalme, Sonora. Winston was inclined to blow, anyway, and when he had "run down" his friend, Deputy Billy Moore, the brother-in-law of the sheriff, it had irritated Jeff, who took Winston in hand, disclosed his duplicity to Shaw, and got him discharged.

Afterwards Moore was sitting at a table in a back room at Charlie Cresham's saloon, reading, when Winston came in, bold with booze, walked back near the door, drew his six-shooter, and shot three times at Moore but hit the door facing every time.

"Now Moore wa'n't afraid of nothin'," even though all he had was a pocket knife. He jumped up and took after Winston, who knocked a swinging door off its hinges in leaving, as Jeff would recall with a hearty laugh and the believable observation that "we used to have lots of fun."

To make the "fun" a little more intimate, all this time Winston was sleeping in the back room of a small dobe house that Jeff had rented. Talk of trouble went on. One day Frying Pan Alzamora rushed up to Jeff near Billy Reed's saloon, saying, "Jeff, don't go in that saloon. So and so's looking for you and gonna shoot you."

"How you know he is?" asked Jeff.

"I know he is. I heard him say so," warned Frying Pan.

"All right, I'll step right up and find out about it," Jeff retorted. "If you're gonna get shot, just well get shot and be done with it. No need to be scared to death all the time." The bad man saw him coming and dodged back into the saloon. "I walked in," said Jeff, "and he was there. But he didn't make any break a-tall.

187

I just sort o' looked him over and talked it over with him. And there was no more trouble after that."

But it took a little longer to straighten out Winston, Hamilton, and Hood. Jeff reached town one day to learn that they had been drinking together and swearing about the saloons that they were going to kill him.

He thought it over as he went home to go to bed. When he entered his room, he heard Winston, who had apparently been listening for him, jump into bed in the back room. He stalked through, jerked back the cover, and without a word hauled Winston out by his heels. As he hit the floor, he began to howl.

"Oh, Milt, what's the matter? What's the matter?"

"Get up from there! If you don't, I'll kill you right here. Get out of this house just as fast as you can."

"I don't have any six-shooter . . ." he complained.

"You're a liar," snorted Jeff.

"Wait a minute 'til I find my six-shooter," whined Winston, "and I'll kill myself."

"If you want to kill yourself," said Jeff, "here's mine. Step right out in the back yard, but don't make a mess in here." It turned out that he had hidden his six-shooter under the mattress. Jeff turned the bed back and found it, kicked him out, and threw his gun after him, saying, "Get out there and blow it off."

"But he wouldn't do it," Jeff would recall with a smile. Winston left with the sobering news that he would be killed if he ever came near the place again, and Jeff went peacefully to bed with only his horses in the back corral for company.

Still he had to meet Hamilton, and once, when he happened downtown, "very foolishly" leaving his gun at home, they met, had a few words, and Hamilton said he'd settle the row.

Jeff retorted, "Wait here just a minute. I'll be back and we'll settle it, shore."

He jumped in Phil Drachman's herdic, rushed home, and stuck his six-shooter in his waistband; but when he got back, Hamilton was gone. Sam Drachman said he was laying for Jeff right across the street in Billy Reed's saloon. When Jeff walked

in, Reed, who was eating dinner out in front with his wife, jumped up and tried to get him out.

"Don't come in here, Jeff, don't come . . . " he cried.

"Get out of my way, Billy, or I'll kill you," Jeff snapped, jerking his six-shooter. "Back away, and do it damned quick." Pushing his gun back in his belt, Jeff walked in. There sat Hamilton, a shotgun in his lap, a six-shooter lying on the table, a derringer in his pocket, and another six-shooter on his hip. He was really armed for bear. Jeff walked up without drawing his gun. He knew that he was fast and that he could hit where he looked.

"If he had started to pick up his six-shooter, I'd a-killed him so quick it would o' made his head swim," he recalled.

"Hamilton, you've been hunting me," he began quietly. "Now you've found me. Everybody tells me you're going to kill me. Why don't you raise up and tend to business." But Hamilton, too smart for that, sat there nursing his double-barreled gun, saying he "didn't want any trouble."

"What're you doing with that shotgun, then?" asked Jeff, ironically. "Now Hamilton, it's kind of dangerous business to be hunting a man with a shotgun. If you don't want any trouble, all

189

right. But don't come out the front door. I'll be across the street watching for you."

Then in contempt Jeff turned his back upon him. He stopped and chatted with the man behind the bar, but kept one eye cocked on Hamilton, in the mirror, above, "because I knew," he said, "that if he moved in the mirror, I had him." Jeff was positive he could whirl, draw, and kill him before he could lift his gun from the table top. But no movement reflected in the mirror, and after a passing pleasantry with the bartender, Jeff strode through the swinging doors to the street, and across to Drachman's. There he waited to watch for Hamilton's appearance, but at last someone came over to say that the unhappy gunman had slipped out the back door and was gone for good. Hamilton soon left for Florida, where he fell off a boat along the coast and was drowned.

Jeff went on with his trading until, late in January, 1890, a horse fell on him and broke his ankle. While he was still laid up in bed, four or five days after the accident, a young man from New York named Southwick C. Briggs came by in trouble.

As Jeff understood, Briggs was a nephew of the great tea merchant, George C. Chase, who had sunk some money in a border venture called El Rosario Mine and Milling Company, under the plausible promotion of a ruthless Irishman named Pat T. Dowling. The mine was across in Mexico, a few miles from Sonoita. Its mill and store were just over the line in Arizona. The hole in the ground in Mexico is still known as the Dowling Mine. Chase kept putting money into the venture without taking any out, but at last, with the skepticism that is a part of sound finance, even in gold and silver, he sent young Briggs down to inspect the properties.

Dowling picked him up at Tucson for the long trip by wagon across the desert to Sonoita. But he wanted no inspection and offered Briggs a thousand dollars and a suggestion to take a vacation in Mexico. The young man declined, and they struck out for the mine. Dowling played upon his credulities by talking about the dangers of the Indians, and sat in camp one night near Quijotoa whetting his knife and observing that he had just as well kill him as to leave him to the Indians.

Naturally the boy was nervous, and when Dowling jumped from the fire into the brush, yelling, "Indians! Indians!" Briggs broke away, too, and soon became lost in the desert. Apparently it was what Dowling intended, for he went on to Sonoita without him. Fortunately for Briggs, he happened upon the telegraph line to Quijotoa, and followed it for two days toward Tucson. At last, completely exhausted, he lay down, dying of thirst. An Indian found him and brought him into town. After his recovery from shock and exhaustion, he took his letters of introduction to the bankers and to Dr. Martin, owner of a local drug store, and asked their advice. They told him there was just one man to take him to the mine and that man was Milton. Thereupon he went to Jeff's dobe room, found him in bed, and told him his tale. Jeff's sense of justice was outraged, but, he said, obviously he could not go.

"Mr. Milton," begged Briggs, "I've got to have you."

"Hell, I can't go."

Again Briggs begged him to do so, and he said, "Go up and tell Dr. Handy to come down here."

Briggs set off at a trot, but when Handy got there and heard the proposal, he said, "You're crazy. You can't possibly go." Briggs looked sick.

"Goddamn it to hell," swore Jeff, who was broke and with a doctor to pay, "Briggs, you pay me twenty-five dollars a day, and put the money up, and I'll take you down there, shore."

Briggs jumped up, looked at him, and without a word turned and left the house. "Now he's gone for good," Jeff mused to himself. But it seems that Mr. Chase could afford the bill, for shortly Briggs was back with a certified check for the amount, paying him in advance.

"You go down to Chris's and tell him to come up to see me," snapped Jeff to Briggs. When the livery stable man came, Jeff told him to hook up a hack with a good team, and fix it with a board on which to prop his leg.

"Why, Jeff, you're crazy. You can't stand this at all," fumed Handy, as he thought of the rough, three-hundred-mile trip that he had in prospect.

191

"I'm going, just the same," said Jeff, with finality.

Then he sent for old Dawson, a good cook and a desert man, engaged him to accompany them, and with bedrolls, a camp out- fit, a double-barreled gun loaded with buckshot, a rifle, and his six-shooter, Jeff propped his leg on a pillow placed on the board, and together they pushed up the rocky trail across the Tucson Hills that led towards Dowling. Days later, with a leg puffed out around the cast in aggravated inflamation, Jeff drove up to the Dowling store near the mine.

Dowling anticipated trouble, for two Mexicans, with rifles across their knees, sat as guards at either side of the door. But Jeff had made his plans in advance and coached Briggs on what to do. His shotgun and rifle leaned against the seat of the buck- board, but as everybody went armed here, the Mexicans thought little of that.

Jeff slid out, holding up his game leg, took his crutches, and hobbled into the store. His guns were left behind, and the guards sat in the sun without getting suspicious. Dowling, of course, knew him from his border service, and, recognizing him, walked up and roared in lusty Irish greeting: "What in the hell are you doing here?"

Jeff dropped his left hand on Dowling's shoulder, let his crutches fall to the floor as he whipped the old .45 out of his belt, punched him in the belly, and told him what he was doing there.

"Make those Mexicans come in and put their guns up," he ordered, "or I'll kill you right here." Dowling looked deep into his dangerous dark eyes, saw purgatory in the offing, and called to them to do so, while Jeff held him with his gun. When they had put the guns up and backed out, Jeff called to Briggs to bring his shotgun, and the rest was easy. He took over Dowling's teams and sold off his harness and the goods in the store—all except a barrel of whiskey and a case of "3H" horse liniment. Then he gathered his unwilling prisoner and took him over to the mine, in Mexico, where hundreds of sacks of ore were stacked in the tunnel. Dowling showed him the samples from a few that were very rich to convince him that the mine was good. Jeff set them aside and examined the others. They were worthless. Dowling had raked up the good pay ore just for show. When Jeff took it over, Dowling howled, "That belongs to me."

"It belongs to the company," Jeff corrected.

He engaged Nigger Joe, at Sonoita, to haul it over to the mill, and ran Dowling off, but not before the Irishman broke down and bellowed that he was ruined, touching Jeff's soul for a little compassion and his pocketbook for fifty dollars.

Jeff's leg was killing him. He cut the cast off, ripped up a blanket, and had Briggs wrap the swollen member in it. Then he opened several bottles of the horse liniment, saturated the blanket, and left it on for the night. "It took the pain out, but next morning all the skin was gone. It looked like a lobster—just as red and pretty as you ever saw."

"You'll never get out of here," wailed Briggs.

"Yes, I will," said Jeff. "Pour some of that stuff on."

Briggs poured on some more of the scalding liniment, and Jeff rolled over with the pain and "vomited like a dog." They laid up for two or three days to work on the whiskey barrel and rest. Then Jeff, learning that the title had not been perfected, took the papers for the mine and struck out for Altar to consult the officials there. When they reached Palomas, a village on the way, he "was pretty near dead," but they found an old Mexican doctor who treated him, put some splints on the leg, and in a few days they were off to Altar. When the business was settled and his leg a little better, they started back.

Upon reaching Tucson they ran into Dowling once more, who again broke down and cried, "Milt, you know I haven't got a cent on earth. I don't know what to do. Would you let me have another fifty dollars?"

Jeff, always generous with his money, let him have it. He got on the train, went back to New York ahead of Briggs, and put up such a good story there that "I'll be dogged," said Jeff, "if they didn't authorize him to come right back and see me."

"Now, Milt," he proposed upon his return, "all you've got to do is to go in with me. Tell them you've made a mistake; that the mine is very rich. They said if you'd recommend it they'd put up $50,000 more. Do, and we'll split it."

"Nothin' doin'," snorted Jeff. "I ain't in that kind o' business." Briggs cleaned up the matter while Jeff was soon headed back into the desert, horseback, with a pair of crutches hanging over the horn of his saddle—and the ankle eventually loosened up in spite of the predictions of the doctors. Briggs happily left for New York with a shotgun that Jeff had given him—one that the noted Pete Kitchen had left for Jeff some time before after he had kept a local bad man from killing the unarmed Kitchen, in Tucson.[8]

And Pat Dowling of the desert, who had given the great Chase a lesson in the frenzied finance of gold, prematurely wound up as a corpse in Casa Grande, thus settling the account but leaving the books unbalanced.

[8] Frank C. Lockwood, in *Arizona Characters* (Los Angeles, 1928), has told the story of Kitchen's shotgun in detail, 59 ff.

194

14
Policing a Palace Car

Tucson offered all sorts of adventure in the late eighties as well as casual opportunity for making a living. When the customs job played out, Jeff's friends were anxious to enlist him in politics, as his "side" needed all the help it could get. For here the healthy tonic of close rivalry between the two parties biennially called those in power to account.

In the elections of 1890 they proposed Jeff as tax assessor for Pima County. It did not sound like a lot of fun, but some favored and powerful few were escaping their just levy, and Jeff's friends thought he would be able to make the collections. The idea of seeking public office was repugnant to a man of his innate pride, and "while I never asked a soul to vote for me," he recalled, "I ordered several not to."

Politics were wisely taken seriously. The "good politicians" made a habit of corralling blocs of Mexican voters the night before election. The Democrats herded theirs into Goodwin Hall, kept them liberally supplied with whiskey until morning, then handed them a registration receipt and a ticket apiece, and flanking them with a squad of guards marched them down to the polls to cast their free and democratic choice for office for a dollar a head. It sounds sort of crude today and the methods have changed, although the party principle is about the same. In such an environment it may be thought that Jeff's novel campaigning brought defeat. It did!

The long period of convalescence with his broken ankle, coupled with heavy meals at Joe Soladini's splendid restaurant, left Jeff fat and flabby—"too big for a man," he said, "but not big enough for a horse." Besides that, he was broke. Being of an old-fashioned turn, all he knew to do when he got broke was to go to work. He hobbled down to the Southern Pacific offices to see

195

J. S. Noble, the superintendent, one of his poker-playing friends, and told him he wanted a job. Noble laughed at the very idea of his becoming a railroader.

Shuckin's," said Jeff, in disgust, "you can go to thunder," and went down to the shops to see Gray, the master mechanic, of whom he was very fond.

"Mr. Gray, I want to go to firing," he said. Gray looked at his generous and genteel frame and laughed.

"Jeff, are you joking?" he asked.

"No, sir!"

"Go back and get your duckin's and I'll put you on," said Gray.

Jeff got back in no time, and Gray sent him out on his first trip—firing an old diamond-stack engine to the top of the hill on a double-header run between there and Benson. It was upgrade all the way, automatic stokers were unknown, and husky men find there is a decided skill or sleight, even in handling coal. Jeff's 250 pounds of flabby beef flew at the job in front of the flaming furnace with a ready will. He came near exhausting his fuel before he got to the top of the hill, and still failed to keep up his steam. He became overheated and dizzy and would have fallen from the cab had not the engineer caught him, shoved him into his seat, and taken the scoop himself to show him how to handle and spread his fire.

In a few weeks his weight was down to 180, and he had a regular run on "number 105," stoking her west past Gila Bend to Yuma, and at times through Lordsburg into El Paso. On one of his return runs, the train was heavily loaded with steel rails and was late as it climbed through Stein's Pass and across the flats to Willcox. The conductor was hot and bawling them out.

"Can't you drop her down," he fumed, as they climbed over the divide toward Benson, and Jeff, piling in the coal, 'lowed that they could. To make matters worse, the engineer was drunk, though Jeff swears "the fireman was sober." As they roared over the ridge and down the long grade toward Benson, the air brakes failed to work, and they literally "dropped her down." Faster and faster they flew. The engineer sat pale on his seat while Jeff leaned on his scoop and cooled off in the breeze. When they came to a long curve and a trestle at uncommon speed, Jeff turned to the engineer and said:

"Good-bye, old stud!" but they took the turn as smooth as silk, just missed the Nogales train that barely beat them to a switch, tore through Benson without so much as saying "howdy-do," and coasted to a stop on the long grade to the west. The conductor finally got up to the engine, still awfully hot, but not in such a hurry.

"They fired the engineer for it," said Jeff. "I didn't care what happened to me, anyway. It was the conductor's own fault. All I was doing was what they told me to do; shoveling in coal. I wa'n't particularly scared, for I knew I'd have to go sometime, and this time would be quick. You wouldn't be crippled up with forty cars of steel on top of you."

Firing locomotives, however, had its problems even for Jeff. He had to crawl into the firebox and clean his engine after each run, and he had to buy his own polish to keep his brass fittings bright. Then when an inspector wanted to be picayunish, he would pull out his handkerchief and run it over the metal to see if he could get any stain. About the time Jeff was deciding he might be a better hand at something else, he met the superintendent of the Pullman Company, E. N. Leemaster, at El Paso.

"Jeff," he said, "why don't you come down here and I'll put you to work in the Pullman service."

"Well, by Jacks, that'll suit me," said Jeff, who forthwith pulled off his duckin's and threw away his greasy cap. Leemaster made him conductor of a run from there to the City of Mexico, and Jeff was happy with the change of scene, the genteel Mexican manners, and the good food and drink at the end of the line.

Vic Wilson came in from California to enlist his help in running down the Sontag-Evans band of outlaws, found him gone to Mexico, returned to tackle them alone, and walked right up to his death.

Jeff's first run south began interestingly enough. He had never slept in a Pullman before. But it turned into a convivial initiation as some of his old friends, among them young Hamp-

197

ton, son of the Southern general, Wade Hampton, were on the car. Somebody suggested a game of poker. Jeff, not knowing it was against the Pullman rules, joined with a hand in the drawing room. They stayed up late, and the porter, puffed up over his change of bosses, failed to follow orders and call Jeff next morning. Jeff did not wake up until the train had pulled into Chihuahua. When he rushed out, the passengers were handling their own baggage, the cuspidors were still dirty, and the car had not been cleaned. Jeff reprimanded the big, burly Negro for not calling him, and asked, "Porter, why haven't yo cleaned up?"

The porter, who felt he had the conductor on a hot spot for breaking the rules, instead of answering got insulting. Jeff picked up the heavy wooden stick that was used in making the berths and "tapped him one," and while he was still out, threw him, bag and baggage, down the steps of the car. Jeff then went into the station and wired El Paso that he was short a porter, and again they rolled merrily on toward Mexico City, while Jeff—with the help of Hampton and other accommodating passengers who had been on a Pullman before—made their own berths and set the rules to suit themselves.

Jeff never ceased to be fascinated with Mexico. This was partly due to the fact that he was still young and gay, and a part of that romantic world that knew nothing of dullness or drabness, but flirted with life and death because they were dressed for him in the brightest of colors. He met "the most beautiful woman" he ever saw on his Pullman in Mexico, and as there is genial compulsion in the courtly tradition, "I just had to tell her so," he recalled. "She didn't seem to mind, though the old duck who was her husband wa'n't so well pleased."

Again, when he openly admired a lovely lady at a Mexico City theater one night, the escort was furious. "He just raised Cain until I told him if he was so redheaded with me that he wanted to fight it out, we'd go outside and do it."

But the offended one was a gentleman and properly challenged him to a duel. Jeff gave his Mexico City hotel address and waited next day for the fun to start. The fighter failed to appear, but a second came and after a little negotiation "squared it off." Jeff went back to his Pullman run to have his troubles with another "lady."

At this time an Irish gentleman known as Lord Beresford had settled in northern Chihuahua. Delaval Beresford had come to Texas as a young man to make his fortune, with plans then to return and marry the girl of his choice. Three years in America without fortune brought him the unfortunate news that his fiancée had taken another man, and sent Delaval off in distress to the remote hinterlands of Chihuahua.[1] There he built up a ranch at some bold springs in the grama meadows at the northern tip of the Sierra Madres, which in time was dominated by a Negro wench with an intolerable pride in her title of "Lady Beresford." Although the ranch is now crumbled to dobe dust and the principals are dead and gone, the stories of "Lady Beresford" are still bandied about in this color-conscious land to cloud respect for a warlike name that stands for honor in the isle of Erin.

Jeff boarded his car at El Paso one day for his run, his Southern blood in commendable repose until Lord Beresford and "Nigger Annie" barged on to his Pullman. He met her in the aisle and said firmly enough, "You can't come in here."

"I am Lady Beresford," she answered, with haughty disdain.

"I don't care who you are," he insisted. "You can't come in here."

"Lord Beresford will take care of you," she said.

"All right," replied Jeff, and stepped out ready to meet his Lordship, to find a tragic figure whom the twin and ruthless mistresses of disappointment and liquor had brought to degradation. After a few words, Lord Beresford and "Lady" went into the day coach, and Jeff went on about his business.

It was the custom of the Pullman Company at that time to send out "spotters" to spy on the conductors to see if they were reporting their total fares. They sometimes resorted to cheap stratagem to test the character of the conductors. Jeff was tipped

---

[1] Lady Clodagh Anson, in her *Book: Discreet Memoirs* (London, 1931), gives something of the history of her people, the Beresfords, and the cause of Delaval Beresford's self-imposed exile, pp. 230–31.

off by a friend at El Paso one day that a spotter, with the initials
"A. B. C." on his bag, would board his car. Now Jeff, while ad-
mitting that some conductors "made lots of money—even more
than the railroad," always had a contempt for devious methods,
and when the spotter climbed on, Jeff had him spotted at once.
He purposely boarded without a ticket and asked the fare to
Chihuahua. Jeff told him "two dollars," took the money, and
started to write out the ticket, but the spotter waved him aside
and asked if he would have a drink.

"No, but I have two quarts in the drawing room which you
can have, if you like," said Jeff. When they reached Chihuahua,
the spotter said he believed he would go on to Torreón, and paid
again, and again waved the receipt aside. The game simply was
for him to count the passengers himself, including his own fare,
and then see if Jeff's report to the company tallied with his own
at the end of the run. Jeff made up his mind to fix him. He not
only wrote up the spotter's tickets and fare, but two or three
spurious extras besides, and took the money from his own pocket
for his report and return. Then when the company checked his
account against the spotter's and found the spy reporting less
than he had, they were convinced that the spotter was as crooked
as he really was and fired him. And they fired him by wire, for
the Pullman Company was really efficient at that time.

Soon after this, Jeff's adventures sent him out of Mexico in a most unusual way. On one of his stops in Zacatecas, he was approached by a prominent Mexican then drunk and mean. It seems a strong but by no means exclusive characteristic of the Mexican either to love you to death or hate your tracks when he is under the influence of liquor. This one took after Jeff. Along the border it was an attribute of good common sense to realize that Mexico is no place for a gringo to get into trouble. Although Jeff had never seen the man before, the Mexican began cursing him. They had a few words, and Jeff started to charge him, but recalled where he was and went back into the Pullman.

The drunk followed him and made more trouble after the train had started. Then he went out to the observation platform and fell off as the train swung around the roadbed at the edge of a precipice, hundreds of feet high. Some peons saw him come tumbling down, and the officers at Zacatecas wired down the line ordering Jeff's arrest for murder. Jeff, anticipating what lay ahead, rustled some old Mexican clothes, went into the drawing room, shaved off his black and sweeping mustache, dirtied up his face, pulled an old sombrero low over his eyes, and took a seat in the day coach like a third-class peon. Officers searched the train for him at every major stop from there to Mexico City, but black-eyed Jeff, heavy and dirty, draped himself over the hard seat beneath his low-pulled sombrero like a Mexican in somnolent ease, and escaped detection.

He knew the Mexican nature, illustrated so well by his *rural* friend of Torreón who had recently captured a robber on one day and tried and had him shot on the next. Detection meant "the dobe wall" for him. He pressed his six-shooter in comfortable fashion against his flank, out of sight beneath his waistband, while his hot eyes watched for the first overt evidence of discovery that would mean certain death for several others and eventually for him. There would be no capture.

Unfortunately they were still running south. Mexico City meant a layover and a change. Jeff eased off the car with the peons. On the way out of the station he passed Superintendent Leemaster, who did not know him. He still had his Pullman collections in his pocket, and thinking Leemaster wanted them, stopped to turn them over. When the Superintendent finally recognized him, he exclaimed in alarm, "Good gracious alive, man, do you know everybody in Mexico is looking for you?"

"I don't care," said Jeff, digging out the money. "I am just trying to get out of here."

Leemaster refused the funds and gave him a hundred dollars more, saying, "Keep that money 'til you get back to El Paso."

Jeff went to a hotel with advice to lay up in his room until he could catch a train by another line, out by way of Laredo. But the confinement was more than he could stand. He dressed up like a gentleman, put a plug hat on his head and his .45 in his belt, and went out to enjoy the town. Leemaster, who was hanging around, protested his insanity without results, but followed at a safe distance, hopeful he would escape detection.

Jeff was enjoying the fresh air and the evening scene until he came to a hauler who had broken his old, overloaded mule down in the middle of the street and was beating the animal unmercifully in an attempt to make him rise. Jeff could never tolerate the abuse of an animal. The sight of the mule, broken down in his loins and beaten by the cruel freighter, threw him into fury.

"I jerked my six-shooter and started to kill him," he recalled. But Leemaster, then close behind, rushed in and stopped him, saying, "Get away from here, Jeff. You're the craziest man I ever saw," and managed to loose-herd him off down the street. After a pleasant walk Jeff sauntered back into the hotel. Then in a Prince Albert coat, "all diked up to beat hell," as he recalled, he caught the next train to Laredo. To avoid suspicion, he bought a ticket only to the first station. Once on the way, the conductor chanced to take a vacant seat beside him, and Jeff, lifting a cautious eyelash, said, "Don't you know me?"

When the man had studied out the loss of the mustache, he recognized him, and thereafter Jeff continued toward the border without the risk of renewing his ticket. Still the Mexican officers were hunting him, and the most noted of all on his trail was one of the best in the entire West—Emilio Kosterlitzky. They were to see much of each other in later years.

Kosterlitzky was born in Moscow, Russia, November 16, 1853, and was educated for the military. He deserted from a Russian man-of-war to the South American coast in 1872, joined the Mexican cavalry, May 1, 1873, and became a leader in the Díaz forces. On April 21, 1886, he was placed in command of the border *rurales* and served with distinction until 1913.[2]

As a young man in Mexico, he became a superb soldier, a leader of commanding physical appearance, ruthless resolve, and undeviating iron discipline. When he was with the Díaz forces, he went into battle riding a mule, he once recalled, and the fight was going against them. A retreat was ordered just as his terrified mount stampeded and headed, hell-bent in spite of the rider, just as mules often do, in the wrong direction. Kosterlitzky's astonished company saw him gallantly leading a charge and fell, pell-mell, behind him, and so unnerved the enemy that they took the field, and Kosterlitzky was the hero of the day. Whether or not his initial fame rested on a cold-jawed mule, his advance to position and power was based on genuine ability and cold courage. Eventually Díaz sent him, with the rank of colonel, to command the *rurales* on the Sonoran frontier. There, later, Jeff was to know and admire him, thoroughly and well. But just now Milton was not looking for Mexican friendships. Kosterlitzky, however, was looking for him.

At last, at Laredo, when the train stopped for the usual immigration and customs clearance, Jeff saw a special detail of a captain and three men board the train and start to search it through. Two unknown Americans sat with him in the drawing room. He shifted his gun into easy position, turned to his fellow travelers, and quietly said, "Pardon me, gentlemen, but we are all Americans here, and there might be something happening in just a few minutes. I suggest you get out of range."

He had made up his mind as to what he would do. He would shoot it out, rush to the engine, and pull it across the river into

---

[2] Charles Hardy to J. E. H., January 1, 1945; E. L. Chalfant to J. E. H., February 1, 1945, and, of course, Jeff Milton. Dane Coolidge, in *Fighting Men of the West* (New York, 1932), has a chapter upon Kosterlitzky. Noah Beery, Jr., in the *Westerners Brand Book* (Los Angeles, 1948), 97–98, gives some fresh and authentic information upon Kosterlitzky.

Texas himself, while standing any pursuer off. But the last threat of capture passed as the searchers went by, looking for a Pullman conductor with a black mustache. And as the train eased past the middle of the bridge over the Río Grande, Texas again looked mighty good to Jeff.

Now, with Mexico out of bounds for him, the Pullman Company gave him another run, this time from El Paso to St. Louis. All went well until he had to brush another impudent porter up on his manners. This porter was a bad one who had beaten up several conductors, and when he was assigned to his car, Jeff went to the superintendent at St. Louis and said, "I'm gonna quit." The superior asked him why.

"You have given me this nigger who has been beating up conductors, and I don't want to monkey with him."

"That's the reason we've given him to you. Go on! Don't quit."

Jeff went on, but at the beginning of the run called the porter aside to advise, "You have had considerable trouble with other conductors. But as long as you attend strictly to business and keep a clean car, we will have no trouble." The porter was dropped off at Longview, on the way down, and, said Jeff, "he had done beautifully all the way." On his return from El Paso, Jeff picked up his car again, and the car was dirty. He ordered the Negro to clean it. As the train approached Poplar Bluffs, Jeff came back to the car and found the passengers standing and smoking in the vestibule. When he inquired why they were not in the smoking compartment, they told him the porter had put them out and closed the door.

"The hell he did," snorted Jeff, as he went inside, where the porter had made down his berth and gone to bed. Jeff told him to get up and take care of his baggage and continued back through the car. Upon his return he found him still in bed, and again told him to get up. He came up with a growl and threw his 190 pounds of savage bulk at Jeff, not knowing that he was ready for him.

"I did not want him to beat me up," Jeff said. "I just took my time, as I knew exactly where to hit him. I tapped him a couple of times with my six-shooter just as the train was checking down.

Then I got him by the collar, dragged him into the aisle, out on the back platform, and dropped him off on the ground about the time the train was stopping. And we went on without the gentleman."

When the train reached St. Louis, Jeff, still hotter than the barrel of an old .45, went to Superintendent Martin's office and found the news was ahead of him.

"Don't you know we don't allow fighting, sir?" Martin began.

"I don't want any words with you a-tall," snapped Jeff. "There was no fighting, sir. I told you I didn't like the looks of taking that porter out. I'm not gonna work for a damned outfit that keeps a porter that beats up its conductors. There's my resignation," he added, pitching down the previously composed document. "I'm through."

"We're not going to accept it, sir," said Martin, who not only quieted down but showed him reports already submitted by a Pullman spotter as well as a high rail official who had been on the train and had seen the fun. So Jeff cooled off and went on about his business.

His business still lay along the Texas and Pacific into El Paso, where he still had lots of fun. But the most amusing incident of his railroad career took place on that long run that stretches six hundred miles from Fort Worth into El Paso. He always carried his gun, either out of sight in his waistband or in his little bag in the Pullman, because it was comfortable company in any adverse environment. Besides that, he might want to shoot a coyote, or kill an antelope for meat, from the railroad tracks in a pause along the way—a not uncommon adventure even for passengers.

One day the train had stopped for trouble, in the valley below El Paso. The passengers were stretching their legs and sunning themselves outside when a young lady, observing some mistletoe high in a near-by tree, exercised that perfectly natural feminine impulse of wanting it.

"By jacks, if I just had my six-shooter I'd knock it out for you," said the gallant Jeff, recalling that his gun just then was in his grip, inside.

In the crowd a dark-eyed, grizzly-faced man not given to

205

banter, John R. Hughes, of the Texas Rangers, looked the conductor over with a skeptical eye, pulled a six-shooter out of his belt, and said, "You think you can hit it with a pistol? You can have mine."

Jeff took it, hefted it in his hand, eased back the hammer with his thumb, and whirled the cylinder to test its condition. Hughes perked up at the familiar fondling, but still nursed his skepticism as Jeff gaily said, "I'll knock it off just where it joins the tree." And aiming at the little excrudescence from which the parasite springs and nurses its life, he hit it dead center, the mistletoe popped out of the top of the tree and floated to the ground, to the delight of his feminine friend.

The gentle Hughes shoved his gun back into the scabbard, saying, "Young man, you ought to join the Rangers."

"Why, I quit them years ago," Jeff said, and Hughes looked at his Pullman garb in wonderment, but could not figure it out. Well, there are periods in most careers that hardly fit with logic.

From El Paso the joint track of the Southern Pacific and the Texas and Pacific took the easy grade of the Río Grande basin to a point west of the Sierra Blanca, and then snaked its way up the ridges around the base of the mountain. Then the rails forked to take their separate ways across the flats and to either side of the Davis Mountains. As the T. and P. trains rounded the range on the north, they stopped for water on the long slope of a rocky ridge at a point on the map—that is still just a point on the map—by the name of Kent. Once as Jeff's train approached the water station, the easy flow of talk in his smoker, in response to the powerful suggestion of that wild and apparently brooding land, turned to holdups.

"Were you ever held up?" asked a confident passenger with the easy familiarity born of a Southern smoker. "What would you do if you were?" he continued.

"I would throw my gun under the seat and crawl in after it," replied Jeff, with a smile.

"If anyone ever tried to hold me up," retorted the other, pulling a gun from his waistband, "I'd show them the smoky end of my old .45."

Directly the train slowed for the water tank at Kent, came to a sudden stop, and was thrown into great confusion as the conductor tore clear back to the Pullman, where with his watch in hand, he shouted to Jeff, "Here, take my watch."

"What's the matter," snorted Jeff, pulling his six-shooter as the conductor hollered, "Holdup!" and then began putting out the carbide lamps which the porter had just lit in the growing dusk.

"Don't put any more lights out in this car," shouted Jeff. "Somebody might shoot into it and there are women and children here."

"They're coming," continued the conductor.

"How many?"

"I think four or five—quite a bunch."

"Let 'em come," Jeff said, as he stepped beside the door with gun in his hand. "If they come into this car, business will sure pick up." Meanwhile the brakeman had shot his six-shooter off and locked himself in the toilet. As none of the "four or five" robbers showed up, Jeff started out to investigate. As he did, he passed a man cowering between the seats, who looked up to say, "Conductor, it's a holdup and I'm taking your advice. I threw my gun under there," said the bold, bad talker, pointing beneath the seat, and Jeff "just had to laugh."

He went forward and found that the train actually had been held up, and the highwayman—a lone cowboy—had gathered some booty from the express car and was already gone. Eventually he was captured, and what Jeff felt sure was the completely honest story of the strangest train robbery he had ever known— and he came to know many—was brought to light.

With his loot in hand this cowboy headed toward Valentine, where, as Jeff understood, he hid his roll of bills in an old-fashioned outhouse and got into a game of poker. But fortune was fleeting and he frequently left the game, retired a moment, and showed up again with fresh money to wager. As a rule Texans never went to their privies to dig something up, and his unusual action aroused suspicion. He was arrested, and, being an entirely honest train robber, readily admitted where he had got the money. 207

He had ridden up to Kent that evening, he said, unpacked his bed, staked his horse, and camped for the night, as drifting cowboys around Kent still do. Then he took a bucket and started for the railroad tank to get some water for a pot of coffee, and, as he did not wish to risk losing his rifle to the Mexican railroad hands living near by, he had slipped it from its scabbard and carried it with him. As he stood at the tank, the train rolled in, silhouetting him in its headlight with his gun in hand. Apparently the engineer, like the passengers in the Pullman, was a man of imagination, and likewise concerned with his hide. He and the fireman jumped from the cab with their hands in air, yelling to the "outlaw" not to shoot. The conductor, "buggered" still worse, ran to the rear to save his watch and warn the passengers that the whole band was coming.

The astonished cowpuncher dropped his bucket, but, with trigger-quick imagination that deserved a better break from fate, said to himself, "If it's that easy, I'm going to take it." And take it he did.

All of this came out on the stand. Jeff was convinced of the cowboy's honest intent. The state of Texas sent him to the penitentiary just the same but left unsolved the problem for cowpunchers still camping at Kent. Should they leave their guns on their saddles while they go for water, or should a man not drink water out there, anyway? It is a serious social problem west of the Pecos that collective society ought to correct, for the entire risk still falls on the individual, thirsty man.

With a land like this, and men like this at the lower end of his Pullman run, it might be guessed that Jeff would eventually quit his comfortable security above the gleaming rails. Just then El Paso was laboring with the birth of respectability, but for the old sophisticate it was not an accouchment of ease. Her wild and wanton period was passing, but not without the pains and paroxysms of deathlike struggle. She needed the reckless courage of youth to see her through. The powerful forces of history which men call fate seemed to decree that Jeff Milton should be there.

208

15

El Paso del Norte

El Paso had come far since Jeff had first known it, but not along the road to respectability. On the contrary, it had been the locus of the lustful, lawless, callous souls seeking life, and often finding death, in that untrammeled license they confused with freedom. Three physical features of location made and kept it so, far beyond its appointed time. It was isolated. No substantial settlement lay within hundreds of miles in any direction; a vast unsettled world hemmed it in. It was a border town against a volatile and turbulent land. It was a narrow pass—*El Paso del Norte*—into which rugged ranges funneled men and traffic between the southern extremities of our land, east and west, and between two nations, north and south.

Racial diversity lent it color without accentuating conflict. Anglo-Saxons and Mexicans dominated the place. Booming business and loose money attracted the lawless without the usual stimulus to law. The thoughtless pride of naïve, youthful men in being rough and tough, worked hand in glove with the sophisticated cunning of those designing to fleece them. Any and everything went. El Paso was a "wide-open" town, tough as an old boot, mean as a sore-headed bear.

In the early eighteen nineties the temper of the town was still largely determined by its rougher elements. Widespread, unrestrained gambling worked cheek by jowl with the traffic in liquor and women. Easy egress to Mexico on one hand and "fixing" of the local law on the other made El Paso the shining sanctuary of the fugitive and lawless and the profitable field of the frontier racketeer. John Selman, the most depraved gunman of Texas—which took in plenty of territory— was constable, levying ten dollars a month on the many fancy houses flourishing on the philandering propensities of El Paso's men. John Wesley

Hardin, the hardest gun-fighter of them all, was shortly to arrive from the Texas pen and begin his practice of law. Charlie Patterson and a host of others were already there.

Patterson, once in trouble for the illicit sale of liquor, was later admitted to the bar, and, with George E. Wallace, developed a practice for the tough end of town in the justice court. Jim Byrnes, owner of a dance hall in the "Tenderloin," as the red-light district was sometimes called, got Patterson to draw his will designed to leave his property to nieces in Iowa. When filed for probate, it provided that his fortune go to Patterson. Wallace was one of its witnesses. It was upheld in the Court of Appeals at San Antonio, the Supreme Court refused the writ, and a few months later Wallace was deeded one-half of the estate. The effrontery of El Paso knew no bounds.

Patterson was in favor, too, with the Mexican element. His dusky clients, finding difficulty in pronouncing his name, called him "Charlie de Pat." W. H. Wheat, a mild, pleasant-faced, blue-eyed constable, summed up the character of Patterson and unconsciously sounded the sentiment of the town when he said, "Charlie de Pat wasn't such a bad man. He just found it was a game of skin or be skunt, and so he skunt 'em."[1]

But the sporting fraternity, which these men both represented and preyed upon, was not building El Paso. It was simply running and living off of it. Legitimate traffic through the Pass, and not the brawling ways of her dives, was the town's economic breath of life. Now sound business brings and begets settled and proper people, slow to positive action but formidable when aroused. At last the ways of her wild men and wanton women began to go against the grain. The decent folks decided on a change.

For some time moral propriety had, politically, ridden a sorry second in the race with sodden vice, but in the early eighteen nineties her fortune looked more favorable. This was partly due to the fact that the town was then closely divided between Democratic and Republican control, and partly due to one of those sensitive human reactions that makes politics about as predict-

[1] Richard Burges to J. E. H., February 29, 1944.

able as the Texas weather. The incident that fanned the issue to the fever heat that generates reform reached from the county clerkship at El Paso to the national convention that nominated Cleveland.

Park Pittman won the Democratic nomination for county clerk over the incumbent, Beverly G. Thomas, in the local convention of 1892. But when John J. Taylor—who along with Pittman's uncle, George Look, was owner of the Gem Saloon at the site of the Paso del Norte Hotel—as a delegate to the national convention helped nominate Grover Cleveland for president, it so rankled the town of El Paso, with its genius for genuine perversity, that it took out its spite on Pittman.

Juan S. Hart, son of the founder of Hart's Mill and owner of the *El Paso Times*, in his zeal for Pittman's scalp, opened fire on the gambling fraternity, which was always closely linked with the liquor trade. Pittman was beaten on the basis of the prejudicial connection, and, somewhat inadvertently, the spirit of reform was prematurely born.[2] Its slender hold on life, however, revolved around the city's choice of council, mayor, and city attorney. And the public careers of these was often as short and uncertain as those of the noted gunmen who went their openly armed way up and down El Paso's streets.

W. H. Austin, cashier of the El Paso National Bank, was elected mayor in 1893, but on account of illness served only a little while. Adolph Solomon, owner of a transfer business and "one of the best men in town," was chosen to hold the place until the next election in April, 1894, when Democrat A. K. Albers, a wholesale druggist and the reform candidate, was the city's choice. But he resigned immediately after induction. The city council chose R. F. Johnson, a wholesale liquor dealer, to take his place, and El Paso had passed through the doubtfully honorable distinction, according to its city attorney, "of having three mayors in two days."[3]

[2] W. H. Burges to J. E. H., August 6, 1939.
[3] W. H. Burges, as cited; *El Paso Times*, April 11, 1894, notes Albers' election, April 17 issue, his uncertainty over serving, and April 21, Johnson's succession "by unanimous choice of the City Council."

Bob Johnson, as he was known, in spite of his preference for the point of view of the liquor trade, had so much pressure put on him by the reform element that he decided either to control or to close the open gambling halls in order to keep peace with Juan Hart's *El Paso Times*. Much of the pressure, and even more of its dominant intelligence, found fluent outlet through the aggressive nature of Will H. Burges, representing the Democratic Citizens League, and his brother Richard, fresh to the West from Seguin in southern Texas.[4]

Young Will Burges, from a more conventional environment and fired with moral courage, exceptional ability, and something of the youthful spirit of reform was elected city attorney in 1893 along with a majority of the council. In 1894 the country had not yet recovered from the depression of ninety-three. The railroads, with the heaviest employment in town, met their pay rolls in hard cash, which meant, Burges recalled, "that next morning most of the workmen had to borrow from the gamblers to get their groceries."[5] So the battle for reform, like some similar battles since, paced its gait with the fall of the business barometer.

Spring wore off without definite action, but the pulse of the public climbed with the mercury of early summer. The *Times* regularly put out its sheets to fan the fire, noting, late in June, that the "anti-gambling spirit appears rampant," although the gambling and liquor elements were battling to retain control.[6]

Then Alderman Lock was arrested for running a gambling hall, himself, and by July 24, the *Times* was saying that gambling was stopped. But five days later it recorded that a gambling house and the Bonanza Dance Hall were open. By then this seesaw between propriety and license had made it obvious to all that the suppression of gambling in this worst resort of the Western gunman was a man-sized job. Somebody, apparently Dr. Albers, thought of Jeff Milton, and Johnson wired him at St.

[4] Owen P. White, in his book, *Out of the Desert: the Historical Romance of El Paso* (El Paso, 1923), credits *The Herald* with the leading role in the fight for morality. See pp. 304–311. W. H. Burges says that it was Hart's paper.
[5] W. H. Burges, as cited.
[6] *El Paso Times*, June 23, 1894.

Louis offering him the job of civilizing the town. He agreed to look it over on his return run, and Johnson noted the change of policy in the *Times*, August 1, 1894, with the news that he had "offered the place to Mr. J. Milton and he will give me his reply when he returns from St. Louis." And the next day the paper editorially observed, "The gambler in El Paso seems more powerful than the law."

All of which made it sound like a "lot of fun" to Jeff, who, on his way back, was peacefully punching tickets until he reached Sierra Blanca, a sort of detached frontier suburb on the way to El Paso. There three prominent gamblers, aware of his coming, boarded his car, told him of the dangerous road ahead, and advised him not to take it. But if he did, they said, they would run him out of town. Jeff "just had to laugh," saying, that if they did, it would "be easy to step across the river into Mexico." Still they insisted.

"My trunk's in the baggage car, and I'm gonna follow it in," he said good humoredly, but added with dangerous undertone, "You fellows take care of yourselves; I'll try to take care of mine."

He followed the baggage car in for his conference with Johnson, Burges, and the city council. He had only one important question to ask: "Do you really mean business?" They assured him they did.

He wound up his affairs with the Pullman Company, and with Bob Ross as his captain, took oath as chief of police, August 10, 1894, and made bond on the eleventh, with Joseph Magoffin, S. F. Freudenthal, and Barney Hamsen as sureties.[7] And the surest thing of all was the fact that for the short spell that El Paso could stand reform, she was in for a radical change.

Jeff suspected, however, that Mayor Bob Johnson, in view of his liquor interests, would probably weaken when the pressure was on, and told Burges, "I'll be removed when I close these gambling halls."

"What's the matter with having you confirmed by the city council?" suggested Burges. "Then the mayor can't remove you."

"Can you do it?" asked the new chief.

[7] *El Paso Times*, August 11, 1894.

213

"Of course we can," said Burges. "We've got the council."

So at their next Thursday night meeting the council approved the mayor's choice of chief of police, and reform broke out all over El Paso with a bang.[8]

A proper appreciation of the violence of its convulsions requires a brief review of a few more of the leading citizens of the town.

John Selman was the most degenerate of the bunch. He had drifted west to El Paso with twenty dead men to his acknowledged credit, had been prospering as constable of Precinct One since 1892, and now was posing a problem for Milton.[9]

The story of Selman's last killing, casually characteristic of the town and time, can be understood only in view of the fact that there comes a peculiar perversion in this lust for blood. This was the nature of the bad man. He took pride in his gory profession. Perhaps he secretly dreaded the best; he surely wanted to kill the worst. And among the worst was a Ranger by the name of Bass Outlaw. His reputation as a fighting man was good; his name as a moral character had got bad. On April 5, 1894, he and Ranger Tom McKidrick were shot down at Tillie Howard's fancy house on Utah Street, and Bass died on a billiard table in the Barnum Show Saloon. "The only man I ever saw," Will Burges recalled, "who died in mortal terror."

"There is no question in my mind," he added, "that he was killed in cold blood. Tillie, the prostitute, showed me where Selman stood behind a fence and shot him down. Selman just wanted another notch on his gun barrel."[10]

To know El Paso, it is not only necessary to understand the brutal character of Selman, but the anomalous nature of Tillie, "whose word," said the accomplished Burges, "was good anywhere." For Tillie Howard, "madam" of a bawdy house in El Paso and lacking the fairest of the feminine virtues, was a woman

[8] W. H. Burges, as cited.

[9] Owen P. White, in his flippant but readable style, exploited "old John" beyond his just deserts. The *El Paso Times* for the period is full of news about him.

[10] W. H. Burges to J. E. H., January 24, 1945. Eugene Cunningham, in his book *Triggernometry* (Caldwell, Idaho, 1941), 236, gives a sketch of Outlaw, but does not say that he was murdered. Jeff Milton agreed with Burges. See the *El Paso Times* and the *El Paso Herald*, April 6, 1894, for contemporary accounts.

214

whose great character deserves a page in frontier history. W. H. Burges, counsel for Standard Oil and other mighty corporations, was likewise Tillie's lawyer, and has left us Tillie's story.

Tillie Howard came to El Paso with $65,000 in cash, an impressive adornment of jewels, and a beautiful tiger skin that she sentimentally cherished all her days. She took her money and opened her house on Utah Street, where for a price vigorous and wayward men sated desire without achieving satisfaction. "But she did as much for little, helpless children in that town as anyone ever did."

As an example, a Negro woman lived in the red-light district rearing a white baby girl. "I don't know what kind of story she told when she came," said Burges, "but whatever it was, it was all right. For this baby's mother was a young lady back in the settled part of Texas who had gotten into trouble. When the baby came, the mother's brother handed the child out of the window to this Negro woman the night it was born. She came to El Paso and was raising it." And now the child was growing up and decency demanded that something be done.

A proper home was found, Tillie put up the money for the child's care, and she grew to womanhood, married, and brought up children of her own, all happily merging into the "best" life of El Paso with no disturbing doubts about legitimate origin. It was typical of Tillie. And while death and the professional honor of the lawyer assure the peaceful anonymity of one, disclosure came within life for Tillie, when a man from Wisconsin dropped into her parlor, looked her over, and said, "You're not Tillie Howard! You are Tillie Weiler."

"Yes," came the answer, "I am Tillie Howard."

"No, you're not," he insisted. "You're Tillie Weiler from Wisconsin." At last she admitted that she was, and asked if any of her relatives were living yet. He told of an infirm uncle and aunt who were about to lose their home because of a mortgage. And, although it had been years since she had seen them, Tillie boarded a train, went back, secretly investigated the debt, and returned to El Paso determined to lift it. She took more than $5,000 in securities to the First National Bank and asked for a

215

loan of that amount. The president said that he had to refuse, because even though the collateral was good, the business was bad, for Tillie still ran a house in the "Tenderloin."

"Well, would you lend the money on the securities to someone else?" she asked, and the banker admit~d he would. She took them to Burges and told him the story. He borrowed the money, Tillie paid off the note, he recorded the release of the mortgage, and two happy old folks in Wisconsin never knew the wayward source of the gracious bounty that brought them to death in ease. Tillie wanted to reward Burges with her tiger hide, but instead he heard her story.

She was born of German parentage in Wisconsin, her mother died at her birth, her father three years later, and she was taken by a near-by family. She labored for them as a child but was beaten unmercifully. After one whipping, when she was about twelve years old, she ran away to a near-by stream at a railroad trestle with the intention of drowning herself. But her nerve failed, and she sat in distress until a train of the Wisconsin Central stopped there for water. The crew heard her sobbing on the bank, picked her up, and put her on the caboose.

For two or three years she rode as a vagrant up and down the line, eating from the crew's lunch pails and sleeping in the caboose. Being an overgrown, healthy, handsome German girl, the inevitable happened and Tillie no longer toiled.

When Sell's circus showed in a town where she was stopping, Willie Sells, their great trick rider, met and took a fancy to her, and for an apparently happy period she traveled the road with him, only to be dropped in San Antonio. There she fell in with Rufe Nimmo and an army captain full of the gold fever for the Rand. Nimmo was a bad one, but Tillie seemed to take to that kind. Off they sailed to Johannesburg, where they bought a wine shop, sold it at a profit, and bought another one. As tensions between the Dutch and the English in South Africa were tightening, Tillie Weiler, with her German background, flourished on the Dutch trade. She shook off Nimmo and his associate, and eventually owned the only wine shop on the principal financial street in Johannesburg. Then she sold out for $65,000, invested in gilt-edge securities, and with her jewels and a tiger skin from Africa, came back to that spot of crimson glory on the edge of Texas and bought a house in the red-light district under the name of Tillie Howard.

It was she who showed and told Will Burges how Selman murdered Outlaw. "And I believed every word of it," emphasized the lawyer with the distinction of a hundred-thousand-dollar fee, and, "further," he added, "I'll argue her case in the hereafter, if I can, though I do not expect to be called as counsel."[11]

People like these, with a mottled herd of others, made up the El Paso that Jeff was called on to subdue. Lack of character at times in high places, and high character at times in low, emphasized the fact that it was an anomalous land where the mettle of the individual was the only thing to count. The new chief of police took the oath, The *Times* reviewed his frontier record next day in a sort of premature epitaph, and Jeff Davis Milton, at thirty-two years of age, was in control of the toughest town in the West. The wise heads watched with obvious amusement to see what he would do.

They had but a brief spell to wait, for Jeff brought the firm conviction, from his seasoning in the West, that "the only way to handle that sort of folks was just to take a-hold of them and do it." The first morning he ran into Old John Selman's ugly talk about where he would stick this young upstart's gun and then kick the handles off. Jeff, who knew him from his Ranger days, found him holding forth in one of the saloons. Selman did not see him until he dropped a firm hand on his shoulder to interrupt his flow of talk and turn him around.

"Hello, Uncle John, how're y'u, sir," greeted Jeff, in quiet and even tones.

Selman looked greatly surprised, hesitated a moment, and blurted, "Why, hello, that you, Chief?"

"Y-a-a-s," drawled Jeff. "How about the six-shooter? I've got it on. Think you want-a use it on me?" Selman tried to laugh it off, but Jeff insisted, "I just wondered if you wanted to try it out, see?" And Selman saw, but didn't.

[11] W. H. Burges to J. E. H., January 24, 1945.

217

Jeff next arrested Selman's deputy constable and threw him in jail when he caught him levying on "the girls" for protection. This infuriated Selman. Jeff met them both on the street one morning after the deputy was released. Selman had his hand on his gun, which he carried in his right pants' pocket. Jeff could tell by "the look in their eyes" that they meant to kill him.

"Come here! I want-a talk to you," Selman growled, beckoning him into the lower landing of an old-fashioned staircase that opened to the street. He started in ahead, with his deputy behind. Obviously their plan was to take him between them.

"Hold on a minute, John," commanded Jeff, shifting his gun into shape, "I'll step in first," and did, whirling quickly, ready to draw, saying, "If you boys want anything, you've shore got it."

Selman, surprised that his notorious record had not awed the Chief, protested his peace: "We don't want any trouble!"

"If you do, you've shore got it," repeated Jeff. "Just make a move and you'll settle things quickly." He really "meant to kill 'em both if they had made a move."

"I just wanted to talk to you, Chief, about that business," said Selman.

"You can't rob those women," Jeff insisted, "and if you try it again, I'll put you both in jail. And if either of you ever starts anything with me again, I'm going to kill you, certain," he added in positive benediction. So the incident passed, and with it passed the levy on the prostitutes in the name of legality.

Next Jeff hunted up a gambler and gave him $100 out of his own pocket for the name of every tinhorn in town. He arranged the names alphabetically, and served notice on ten each day to be out of town on the next train or he "would bag them." When they hesitated, he locked them up as vagrants in the county jail. The exodus started.[12] Of course there was dispute, for somebody was bound to call the Chief's hand, and all who could were waiting to see it done.

The city council approved his action, repealed the ordinance

[12] Lordsburg reported a heavy immigration from El Paso. *El Paso Times,* August 19, 1894.

which authorized gambling, and refunded the unexpired portions of the license fees. At first the toughest said they would never close.

"You'll be closed, you'll be in jail, or I'll be dead," retorted Jeff, and he meant it. Next day they were closed.

Mayor Johnson, fearing the worst, left town, followed by another leading citizen, Charlie Davis, collector of customs. Feeling was running high when Jeff met one of the biggest gamblers on Magoffin Avenue soon after he issued his order.

"Come here, I want to talk to you," the gambler growled, who then swore that he and everybody else were going to open up that night. At last he snorted, "You heard what I said, didn't you?"

"Yes, sir, I heard you," the Chief answered quietly.

"Well, what are you going to do about it?"

"I'm gonna put you in jail five minutes after you open," Jeff snapped.

"There ain't enough men in Texas to put me in jail," the gambler snarled.

"Don't need anybody to help me a-tall. In you go, certain, or anybody else that opens up." And, Jeff added, "they didn't open."

Next their main fighting man, a German who had "killed a man or two around there and considered a pretty bad bully," met him on the street in front of Dr. A. K. Albers' drug store, raised an awful row, and told him what he was going to do to him if he did not relent. "He was gonna just raise this, that, and the other with me," Jeff continued. "And he give me quite an explanation of what he was gonna do, right there in front of a dozen to twenty men. I never said a word. What I wanted was advertisement to begin with."

"Now," he says, "I'll explain to you again tomorrow if you put anybody out."

"All right, sir," came the answer. Albers was dumbfounded and so angry that he refused to speak to Jeff, but strode into his store in bitter disappointment. Jeff went ahead and shipped some more gamblers out that evening. Next day he waited until the fighter had time to get half-drunk and doubly bold before going downtown. When the fighter saw him coming, he charged at once and again started his abuse.

"I planned to kill him," said Jeff, "but I wanted everybody to see the fun. I was waiting for him to call me a s——o——b—— and then I was gonna kill him. But he never said it."

"Didn't I explain to you what I was going to do to you yesterday?" he shouted at last.

"Yes, sir," answered Jeff, by which time the crowd had swelled to a mob.

"He was just getting ready; having lots of fun," Jeff laughed in later years, "and I was ready for him to get there."

"Goddamn you," he swore, "don't you think I told you enough yesterday?"

"I shore do; I think a-plenty," snapped Jeff, grabbing him by the ear with his right hand, spinning him around, and kicking him off the sidewalk, his six-shooter out of his hip pocket. It fell in the street near the fighter, who landed face down in the dirt. Jeff's gun was out and on him as he fell, but he groveled there in the street, while Jeff stepped out, kicked him a time or two, and stomped his neck, saying, "Get up and pick that pistol up."

He began to howl that Jeff wanted to kill him. Jeff told him again, and he reached for the barrel of his gun.

"Pick it up by the handle; if you don't, I'll kill you," commanded Jeff, which he did, still on his knees.

"Get up from there, crawl across here, and put that six-shooter behind the bar," continued the Chief. "And let me tell you another thing; next time you speak to me, come up and take your hat off. And don't pass me on the street without taking your hat off—at no time! If you do, I'm gonna tend to you right!"

"And I explained to that gentleman thoroughly," he recalled, "after which they sorta quieted down, and about a week or ten days later he went up to Albuquerque, and he never bothered me no more."

During the first few days after Jeff's order, however, one hall was opened. Jeff was informed of its plans and waited until the gambling got in good swing, eager to catch as many as possible. Then he dressed in some Mexican clothes and big hat; and with

220

Henry Heep, one of his men, in plain clothes just behind him, Jeff, acting "drunker'n seven hundred dollars," went staggering along the street until opposite the guard posted at the stairway that led up to the gambling hall. Just as he got even with the door, Jeff staggered against the guard, grabbed him by the neck, and threw him into the street to Heep, who immediately choked him down. At the head of the stairs Jeff stepped in with his six-shooter in his hand, shouted to the house that he would kill the first man who made a break, and then marched the gamblers all off to repent in jail. No more opened up.

Big and little, bad and worse, they all looked alike to Jeff. He had few better friends in town than Juan Hart and Charlie Davis. But in El Paso there were now no exceptions to the rule of law and order. One day he found one of his policemen outside Luke and Taylor's saloon, where an awful racket was going on.

"Chief, don't go in," the man advised, with an eye to political power, wealth, and influence. "Juan Hart and Charlie Davis are raising sand in there."

"You been here listening to that and didn't do anything," answered Jeff, severely. "Let me have that badge," he added, reaching and taking it off, and marching inside himself.

"Come with me, Juan," he said, crooking a finger at Hart. When he turned to Davis, that outraged worthy made a motion toward his shirt—inside which gentlemen sometimes carried their guns in a shoulder holster—but was brought to his senses when Jeff warned, "If you don't keep your hand out of your shirt, Charlie, I'll have to kill you."

Davis was dumbfounded, but the newspaper owner broke the tension. "Come on, you so and so," said Juan to Charlie, good naturedly, "I rather go to hell with this fellow than to go to Heaven with you." Jeff took them out the back door, sent them across the river to Juárez to sober up, but told them they would go to jail, certain, if they disturbed the peace again.

In such a place anything could happen and usually did. There was the case of the man stepping out of his house to get a drink and having his hot cookstove stolen, to be recovered by Chief Milton while in use an hour later in a situation that "was plumb

221

reedic'lous." But the most outlandish incident took place at an undertaker's in the middle of town. Jeff was sauntering by one day when a man, completely naked, broke out of the grisly depths of the place and headed down the street at a dead run. Jeff caught him and heard his charge of attempted murder by the undertaker, but led him back to get his clothes and hear the defense. The undertaker claimed the man had been brought in dead and laid out on a cooling board. And dead he was, but dead drunk. When the undertaker started jabbing his instruments in to drain him, the corpse, along with everybody else, had immediately come to life and broken out of the place, yelling bloody murder.

Then there was the editor of a jerkwater paper who, becoming peeved with his elderly landlady, abused her in his paper. Jeff picked up a quirt at a saddle shop and called on the lady to console her, suggesting that she come with him and give the offender a public quirting.

"Do you mean it, sir?"

"Certainly, madam," he answered. "He won't bother you a-tall. I'll guarantee that."

So together they called on the gentleman and Jeff held his gun on him saying, "Stand and take it." And he stood and took it. "You had to handle those people, then," he simply said in explanation.

Still there were others who called for more rigorous treatment. When he went in as chief, he cleaned out the whole force because "they were worthless." Among his new force was John Selman, Jr., the son of Old John, because "he was the best boy to have the sorriest daddy" that he had ever seen. So he hired young Selman and gave him a beat of his own in the Tenderloin end of town.[13]

There a saloon man named Nelson had a colored virago of around 220 pounds called Annie Rooney. She acted as a sort of bouncer and beat up everyone who incurred her displeasure around the dive, the toughest sort of a joint and a continual sore

---

[13] John Selman, Jr., in "John Selman," *All Western Magazine,* November, 1935, 44–61, has given some recollections of his father and this period.

spot for the police. She refused arrest after one of her own drunk-
en and frequent disturbances, and the patrolman, not wishing
to hurt her, reported to the Chief.

Jeff went down, himself, and called to her, "Come on, Annie."

"Sho', Chief," said the haughty Amazon. "I'll go wid you, but
no audinary p'l'cemun gonna 'rest me."

Annie's testy temperament was simply in keeping with Nelson's nature. He had a police whistle, which he blew on occasion
for the fun of seeing the cops come a-running, and when Young
John Selman wasted words with him, he cussed the cop. Selman
let the insult pass and reported to the Chief for instructions.

Jeff was furious. He called his entire squad to tell them, one
and all, that, except for drunks, if he ever heard of another policeman taking a cussing from anybody, he would fire him. John
went back to his beat. Next night another row started in Nelson's
dive, and young John, a big six-footer, rushed in to quell it. Nelson again cussed him out, and Selman followed the Chief's
advice.

Jeff was closeted with the city council, but Captain Ross
came up and called him out: "Chief, can I see you a minute?"

"What is it?"

"John Selman has beat this fellow Nelson to death—at least
they think he's dead."

"What did he do it for?" asked Jeff.

Ross explained the incident, and wound up by asking, "What
shall I do with John?"

"Where is he?" asked Jeff.

"I've got him under arrest," said Ross.

"Send him back to his beat, and tell him if anybody else does
the same, to kill him, shore. And if anybody doesn't like it, tell
him to kill them."

"What do you mean?" asked some of the council in alarm.

"Just what I said," Jeff replied angrily. "We'll kill 'em all or
stop this stuff," and, he added in retrospect, "we did." As to the
will to do, Jeff said it was simple: "It's no trouble a-tall to make
up your mind. If you're right, either kill 'em or be a cur."

Nelson went to the hospital for a month. After he had re-

223

covered enough to talk, he sent for Jeff. The Chief ignored him. But back at his saloon he and Annie had definitely undergone a change of life as well as politics. Across the front of his dive he erected a sign portraying a big bad wolf at the throat of a lamb, and beneath it this large and telling inscription: "I once was a Democrat but now I am a Republican," and Jeff just had to laugh at the way he was converting them.

Gradually his troubles with the toughs threatened to simmer down completely. Still there was always something to make life worth while. Although it was against the law, an organization of young men called "The One-Lunger's Club" wanted to stage a prize fight. Jeff told them he could not give them permission but added that if they put one on, a policeman would not be there. That was all the encouragement they needed. They groomed Red Sullivan, their local fireman, into condition, and challenged another fireman from Denver.

Jeff, familiar with the frontier, figured there would be trouble. He sent a policeman to post himself outside, with orders not to interfere, even when the riot started, but "Just let 'em fight."

Jeff then went to bed. Prize fights were properly named, for when the bout opened, a local fan piled into the ring and fell upon the visiting fighter. The referee jumped on him, and Red Sullivan began to beat up the referee. From then on, the fight grew into a good one. Everybody got in. Then Jeff heard the frantic cries of the president and some members of The One-Lunger's Club at his door.

"Chief, Chief," they yelled. "Come on up to the fight. We're about to get a bunch of men killed." Jeff dressed and made his way to the arena. He found, of course, that the visiting fireman had got whipped, and everybody was touseled and torn, while Red Sullivan had grabbed the gate money and run off to the fire station.

A few days later Jeff said to the president of the club, "I've decided to let you boys have a fight every time you want to."

"Nothing doing," said the promoter of El Paso's pugilism. "We've had all the fights we want."

But even here Jeff found occasion to temper the hard fist of

224

justice with the warmth that kindled deep in his heart. When a wealthy man from the East was fleeced by a confidence man in Juárez, he made complaint to Milton, describing the man who had taken him in for several hundred dollars as well as a fine watch. Jeff knew the offender from his description, a man afflicted with tuberculosis who lived at the old Lyons Hotel. Jeff went over and knocked on his door. He did not open it, but Jeff, knowing he was in, demanded that he do so. At first he refused.

"Then I'll kick the damned thing in," said Jeff.

He opened it and then crawled back into bed. Jeff told him of the complaint. He admitted getting the money, gave up a pawn ticket for the watch, and then asked Jeff to read a letter from his wife and children in Denver, which showed their destitute straits. Then he produced the express receipts for the missing money which he had sent to them. Jeff left him alone but took the pawn ticket to the complainant, who still protested the loss of his money and the man's escape.

"Dammit, you expected to win when you got into the game, but you lost. Besides, that happened across the line. It's none of my business!" said Jeff with finality.

"But I wouldn't a-done anything about it," he added in mellow retrospect, "even if it had o'been."

16

"Wes Hardin Will Git You"

The late W. H. Burges said that when he was a boy in South Texas, the mothers of that section warned their children to good behavior with a modified, but currently blood-curdling version of "Little Orphant Annie's" goblin threat:

"Wes Hardin will git-chi if you don't watch out."

And for terrifying the Texans of that period it was the most direful threat that anyone could utter. For although John Wesley Hardin was the son of a Texas preacher, the namesake of the great churchman never qualified among the faithful. But as a Texan ever willing, even anxious, to rush perverse souls prematurely to Heaven, he was the best—or the worst, depending on the proselyte's point of view.

Like most gunmen who rose on the flotsam of that period to notoriety if not respect, he was a product of his land and times. The South had long produced its men of high honor and petulant humor. The degradation of defeat and military subservience during Reconstruction fanned their fury to continued individual rebellion. The arrogance of an ignorant race recently released from servitude often led to Negro killings, the killings induced outlawry against a carpetbag regime, and the hardest outlaws captured the affection of decent but oppressed people as riding Robin Hoods.

So it seemed at first with John Wesley Hardin. But the universal affection for unadulterated bravery often leads to false judgments. While there is no invariable formula for the psychology of a killer, those frequently justified to begin with soon dulled in the delicate art of discrimination. The best of the indiscriminate killers became notorious outlaws; the best of the decent gunmen became great officers. Hardin's career boomed with brilliance. By the time he was twenty-one, with some thirty-nine dead men accounted for by his fast and flashing guns, he had passed well to the other side of that tenuous line between legitimate fame and outlawry, and was a feared and hunted man.[1]

He engaged in reckless gamblings, trail ventures, and killings all over Texas from the time he was a callow youth. He was a dead and willing shot in the Taylor-Sutton feud in South Texas. He was taken prisoner in Florida, returned to Comanche for trial, and sentenced to twenty-five years. He was discharged from the penitentiary, February 17, 1894, and granted a full pardon and restoration of citizenship by Governor James Stephen Hogg a month later.

His term in the penitentiary was characterized by recurrent plans for escape and a decided disinclination to labor. He did read up on theology without breaking out with conversion, and left with a smattering of law that enabled him to take a certificate. He first hung out his shingle at Gonzales, a town with a fighting tradition that he had embellished somewhat in his youth, himself. There he fell into a heated campaign being waged for the office of sheriff, and soon after decided to go west.[2]

He was retained for the prosecution of Bud Frazier, of Pecos, after Frazier's shooting scrape with another noted Texas gunman, Jim Miller. In the pursuit of his new profession he dropped into El Paso with two confederates and began prowling around the town.[3] Chief Milton had wind of his coming, and, anticipating trouble, had "stashed"[4] four or five semiautomatic shotguns with folding handles at convenient spots.

Jeff heard that Hardin and his men were making the rounds

---

[1] The primary source of information on Hardin is his autobiography, printed posthumously at Seguin, Texas, as *The Life of John Wesley Hardin* (1896). Cunningham, in *Triggernometry*, has a good account of his career. Owen P. White, and nearly everybody else who aspires to paint the West with red pigments, profitably portrayed Hardin without adding to his history or even detracting from his fame.

[2] *The Life of John Wesley Hardin*, 76, 132–35.

[3] Cunningham, *Triggernometry*, 58. G. A. Frazier shot and wounded Miller at Pecos, April 12, 1894. *El Paso Times*, April 13, 1894.

[4] This word, not yet found in the Oxford Dictionary, is a Southwestern corruption of the French *cache*, and likewise means "to hide"; not after Webster or even Mencken but after Milton and equally authoritative others.

with their six-shooters on and Winchesters in their hands. Six-shooters were expected, if prohibited, but a party of men with rifles at harmless social diversion was sort of obvious. Jeff never carried a troop or squad on his worst missions. Somebody would blurt an unwise word or make an overt move, and hell would pop. It always caused trouble. The way to prevent it was to make his missions alone. He met Hardin and his men in McClain's saloon; and, although he had never seen this noted gunman, he knew him at once by his bearing, walked directly to him, and said, "I am Milton, chief of police. I don't permit six-shooters to be worn on the streets of El Paso. You will have to take them off and put them and your rifles behind the bar."

Hardin looked him over with his narrow, cold-gray eyes, noted his cool and calculated demeanor, and said, "Do you know who you are talking to?"

"I evidently do, sir," said Jeff. "And I think if I were you—all of you—I'd take 'em off right now, before anything starts."

There is a powerful compulsion in the quiet manner of men who are right and never afraid to die. Hardin looked at him for another minute, and then said, "All right, Chief, we'll abide by the law."

"That's all I ask," said Milton, strictly businesslike, as he turned and went back to the station, never forgetting the natural dignity implicit in the proper relations of all men, nor inviting the flippant familiarity that leads to loss of respect and trouble. To begin with, Hardin gave him none at all.

Yet there was, even then in the making, one of those complicated webs of human device that was to bring death to Hardin and others and high adventure to Jeff. Its origin lay in part in the complicated psychology and traditions of Texas gunmen, and in part in battles for beef on the open range. It was drawn to tragic dimensions by a blonde, by booze, and by bad blood in Paso del Norte. It was liquidated in the lives of fighting men on the banks of the Río Bravo. And the skein of its web is spun in history.

Among those dangerous men who followed the longhorn herds up the Pecos was one named Martin M'Rose. He wasn't

228

the best of cowboys, but he rode with a long loop, an inquisitive eye for a stray beef, and a nose for business.

Back of that he was a Polander, or Bohemian, from a settlement of the breed near Helena in South Texas. About 1880 he drifted out to the Atascosa River ranch of the McGowan brothers south of San Antonio to learn the cow business. They put him in camp with a cowboy named Dee Harkey, where he stayed for three years, learning to speak English and also learning to commune with cows. He was a big, rough, blue-eyed blonde who wore neither underwear nor boots, but went about in a pair of brogan shoes. Hence he was suspected of a total lack of imagination and devoid of all duplicity. Thus when he wanted to borrow a good saddle horse named Red Bird to ride to town, the Mc-Gowans willingly let him go. He never stopped at the local village but sailed right along on Red Bird until he reached the vast Pecos ranges of southern New Mexico.[5]

That region then—in fact since the days of the Lincoln County War—was decidedly the place for the free lance of the open range. Those who had been on the winning side of that bloody conflict, and hadn't been buried, were still riding high and wide. Tom Finnessy, who had killed John Northern at the rip-snorting village of Seven Rivers, just up the Pecos,[6] was range manager for the VVN's, the Eddy-Bissell Cattle Company. He liked M'Rose, put him on as a hand, and made him a trail boss, driving VVN herds to Dodge City and to their Colorado range. M'Rose grew rough and tough enough to become genuinely acclimated to the Pecos. He had plenty of daring to get into some shooting scrapes, and enough design to keep himself out of serious trouble. While on the trail he stopped off at Cripple Creek to take a shot at Bob Ford, in Ford's dance hall. Ford slammed the door to shut

[5] D. R. Harkey to J. E. H. and Hervey Chesley, February 24, 1945. There is much dispute about the spelling of M'Rose's name. He is usually called "Monrose." Some say he spelled it "Morose," although the spelling used here is the printed spelling of the period. There is no dispute about his character. B. A. Oden to J. E. H., February 27, 1944; Bob Beverly to J. E. H., May 11, 1944; Mrs. Jerry E. Dunaway to J. E. H., June 23, 1937. A. P. Black, MS, "Martin M'Rose," in the Earl Vandale Library.

[6] Mrs. Jerry E. Dunaway to J. E. H., June 23, 1937.

him out. M'Rose drilled a hole through it, but missed, and Ford, refused to step outside.[7]

Then the southeastern corner of New Mexico was organized as Eddy County, and Dave Kemp, an outlaw from Hamilton, Texas, became its sheriff. J. J. Hagerman was interested in the Pecos Valley, and C. B. Eddy, a broad-gauged man of the lower Pecos, spread out from ranching to irrigation and colonization. Talk of ditches and railroads was as thick as the dusty, alkaline air, and the town of Eddy, which turned into Carlsbad, grew in spite of the prohibition clauses restricting the use of its lots. Vice in the ascendancy, however, easily evades the legal limits of virtue, and a settlement devoted to pleasure was started on the river a mile and a half away with no limitation in title. With ill-concealed irony, its promoters called it Hagerman, after the high-minded gentleman developing the land they designed to exploit.[8]

Liquor flowed freely to offset the alkaline nature of the Pecos water, and Dave Kemp, the sheriff and a warm friend of Martin M'Rose, and Walker Bush, another Texan, opened a dance hall and sporting house there. M'Rose got a contract to supply one of the Pecos projects with beef, and, in partnership with Bill McClendon, was running a herd of horses and cattle on the side. He got into a row and killed a man about this time, but that was of precious little moment on the Pecos.[9] Finnessy, Kemp, McClendon, and another hard case named Vic Queen were his close friends, if not cohorts, and all were prospering.

Meanwhile, Eddy was growing, and among those who reached that drab and gyppy flat above the river in 1890 was Dee Harkey, a wiry little puncher with bright blue eyes, a long

[7] A. P. Black, as cited.
[8] Stem Daugherty to J. E. H., February 29, 1944. This suburb of Carlsbad is not to be confused with the present town of the same name in the Pecos Valley. See W. A. Keleher's splendid book, *The Fabulous Frontier* (Santa Fé, 1945), for a sketch of Hagerman and his work.
[9] Black and Harkey, as cited. Walker Bush walked into a religious meeting at Hamilton wearing a six-shooter. He was tried and convicted of disturbing worship, but the higher court, in a discriminating opinion, reasoned that he had made no demonstration with his gun and freed him. *Texas Appeals Reports*, Vol. II. He is reputed to have dabbled as a lawyer at Sweetwater before going on to New Mexico, and some say he turned to the ministry in Arizona.

nose, and bat-wing ears, from the Atascosa River in Texas. When he and another cowboy, Hall Herring, walked into a restaurant soon after Harkey's arrival, Herring pointed to a prosperous gentleman at the counter and inquired, "Don't you know old Martin M'Rose? That's him. Come out here, shot a fellow's head off, got rich and important."

Harkey walked up to his early apprentice in a cow camp, and during their visit inquired, "How in the hell, Martin, did you ever accumulate all this property?"

They were bold and honest thieves and the answer was not surprising: "I jes' went up the trail for old mans Eddy," he said benignly in his broken English, "an' when we gets to Dodge City, I had more cattles dan Eddy did."

His profession was common talk, for Charles Ballard, an old-timer in the Valley, recalls that when once a jovial crew rode by an old discarded stove grate on the trail near Roswell, some wag pointed it out to say, "Why, there's Martin M'Rose's stamp iron."[10]

It was an apt comparison, for M'Rose called his brand the "golden ladder," a latticework on rawhide that could be made to cancel out any angular brand. Simply on the face of it, a man branding a ladder in the West was always open to suspicion. And this ladder iron, suggestive of a stove grate, kept canceling out other people's brands, to M'Rose's golden profit, until those tolerant Texans who had settled the Pecos could no longer stand his prosperity.[11]

Although Eddy County had been organized, Dee Harkey says that most of the citizens were outlaws and thieves. But some respectable few succeeded in getting him appointed Deputy United States marshal, and J. C. Loving, of the Texas Cattle Raisers Association, hired him to put a damper on rustling. The thieves held a meeting in the Tansill Building in Eddy and,

[10] C. J. Ballard to J. E. H. and Hervey Chesley, June 9, 1939; D. R. Harkey to J. E. H. and Hervey Chesley, February 24, 1945; Edgar Harral to the same, June 13, 1939.

[11] Harkey, as cited. Bob Beverly recalls that his cow brand was Ladder 7; his horse brand the "Fiddle Case," "which you can see would cover a lot of other people's brands." Beverly to J. E. H., May 11, 1944.

with Martin M'Rose as spokesman, Vic Queen, the sheriff, and nearly everybody else in attendance, called Harkey over for a conference.

"Dees," Martin said, "we want to make you a proposition. We have all got rich. Deres nothin' out here but dese big cattle ranches and big foreign companies. We pay you as much money as de Association and brand you a thousand calves a year if you let us alone."

"Martin," began Dee Harkey distinctly and slowly, "I wouldn't accept your proposition; can't do it anyway. But I will tell you what I will do. You have told me about your stealing; how you got this money and all that damn stuff.[12] I am going to take this job, and if you fellows will stop stealing, and you who are renegades will quit—and half of you are—then I will forget the past and we will start over from here."

But Martin M'Rose, Vic Queen, Tom Finnessy, and their twenty-five to thirty confederates would not agree. Instead, M'Rose and Queen went over to the nearby VVN's and stole a bunch of horses. Harkey filed on them, and they left for parts unknown "before God could get the news."

M'Rose headed east across eighty miles of sagebrush, shinnery, and sand to the Half-Circle 84 headquarters of that old Texas trail-man, Jim Daugherty, on Monument Draw. Leaving his horses there, he rode into Midland with Stem Daugherty to meet a voluptuous blonde with "big, baby-blue eyes," whom he had met and married at the sheriff's whore-house at Eddy. She had come up with a tiny baby from down in Texas, had improved her estate by marrying M'Rose, and by arrangement was staging her way to Pecos to take the train to Midland. M'Rose, as a fugitive, was taking the safer horseback course of 150 or so miles across the open range.

The $6,000 in cash that he carried was more than he wished to risk on the dodge. So leaving $2,500 with Daugherty and giving him a bill of sale to his horses, M'Rose met his wife at Midland and, as unobtrusively as a man with an attractive

[12] "Stuff" is generic for cattle—"dry stuff," "fat stuff," "good stuff," "poor stuff" are all stuff out West.

blonde in a hot-blooded environment can, caught the train for El Paso and crossed into Mexico to join Finnessy and Queen, where he hoped to buy a ranch.[13]

Then the news that he was wanted, with a heavy reward for his capture, reached El Paso, and through Jeff's intercession with the Mexican officers, Queen and M'Rose were arrested, April 6, 1895, and thrown in the Juárez *juzgado*.[14]

In the meantime J. D. Walker had become sheriff at Eddy and with Dee Harkey, of the Cattle Raisers Association, began working on their extradition. On May 1 the *El Paso Times* reported that the governor of Chihuahua had granted it, and predicted their removal by Sheriff Walker and George W. Baylor, veteran captain of the Texas Rangers. Then Walker began getting telegrams from M'Rose and Queen saying that they were coming back to kill him.[15] Fearing they might and being jealous of Harkey's unofficial position, besides, Walker dillydallied in the fight for extradition. Harkey claims that this gave "General" Gene Mackenzie, a friend of M'Rose and a prominent cowman from the Monument Draw involved in range troubles there, time to reach Juárez by way of Midland and, with $4,000 judiciously distributed, effect their release by "fixing" the officials.

"All hell," Harkey conservatively observed, "couldn't get 'em out of Mexico then."[16]

Negotiation knows no end, however, in Mexico. It went on and on, to help drag John Wesley Hardin, the greatest gunman, and George Scarborough, one of the best officers of the time, into this tangled web of intrigue and passion.

Jeff had known Scarborough as a cowpuncher in the Fort

[13] A. P. Black, one of his cowboy associates in New Mexico, heard that he had $15,000. MS, as cited; Harkey and Daugherty, as cited.

[14] The *El Paso Times*, April 24, 1895, somewhat reviewed the case. D. R. Harkey to J. E. H. and Hervey Chesley, February 24, 1945.

[15] It was reported in El Paso that M'Rose foiled the efforts toward removal by swearing allegiance to Mexico, though the Mexican consul later denied that he had taken out papers. Harkey, as cited. *El Paso Times*, May 1 and July 2, 1895.

[16] The story of "the Mackenzie War," as it is still called in the Pecos country, while tying in with the trouble on the Pecos, is a separate saga. Beverly, as cited. B. A. Oden to J. E. H., February 27, 1944; Harkey, as cited. Milton once observed that extradition failed because of faulty preparation of the papers. *El Paso Times*, June 30, 1895.

Griffin country in the seventies. He was the son of a Baptist minister, a popular, forceful young man handling hot disputes over burned and blurred brands on the Brazos in the middle eighties, renowned sheriff of Jones County later, and now was eagerly sniffing the air for troubled spots in Paso del Norte. Of medium height and build, ruddy, healthy complexion, clear and quick blue eyes, rather prominent teeth but determined mouth, he lusted for the worst that walked and hoped they would go for their guns. M'Rose had the name of being tough and hard. So Scarborough wanted M'Rose and he wanted him bad.

During this period,however, El Paso had gotten fed up on reform. Mayor Bob Johnson, the Democrat, had resigned, Floyd Payne had served in the interim, and an election,[17] much like those Jeff had witnessed in Tucson, had been held. The night before, the rival parties scoured the town for Mexican voters, gathering them where they could find them and taking them in charge. The Democrats dropped their captives into a large cellar near the depot, stocked with food and liquor. The Republicans shamelessly herded theirs into a corral they had erected on El Paso Street out of 1" by 12's". But with diabolical device the Democrats slipped some spies into the rival bull pen. Just before daylight these saboteurs pried a board off the back side, paid some extra money to these "qualified voters," and before the Republicans knew it had deposited about a hundred head of them safely in their cellar. Such stealing of votes, of course, was dirty politics, and the Democrats did not deserve to win. And with the stigma of reform, they did not.

Republican candidate R. F. Campbell, nicknamed "Poker Bob,"[18] was elected mayor, April 9, 1895, over Charles F. Slack,

[17] W. Floyd Payne to J. E. H., February 28, 1944; *El Paso Times*, March 31, 1895.

[18] The *St. Louis Republic* had so alluded to him when he was an applicant for collector of customs, suit for libel had been filed, and the Burgeses had represented the defendant. The paper was technically in error, for the article said he was "indicted for keeping a gambling house," when he had been "charged" with doing so. Suit was settled for $1,000 damages, a bad jack pot for such big game. W. H. Burges to J. E. H., as cited; Richard Burges to J. E. H., and Hervey Chesley, December 19, 1938.

and next day the *Times* recorded that Chief Milton "was con-
gratulated on all sides for the admirable manner in which he
preserved the peace." Also it went on to note that: "Constable
Selman says that the highest price bid for a vote yesterday was
$1 and that he bid that amount because a preacher had offered
50 cents for the vote."

The *Times* continued its support of Milton, but the people
of El Paso, fed up on reform, called for a change. Campbell was
rumored to favor Colonel Ed M. Fink for chief of police, a man
Jeff had fired off the force, and the *Times* regretted that " . . . this
is a clear indication that El Paso is to lose the most efficient officer
and fearless chief of police she has ever had."[19]

But Jeff got another chance. The official fixers called on him
to say that he could keep his job, with much better pay, if he
would go along with them and throw the town wide open. They
got their answer at once.

"Boys, I can't play hot and cold the same day. I don't want
the job."

Late in April, Campbell announced Fink's appointment, and
Jeff left on a trip to Chihuahua City with United States Consul
Buford, apparently on the M'Rose matter. His enemies started
the rumor that he had left town to evade indebtedness, but to
their consternation he was back in a few days and hot on their
trail.[20]

The gambling halls opened at once with refurbished splen-
dor, and the *Times* of May 2, observed that "El Paso is no longer
bad medicine. Last night a quiet game was opened in the Gem
Building." The most notable reaction came from John Wesley
Hardin.

When the news reached him, he hunted Jeff up to inquire,
"Chief, are you going out of office?"

"Ya-s-s," Jeff answered.

"You wouldn't bother nobody in town?"

"I certainly wouldn't."

"I'll have mine tonight," said Hardin gaily.

[19] *El Paso Times*, April 25, 1895.
[20] *Ibid.*, May 9, 1895.

He went to the club room—the gambling hall above the Gem Saloon—that night, and began to play. After losing a lot of money, he whipped out his six-shooter, scooped up everything on the table and what was in the bank, and walked off with it. Then, hoping somebody had resented his high-handed action, he walked back to challenge anyone who did "not like his play" to trot out, and, as a witness testified next morning in court, "As no one trotted out I guess they liked the play."[21]

The whole thing was so amusing to Jeff as to be "plumb reedic'lous," but it was not so to official El Paso. City Attorney Burges agreed to prosecute the high-handed action if anybody could be found who would file the complaint. Justice of the Peace W. D. Howe, an observer at the Gem, said he would do so, and the warrant went to Sheriff Frank Simmons for service.[22] Simmons hunted up Jeff and asked if he would make the arrest.

"Certainly," he said, taking the writ. Upon finding Hardin, he advised, "Hardin, I have a warrant for you."

Hardin looked a little surprised, answering, "Milton, I thought you had quit the business."

Jeff admitted that he had but said he was serving the warrant just to accommodate his friend, the sheriff.

"Do you want to go with me?" he interrogated, getting back to business.

"Sure, I'll go with you," agreed the gunman. "But how about my pistol?"

"You will have to take it off," advised Jeff.

"If anything starts, can I reach and get it?" asked Hardin, with the eternal suspicion of the hunted man as natural as his breath of life. Jeff assured him that he could as he stuck the six-shooter in his belt opposite his own. And Hardin, knowing that he meant it, followed him off to the justice court, where Burges pressed the complaint. The office was full of fighting men, and the observant Burges, in passing, told Howe that they were the only ones present who had not killed some men. Undeterred by that, however, for the boldest of all was his own warm friend,

21 *Ibid.*, May 16, 1895.
22 W. H. Burges to J. E. H., August 5, 1939.

Burges filed on Hardin on three counts: gambling in a public place, display of firearms, and robbery with firearms—the last a capital offense and not subject to bond. Burges just knew he would at least land John Wesley in jail.[23]

But he reckoned not with El Paso's tolerant nature. Hardin was released on a writ of *habeas corpus* on a $100 bond, and eventually fined $25 for carrying a gun. He was still well ahead in the Gem game.[24] Hardin's plea in defense had been that he might be attacked any day by Martin M'Rose and his men.

Although he always had a gun, the peculiar plea that Hardin had made was now a substantially valid one. From being an outlaw's lawyer he had progressed, through the amorous intrusion of passion, into an open, acknowledged consort of Martin M'Rose's wife. While M'Rose was in jail in Juárez, she apparently had sought his defense by Hardin, and Hardin's little "serpentine eyes" had appraised her personal appeal and sinuous carriage approvingly. He was immediately retained, body if not soul. For him it was simply too good to be true. She was blessed with Martin's money, fair looks and voluptuous flesh, and the wayward spirit that first brought her west. It was illicit love made to order. Hardin warmed up to her but cooled off on M'Rose, who could fume and swear in Juárez, while he enjoyed himself in El Paso with the deference due the greatest gunman of all. Well, almost, but not quite. The Texas frontier was downright irreverent of fame. Greatness with guns was always subject to dispute.

Even before Jeff's dismissal as chief of police, the tensions of the M'Rose matter were drawing the nerves of them all to a bloody showdown. M'Rose and Queen had been reinforced by the fighting Finnessy, Sam Kaufman, a man named Lightfoot, and another friend. They just stayed there, strong in numbers, courageous individually, and immune to removal. M'Rose's money was in his wife's hands in El Paso, and her fickle affections were now lavished on Hardin. And M'Rose, quite naturally,

[23] *Ibid.*

[24] *El Paso Times*, May 17, 1895. The newspaper tells of the complaint and fine; the details of arrest are from Milton; the other from Burges, as cited.

237

was boiling to kill him, but deterred by the double hazard of death or capture at the hands of Milton and Scarborough.

Sometime earlier a Santa Fé detective, lured by the reward, tried to induce M'Rose across by assuring him of official protection. Then he gumshoed his way over to the Chief of Police to get him to go in on the scheme, for M'Rose had said, "If the Chief will give me his word that I won't be bothered, I'll come over."

"Nothin' doin'," snorted Jeff. "If M'Rose crosses the river, I'll catch him or I'll kill him."

"Why, won't you frame a fellow to catch him?" complained the detective, impatiently.

"I'm not in that kind o' business," said Jeff. "That wouldn't be fair. When I give a man my word, I carry it out." And the detective left in high dudgeon.

Then in order to keep M'Rose and Queen from suffering any misapprehension, Jeff sought them out at a saloon in Juárez and told them where he stood. "If you cross the line, you're mine, certain!"

This talk soured on the sensitive stomach of big, bluff Vic Queen, who bruited it about the dives of Juárez that he wanted to "smoke up" Milton and Scarborough. Borders are never barriers to incendiary talk, and of course it came to Jeff. He suggested to George that they go over the river to see them. That sounded like the stuff to him.

"We'll just start something ourselves," he said, "and then kill them all."

"No, George," Jeff overruled. "No use of us startin' anything; we'll just go over and let them start it."

They set off on their zestful mission, found the New Mexico gang in a saloon, and walked in on them with Jeff's pleasant but significant greeting, "Hello, fellers! Understand you been wantin' to see us!"

They certainly had, they assured them cordially, invited them to a social drink, and battle at once died a-borning. But the deadly subtle significance of the call was not wasted on M'Rose and his men.

By this time Wes Hardin was openly anxious and enlisted in

238

the attempts to get M'Rose removed from the scene and safely out of the way. The legal way of course—and Hardin was even willing to resort to that—was to effect his extradition into the anxious hands of the cowmen of New Mexico.

On a Sunday evening late in April, 1895, John Wesley was making his way down a Juárez street with his mind on anything but the Lord's business when he ran into Finnessy, Lightfoot, and other friends of M'Rose, who tried to badger him into a fight. Hardin knew enough to know that these veterans of the Billy the Kid tradition were not to be taken lightly, and he let the goading pass, "though they grew quite saucy in their talk" to this man who boasted that he "took no sass but sassparilla."

To add outright insult to injury, they wrote him, he claimed, telling "him that he would never be allowed to get M'Rose to this side of the river and that he had better make himself scarce in Juarez."[25] Which was not only "saucy talk" but "sass" compounded with contempt.

Hardin just had to go back to Juárez. The odds were definitely against him. But a heavy reward was on Queen and M'Rose, and Jeff and Scarborough still wanted them. Again the two were in Juárez together, and when passing Deiter and Sauer's saloon, at the corner where the streetcar turned and disgorged thirsty and adventuresome Americans for years, they met Hardin and one of his friends. Hardin invited them in for a drink. They passed the bar to the privacy of the room for parties in the rear— Jeff rather suspected by prearrangement between Scarborough and Hardin—to walk in on five of the band in animated talk with Mrs. M'Rose.[26] Jeff thought to himself, "This looks like business; better keep an eye on your gun."

But, as the *Times* next day recorded, "to have backed out of the room would have looked like retreat, so the four friends entered, saluted and took seats. The conversation soon became general. M'Rose's case was brought up and hot words passed between Hardin and Finnessy. Both men sprang to their feet.

25 *El Paso Times*, April 24, 1895.

26 Among these were Tom Finnessy, Vic Queen, Sam Kaufman, a man named Lightfoot, and an unidentified other. Who was with Hardin is not known. *El Paso Times*, April 24, 1895.

239

In an instant Mr. Hardin had slapped Finnessy's face and had his gun at his breast. In another instant Finnessy would have been a dead man, but quick as thought Chief Milton grasped the pistol and was struggling with Mr. Hardin. In the meantime the two gentlemen who accompanied Chief Milton and Mr. Hardin had the M'Rose party covered. At the request of the Chief, Mr. Hardin returned his pistol to his pocket; but his blood pressure was up and remembering the occurrence of Sunday night, he walked up to Lightfoot and gave him a slap in the face that could be heard for a block. Chief Milton, as cool as if he had just stepped out of a bath, placed his back to the door of the room and stated it was best to settle the little trouble right there and then if it was to have a continuance."[27]

But no one dropped his hand to open the ball, and another incipient battle had passed.

Jeff went back and hunted up Will Burges.

"We are booked for trouble with Hardin," he stated and told him the story of Hardin and Finnessy. "It was perfectly evident to my mind," he said, "that Hardin was trying to pick a row, and I decided I'd stand on my feet, so if I had to act, I could act as quick as anybody, I was wrong about part of it.

"Hardin is the fastest thing I ever saw in my life with a gun. There is nobody that is a match for him as far as that is concerned. Before I could get my gun, he had pulled his and had it in Finnessy's belly."[28]

He left Burges a little gloomy, for, he thought, "if Milton wouldn't have any chance with Hardin, nobody would." He was thinking, of course, of a good straight fight, and not of the perfidy of Old John Selman.

Thus the attempts to capture Martin M'Rose rocked dangerously into the summer of 1895. Scarborough, however, was busy, and on the night of June 29 told Jeff and Ranger Frank M. Mc-Mahon, his brother-in-law, that M'Rose was to meet him that

[27] *Ibid.*

[28] W. H. Burges to Hervey Chesley, March 10, 1938, with this correction: Judge Burges thought that Hardin had struck Queen.

night on the Mexican Central Railroad bridge, and for them to be near the end on the Texas side. They were there. At 11:30, out of the dusky obscurity that was night on the mountain range in Mexico, two darker spots took form as Scarborough and M'Rose. Jeff and McMahon rose up to take M'Rose, but at their order, "Throw up your hands," he went for his gun and opened fire on Scarborough. Jeff shot him down with his Colt .45, but M'Rose, a powerful man in his prime, got up from the ground and shot again. Scarborough, too, was in action.

"M'Rose was the only case I have ever known," recalled Will Burges, "where a man was shot through the heart, got back up, and shot again, himself." Justice W. D. Howe performed the inquest and found only two bullet holes, "one through the heart, and the other right close—through the pericardium."[29]

Vic Queen afterwards had the audacity to write Judge W. D. Howe that he was across the river with a rifle at the moment, and had he known what had happened, he would have smoked the whole bunch out. But he did not know until the next morning when the papers were out with a lurid account of the death of M'Rose, "the outlaw" who "met his end . . . riddled but died

[29] W. H. Burges to J. E. H., January 24, 1945; W. D. Howe to J. E. H. and Hervey Chesley, December 20, 1939.

game . . . pierced by eight bullets. Some of the wounds were made by pistol balls and some by buckshot." His six-shooter, still cocked, was picked up from beside his body.[30]

Jeff, Scarborough, and McMahon were placed under arrest. Jeff called Burges, who went down, arranged their bond of $500 for appearance before the grand jury, and observed that Jeff was not nervous or concerned at all.

At the hearing next day Scarborough took the blame for the killing, while the local papers noted that M'Rose "had made several threats that he would kill John Wesley Hardin," but had been afraid to cross the river for fear the officers would get him. Scarborough said that he had been in touch with M'Rose for a month; that he had talked with him in Juárez on the twenty-fourth of June; that he had delivered a message to "a party" in El Paso whom M'Rose wished to meet; that the party refused; and that the trip last night was planned.[31]

Now whether Scarborough enticed him across to appeal to his wayward blonde, or whether he came to battle with Hardin, is a matter of speculation. Burges said he was baited with the hope of killing Hardin, although it could easily have been both. In his pocket was a letter addressed to "Miss Beula M'Rose."

In his statement, Milton reviewed the fact that he, "a special ranger" of the state of Texas, had originally effected the capture of M'Rose through the Mexican officers, that he had a warrant for his arrest, that Scarborough had notified him that he was coming over, and that they had called in McMahon in the hope that the desperate man would give up without a fight against their superior numbers.

And while the body lay on a cooling board in the Star Stable Undertaking Establishment, outraged Vic Queen shot a verbal broadside across the river, claiming that Scarborough had followed a "systematic course of deception to inveigle Martin M'Rose . . . across . . . on the pretense of getting a division of the community property his wife had in her possession." Scarborough, he claimed, represented that she was ready to divide

[30] *El Paso Times,* June 30, 1895.
[31] *Ibid.*

the money. M'Rose's friends had urged him not to go but he slipped out and "kept his ill-fated appointment."[32]

For Milton, McMahon, and Scarborough, it was an old story in the thankless job of the enforcement of the law. With that peculiarly American perversity for the repudiation of courageous duty, "public opinion condemned the killing," and "the talk of the town was against them." They were indicted but released on bail. Yet, on the other hand, "not a soul accompanied the hearse to the cemetery." When it got there, a callous couple was waiting to see the box go into the ground—one through unfeeling serpentine orbs, and the other with mixed emotions that spoke silently and a little fearfully from "big, baby-blue eyes."[33]

But the plan to rob the Sunset Line "on this side" that night was buried, too. Queen was eventually killed near Silver City, and M'Rose's faithful men scattered with the western winds.

Not so his wanton wife. She and Hardin stayed on, a little uneasily, and with more frequent resort to the unstable diversion induced by drink. His landlady, who felt her "very bones chill" when he looked at her with his "darting, serpentine eyes," noted that he carried his whiskey up by the gallon, "and at all hours of the day and night" she could hear the rattle of his spoon "stirring his toddy." She noticed, too, with the inquisitive eyes that landladies develop, that he paced the floor more nervously than of old, and that he practiced his draw continually with his two double-action .41 Colts.

"I have seen him unload his guns," she said later, "put them in his pocket, walk across the room and then suddenly spring to one side, facing around and as quick as a flash he would have a gun in each hand clicking so fast that the clicks sounded like a rattle machine. He showed me how he once killed two men in that way. They demanded his guns and he extended them, one in each hand, he holding the muzzle as if to surrender, and when the men reached for the guns he tossed the pistols over, catching the handles, and killed both men while their hands were ex-

[32] *Ibid.* The prejudicial point in the case was the obvious fact that Scarborough had tolled M'Rose across the river.

[33] *El Paso Times,* June 30, 1895.

tended for the weapons." That was the way he took Wild Bill Hickok by surprise.[34]

Not only was he continually practicing his draw and drinking heavily, but, as is characteristic in such relations, he was having trouble with Mrs. M'Rose. She swore out a warrant for him because, she claimed, he not only threatened to kill her, but, she told the landlady, "he had forced me to write a letter saying that I had committed suicide."

So Hardin was again arrested and again released on bond. He was surly as an old bear, however, and intimated that he was out of sorts with Scarborough, and had something to tell about the killing of M'Rose.[35] The town was an armed camp and momentarily expected trouble. Daily young Richard Burges and his associates trotted out to the mesa, back of town, for extended pistol practice on the prickly-pear leaves, anticipating that final homicidal mania so often the upshot of reform.

But Jeff Milton, not a reformer by nature, keeping largely to himself and tending strictly to his own business, went serenely on his way until he received a note in a feminine hand warning him not to pass the plaza on a certain day. The implication was that Hardin would kill him if he did. He not only passed it frequently on the anticipated fatal day, but he spent at least half his time in the park on a bench "waiting for the fun to start." But a little regretfully he recalled "it never did."

It seems entirely human for men of diabolical depravity to hate and hold in contempt those of courage and integrity. Hence it is not surprising to find Wes Hardin, his arrogant blood running strong with the additional stimulus of liquor, boasting about El Paso that he had hired Milton and Scarborough to kill M'Rose so that he could get his woman. It was a dangerous blunder.

Jeff caught Hardin in front of Con Ryan's Parlor Saloon that night, dangerous and duly sober. Hardin stood, back to the wall when Jeff came up with death in his hot black eyes. Will Burges and others, who had heard the story, watched at a respectful distance.

[34] *Ibid.*, August 23, 1895; *Life of John Wesley Hardin,* as cited.
[35] *El Paso Times*, August 7 and 23, 1895.

"Hardin, I understand you told Captain Carr that you hired me to kill M'Rose so you could get his woman," Jeff began, quietly. "I told them you're a goddamned liar and I've come to get you to tell them the same." Hardin straightened up, said Burges, "as if ice water had been thrown in his face, and a nervous twitching showed in his features."

"Why, Captain Milton," he answered, "I don't let any man talk to me that-a-way."

"I'm telling you that," said Milton, "in fighting talk. If you don't like it, help yourself. But you're going to do it."

"I don't want to have any trouble with you," countered Hardin.

"Well, you took a damned poor way to keep from it," said Milton.

"You're armed, and I'm not," parried Hardin.

"Oh, yes, you are. You're always armed."

"No, I'm not," he said, lying again.

"I know better," said Milton. "But it's only two blocks to your room, and if you want another gun, go get it. I'll be right here when you come back, and when you come, come a-fighting." Again Hardin contended that he wanted no trouble.

"The trouble with you, Hardin," Milton continued, "is that your nerve's failed you. You're not only a goddamned liar; you're a goddamned lying son-of-a-bitch, and you are now going to tell these gentlemen you are."

"Gentlemen, when I said that, I was drinking."

But Milton, in an entirely different tone of voice, the last word, posing death for Hardin, said, "That don't go. Tell them you were a goddamned liar when you said you hired me to kill M'Rose."

And Hardin, fearing for once he could not beat his antagonist to the draw, knuckled down, "Gentlemen, when I said that, I was a goddamned liar," and then let his voice trail off in a mumbling.

"Dry up. I don't want to hear anything more from you," said Milton, turning on his heel and walking straight off up the street. Burges, with his Prince Albert tails flapping off his own six-shooter protruding from his striped pants, fell in with him. Without

245

a word they stepped into the entrance to the stair to Burges's office, where Jeff stopped, leaned against the wall, and smilingly said, "Now don't that beat hell. I wouldn't have believed it was possible. Believe I'll go home and go to bed." And the admiring Burges followed suit.[36]

Unfortunately for the frail of the human race, fortitude for life never comes capped in bottles. Yet the substitute is eternally and understandably tried when courage falters, and memory is momentarily drowned in drink. It is often the last resort of souls in dire distress. Hardin's mistress got drunk and made a gunplay of her own in the middle of town. Wes was away, and Young John Selman, still on the police force, arrested her. Upon his return Hardin was furious, and upon meeting Old John gave him a thorough cussing for having sired such a contemptible son. John, too slow on the draw for the peerless Hardin, let the insult pass. But with a reputation built high on a stack of dead men of his own, and jealous of the greater glory of Hardin, he nursed his resentment with a little liquor just to keep it warm.[37]

At this time Hardin was prepossessed with that powerful urge that frequently falls on the truly great to recall the past in reminiscence. He, too, was writing a book, with an obvious advantage over many who do, in that he really had a tale to tell. His landlady, torn between a dust rag and a meddlesome mind, kept pace with his gory progress, firing questions at this border Benvenuto as she stirred the dust in his room.

"What are you doing now," she quipped one morning with the easy familiarity born of knowing too much of what goes on in a boardinghouse, "telling how you killed a man or stole a horse?"

Now authors are strangely human, and, complimented by the interest of a prospective reader, Hardin answered that he

[36] W. H. Burges to J. E. H., August 6, 1939; W. D. Howe as cited; Richard Burges to J. E. H., December 19, 1938; El Paso Times, August 7, 1895; and Cunningham's *Triggernometry*, 61. Milton casually alluded to the incident, very lightly, for "'twa'n't nothing to it."

[37] John Selman, Jr., in his article, "John Selman," *All Western Magazine*, November, 1895, 55–56, tells of the episode, which is touched upon, too, by the El Paso papers after Hardin's death.

was just then engaged in stealing a horse. But that reminded him that there was just one more man who lived near by and who had helped in the "lynching" of his brother Joe years ago, at Comanche, whom he really wanted to kill.[38]

He practiced his famous draw long and daily. No one ever entered his room and found him sitting; he was up, on his feet and ready for action. But instead of the hundred-dollar bill that he usually carried in the empty chamber beneath the hammer of his Colt .41, Jeff said, he now had it stuffed with a five-hundred-dollar note. He seemed to be heading for the showdown. He put Mrs. M'Rose on the train and billed her for Phoenix, but she stopped off at Deming and with deadly premonition wired, "I feel that you are in trouble and I'm coming back."[39]

Although he carried liquor to his room by the gallon, it should be remembered that there must be a powerful spiritual stimulus to real literature. His story grew with his restless pacing of the floor far into the night and the tinkle of his spoon as he stirred his toddy. The only evidence of excessive drink, however, was his "extreme politeness and the peculiar snake-like glitter of his eyes." Old Wes approached the peak of his story and immortality with proper fervor. On the morning of the nineteenth of August, 1895, he told a friend that, with 350 hand-written pages, his opus would be done the next day.

That night he walked into the virtually empty Acme Saloon, raised his left foot in familiar posture on the rail, dropped his chin in his left palm, supported by his elbow bent on the bar, and began rolling dice with the tender, Henry Brown, for a quarter a throw. Hardin shook first and tossed the ivories out.

"Four sixes to beat," he said, as Brown picked up the dice.

Just then the carefully elusive figure of Old John Selman eased in at the swinging doors behind him and cut loose with his .45. Hardin slid to the floor while Selman still pumped in the

[38] This was obviously Jailer J. C. Jones, of El Paso. *El Paso Times*, August 23, 1895. "A nobler man never lived than my brother, Joe," Hardin said. When infuriated citizens dragged him out of jail and hanged him, they went to his room and found it replete with equipment for forging and aging land papers. James Bonner to Hervey Chesley, 1932.

[39] *El Paso Times*, August 20, 1895.

247

lead. Captain Frank Carr, of the police force, was there in a few minutes "after the shooting and he found two guns, Colts forty-ones, but . . . no sign of the mail shirt" Hardin was rumored to wear. And the writer for the *Times*, aware that the hardened Selman was still alive, gave him that partisan portrayal now known as "a good press," saying, "The first shot did the work. It entered the eye and came out at the back of the head."[40]

Justice W. D. Howe was called for the inquest. Jeff went down for a last look at Hardin, who, with forty-odd notches on his guns, was now comfortably dead in the middle of the Acme floor. His ready eye saw where the bullet had hit. At a table near by sat Selman, wearing a comical little hat, sweating like an Alabama Negro on election day and receiving the acclaim of the mob. Extending a nervous paw to Jeff, he said, "Shake hands with me, Cap, I've killed the son-of-a-bitch. I shot him right in the eye."

"I don't mix with a murderer," said Milton with contempt. "You shot that feller right in the back of the head. You can't shake hands with me, certain!"

Next day the *Times* revised its original report. Selman was arrested, but his attorney, Charlie de Pat, got him out on $10,000 bond, while the preliminary hearing was full of ghastly humor resulting from release of the tension.[41]

The police force breathed a sigh of relief, and the *Times* editorialized on the "climate," claiming that the reputation of the town "as a health resort is already firmly established."

But when George H. Higgins, an Episcopal minister trans-mogrified into a homeopathic surgeon, was put on the stand after examining the corpse, to determine if it was really murder, if Hardin was really shot in the back of the head or in the eye, he sounded the humorous good sense of the whole town.

"If he was shot in the eye," came his conditional answer, "I'd say it was excellent marksmanship. If he was shot in the back of the head, then I'd say it was excellent judgment."[42]

[40] *Ibid.*
[41] *El Paso Times*, August 21, 1895.
[42] W. H. Burges to J. E. H., August 6, 1939; Richard Burges, as cited; *El Paso Times*, August 21, 1895.

Selman strutted his stuff after Milton was gone, but Scarborough was still on hand. Young John was thrown in jail in Juárez charged with white slavery, although he contended that he wanted to marry the girl. Old John raised a racket in trying to get him out, and then returned to El Paso to bump into Scarborough on the night of April 5, 1896.

"George, I want you to go across the river with me in the morning to see John," Selman said as they walked toward the back door of the Wigwam Saloon. "We must get the boy out of jail."

"All right, Uncle John, I'll go with you," Scarborough testified to saying, "but there must be no play like you made over there yesterday, as that does harm."

Selman disliked to be crossed, but Scarborough had the reputation of a great fighter, and in spite of his friendly manner, said Jeff, "Old John just wanted to kill him for reputation."

They walked out of the back door of the Wigwam, Selman dropping his left arm around the marshal's shoulder—thus figuring on having him at too close quarters for Scarborough to use his right—and drew with his own right hand to take him. But Scarborough was too wise and quick for that, and Selman, shot three times, went down himself in the alley back of the Wigwam. The case against Selman for the killing of Hardin was still pending, the *Times* recorded, "when Scarborough's bullet transferred it to a higher court."[43] And Old John really faced the bar of final judgment with trepidation, said Jeff, for before he died, "he just prayed to beat the band. Said he hadn't been a bad man, and told God all about it."

Scarborough said his first shot knocked Selman down, but he got back up, and he shot him twice more. Selman's gun was not found, leading to the illogical, sentimental conclusion that he was not armed when killed.[44]

He "had met the same fate as all bad men who come to El Paso looking for a fight," the *Times*, with unwarranted smug-

[43] *Ibid.*, April 7, 1896.
[44] The gun was later found. W. H. Burges, as cited; *El Paso Times*, April 5–7, 1896; *El Paso Herald*, April 6, 1896.

ness, observed. And though all hands heaved another sigh of relief, they agreed with Richard Burges that they "had never experienced a more interesting time" than this, when, in the idiom of the cotton patch the "bad men thinned one another to a stand."[45]

Jeff had already gone west to work for Wells Fargo. But he, Scarborough, and McMahon were still under indictment for the murder of M'Rose, and the district attorney, catering to the rougher elements, was continuing the case just to chouse them around. Then John Dean, Jeff's friend and hot-blooded prosecutor from the Fort Davis country, came into office, announced ready for trial, and Judge Falvey called the case on April 28, 1897.

W. H. Burges, for the defense, had been ready for two years, though a little uncertain of the public reaction until Charlie Newman, a willing witness, appeared at his office. He was an employee at the station on the Stanton Street Bridge, just up the river from the Mexican Central on which M'Rose had crossed. He had stepped out on the dump in the dark that night, just happened to be facing the scene of the shooting when it started, and told Burges he had seen the first flash, "which came from the side next to the river." Thus M'Rose had undoubtedly fired first, which, with Milton's warrant, said Burges, left "no question of his right to kill him." And so Burges had pressed for trial at once.[46]

On the stand, Jeff, of course, admitted the killing.

"Did you have a warrant for M'Rose?" he was asked.

"Yes, sir," came the answer.

"Where is it?"

"Down in the vault of the bank."

Judge Falvey dismissed him to get it. Upon his return, Falvey looked it over, turned to the jury, and instructed its verdict: "Not guilty."[47]

[45] Richard Burges, as cited, February 29, 1944.
[46] W. H. Burges to J. E. H., January 24, 1945.
[47] Criminal Cases, 1902, 1903; District Court Minutes, El Paso County, VIII, 453, 456, and 634; ibid., IX, 268–69.

Jeff walked out of the El Paso courthouse, left Texas, and headed farther west to where the worst outlaws still alive were giving Wells Fargo lots of trouble. His work was now with them, and he dismissed the M'Rose matter by saying, "I just went on about my business." Business for him was to take the trail of trouble.

17
Wells Fargo Agent

Soon after Milton left the office of chief of police, he became a deputy United States marshal under Dick Ware as well as a special Ranger of the state of Texas.[1] Ware's headquarters were in San Antonio and, with two such wheel horses at war as Milton and Scarborough, had little worry with the western end of Texas. Ware and Jeff had been friends since their Texas Ranger days; Jeff had helped cure him of a spell of rheumatism, with rattlesnake oil, and they were warm friends.[2] Together they carried shipments of federal prisoners to Detroit, Michigan, and to Ottumwa, Iowa, but the job paid little, and Jeff again headed west to work for Wells, Fargo & Co.

The company had found that he tended strictly to business, and that he could not be bought or scared. When he became chief of police in El Paso, the superintendent of the Southern Pacific had tried to pay him a bonus of $100 a month for special protection of their properties.

"Nothin' doing," he had answered, "the city pays me for that."

Such news as this gets around to substantial interests always looking for sturdy men. In 1895, when Wells Fargo had a shipment of several million dollars in gold for the West Coast, their El Paso agent asked him to get some extra guards and take it through. He refused the job if there were to be additional guards. He knew what he could do; he was not so sure about other men. The superintendent talked it over and agreed.

[1] *El Paso Times,* June 8, 1895.

[2] The Colorado City country was full of snakes in the early eighteen eighties. The Rangers skinned them, rendered the oil, and rubbed it in, after which the patient got "as limp as a dishrag" for about two weeks and then recovered. Of course the oil had done the work.

Jeff got some jugs of water, a sack of grub, and his bedroll and climbed aboard, armed with his rifle, six-shooter, and one of the semiautomatic shotguns he had bought for possible use on Hardin. He stayed with the gold night and day until it reached San Francisco, and nobody bothered it.

Then Wells Fargo offered him a job in Mexico City, and he went down to look it over. He found that it paid so little that he could not afford to take it, and returned to the states. Then Ed Crumb sent him a telegram offering him a job as a Wells Fargo messenger on the rail run from Benson, Arizona, through Nogales to Guaymas, on the west coast of Mexico. He took it.

He was not a shotgun messenger in the old sense of the stagecoach term, but he was express agent and guard combined, and subject to call to any point in the Southwest where trouble was brewing. He furnished his own shotgun, rifle, and six-shooter. He handled everything from crates of quinces to bars of silver and gold. He spent a lot of his time off the express car and in the saddle, hunting the highwaymen who swept in from the great ranges of southern New Mexico and Arizona to rob the Southern Pacific trains. In his eighties, when he had aged a little, he observed v   t a fool he had been—"riding and fighting for them all the time at eighty-five dollars a month." But the thought never occurred to him at thirty-five.

He and the other messengers could stop off only at the end of their runs. But the crew stopped the train on occasion at Santa Ana, in Mexico, where schedule was always subject to whim and change, locked up the cars, and went off to dance a pleasant hour with the girls before going on.

He placed a little stove in the express car so that he could cook his own meals and lived high off sacks of luscious Guaymas oysters and slabs of fish in season. He carried his cot and bedding, too. His cargoes were valuable ones, for the railroad tapped a mining country, and he was often loaded with gold and silver bars. The small gold bars were locked in the safe; the silver bars, from 50 to 150 pounds in size, were stacked against the wall. Once when he had them stacked high at the back end of the car and was sleeping on his cot directly in front of them, the train jumped the track and plowed into the ditch. The highest bars catapulted over him and went through the floor of the car. "Never touched me," he said. "Lucky, wa'n't it? But after that I stacked them in the front of the car."

He laid over a night at Nogales, his headquarters, at the end of every trip. He got a stable and corral for his beloved horses, always kept some dogs, and shared a room with the resident Wells Fargo agent, "a little mite of a man just five feet, six," William F. Overton, who endeared himself to Jeff because he was "one of the gentlest, nicest men—quiet and such a gentleman."

At the end of his run Jeff would dress in his best, slip his .45 in his waistband, drape a flowing cape across his broad shoulders, drop by the Bird residence to pick up his girl, and cut a handsome figure down Morley Avenue with Bess Emory daintily clinging to his arm. Such trips not only left other feminine hearts aflutter, but were of dire concern to the Nogales boys.

For the jovial Jeff, in his spare moments, was teaching them how to ride and shoot. From their elders they heard enough of his exploits to build him into a sturdy Scottish knight, a fabulous figure in that drab and dobe town. Thus they were greatly concerned over the fate of Milton, but only at the hands of a woman, and Allen T. Bird's boys scurried from the office of *The Oasis*, as Bird's weekly was called, to take their fears to their mother, hopeful of reassurance.

"Aw-w-w, I don't think she's good enough for Mr. Milton," they argued with their well-poised mother busy at her domestic chores, who countered with an irrefutable remark, "Why, I like Bess very much." But they would "a-w-w" again and go off to nurse their jealousy and their impatience with feminine indirection in disgust. They just knew it would ruin a dashing man like Milton to marry.[3] Then Charlie Marlowe, a child of six, burst back upon Mrs. Bird at her darning to declare, "Mrs. Bird, I think Tracy is going to be the bravest man in the world—just like Mr. Milton."

There was always something going on to brace him up. The

[3] Mrs. Allen T. Bird to J. E. H., November 18, 1945.

United States consul in Nogales, Sonora, was a fresh young fellow who once walked into the room at the Bird residence occupied by Bess and her friend, Mary Dow, while the two young ladies were still in bed. Jeff heard about it, collared the gentleman, took him to the house on pain of death, forced him to apologize on his knees for his boorishness, and advised him never to see them again. Liberty then certainly imposed personal responsibility, and Jeff was willing to see that it was carried out.

Unlike most of the settlements of that border region, Nogales was a new town. As the natural gateway for the traffic of the western slope from Mexico north, it came into important use with the completion of the railroad from Benson to Guaymas. In 1880, a Jewish peddler named Jacob Isaacson, with the keenly observant and aggressive nature of his race, loaded a wagon with goods and made his way up Nogales Creek, that natural pass into Mexico. He stopped at the border, along the survey of the New Mexico and Arizona Railway then projected south from Benson to meet the Sonora Railroad the Santa Fé system was pushing north from Guaymas. He opened a store in a dirt-roofed, dobe house fenced in with prickly *ocatillo* stalks, hung out the sign, "General Merchandise," and called the spot Isaacson.[4]

William Raymond Morley, chief engineer for the Santa Fé, moved his family by boat through Guaymas to Hermosillo, and pushed the construction from both ends of the line to complete it in 1882. When he was accidentally shot and killed next year while surveying the Mexican Central Railroad out of Chihuahua, the principal street that necessarily parallels the railroad, following the canyon, the length of the town that was now called Nogales, was named Morley Avenue in his honor.[5]

As already noted, the mining camp of Oro Blanco, seventy miles west, was the first substantial settlement in that direction

[4] *Douglas Dispatch*, January 22, 1910; *Nogales Herald*, February 14 and March 14, 1942.

[5] Morley was born in Springfield, Massachusetts, September 15, 1846 and died January 3, 1883. Mrs. Tom Reynolds to J. E. H., February 26, 1945; *Nogales Herald*, February 14, 1942. Agnes Morley Cleaveland, *No Life for a Lady* (Boston, 1941), 12–17, gives something of her father's background and work. H. H. Bancroft, *Arizona and New Mexico*, 604, notes the railroad development.

until the weary traveler reached Sonoita. Nearer was the mining camp of Duquesne, owned by Westinghouse, whose representative came from the East, Jeff recalled, about the time the social world was agog with the sparkling news that Lily Langtry, the lovely actress, had taken a bath in pure champagne.

This mining man, stimulated with the high, dry climate of southern Arizona and a proper amount of dry and ancient mescal, was not to be outdone. Disregarding the fact that outdoor men here accumulate nothing that soap and water will not cure, he boasted around Nogales: "By golly, if Lily Langtry can take a bath in champagne, I can, too." He bought up all the stuff in town, emptied it into a bathtub, and outdid Lily in everything but looks. Then, Jeff recalled, the Mexican and Negro help drank his champagne.

A number of noted characters lent color to the town. Johnnie Jund dispensed the oldest and finest liquors, domestic and imported, from a hole in the wall on the Sonora side that served as a saloon. He sometimes had $20,000 in cash in his safe, and bought his liquor by the carload from the States, shipped under bond for sale outside—and hence escaping the internal-revenue levy, His pet crow disturbed the neighborhood and stole every trinket lying loose about the town. Anything missed that the bird could carry was suspected of being cached on Johnnie Jund's premises. To add to the eerie appeal of his place, Jund kept a boa constrictor about eight feet long as a house snake—a reptile that insinuated its way into Johnnie's jovial company, and gave many a man a premature case of delirium tremens. Besides, he kept down the rats. No liquor found market at Johnnie's that was less than seven years old, and it went at fifteen cents a drink. No wonder old-timers recall Johnnie Jund.

M. M. Conn owned the Palace, also across the line, while Jack Gates owned a saloon on the States side. John M. Brickwood, an educated man who left the impression of having come West from better background, kept bar in a building built directly alongside the line. He kept his cigars in his window opening into Mexico, so that whoever bought them made his purchase from over in Mexico, and hence the sale was exempt from internal-

256

revenue tax on the American side. Likewise, his back door was a convenient exit for any elusive person anxious to step into another nation without being obvious.

Living there, too, was a German named William Schuster who had been president of Guatemala for a day. He had gone in by revolution and out the same way the following day. His principal business now was the promotion of mining and the drinking of liquor, and being the butt of the jokers as the "President of Guatemala." The contemporary history of the place was set down by Allen T. Bird, who had come in 1893 to found *The Oasis*, the files of which are still preserved.[6]

A number of Frenchmen had drifted up the west coast from Maximilian's scattered forces, and it is thought that the owner of the most noted café on the border west of El Paso came with them. At any rate, Pete Cazabon's restaurant, owned and operated by this big, burly Frenchman on the Sonora side, was the place to eat; and Jeff, with an appreciation of good food and drink, often enjoyed turtle soup there.

Once Jeff went into a little café a few steps from the line and, being hungry for Mexican cuisine, ordered a dish of *menudo*. With him was an American mining man who had been wanting to start a fight all evening. Jeff had held him down. But the world is generous with those who are only satisfied with trouble. Shortly a prominent but drunk Mexican came in, took a seat across the table from them, and began cursing Americans in general. Jeff got up with his *menudo* and moved to another seat. But his friend, providentially provided at last, swung on the Mexican and caught him with the edge of the open hand across the throat, nearly breaking his neck and knocking him out.

A Mexican officer rushed in to arrest them, but Jeff beat him to the draw, poked him with his gun, and said, "Give me that six-shooter." The officer complied, just as another rushed in, and Jeff dropped down on him, again with the order, "Give me that six-shooter," and he took it, too.

6 Mrs. Ada Jones to J. E. H., February 1, 1945; Mrs. Bird, as cited; Duane Bird to J. E. H., November 18, 1945; E. L. Chalfant to J. E. H., February 1, 1945; files of *The Oasis*, 1890–; Harry W. Kelsey to J. E. H., February 1, 1945.

"Let's go," his friend called, as he started for the boundary line some six feet away.

"No," Jeff answered, "I've paid for this *menudo* and I am going to eat it."

"Gentlemen," he said, turning to the disarmed Mexicans, "we are all officers here together. Have some *menudo*." But they refused to eat. So he sat down and finished his supper alone while he kept them standing near by. Then he got up and handed them their guns, saying, "Boys, here are your six-shooters," and walked across the line. Next morning, a little conscience stricken, he went into the judge's office to admit that he was the man involved. "But I didn't resist any officers," he firmly contended. "I just stopped them before I had to resist them."

Again, as he was coming north from Guaymas, a Mexican insulted him, and he knocked the gentleman down. Then he picked up a wire from Overton, at Santa Anna, with the news that the officers in Nogales, Sonora, planned to arrest him upon arrival but that he was sending a man south with a horse and gun to meet the train above Imuris, eight miles out of Nogales. There they should stop the train, turn the express car over to the relief, and, Jeff, by riding back, could circle the town and escape to the American side. They made the stop and Jeff took the horse but, reluctant to be a fugitive again, rode straight into Nogales, submitted to arrest, and got a friend to "fix it up" next day.

One of his most notable experiences in Mexico took place at Pete Cazabon's café. Jeff walked back through the bar to enjoy a steak and sat at a table served by Cazabon's nephew. When the meat was served, he found that it was tainted. He dressed the waiter down good and proper and ordered him to take it away.[7] The infuriated waiter reported the incident to Pete, at the bar, in front. As Jeff started out, Cazabon stopped him, charging that he had insulted his nephew. Jeff told him he did not want a word out of him; and Pete, a very active man who had built quite a

[7] Frank King, Jeff's friend and pioneer of the Nogales country, recalled that the steak was too rare, and has printed the story among his remarkable collection of anecdotes in the *Western Livestock Journal*. Jeff says the meat was "rotten."

reputation as a fighter by whipping several men, jumped over the bar to get at Jeff. But when he hit the floor, Jeff's six-shooter was out and in his ribs, and a big Italian waiter standing near by grabbed his arm and pulled it aside, forcing the gun to go off. The bullet passed through the bar, and Cazabon's hands flew up.[8]

A Mexican policeman came running in with his six-shooter in hand, but Jeff threw down on him and took it. Again he could have stepped across the line, but he refused to do so. He was working in Mexico and he would stay and see it through. Cazabon demanded that the Mexicans arrest him, while one of Jeff's friends, Morales, a porter who worked under him for Wells Fargo, ran up, shouting, "Make him arrest Cazabon first"; and Jeff, still with the policeman under control, made him take charge of Cazabon and the Italian waiter who had interfered. Then he returned the officer's gun and gave up his own. Off they were marched in triumphant Latin fashion to the Mexican *juzgado*, where they started to throw him into a cell, but he protested so vehemently that they turned him into the bull pen with the common run of prisoners. The news flew all over town, and in twenty minutes one of Jeff's friends showed up with whiskey for the jailers and a request to see the prisoner. The Mexicans took the liquor and let him in.

He visited awhile, turned his back to Jeff, and whispered, "Reach under my coat and get that gun." Jeff did, and slipped it under his shirt and down beneath his belt, although he still had one concealed under his arm, in a shoulder holster, which he had not surrendered upon his arrest.

The visitor went off, and shortly Overton showed up with some whiskey. He was admitted, casually visited, and whispered as he turned to go, "Reach under my coat and get that gun." Jeff did, and slipped it in his waistband.

A little later Johnnie Jund showed up at the jail with a bottle of real liquor and asked to visit his friend. He backed up to Jeff and said, "Scratch my back and get those guns."

"Why, man, I'm a walking arsenal already," laughed Jeff. Jund went on to advise that the boys from across the line would

[8] Frank King recalls that Jeff wounded Cazabon in the leg.

storm the place on the morrow and take him out, for there was a limit, they let him know, to what national pride and honor could stand. Jeff vigorously rejected the plan.

"Tell 'em to let me alone," he said, conscious of the fact that he had to keep peace with Mexico since he was working there. "I can walk out of here any time I want to," he added. Meanwhile Frank King and other friends, fearing the Mexicans were going to have him shot, struck out to intercede with the commandant of the district, Colonel Finnocio.[9]

Then Colonel Emilio Kosterlitzky, head of the *rurales* in the field and living at Magdalena, heard the news, caught the train, and came up to see him.

"Jeff, they're going to have to fine you," said the Colonel.

"That's all right," he replied. "I won't mind paying a hundred dollars."

"One hundred dollars, hell!" the Colonel exploded. "Don't you think about paying over fifty."

So they took Jeff into court with ten or twelve prominent Mexicans in attendance. Kosterlitzky, erect and precise, dark eyes flashing and mustache a-bristle, was there to see justice done. The evidence was heard and the judge imposed the fine: "Three hundred dollars!"

Kosterlitzky popped out of his seat like he had been stuck with a pin. "Three hundred, hell!" he shouted at the judge, and others in the audience jumped up, too, to protest the gross injustice.

Jeff saw that the Court, obviously not abreast of the progressive thought of the times, was about to be embarrassed by pressure, and he, the prisoner, rose to say, "Your honor, I'm ready to pay a fine."

"What do you think would be reasonable?" asked the Court.

"It seems like about fifty dollars would be reasonable," suggested the prisoner, reversing the legal procedure by leading the judge.

"Are you willing to pay that?" inquired his honor.

"Certainly, sir," Jeff agreed. And so the fine was imposed, al-

[9] Frank King, *Mavericks* (Pasadena, 1947), 83–84.

though justice was tempered with mercy, as Jeff stepped up and paid it, waiving the receipt and starting to go.

"Hold on a minute," insisted the judge. "Mr. Milton, resisting an officer is a very serious offense in Mexico. But I will give you a police commission so you won't resist officers any more." And he did, which, as Jeff recalled, "was kinda nice, you know." When it comes to accommodating friends, Mexico simply cannot be beat.

Another of his friends was a Wells Fargo employee named Fred Kiel. In the easy manner of the time Kiel had lent a friend two hundred dollars of company money, which, too, in the easy manner of the time, slipped away without being repaid. The day for the inspection of company accounts approached, and Kiel, out the money and out a friend, told Jeff he was in a jack pot. Direct action was the only redress of grievances that Jeff knew anything about, and together they located the delinquent at Jack Gates' saloon in Nogales. Jeff called him outside while Kiel waited in the alley.

"You owe this man two hundred dollars. I want you to pay it back and pay it right now," Jeff advised the debtor.

"I don't have it, and I can't get it," he answered. But when he saw the dangerous glint in Jeff's eyes, he knew that the moratorium was over and the resumption of specie payments was at hand, and he rustled the money from Gates and handed it over. Thus Kiel's honor with the company was sustained, and another good man was "kept out of the pen."

When Jeff and his friends wished other diversion, they could find it down the railroad at Guaymas, Mazatlán, or even farther along the coast at the capital of Nayarit, the city of Tepic. There Jeff, the mild and dignified Overton, and another friend, Captain Charles Beaty, made a visit together. A bullfight was in progress when they got to their hotel, and Jeff, in his usual spirit of fun, wagered his friends that the governor of the state would visit them before the evening was over. Then he wrote a note to the governor, conveying their regards as well as their regrets at arriving too late to see the bullfight, and signed it: "General Beaty, Colonel Overton, and Captain Milton." Overton and Beaty were both so quiet and dignified, he recalled, that "somebody had to start something."

The Mexicans are noted for appreciation of protocol—a high regard for official dignity. Posthaste the runner returned with a note from the governor, inviting the honored guests of the city to the Capitol. Posthaste Jeff sent him back with another note, advising his Excellency that they were "very busy gentlemen," there on matters of grave import, demanding the most of their time, but they would be glad to have him call at the hotel. As for business, they had been out to see some Indians and Jeff had bought a leopard skin. The governor came at once and entertained them with good drink at his expense.

And at last, when their vacation was up and they were ready to board the train for Nogales, there to see them off was the governor and his daughter. Jeff's appreciative eye measured her attractive features and form as quick as he could cock a gun, and he turned to his companions, stiff in the self-conscious style of conservative folks in strange surroundings, and shivered their composure by saying, "By jacks, I sure would like to have my arm around that girl."

"You'll get us all killed," censured Captain Beaty.

"Bet you ten dollars I have my arm around her in ten minutes," he said, and unfortunately they called him. Now the vigorous Jeff was nothing if not gracious and handsome, and the challenge that twinkled in his quick, black eyes was certainly not that of war. Approaching the governor's party, he swept off his hat and bowed with the gentle ease of his native land, meanwhile pulling a little camera from his pocket.

"I have taken pictures of some very pretty girls in my time," he complimented the daughter, "but I believe you are the prettiest girl I ever saw. I would like to put this leopard skin around you and take your picture."

"*Seguro que sí, Señor,*" she replied in rippling Castilian, and spoke softer still with deep black eyes in terms that never need translation. With courtly grace Jeff wrapped the leopard skin about her shoulders and held it there with a willing arm until his astounded companions were anxious to pay the debt. Then

262

he took the picture which is still to be seen in the Milton album. After all the Southern tradition certainly has its advantages.

Gay diversion is simply an interlude, however, in the pursuit of duty. Wells Fargo did not pay Milton eighty-five dollars a month to frolic in Mexico, even with the governor of Nayarit. It paid him to "rassle" crates of quinces and bars of silver into express cars on regular runs and risk his life and limb in wild pursuit of Western desperadoes depredating upon its consignments of coin. He left the land where romance dances in bright colors and dark eyes, and "just went on" about his business.

And business with him was not the commendable accumulation of goods, but loyalty to and unlimited effort in the interest of the people who had him hired. That, too, was a part of his upbringing; that, too, was in keeping with the gallant tradition. The logic of history accentuates the contrast in attitude and time. He lived in a strangely uncivilized world that now seems "far away and long ago."

18

Black Jack's Band

It is not surprising that Wells Fargo—with the wisdom that characterized the great and growing organizations in American business—frequently let Milton off to take the trail of outlaws. These trails were never easy, but were all tied up in knotty problems across forbidding terrain.

Tough topography seems to exercise a tenacious grip on the fates of men who live in close touch with hard soil. Mechanization may ameliorate its harshness; it cannot obscure the fact. Hard hooves shape up on rocky ranges, rawhide draws tighter in arid air, and tough fiber develops on lean land. Any cowboy knows as much. The physical influence operates as well on men. Down in the Southwest, geography gets all mixed up in gunplay. The affiliation is perfectly natural.

Deep spiritual emotion sprouts in desert zones, imagination runs wild in vast and open lands, and nervous tension draws tighter in high and dry places. Such regions have made messiahs with great religious philosophies; they have produced notorious renegade warriors with blood upon their sleeves. Strikingly similar the fervor of spirit that sometimes seized them both!

The Southwest—high, dry, and windy enough to stimulate almost any extreme in human emotion—has, thus far, specialized in its John Wesley Hardins and Billy the Kids. But the progressive world should not despair; it still has time and room for penance and meditation.

Why its outlaws have been so bold may be explained in part, perhaps, by the fact that the unassuming men who live in continual struggle with its stark, eternal realities seem less afraid to die. Some contend it is simply fatalism; others call it courage. It matters not, for semantics gave way to six-shooters in subduing outlawry on the range. Guns were in the hands of men who would walk straight up to death and use them.

The impact of geography is inescapable. The isolation of vast space, with the refuge of rugged ranges of mountains, encouraged a lot of bold but not essentially bad men to turn their lean hands to outlawry.

Most of them were cowhands and some were mighty good ones. Encroachment of settled ways had pushed them into the broad cattle ranges of the lower and adjoining corners of New Mexico and Arizona. The physical features that made this a forbidding land to frontier travelers made it attractive to them. Struggle with that stern environment tempered their own tough natures, wild imagination conceived their reckless and fantastic schemes, high emotion rode with courage to drive them through, and a wild terrain swallowed them up in that space and anonymity that even good men often find consoling.

The Southern Pacific cut across the high and dry divide west of Deming, and across the flat and usually waterless playas, or lakes, beyond Lordsburg, to follow the course of the Butterfield Trail through that break in the natural barrier between Arizona and New Mexico called Stein's Pass. Today, great double-headers belabor their way up its grades to drop their rolling stock down the other side. Their progress is still slow, and Stein's Pass is a likely spot to hold up a train. At least it appeared so in the late eighteen nineties when Jeff was riding for Wells Fargo. The nature of the land about contributed to this conception.

The first business of robbers after a holdup was to get completely gone. Their idea then was not to lose themselves in a heterogeneous mass of humanity called a city but to fade away in space or natural obscurity. And for this, southern Arizona, in any direction, looked something like the promised land.

By the left hand, to the north, ragged ranges rose from the hazy depths of broad valleys to lose their identity in the distance among the jumbled mass of the Rockies known as the White Mountains. Directly to the south, nature had scooped out the wide and massive valley of San Simon to open a view for a hundred pellucid miles, clear into Mexico. On the west, the serrated spires of the Chiricahuas punched holes right into the sky, and bounded the San Simon[1] with an impassable barrier of bluff and canyon, cliff and crag, the length of its glaring and grassy bowl.

Over the Peloncillo Hills, the parallel range to the east roughly along the state line, much of the country was held if not owned by one great ranch known as the Diamond A's. Originally it was the Head and Hearst outfit whose range, in 1883, ran for eighty miles, from Warm Springs south into Mexico.[2] Its business headquarters was handled by capable men at Bakersfield, California, and its magnificent miles of grass and great herds were now under the resident management of Walter Birchfield, a Texan raised in Uvalde.

The San Simon Valley was under the undisputed dominion of Texans, and loosely administered by capable men living in Abilene. It came into being with the venturesome spirit of free cowmen spurred with the want of grass. In the eighteen eighties crowding herds began to pinch their province in Texas, and Jim Newman, of Sweetwater, discussed the need of new range with J. H. Parramore, of Abilene. Newman, who had seen the San Simon, suggested, "You know there is a paradise in Arizona, with nothing on it but grass, game, and outlaws."

That sounded good to Parramore, and they went and inspected the range. Then, in 1883, Parramore, Clabe Merchant, and several other Texans with more cattle than country, put up herds of some 1,500 head each, and moved between 10,000 and 12,000 cattle to Arizona. They set up their headquarters at the San Simon *ciénega*—the marsh and seep springs in the valley— twenty miles below San Simon siding on the Southern Pacific.

In 1885 they incorporated their holdings into the San Simon Cattle Company, and, with widely scattered cow camps appropriated a country sixty-five miles long and twenty wide. They worked the range after the apparently casual but thorough fashion of Texans, and handled the business end just about as loosely as Texans usually did.

It is yet recalled in the ancestral homes of the owners at

[1] Chiricahuas is pronounced "Cherry-cows"; San Simon, "San See-moan."
[2] *Albuquerque Journal*, May 13, 1883.

Abilene that they did not bother with inventories or tallies. They never knew for sure how many calves their bosses had branded, and they never really cared. The method in this apparent madness was characteristic of the time. Keeping books is bothersome business for cowmen, on the one hand, and it is hard for a tax collector to levy on what nobody knows he has, on the other.

The important feature of the venture was the fact that thousands of steers on their way to market annually stirred the dusts of the San Simon flats for the better part of thirty-seven years.[3] During much of this time the great space of the San Simon, peopled with few men, was attractive to outlaws.

For the ranch was worked by Texans who had come to profit on beef and not to reform the land. When not downright dangerous, it was certainly a rude violation of the proprieties of a cow camp to inquire into a man's connections or character. Any cowpuncher could drop into any cow camp without suggestion of suspicion, and be taken at face value, and not critically at that.

For these cowboys, in long evenings around campfires with no diversion except the cryptic conversation of daring and imaginative minds, there were two traditional resorts—retreat into sober philosophy or conception of reckless enterprise. Philosophy, however, was for the damned drudges who herded sheep. Meditation was not for them. They were bowlegged vikings on the humped and hurricane decks of mustang horses. Why not do something profitable and exciting? Why not whip and take Mexico—they were always going to complete the conquest started by their sires in Texas—or at least hold up a train? They could do either one that night and gather the rest of the snaky cattle out of Skeleton Canyon tomorrow. The picture is not overdrawn. That is the way they thought; that is the way it was planned and done—well, almost.

About the time Jeff Milton left El Paso, two other noted characters were heading west, but for a different reason. In the early summer of 1895, Will and Bob Christian got crossways

[3] D. D. Parramore to J. E. H., September 26, 1946. Oscar Cochran, a cowboy there from 1892 until he became a boss in the early nineteen hundreds, indicates that their brandings ran around 7,000 head. Cochran to J. E. H., March 11, 1945.

with the law at Guthrie, killed an officer, and were sentenced for the crime.

They broke jail, and for two months rode and robbed almost at will through Indian Territory. At last they headed for New Mexico, stopped awhile in the Seven Rivers country, and then caught fresh horses and rode for Arizona.[4]

Bill Christian showed up in the Sulphur Springs Valley under the name of Ed Williams, while a man with him thought to have been his brother was known as Tom Anderson. Bill was definitely the leader. He was an "awfully well-met" man, a jovial, powerful, handsome, broad-browed, dark-complected six-footer, whose appearance and self-assurance, before the camera and elsewhere, should have suggested a career in Congress instead of outlawry on a cattle range.

There in the Valley, west of the Chiricahuas, he went to work breaking mules for Jim McNair. Later he joined Tuck Potter, on the IX ranch of the Duval Cattle Company, in sapping out a bunch of broncs. He weighed 202 pounds then, Potter recalls, and in that region addicted to nicknames was sometimes called "202." He was a real rider, so big and powerful that he could manhandle a broomtail bronc, and as quiet and unpretentious as the average cowpuncher, for he was a genuine hand.[5] Eventually, on account of his Indian-like looks, his cowboy associates called him "Black Jack."

Apparently no one there suspected his predilection for lawless danger until he and four other would-be robbers rode into Nogales, at noon, August 6, 1896, and climbed off their horses in front of the International Bank while nearly everybody was out at dinner. Jess Williams and Bob Hays got off and went inside, while Black Jack, Three-Fingered Jack Dunlap, and George Muskgrave sat on their horses to take care of the approaches. Only Fred Herrera, a clerk, was at the bank, and the streets were

[4] For Christian's origin, Sam Hayhurst to J. E. H., December 17, 1946; for some of his early outlawry, see Lorenzo D. Walters, *Tombstone's Yesterdays* (Tucson, 1928), 124–28; D. R. Harkey, as cited; *Edmond Sun-Democrat*, July 5 and August 16, 1895; *Oklahoma State Capital*, May 14, 1895; *Daily Times Journal* (Oklahoma City) August 3, 6, 20, 22, 1895; and *Daily Oklahoman*, March 25, 1898.

[5] Tuck Potter and Sam Hayhurst to J. E. H., December 17, 1946.

almost deserted. Ed Roberts, a cowman on the San Pedro, was crossing a herd from Mexico and had arranged for $30,000 in "dutiable money"—specie and federal bills. Herrera had counted it out on the counter to be picked up at one o'clock by the cowman.

Everything was working on schedule as Hays and Williams scooped it into two sacks. But just at that moment Frank King, noted cowpuncher turned reporter, ambling down the street from the customs house headed for something to eat, saw the three heavily armed men on their horses, divined what was up, pulled his short-range .41 double-action Colt, opened fire on the three outlaws, and began to make some news. A second or two before, however, a passing whirlwind had slammed the back doors of the bank, so exciting Hays and Williams that they ran together in getting outside, fell, dropped their sacks, and never stopped to recover them.

By this time King and the mounted outlaws had opened a fusillade, although King was handicapped on account of his light gun. Once outside, Hays and Williams jumped on their horses in the midst of the fire, and despite the fact that King wounded two of their mounts, the entire band left town at a high lope. Herrera grabbed a gun, shot a hole in the roof as the robbers ran out, and, following them outside, shot again, killing a Mexican wood-hauler's horse hitched to a wagon just below the bank.

269

The town constable formed a posse but lost the trail. King grabbed a buggy horse tied to a rack in front of the Montezuma Hotel, threw a half-hitch on his nose, jumped on him bareback, and came near getting thrown as the surprised old fellow crow-hopped all over the place. He then ran up to a cowpuncher riding into town on a real mount, yelling for him to get off and give him his horse, and he, thinking King had killed a customs inspector with whom he had had trouble, fell off and handed him the reins so he "could get away." King shortly caught up with the outlaws, but, being alone, turned back after getting into another shooting scrape with them.

Then with a posse of his own he took their trail again, followed it out through the San Antonio Pass in the Pajarito Mountains, and lost it that night before they got as far east as Lochiel.[6] Sheriff Bob Leatherwood, with a posse from Tucson, set out to help, while Bisbee officers, with a coming bad-man deputy named Burt Alvord, also took to the saddle to apprehend the band, now obviously headed for familiar haunts in Cochise County. The trail led through the Swishelm and Chiricahua Ranges and crossed the San Simon Valley, Black Jack and his men changing horses by gathering remudas and catching mounts they knew along the way.

Leatherwood's party came up on them near the New Mexico line, in Skeleton Canyon, where the outlaws killed Frank Robson, one of his men, and routed the others. John Slaughter and Sam King, customs line rider, cut across from Slaughter's San Bernardino ranch to help, but got there too late for the fight, else it would have been another story. For Slaughter was noted for reading his warrants to culprits after the shooting was done.

"I say, you're a fine bunch of officers," he chided. "If there was any ambushing to be done, why in the heck didn't you do it?" But Black Jack and his band by then had got "plumb away," apparently into Mexico.[7]

---

[6] Frank King to J. E. H., November 17, 1947. *The Arizona Daily Citizen*, August 6, 1896, gives a garbled account of the affair.

[7] Frank M. King, *Wranglin' the Past* (Los Angeles, 1935), 243–47. *The Arizona Daily Citizen*, August 14 and 16, 1896, followed the progress of the pursuit and noted the defeat of the posse.

Jeff, out of Nogales at the time, did not get in on the fun. Wells Fargo willingly let him take his horses, enlist Billy Stiles, Felix Mahugh, and another man who he knew would fight, and hauled his party in a special car up to Benson and east to Bowie. From there they took a pack outfit and struck south to pick up the old trail at the lower end of the San Simon.

Meanwhile the band came to be known as the "High Fives," and was joined by Tom Capehart and Bob Anderson. Muskgrave —known also as Jeff Davis—Capehart, and Williams had all worked as cowboys for Walter Birchfield on the Diamond A's.[8]

Naturally, now they did not settle down but kept pretty generally on the prowl. They swept back and forth through 150 miles of Diamond A, San Simon, and Sulphur Valley ranges, knowing the friendly cowboys in the scattered camps and the remudas of all the outfits. They would ride until their horses grew leg-weary, round up a fresh bunch wherever they were, unerringly catch the best, and sweep on across that great and wild terrain ahead of all who hunted them. They were definitely in the saddle, and they knew it.

Walter Birchfield, managing the Diamond A's, never asked hands their names upon hiring them—"I just asked what their traveling name was; what name they wanted their checks made to. At least half the people in the country then were not going in their right names."[9] Thus cowboys with obscure pasts welcomed the outlaws at their work and let them levy on their horses. And, remarkable to recount, the San Simon, through all the years of outlawry, never lost a horse. When not dropped, gaunt and weary, on their own range, the San Simon hands always got word —from distant ranges—that their horses had been left there.[10]

Black Jack and his band, with the break definitely made, ventured boldly from now on. They swung north to rob Weem's store, at Separ, between Deming and Lordsburg. A posse of eight officers, among whom were the noted Fred Higgins and Les Dow, from the Pecos, and Baylor Shannon, sheriff of Grant County, in charge, thinking their trail led to the Diamond A, Deer Creek ranch, headed for the Deer Creek horse camp.

[8] Walter Birchfield to J. E. H., November 2, 1939.
[9] Birchfield, as cited.　[10] D. D. Parramore, as cited.

271

Early that morning after their arrival, while the Diamond A hands were catching horses at the corrals, the posse saw four men riding up. Some of the officers dropped down behind a tank dump, and Higgins posted himself inside a picket corral. A cow-puncher, friendly to the High Fives, walked across the pens and unobtrusively waved in warning to the approaching men, but apparently the signal was not seen. When the band got within forty to fifty yards of the dump, the officers rose up and called on them to surrender. Instead, they swept their free right hands to their six-shooters and the fight began.

A Diamond A cowboy from Arkansas, called Sam, grabbed a six-shooter that his prankish associates had daubed with sour dough, rushed out to join the fray, and won renown forever with them as "Sammie Behind the Gun." At the corrals hell was popping, but the marksmanship was not commendable.

"Les Dow shot at Black Jack five times," Birchfield said, "and it looked like every shot hit him." Bob Hays had his horse shot down within thirty steps of the tank dump but stepped off and shot three times at Higgins, knocking splinters in his face. Hays was shot twice. But in spite of the fact that the outlaws were out-numbered two to one, the posse was under shelter, and the fight at close range, Black Jack got away afoot after they had killed his horse, and his two confederates went with him. Walter Birch-field put Bob Hays' body in a wagon, and with "Sammie Behind the Gun" driving, sent it to Deming.

But this did not put an end to their plundering, for the High Fives robbed the station at San Simon, where Langlotz, the agent, had made some talk that he would kill every outlaw that darkened his door. His talk reached Black Jack, who accommo-datingly rode down and raided the place. Boasts are poor sub-stitutes for bullets. Black Jack made the agent shed a brand-new colored coat he had got from Sears and Roebuck.

"I've just bought it," he wailed.

"We don't give a damn," Black Jack said. "You've been mak-ing a lot of talk. We want it." And they took it, as well as the change he had in his drawer.[11]

[11] Oscar Cochran to J. E. H., March 11, 1945.

272

Then they rode in and raided D. W. Wickersham's store at Bowie, cleaned the change out of the post office, sheltered in the same establishment, and rode out of town, south toward the Chiricahuas. They stopped and butchered a beef, and reached the old Joe Schaefer ranch, a small outfit, at sunup next morning. Only Mrs. Schaefer and her two daughters were there. They asked her to fix them some breakfast, tied their horses to the front-yard fence, respectfully stacked their guns on the porch, washed up at the usual basin outside, and ate their breakfast as quietly as genuine cowboys habitually do.

When Black Jack got up to leave, he pitched two Bull Durham pound-sacks—it then came in generous quantity—down on the table, each full of change from the post office at Bowie.

"You don't owe anyone here for your breakfast," Mrs. Schaefer protested.

"It's too heavy to carry," he explained, as he left it there. "You needn't worry about us bothering any of your stock, or killing your beef, or taking any of your horses. We just work on the big outfits that can afford it," he added, in keeping with that progressive outlaw philosophy that still has a familiar ring.[12]

From here they continued down the west side of the Chiricahuas to the Riggs ranch, where the owner, another old-timer, asked them to dinner. With characteristic cowboy humor, they declined, saying they had eaten breakfast "and weren't used to so many meals a day."

"We just want a change of horses, Mr. Riggs," they told him, "if you'll send your boy out to bring some in."

The old man, quick spoken and prompt, hustled his hand off after his remuda. Black Jack's men started roping out the best, and Riggs, whose horses were really good, began to protest. "I'd rather you wouldn't take that horse; he's one of my favorites. I'd rather not see him go."

"Mr. Riggs, we want good horses," they patiently explained. "We're not s_ealing them from you. When we make a change, we will drop you a card so you can come and get them." And they

[12] The Schaefer ranch was established in 1881. Joe Schaefer to J. E. H. and Hervey Chesley, February 28, 1945.

took the best, for they knew his mounts. They went south through the Sulphur Springs Valley, through the pass of the Chiricahuas to the east, across the San Simon again, and over into the Las Animas Valley in New Mexico, to change to Diamond A horses, which they knew even better. At last Riggs got the card, saying that his horses were there, with the accommodating suggestion: "You can send and get them." And of course he did.

After the fight at the Deer Creek horse camp, the High Fives were hard to catch. Milton and his men trailed them in and out of the Chiricahuas, sometimes over country that cannot be traveled on a horse. Jeff split his party, left their supplies and saddles in a cave, arranged a few pebbles in front that would be disturbed if anybody entered, and began to trail in pairs, working out the roughest regions afoot. The range was full of deer and bear, but Jeff warned his boys to be quiet, saying, "Don't shoot. I'll bring the meat in." Then, pointing out a spot at a distant canyon where they would meet and camp that night, he took Billy Stiles with him and set out. As they made their way toward the camping place late that evening, they jumped some deer and Jeff started to shoot one for their supper and breakfast.

"Mr. Milton, I never killed a deer," said Stiles. "Let me kill him." Jeff readily agreed, but Stiles shot at a little buck six times and never did hit him. So Jeff killed one and as they packed the meat toward camp, Billy said, "Mr. Milton, if you don't mind, I'll tell the boys I killed this deer." Jeff did not mind at all, and Billy killed the deer that night all over the camp.

The next day they set out again. Jeff took Felix Mahugh and let Billy go with his fighting cowpuncher. Late that evening they came to an oak thicket, and Jeff, knowing that deer would be browsing on the acorns, told Felix that here they would get their supper.

"Mr. Milton," Felix said, "I never have killed a deer in my whole life. Let me kill this one." But Felix missed his chance, and Jeff killed a fat buck. Felix heard the shot, hunted him up, and, terribly disappointed, suggested, "Mr. Milton, Billy killed that other deer. Do you mind if I tell him I killed this one?" Jeff, who just had to laugh, "didn't mind it a-tall." And so their search went on.

At last he and Billy returned to their cave one night and found the pebbles disturbed. They decided it unwise to go in until they could see, and tramped off half a mile to spend the night with an old settler, S. B. Reed, on Cave.Creek.

Reed was a generous soul, and Jeff and Billy were welcome. When they were settled before the fireplace that night, Reed started a story about killing a bear that had killed a cow of his many years before. The cow, however, had a heifer calf that he had raised from a dogie. And this heifer, as good heifers do, had a calf, and so on he told the story of ten generations of cattle that had come from that heifer calf whose dam was killed by the bear.

Outdoor men grow drowsy when baking their shins before a genial fire after a day in the cold, and Jeff lay down on the floor and went to sleep. At length he awoke and listened for the actual killing of the bear, but old man Reed was still involved in the flowering offspring of that one cow, and Jeff dozed off again. Another hour passed, and he woke once more to find Billy asleep on the floor, and the bear, at last, was dead. He always wondered how Reed had killed him.

The next day they went back to the cave and found their saddles and supplies intact. Evidently pack rats or chipmunks had disturbed their pebbles. Then Jeff and his cowboy deputy dropped into T. R. Brandt's store at San Simon.

"I was never so glad to see anyone in my life," Brandt began. "They've held me up once and I expect them to again, anytime now." Jeff replied that he and his men would sleep there that night and nobody would bother his store, "certain." And, as he was tired, he lay down on a pile of Navajo saddle blankets stacked on the counter. A big cowpuncher from the Chiricahuas came in, and, not knowing Jeff, began blowing around that Black Jack was running the officers instead of the officers running him. Finally, he boasted that he himself, "could run the officers out of the country with a smoking corn cob."

Jeff raised up, motioned his man, and said, "Go up there and box his jaws. I'll be a-watchin' him, and if he beats you to the draw, I'll kill him."

"Sure, it'll be a pleasure," said his deputy, who walked up and roundly boxed the bad man's jaws, and, Jeff said, "I didn't see no smoking corn cob."

While on this hunt, Jeff sometimes stopped in camp with a cowboy friend, "a hell of a fine fellow who got to talking about robbing trains."

"Milton," he suggested at last, "you know how to hold up a train. You and me could do it, get away with it, and live easy the rest of our lives." And so he held forth far into the night about their golden opportunities of holding up trains. Again Jeff stopped to spend the night, and again his host emphasized what they were missing.

"Might do that," Jeff agreed at last. "But if I ever rob a train with anybody, I'll kill him immediately, so he can't turn state's evidence."

"My God," said his host, "I'm not gonna rob any trains with you, for certain."

But in that wild domain there was one rugged soul who never catered to outlawry and was never intimidated by Black Jack's gang. He was an old preacher who had homesteaded a tiny place in the San Simon, where he dug a ditch for an irrigated patch, and tended strictly to his own and the Lord's business. He sent Black Jack word that if he ever stole a horse from him, he would hunt him up and kill him "just as shore as hell," even if he had to follow him to Kingdom Come. Black Jack never bothered the Reverend J. A. Chenoweth at all.

Oscar Cochran, once boss of the big San Simon outfit, recalls that "Parson Chenoweth would run you a race, jump with you, rassle with you, or fight you. He wouldn't stand for any monkey business. He knew the Bible though and would preach—hell yes, he'd preach."[13]

He once killed a man at Galeyville, a ghost village in the

[13] Cochran and Schaefer, as cited. Chenoweth was born in Tennessee in 1813, came west in 1854, and died in the San Simon Valley in 1913. Mrs. Ola Martyr to J. E. H., November 24, 1947.

Chiricahuas, Jeff recalled, and then preached his funeral. Understandably, Indians, outlaws, and everybody else left him strictly alone unless in a hurry to get to Heaven. Jeff admired him immensely. He and his men rode up to his ranch one day, heavily armed of course, unshaven, unkempt, and pretty rough looking after several weeks in the weather. He asked if they might get some dinner. The Parson was away, but Mrs. Chenoweth readily agreed to "fix" their dinner after killing some chickens. Jeff protested this bother, but she told him to wait. She went out in the yard, caught and killed several chickens, picked and dressed them, and after the lapse of a couple of hours had them fried and on the table.

Then she slowly served the meal. It was some time before Jeff discovered why it had taken so long. She had mistaken him and his partners for Black Jack and his band, and while the chickens were making their leisurely way to the frying pan, one of her boys was quirting his horse at a high lope twenty miles to the village of San Simon to get the agent to wire the officers. When he got there, the agent began wiring all over the country for Jeff Milton. After the meal was over, Jeff paid for it, told Mrs. Chenoweth who he was, gathered his guns from where they had stacked them in all propriety on the front porch, and again took up his search.

In very cold weather they followed some horse tracks into Dave Rook's cow camp, Jeff thinking sure he at last had cornered the band. They left their horses and all four eased up to the door. For protection from the wind, Jeff had been riding with a bandana around his face. He felt sure there would be more shooting, but he told his men that they would step right in and take them. He pushed the door open and jumped in with his cocked gun in hand. Four men sprang to their feet while Jeff poked his sixshooter into the belly of a big cowpuncher near him, saying, "Back up; let me look at you all!"

"Don't shoot! Don't shoot!" shouted the man. "We'll give you everything."

When Jeff saw that they were not Black Jack's band, he pushed his gun back into the holster, told them who he was, and

277

explained the mistake. "It was right funny," to him, for when
they saw the handkerchief over his face, they thought he was
the notorious Mexican outlaw, Augustin Chacon, who killed
some twenty-nine Americans in that region before he was hanged
in 1897 at Solomonville.[14]

But Jeff found it downright ludicrous when he turned around
and saw that only Billy Stiles had followed him in. Back outside
he said to the other two, "What in the devil are you doing out
here?"

"We thought we had better stay out where we could protect
you," one of them answered. And it was the second time in his
life, Jeff recalled with disgust, when "men had stayed behind
to protect me."

Again in the same section, he and Sheriff Scott White, of
Tombstone, followed some tracks to an isolated camp while after
a man. Jeff pushed the door open and walked in. A cowpuncher
fugitive was standing, shaving, in front of a mirror hanging on
the opposite wall. He never turned but simply looked at Jeff
through his reflection in the mirror, saying, "Don't shoot," and
went on shaving.

"Nobody else around here but you?" Jeff inquired.

"No, I am the only one here, and I am going as fast as I can.
I found some grain for my horse and got something to eat. I was
told by a cowpuncher to look out, that there were officers around.
But I will be in Mexico before they get here."

"I will, too," said Jeff, seeing that the man took him for an
outlaw and deciding to get in on the fun. "We've got to cook
dinner, but we'll probably overtake you before you get to
Mexico."

"You won't catch me," the fellow said, mounting his horse
and heading south.

"What do you think about it?" White asked of Jeff as the
fugitive started away.

[14] Dane Coolidge, in *Fighting Men of the West*, 267 ff., gives an account of
Chacon. Also, B. C. Mossman to J. E. H. and Hervey Chesley, February 25, 1945,
and Jim Parks to J. E. H. and Hervey Chesley, February 27, 1945.

"Let him go," said Jeff. "We don't know him. If he had of hurt anybody in this country we'd o' heard of it."

And so with humorous incident to spice their chase, Jeff and his men kept after Black Jack. It was not their luck to catch him. He pulled out of southern Arizona and made an unsuccessful attempt to hold up a Santa Fé train. He killed one of his own men whom he suspected of betrayal, and with two confederates rode south across the White Mountains and took refuge east of Clifton in a cave in a wild gorge still known as Black Jack Canyon.

On the early morning of April 28, 1897, a posse made up of Ben R. Clark, Crook-Neck Johnson, Deputy United States Marshal Fred Higgins, and two other men, having received a tip, hid along the canyon and ambushed the outlaws. Black Jack fell in a thicket with a bullet in his side. The posse, however, was afraid to investigate and went back to Clifton, while the other two outlaws caught their horses and "left for the tall uncut."

Later that day the owner of a near-by goat ranch saw his horses shy from the trail as he took them to water. He rode to the spot and found Black Jack Christian, now almost dead. He died in a little while and a passing Mormon freighter placed the body on top of his load of lumber and bounced it into town.

A reward of $2,000 was on his head for four early robberies of the White Oaks–San Antonio, New Mexico, mail coach. The same rewards, $6,000 in all, reposed on George Musgraves and Tom Anderson, but they were gone.[15] Bob Hays had been killed on the Diamond A's, and Code Young, another who had joined the band, was killed in a train robbery at Río Puerco, New Mexico.

With Black Jack's death, the High Fives fell into the discard, and Jeff Milton turned his attention to another band around Stein's Pass.

15 Walters, *Tombstone's Yesterdays*, 129–31; Parks, as cited; Ben R. Clark, MS, "William Christian, alias Black Jack"; Mrs. George F. Kitt, MS, "Reminiscences of Leonard Alverson," in Arizona Pioneers Historical Society, Tucson, 21–22; *Florence Tribune*, January 16, 1897; *Arizona Daily Star*, May 9, 19, 23, 1897. Muskgrave and Jess Williams went into Mexico. Frank King to Mrs. J. D. Milton, November 24, 1947.

19

Holdups and Holdouts

Black Jack Christian's band had apparently pulled out of the Chiricahua country in February, 1897. Christian was killed in April of the same year. A persistent rumor that he was alive was bolstered by the story of a San Simon ranchman that he had seen him, now with a band of twenty to thirty men, in the vicinity of Rook's Well, in Cochise County.[1] And further to befog confusion, the man shot down in the canyon east of Clifton, the stories ran, had been identified as Tom Ketchum. It was an interesting case of mistaken identity so interwoven with fact and fancy that it almost defies thorough unraveling yet.

Black Jack Christian really was dead. Black Jack Ketchum was very much alive. Ketchum, an outlaw from San Saba County, Texas, had been joined by his brother Sam, and come west to Arizona for refuge and further venturesome occupation. He reached the Chiricahuas soon after Christian left.[2] The conflict in identities, however, further confused with the flight of time, has done no discredit to either band. Both were bad enough.

Tom Ketchum, likewise of swarthy complexion, logically inherited the role as well as the nickname of Black Jack. He and Sam were acknowledged leaders. Another Texan, Dave Adkins, was a big help. Will Carver, also from Texas, left the Erie outfit and regularly engaged in their bold and bad pursuits, while Tom Capehart and John Cush were "thicker'n thieves" with Ketchum and his friends. Others came and went, either habitual outlaws or on the high-spirited impulse of the moment. And so outlawry continued to flourish through 1897 in southern Arizona.

[1] *Arizona Daily Star,* May 19 and 23, 1897.

[2] Mrs. George F. Kitt, MS, "Reminiscences of Leonard Alverson"; Albert W. Thompson, *Early History of Clayton, New Mexico* (Clayton, 1933), 63–83.

Milton had planned to meet Colonel Emilio Kosterlitzky, the great leader of the *rurales*, at Slaughter's ranch at San Bernardino. They designed a sweeping campaign against the bands playing back and forth across the line.

Jeff had arranged to keep his horses at Cap Tevis's corral in Bowie. He picked up Sam Webb, Scott White, and another young deputy named Cooper and came to Bowie by rail. He packed his mules, saddled up, and on the evening of December 9, 1897, got away from Bowie and camped that night at Rook's Well, a few miles down the San Simon Valley.

That same evening another party made up of Black Jack Ketchum's men was jogging gently up the Valley towards Stein's Pass under the leadership of Dave Adkins. With him were Bill Warderman, Walter Hovey, *alias* Fatty Ryan, Ed Cullin—"Shoot 'em up Dick" of the San Simons—and possibly Tom Capehart and an Erie hand named Alverson.[3]

Cullin, a late recruit, was moodily sweating Sam Hayhurst's camp at the site of Naco until ten days before, when he decided to drift on his way. He asked Hayhurst for a ranch horse. Hayhurst, who was working for the great Erie Cattle Company, with headquarters twelve miles up the Valley from the site of Douglas,[4] demurred. "Well, Ed, you know I cain't hardly do that. Those horses ain't mine, but there's a couple of flea-bitten gray Mexican strays. You might rope one of them. Which way you figuring on drifting from here?"

After a moment's hesitation, Cullin answered, "Think I'll hunt up some of Black Jack's gang and throw in with them."

Hayhurst shook his head. "I've lived among bad actors all my life, Ed, and never throwed in with them. Know too much about how it turns out in the end. I'd steer clear of that outfit if I was you." But Cullin turned down the advice, rode off on the flea-bitten horse, and a fortnight later the crows were picking his brains off the crossties at Stein's Pass for breakfast.[5]

There was no deviation from his decision. Ed Cullin came of

3 For some reason Tom Ketchum later said that he was with the band, but this seems unlikely. Will Carver, too, was absent.
4 Sam Hayhurst to J. E. H., December 17, 1946.
5 Mildred Taitt Milton, MS, "The Alverson Affair."

281

stubborn stock in Texas. He had worked as a cook for the San Simons where he acquired the dubiously honorable nickname of "Shoot 'em up Dick." He had gone into a Chinese restaurant—southern Arizona had plenty of them then—had eaten a meal, the story ran, and refused to pay for it. The indignant cook remonstrated and Cullin said, "You must not know who I am. I'm 'Shoot 'em up Dick.' "

The Chinaman rushed out and reappeared with a sizable six-shooter which he dropped across the counter into Cullin's chest, and wildly shouted, "I'm slute 'em up Slam! You payee!"

And Cullin paid. When the story got back to the San Simon cowpunchers, they seized upon it with relish, and the reputation of Cullin, their cook, was made as "Shoot 'em up Dick."[6] It was a mean reflection upon the fierce pride of his people in Texas. Why not join Black Jack's band, where some brash exploit would refurbish the family escutcheon!

At any rate, this was the group that was jogging along with the slanting sun of December warm on their backs, as they made their way from their hide-out in the Chiricahuas to hold up the Southern Pacific at Stein's Pass.

They rode into Stein's that night just before the 8:35 westbound was due, robbed the agent and the section foreman, cut the wires, and waited for the train. When the engine puffed up the grade to a stop, vibrating like an old horse with the heaves, four of them climbed aboard and forced the crew to take it three miles farther west, to cut the engine and baggage car loose from the train, and stop at a point just east of the Arizona line where one who had taken their horses had built a fire and was waiting for them.

There they ordered the crew to cut the express car off from the engine. While the engineer was having difficulty with the coupling, two guards, who were hidden on the car, drew back the door and opened fire in the darkness. The shooting became general, and the engineer, caught in the cross-fire, lost all interest in the coupling. Ed Cullin was shot through the head and fell on the railroad tracks. Fatty Ryan was wounded in the leg.

[6] D. D. Parramore to J. E. H., September 26, 1946.

The robbers drew off in a hurry, leaving a saddle, a pair of binoculars, a hobbled horse on which they had intended to pack the loot, and Cullin's fresh mount in the Erie Cattle Company brand tied to a bush. They hit their saddles and headed for their holdout, far to the southwest, across the valley of the San Simon.

Jeff and his boys were warming their shins before a little fire at Rook's Well when the westbound train pulled on to Bowie and the crew sounded the alarm. An engine with a boxcar was sent out the line a few miles east, the engine continuously blowing its whistle as the crew tried to attract Jeff's attention. He heard it but could not surmise its significance until a man walked down across the flat within shouting distance of his campfire. Fearing to come in without making himself known, he called and told what had happened.

Jeff and his men immediately caught and unhobbled their horses, packed up, and hit a lively gait for the point where the locomotive was held in waiting. There, with boards nailed together to form a ramp, they loaded their horses, and, within two hours after the attempted robbery, had jumped them off at the site. In the brilliant moonlight reflected from the white-grassed valley of the San Simon, Jeff picked up the trail at once.

On fresh and grain-fed horses he knew that he could take the trail and catch the holdup men easily that night. But he knew too, that in the trial thereafter, it would be hard to make a jury believe that he had actually trailed them in the dark. So he turned back to the campfire and waited for day.[7]

They again saddled up and made a last inspection of the place as day was breaking. Cullin's body had been moved. Upon a crosstie, where he had fallen with the top of his head shot off, lay a lobe of his brain. A raven, following the course of travel for food carelessly tossed out by human beings, as wise old ravens do, spied the morsel on the crosstie and spread his wings to a stop as Jeff surveyed the spot. He gobbled up the lobe with evident relish between tolerant glances at Jeff, seeming to him to say, "This is certainly good."

At the time the bandits were riding right by the horse corrals at the San Simon ranch, some twenty miles below. With observant eyes Jeff pushed down the Valley hard upon their trail. It skirted the southeastern tip of the Chiricahuas, crossed Shake Flat, and turned up Shake Canyon to John Cush's ranch.

Cush was a hard case who once had owned "The Bucket of Blood" Saloon at the mining town of Pearce. He had moved into the southern end of the Chiricahuas, from where, always mounted on a good horse, he rode that rough range with an acquisitive eye for stray Mexican stock from across the line, and an open hand for the hard and fugitive men who came that way. There, at Cush's camp, Jeff and his men took Capehart, Warderman, Ryan, and an Erie cowboy named Leonard Alverson by surprise, because it was incomprehensible to them that anyone could be on their trail so soon. They surrendered without a fight. Jeff turned them over to Sam Findlay and another guard, and sent them to Tombstone, while he and George Scarborough, who had joined him, and the others, continued their search for Black Jack Ketchum, Adkins, and "Old" Cush, whom they figured was an accomplice.[8]

They got wind of a holdout just over the crest of the range,

[7] Mildred Taitt Milton, MS, "The Alverson Affair."

[8] Years later he learned that Findlay had collected a reward for the capture. Carson Morrow, of the Border Patrol, says he found the inscription, "J. P. Whalen, 1865," on a log cabin at the Cush place, so it was evidently, for that section, an ancient holdout. Morrow to J. E. H., June 11, 1939; Oscar Cochran to J. E. H., March 11, 1945; Sam Hayhurst to J. E. H., December 17, 1946.

and laid plans one night for raiding it. It looked like a tough task, for they knew that Black Jack's men would really fight.

"Get your outfits together," Jeff advised. "Leave everything in shape here, so if anything happens we'll know what you want done if you don't get back."

One of the boys spoke up to say, "Mr. Milton, I've got a wife and children, and I can't afford to go."

Another chimed in, "Milt, I'm married too, and I'd hate to get killed."

And then the third added, "I'm not married, but I'm gonna be next month." It was "plumb" amusing to Jeff.

"When are you goin' up there," snorted Scarborough.

"Right away," said Jeff.

"Milt, you know I'm married and got a wife and a lot of children," George answered impatiently, "and damned if they can't take care of themselves. Let's me and you go."

"You fellers suit yourselves," Jeff said to the other three. "I shore don't want anyone with me who doesn't want to go. But I'm going, for certain." And of course he and Scarborough went.

They found the holdout on a little bench in the canyon. Black Jack and his men had been gone four or five days. But they had cut two pines so that they had fallen into another, and high in the crotch thus formed had stored some loot—molds for counterfeiting, Indian blankets, potatoes, and cans of honey, wrapped up in a big bed tarp. But a bear had found it, torn it up, hammered the cans of honey to pieces on the rocks, and scattered the supplies all over the flat. Jeff and George gathered up the Navajo blankets and worked their way back to camp.

Their conservative companions were greatly interested in their story and the plunder. Just for fun, and he always had time for fun, Jeff contrived a game for the disposal of the blankets. He marked off a barrel lid by drawing lines through the center, like the spokes of a wheel, making more spokes than prizes, although the sections calling for prizes could not be distinguished at a distance. Then all took turns shooting at the center of the lid, and those whose shots hit in the lucky sections won the blankets. But Jeff and George, the deadliest shots in the party, won nothing, proving, perhaps, that there is no justice in gambling.

Jeff kept on the trail of the missing robbers. Ketchum and Adkins pulled out of the Chiricahuas while Jeff and George closed in on John Cush. As they rode up to his place again, Scarborough suggested, "Wells Fargo won't mind, so let's just kill old Cush."

"We can't kill him in cold blood," Jeff countered.

"We'd get rid of a good nuisance," Scarborough argued, with logic.

And so they jogged on with their thoughts to themselves, but at the ranch Cush again showed up missing. Jeff left George there, scouted through his pasture, and met him and another rider, both heavily armed. They exchanged casual but suspicious greetings and started to ride on. Jeff turned back with them, but Cush "cussed a little" and allowed they "didn't need" him there. Jeff knew that things were moving to a sudden showdown, and, to make matters worse, he was mounted on a high-strung horse that "would pitch at the drop of a hat." Knowing that he would have to act in a hurry, he reached for his rifle in the scabbard under his leg.

The horse felt the movement against his side and "broke in two" as Jeff started to quit him, rifle in hand. The horse threw him off and he hit the ground all spraddled out, "but when I did, I was looking down the sights," he said, "right between old Cush's eyes. And I took him right there. But we let the other fellow go, as we had nothing against him."

On trial later Cush testified that "Milton came there to kill me. I could see it in his eyes. I never saw such eyes," he added.

Years later Jeff dismissed the incident with a jest, but he knew it was well for Cush that he had not ridden into the ranch and met Scarborough, alone. The execution of justice would have been complete and the costs considerably less.

Now, with the bulk of the outlaws rounded up, Jeff took Scarborough's son Ed and rode south to San Bernardino to join Kosterlitzky. The dynamic Russian Colonel was in personal command of a squad of twenty well-disciplined, fighting Mexicans, with mules to pack their supplies. They operated under joint orders of the two governments in an attempt to run down "Black Jack" and "members of his gang" known to be at a rendezvous near Chuhuichupa.

They found the rendezvous, with pines round about riddled with bullets where the band had been practicing. But the outlaws were gone. They passed over the range to the Mormon colonies and dickered for horses to replace their worn-out mounts.

While riding one day in the Sierra Madres, Kosterlitzky casually mentioned to Jeff that he had been after him once, when he was a Pullman conductor. It was Milton's first clue that Kosterlitzky had connected him with the unfortunate death at Zacatecas, and he cut a quick eye to see if at last they were going to try to take him here. For Kosterlitzky, with a wild Cossack's sword at his belt, with his hot and hard resolve in pursuit of fugitives, and with the pride of a born military leader, was not to be taken lightly. He was a dangerous and dominant figure, followed by tales of ruthless discipline of his own men, of captives who dug and died in their own graves, and of frequent resort to *ley del fuga*—the law for those who died in flight. Naturally Jeff appraised him with a calculating eye after this apparently casual observation. Nothing in his manner suggested guile, however, and with Jeff's suspicion allayed they rode on their way in search of outlaws.

Then an incident occurred that completely won the Russian to him. As they rode up to a mountain cabin, a man broke for refuge in the woods, and then jumped behind a tree a hundred yards away and shot at the Colonel. As he did, he exposed himself slightly, but enough. Jeff, with quick gun and unerring eye, killed him. Thereafter Kosterlitzky was his loyal ally, whether in personal escapade or in the deadly serious business of hunting desperate men.[9]

After their trip through the Sierra Madres, Milton and Kos-

---

[9] *El Paso Times*, quoted in *The Border Vidette*, January 14, 1898. Dane Coolidge, in *Fighting Men of the West*, has given a vivid description of this iron-handed man.

terlitzky swung down the eastern slope to the Mexican Central Railroad at Casas Grandes, Chihuahua, where Jeff got a telegram from Wells Fargo suggesting that he return. He caught the train out by way of El Paso and at last reported back on the job in Arizona, where other outlaws were giving trouble.

For another cowboy, called Bronco Bill, had cut loose to assert his own uninhibited ways with other people's property. He, too, had been a hand on the Diamond A. Walter Birchfield had put him in camp at the Lang ranch, at the head of the Animas Valley, with a boy from Kansas known as Sage-Brush Bill. They were camped almost in Mexico, and close touch with that wild border still seems to place a strain on a man's morals and puts outlandish notions in his head. The Diamond A headquarters was at the Ciénegas, forty-five miles northeast, in the Playas Valley. Thus the two Bills were in private quarters and definitely on their own.

Bronco Bill Walters, apparently another Texan, was of mysterious origin. One account credits his birth to Georgia with some seasoning as a fighter in Texas.[10] His first appearance on the Diamond A range, as Birchfield recalled, was under strange circumstances for that land of horses and horsemen, for he came out of Mexico, and he came on foot. He was a slim, small man, weighing but 135 pounds, distinguished with dark skin and eyes, a soft-spoken manner, and a sort of a cast-iron set to his jaws.

"You wouldn't have taken him for an outlaw," said Birchfield. "But he was a dead hard *hombre* and had been one all his life. I just asked him what his traveling name was and put him on. He was a good worker, and you could trust him as long as he was working for you. He wouldn't steal a thing. He'd kill a man once in a while, but as long as he was with us, he was a real ranch hand. He'd wrangle horses, cook, clean out mud holes, punch cows—anything. You could trust those cowpuncher outlaws if

[10] Carl Pyne has a readable but not reliable account of his career in *Ranch Romances*, January (first number), 1937, 108–14. Jack Thorp, as told to Neil McCullough Clark in *Pardner of the Wind* (Caldwell, Idaho, 1945), 148, says he was really Walter Brown, "son of the sheriff after whom Brown County, Texas, was named," which would be more convincing had the county really been named for a sheriff.

they were working for you. They'd do anything for you; even risk their lives for you."

Birchfield had Bronco and Sage-Brush Bill cleaning out a spring for stock water at the Lang ranch. It has often been said that two women cannot live in the same house, and it might be added that, temperamentally, two confirmed cowpunchers keeping bachelor's camp are worse still. Birchfield says that the two Bills soon got "cross-ways." Sage-Brush would come in ahead of Bronco, cook just enough dinner for himself, throw out any that might be left, and leave Bill to fix his own. Such relations are terribly abrasive on the souls of sensitive men, and when Bill unsaddled a little late one day, and wobbled his bowlegged way from the corral to camp to find that Sage-Brush had again violated the strong proprieties of the range, he picked up his gun, and suggested, "Sage-Brush, cook me some dinner!" and, said Birchfield, "Sage-Brush cooked a splendid meal."

Bronco ate it with evident relish, and rose to say, "This camp ain't big enough for both of us. I guess one of us will have to move and it ain't gonna be me."

And it wasn't, for Sage-Brush trotted off without his horse, his saddle, or his bed. It was a long way to the Diamond A headquarters, but with proper provocation even a cowboy can walk. Birchfield heard his story and saddled down to the Lang camp.

"I guess you're gonna fire me," said Bill, with fatalistic resignation, "but I just wanted to teach him to cook."

"Not a bad idea," replied the boss, seasoned in the ways of the waddies. "We need good cooks."

They sat awhile in silence after that, as real cowboys with ample time and few words still do, until Birchfield announced his decision, saying, "No, I'm not going to fire you or him either. He wants to work and so do you."

And so Bronco Bill stayed on with the Diamond A's until he quit of his own accord, again to turn down the zestful trail of horseback outlawry. His influence was not completely bad, as Birchfield observed, for "Sage-Brush was a good cook, who would fix a meal for anybody, and clean up too, ever after that."[11]

[11] Walter Birchfield to J. E. H., November 2, 1939.

Thus Bronco Bill Walters left the Diamond A Ranch, and soon all of Arizona and New Mexico—as well as Sage-Brush Bill —knew something of the nature and the temper of this tough little man. Jeff took his trail immediately after returning from Mexico, and would have caught him near Stein's Pass in February, 1898, had he, himself, not ridden into Stein's one night after making camp. When he walked into the railroad office, the operator exclaimed, "They've been telegraphing all over the country for you. They want you at the robbery trial." He took off for Silver City the next morning. So Bronco Bill got away and headed north into that jumbled range that spreads in a riot of crag and canyon all over central Arizona.

When Jeff arrived at Silver City late in February, he found six of the Stein's Pass band arraigned on seven counts in the court of Judge Frank W. Parker. He took one good look at the jury and said to himself, "They'll turn them loose as shore as shootin'!" He left the courtroom and went and swore out fresh warrants for the whole bunch for the federal offense of attempted robbery of the mails.

As he suspected, the jury found them not guilty, March 8, 1898, and as their friends rushed up with congratulations, he jumped up and shouted, "Hold on there, a minute."

Judge Parker, outraged by the action of the jury, rapped vigorously for order.

"I've got warrants for all these men," Jeff continued. And to their consternation he placed them under arrest again, while Parker upbraided the jury.

"This is the worst disgrace in a courtroom I've ever seen," he thundered. "As long as I'm on the bench, I will never hold another session of court in Silver City."

So again the outlaws were thrown in jail, the cases were transferred to federal court at Las Cruces, and at last, after another long trial, three of them were sentenced to the penitentiary from there in September.[12]

[12] Records of the United States District Court, Santa Fé, Case No. 1217, and 1218, and Record E. Page 172, through letter, Wm. D. Bryars to Edwin Mechem, May 13, 1947. Leonard Alverson was pardoned March 29, 1904, after one of

While Jeff and Scarborough were there for the trial, Pat Garrett, newly elected sheriff of Doña Ana County, solicited their help in running down Jim Gililland and Oliver Lee, and he needed it. But Jeff's old friend John F. Cook, deputy sheriff at Socorro, came down to advise them against it. So when the trial was over, they returned to Arizona, where they had plenty to do anyway.[13]

For now Bronco Bill, footloose and fancy free, was playing hide and seek with the officers of Arizona and New Mexico, all the way from the Río Grande to the Little Colorado, and from there to the boundary of Mexico. From the rusty volcanic cones on the northern rim of that rocky mass of confusion called the White Mountains, Bronco had recruited three considerable confederates.

One by one they had cut their eyeteeth on trouble at Springerville, had resisted arrest, and had ridden south to punch cows on the Double Circles, that great outfit built up by Joe Hampson. There the diminutive but dangerous man who had converted Sage-Brush Bill into a willing cook likewise came for refuge in 1898, and there these novices from north of the mountains recognized him as a leader with experience.

They swept north to attempt the robbery of the Santa Fé train west of Gallup, and there one was wounded, and left on the back trail to the White Mountains. A posse pushed close behind, but once in the Double Circle range, Bronco and Bill Johnson doubled back to waylay their pursuers. After a fight they pushed on toward the ranch headquarters, on Eagle Creek, fifty miles farther inside the rocky fastness. Then Burnett, another fugitive from Springerville, joined them. But he was talkative, and after another fight with the officers, they suspected that he had tipped their pursuers off, and when Bronco and Johnson showed

the cell-keepers in the Santa Fé penitentiary made affidavit that Sam Ketchum on his death bed had admitted the Stein's Pass robbery, and, it is claimed, had exonerated Alverson. A copy is in the files of the Arizona Pioneers Historical Society, Tucson.

13 Cook, a Virginian, came to Socorro in July, 1881. George Cook to J. E. H., March 6, 1944. W. A. Keleher, *The Fabulous Frontier*, 71 and 211 ff., gives a splendid account of these troubles.

up at one of the camps, and Evans Coleman, a Double Circle
cowboy, asked where Burnett was, they simply said, "We don't
know, but we'll bet he doesn't tip any more officers off."

The cowboys were their friends, and they came and went
without let or hindrance. They knew the truth of the Argentine
axiom that "A man without a horse is a man without legs," and
they kept two good mounts well conditioned on Double Circle
oats, exercising them daily. Thus, when they left on a foray,
they were mounted on horses that would "take them there and
bring them back."

They covered a lot of country. They robbed the Wells Fargo
safe, on a train, near Belen, where it is claimed they took $20,000
in currency. They headed west into the mountains while Sheriff
Vigil of Los Lunas, gathered a posse of Indians and Mexicans
and fell on their trail in hot pursuit.[14]

H. O. Bursum, sheriff of Socorro, jumped in his buggy and,
with a good team of traveling mares, struck west to the Mexican
village of Puertocito to recruit a posse and take the trail. The
Spanish-American War was on, and the report that he was after
recruits for the army outpaced his splendid team. When he got
there, the patriotic men of Puertocito had fled to the hills.[15] He
returned to Socorro, made up a posse from among the men in
jail, shipped his saddle horses to Magdalena by rail, and from
there struck a long trot to intersect Bronco's trail north of the
Datils.

Meanwhile, Vigil and his Indian deputies caught up with
Bronco and Johnson on Alamosa Creek, where one of the hardest
fights in Western outlawry took place. Milton understood that
the Indian trailers found their camp while they were still asleep,
and proposed to slip up and kill or disarm them. Vigil refused
and waited for day. The outlaws had ridden hard and far, were
tired, and slept late on their saddle blankets. When the sun
filtered through the trees to wake them up, Vigil and his Indians
were ready to waylay them. As their hobbled horses had grazed

[14] Evans Coleman, MS, "A Little Outlaw Gang," Arizona Pioneers Historical
Society, Tucson.
[15] H. O. Bursum and Hal Kerr to J. E. H., March 6, 1944.

292

off some three hundred yards, they went to get them, feeling so secure that they left their rifles in their scabbards on their saddles, and walked off armed only with their six-shooters. On their return they discovered the posse above them, and the fight commenced. Dropping their horses, they made for their saddles, where they got their guns and opened up in deadly earnest.

The posse was in the cedars and boulders along a bluff to their east, while a little wash cut through the floor of the canyon just west of where they were camped. Johnson killed Vigil with a shot between the eyes and went down himself with a bullet through his neck. Bronco, having already killed one of the Indians, started to Johnson, fearful he was dead, when some of the posse, having got in the wash, opened on him from the rear. He whirled to see an Indian stick his head over a log about thirty steps away, and caught him with a quick shot between the eyes.

Then Johnson came to, and began trying to get up. Bronco grabbed his rifle and the money, caught him in the collar, and though by this time wounded in the hip and shoulder himself, and carrying two rifles and the money, managed to get him across the wash and away from the exposed camp, afoot. They left the sheriff and two Indians dead and the other four Indians on the run. Somehow, they hid their money and reached the W Slash ranch, where they got their wounds dressed. When they showed up on the Black River range again, they were "riding two small ponies and two old saddles," and were, themselves, still "bloody, dirty, haggard, and worn."

They put up at the Double Circle horse camp and sent George Felshaw, who was tending the horses, into Fort Apache after some drugs. He came back with a silk handkerchief and a bottle of medicine, and, being an experienced cowboy, began doctoring them just like "a calf with the worms." He would punch the silk handkerchief through the bullet holes with a sharp stick, pull the stick back out, draw the handkerchief through, and pour some medicine after it. Of course they got well, backtracked after the money, put two more good Double Circle horses on grain, and got ready to go again.[16]

[16] It should be kept in mind that this region was impenetrable for almost a

Their exploits were noised far and wide, and Jeff made plans to take them. He asked Wells Fargo for leave, which for some reason was refused. As he prepared to resign, word went up and the leave came through. Colonel Epes Randolph, division manager of the Southern Pacific at Tucson, furnished a car for his horses and transportation wherever he wished to go. He·wired George Scarborough and took Eugene Thacker, youthful son of a railroad detective, who joined him largely for the experience, and set out. Bronco Bill, having heard he was coming, contemptuously sent word for him to bring plenty of good horses and blankets, as he needed them.

Jeff loaded his outfit in a special car, picked up Scarborough and Martin, a Diamond A cowpuncher, at Deming, and swung around to Holbrook, in northern Arizona, as he got wind that the band was planning a holdup there. He and Scarborough rode the express cars for several weeks hoping Bronco Bill would come. But he never did, and after tiresome watching and waiting, a wire came in July, 1898, saying that Bronco Bill had held up a Fourth of July dance at a schoolhouse near Geronimo, on the other, the south, side of the White Mountains.

The dance was under way when the band stepped into the doorway, covered the merrymakers with their guns, and announced, like discreet gentlemen, that they had come only to dance. While Johnson and Red Pipkin stood guard, Bronco moved down the line of flustered young ladies sitting with their uneasy escorts on benches against the walls in front of the open windows, proposing to each in turn, "May I have the honor of this dance."

Each lady in return, prim and precise as a Spanish dagger, replied, "I beg to be excused."

This continued with monotonous regularity until he reached redheaded Tilly Windsor at the end of the line, who declined because she "was too tired."

Now there is a limit to the Chesterfieldian ways of the West, and Mr. Walters, nettled at this affront to his manly pride,

hundred miles square except on foot or horseback. Evans Coleman, as cited; Coleman to J. E. H. and Hervey Chesley, February 27, 1945.

294

whipped out his six-shooter, saying, "Damned if I don't see that you do," and opened a fusillade into the floor about her feet, while Johnson and Pipkin began shooting out the lights. Tilly's partner was a local deputy sheriff, but she later told Jeff that she never knew whether it was she or her escort who "tore the window out going through it." Anyway the dancers leap-frogged through the lattice-like windows in commendable unison, if not rhythm, to the staccato music of Bronco Bill's six-shooter shots. There was something of providential wisdom in the fact that even the early Arizona schoolhouses were built with plenty of windows.[17]

Milton loaded his horses on his special car, was picked up by a passenger train, and again took roundance of the rough country that lay between Holbrook and Geronimo by going over the Santa Fé to Belen, thence down the valley, and west to Bowie by the Southern Pacific. There he was picked up by a special engine and a crew ready to take him wherever he wanted to go.

"That night we ran up to near old Fort Thomas," he said, "jumped our horses out of the car, and made camp in the brush." He and Scarborough rode into town and got all the news they could from Miss Tilly's gallant deputy, came back to camp, saddled up that night, and headed toward San Carlos, a military post now covered by the Coolidge Lake. The rainy season was on, and they made the ride through a severe electrical storm and downpour that lashed the mountains in violence. At last they made uncomfortable camp outside the post.

The next morning Milton and Scarborough called on the commander, to whom Jeff had a letter, who gave them two Apache trailers and guides. But as they did not suit Jeff, he soon sent them back, and the little posse pushed on by itself. From Government Crossing, on turbulent Black River, they made their

[17] *The Arizona Republic*, July 25, 1898, records the incident with the observation that "Bronco Bill does most of the dancing, while Johnson stands watch around the door." It noted, too, that "Bill got too much liquor on board at the dance, and because a girl refused to dance with him, he pulled both six-shooters and cleared the hall."

Mildred Taitt Milton's MS, "Bronco Bill's Last Battle"; *Bisbee Daily Review*, May 6, 1934; Mrs. Edith Kitt, in the *Arizona Star*, August 16, 1936; and Michael Williams, "Real Men of Arizona," in *The Golden West*, May, 1938, touch upon or relate some detail of this incident.

way into Fort Apache, where they picked up additional supplies but kept their mission to themselves. For the scattered settlers of that section, having little business with officers, did have frequent association with the outlaws, with whom they lived in appeasement—a sort of a frontier variation of the tactics that brought "peace in our time."

Day in and day out they hunted for Bronco Bill through those tortuous intricacies of torn terrain that make up the White Mountains. They were blocked by windfalls in its dark forests, and they followed the tantalizing trace of a trail into the bright world above the timber line, directly across the barren crest of Old Baldy. There they found a cairn of stones, and in it a tin can on which was scratched the Diamond A brand. It was the most significant trace they had found. Cowboys, in laborious carvings on gunstocks, in embossments of silver on bits and spurs, and in idle scratchings with sticks in the sands, unconsciously trace the patterns of their lives in brands. They felt sure that Bronco Bill, Diamond A cowboy and converter of cooks, had put it there.

"Bill's work, or I'll eat my hat," said Martin, and Jeff and his party pushed on with zest.

At length they reached the Burnt Corrals—a pen made of pine logs crisscrossed with interlocking ends, and at times used by the Double Circle as a horse corral. As it was a likely stopping place for passing outlaws, Jeff decided to post a guard and watch there for a while. During his turn on guard the second day, he was watching through the dead branches of a fallen pine at the edge of the pen when a cowpuncher drove in some horses. When he got down to change mounts, he turned and looked through the limbs, directly into Milton's eyes.

"Stick 'em up!" called Jeff and stepped out and disarmed him. The man was John Gibson, a square-shooter who had no desire to stand in with the outlaws, and who agreed to lead them to McBride Crossing and the Double Circle horse camp. They saddled, packed, and pulled out.

It was dark when they reached the Crossing and Gibson pointed out the camp—a tent in a glade on the west of the river, at the foot of the trail from Fort Apache to Solomonville, which

296

twisted down from a high mesa on the east. It happened that a crew was there. Jeff and Scarborough slipped up to the tent, threw back the flap, and covered the crowd inside with the command, "Hands up, men!" and up went the rough paws of everyone there.

Eight cowpunchers and a bear hunter made up the haul. They disarmed the force at once. Not a man would admit that Bronco Bill had been there, although Jeff later found that he, Pipkin, and Johnson had ridden off that day and were expected back on the morrow. Jeff put the Double Circle crew under guard and spent the night there.

The next morning Martin went up on the mesa to the west to look for horses, while Scarborough and the Thacker boy were guarding the cowboys. Jeff took Tom Bennett, one of the Double Circle men with him, and walked a hundred yards down the river to catch a mess of trout. He had just dropped his hook in when shots rang out from the side of the mesa to the east. He looked up and saw three horsemen coming down the steep trail. At the same instant his cowboy hostage ran behind a boulder, exclaiming, "I'm going to get out of here. Somebody's going to get killed."

Jeff jerked his six-shooter and stopped him, saying, "If you don't be quiet, somebody will get killed. Lead isn't flying this way," he added, as he had heard no bullets whine. "They're not shooting at us. Who are those men?"

"Damned if I know?" said the Double Circle cowpuncher. With seeming casual indifference Jeff stuck his pole in the bank, and ordering Bennett to walk slowly alongside him, he went back to camp. He passed his shotgun, lying across his bedroll, and walked on to where his rifle leaned against a tree near where Scarborough stood, his sharp blue eyes on the approaching horsemen.

"Who do you think they are?" Scarborough inquired.

"I don't know, but I think it's our gang," said Jeff, as he picked up his rifle. Meanwhile the lead man had ridden into the glade, stepped off his horse about thirty yards away, and was quietly talking to Henry Banty and J. E. Howard, two of the captive cowpunchers who had the free run of the opening.

The other two had ridden upon a rattlesnake along the trail above and, unaware of the presence of the officers, began shooting at the snake with their six-shooters. But the leader had ridden into camp, had seen that "the sign wasn't right," and had jumped off to talk with the first friends he met. Howard gave him a wink and told him to leave. At once he started to his horse as Milton called, "Hold on there, Cap, I want to talk to you a minute."

But he jumped into the saddle, drew his six-shooter, whirled his horse, broke into a run, and began shooting back at Jeff. Two bullets whipped up the dust from between his legs, and both Jeff and Scarborough went into action. Jeff's first shot hit his extended arm, in the elbow, plowed directly up it, shattering the bone, passed clear through his chest, and lodged on the other side under his left arm. He rolled from his running horse and Milton and Scarborough turned their attention to the two on the side of the canyon, above them, who had already got into the fight. They immediately killed the horse from under one, and the rider ran like a deer into the brush. But the other, wise and game, jumped off behind a juniper and began shelling them with his heavy-caliber rifle. From the corner of his eye Jeff saw the dust spurt up behind Scarborough.

"That hit you, George?" he called.

"Never touched me," Scarborough replied as he placed a bullet in the bark right under the robber's nose. This caused him to jump back, exposing his hips on the other side of the tree, and when he did, Jeff's next shot caught him there and bowled him over, where he lay screaming with agony.

Martin came running down from the mesa to get into the fight, but it was all over. The Double Circle boys bobbed up from behind the boulders and trees, and carried the man down from the side of the canyon, whom they identified as Bill Johnson. Jeff went over to the first one shot, and, thinking him dead, started to drag him into camp by his heels. When he did, the blood rushed out at his mouth and the man gasped for breath. That jerk by the heels, the doctors later said, loosened the flow

298

of blood that was clotting in his lungs, enabled him to get his breath, and saved his life. The cowpunchers then told Jeff that this was Bronco Bill Walters.

Red Pipkin had got away. The cowpunchers were worried, saying Pipkin would gather his friends and return to give them battle. Jeff and Scarborough kept the entire bunch under arrest except for "Climax Jim," so called from the fact that his principal "eating" tobacco was the "Climax" plug. Jeff told him to hit a high lope for Fort Apache, twenty-five miles away, after a doctor.

He tore a leaf from his daybook and wrote a message to be sent over the government line to the sheriff of Solomonville. "Climax Jim" saddled up, pushed a quid into his flexible cheek, and began knocking the sparks out of the rocky trail towards Fort Apache. He delivered the message, which read, "Send a coffin and a doctor." It was typically terse. Frank King, cowpuncher reporter, picked it up and sent it out in a news story to add to the Milton tradition, while the post surgeon was so afraid of the trip that he went only under compulsion of the commander's orders.[18]

Meanwhile Pipkin reached the friendly Allen Chitty ranch by foot, and Chitty rode into the fort to report that there was "a bunch of officers out there killing everybody in the country." But it was only a brief stop for a mount for Pipkin. He pulled out in a hurry.[19] Jeff, knowing they had no friends in the region, put all who rode up that day under arrest and immediately disarmed them.

The doctor arrived with an escort of soldiers just after dark. He was scared to death, and after a cursory examination of the wounded men said neither could live. He administered some morphine, gave his meager supply to Jeff, and hurriedly left for the fort. That night Jeff cut the bullet out from under Bronco's arm, but there was little he could do for Johnson, as the shot had shattered the bone in his hip and ranged up through his abdomen. As he was in great pain, Jeff gave him a shot of morphine.

[18] It is usually told, "Send two coffins and a doctor." Frank King notes in author's files and Mrs. Jeff D. Milton to J. E. H., May 7, 1941.

[19] He died many years later in the Gallup country, after having served a term in the Yuma penitentiary. See Coleman, as cited.

He died that night, and the next morning they buried him there by that rocky trail where the rattlesnake had sounded his sinister warning of death to him, where he had foolishly shot the reptile in return, and thus had given warning of danger to Jeff in time to enable him to reach his gun. After that, Milton would never kill a rattlesnake.

"He won't bother you unless you do him," he would explain. "And then he'll notify you, which is more than lots of men will do."

Jeff took a cold chisel from his pack and cut Bill Johnson's initials on a rock which he placed above the grave. "I felt pretty sorry for Bill Johnson," he recalled in regret. "Wa'n't no use being sorry for those fellows, but couldn't help it. So we buried him." But a bear soon dug him up.[20]

They arrested and disarmed all who rode up that day, impounding them with the others, until they had about twenty men on hand. Then a posse under the leadership of a deputy sheriff, getting the Allen Chitty report, came sweeping in well armed with six-shooters and rifles to take matters in hand. Jeff, who knew the leader, stepped out to meet him, saying, "Let me talk to you."

"If these fellows here should see me talking to you . . . " the leader began, indicating the hostile men Jeff's little posse was holding—but that was as far as he got.

"Goddamn you," snapped Jeff, black eyes ablaze, "what are you doing here if you ain't our friends? Get out of this camp and get out right now. We don't need any such damned deputy sheriffs in this neighborhood." And they took his advice at once.

Then he made splints for Bronco's shattered arm, and dressed and tied it across his chest. They rigged a cradle on the back of a horse, padded it with blankets, and tied him on. Then they turned their captives loose and took that rugged trail for nearly forty miles out of the mountains to Geronimo—a ride that is enough to try a well man. Bronco could not stand the pain in the

---

[20] J. E. Howard to Jeff D. Milton (letter in files of author). Howard was one of the Double Circle cowboys under arrest. He had nothing but praise for their treatment by Jeff.

litter long, and thereafter they supported him in his saddle. They got there with him still alive, that night, put him on the train next day, and started to Socorro where he would come to trial.

At Solomonville a crowd gathered on the station platform to look in on the notorious outlaw. They packed about the open window in ghoulish curiosity, and Jeff leaned over to whisper to Bill, "Do you suppose if I raised up your head, you could say 'boo' at those fellows?"

"I will try to say it to the sons-a'-bitches," he answered.

Jeff eased him up on his arm and little Bill shouted, "Boo-o-o!"

The crowd fell all over itself, knocking those down in the rear and shoving others clear off the platform. It tickled Bill so much that "it liked to have killed him."

He recovered from his wound and was sentenced for life to the penitentiary at Santa Fé. He was pardoned after twenty years, returned to work on the Diamond A—where utility, not reputation, was the measure of a man—and where, while greasing a windmill, he fell off the tower and died from the fall.

About a month after the fight, Pipkin and two friends rode into the Double Circle headquarters and threatened Joe Terrill, the foreman. But it was a futile gesture, for the band that Bronco Bill Walters had led with warlike zest was "deader than a door nail."

Jeff Milton knew it. He let his posse go, and as his job was really that of an express messenger, he went back to his Wells Fargo run down the sunny side of Mexico to Guaymas.[21]

[21] In addition to the articles already cited, details of this incident are to be found in Frank King's reminiscent columns in the *Western Livestock Journal;* *Arizona Republic,* August 4, 1898; *Tombstone Epitaph,* August 3 and 10, 1898; *Graham County Bulletin,* September, 1898; Evans Coleman, as cited; as well as the author's voluminous notes from Milton on the subject.

20

The Fairbank Affair

J eff went back to his run with Wells Fargo between Benson and Guaymas. But even then there was an alliance of outlaw spirits in the making that was to cause him trouble, and the principals in the plans were Burt Alvord and Billy Stiles, who pretended to be his friends.

Billy came from Casa Grande. He was a likable fellow but as wayward and variable as a desert whirlwind. He had served as a deputy under Jeff, and when Jeff was in the lead, he would follow and he would fight. But he would never stay hitched. Stability was not in his nature. When he was twelve, the story goes, his father gave him a whipping. Billy got a shotgun, waited for his father to round the corner of the house, and blew his head off with bird shot at close range. Whatever the merits of the story, Billy Stiles was unpredictable, with or without provocation.

Burt Alvord, a stocky, swarthy, bald-headed roustabout who grew up at Tombstone, was of meaner and more designing character. He was known as a bad man, a murderer at heart who would not hesitate to kill when the advantage was with him.

Now Willcox, at the upper end of the Sulphur Springs Valley and the trail town for much of southern Arizona, was having trouble with its celebrating cowboys. In an attempt to hold them down, its leading citizens sent over to Pearce, where Alvord was taking his ease, and offered him the job as constable. He took it.

It has long been noted that the pulse of authority in the veins of men is peculiarly perversive of their better natures; in the blood of venality it becomes criminality compounded with the power of legal compulsion. Burt Alvord, good with a six-shooter and fresh from thieving adventures into Mexico, took the job with relish and almost immediately murdered a cowboy named Billy King.[1]

302

Feeling at once ran high between him and the cow outfits. He got an isolated house on the flats two miles west of town to camp in and looked around for help.

Billy Stiles, always flirting with temptation even when engaged in legitimate work, became his deputy. But Burt wanted two. He found another in Bill Downing. Compunction of conscience in careless killing was not in Downing's nature. He, too, was handy with a gun, a tough customer from Texas with black eyes, a high forehead diabolically lifted at the edges by a receding hairline, and a low-slung mustache that emphasized the length of a face shaped like a longhorned cow's.

This unholy trinity was engaged to bring the blessings of peace to that village on the alkali flats called Willcox.[2]

Another salty cowboy standing out in Willcox like a black muley steer in a white-faced herd was Matt Burts. He had grown up on the Colorado in Texas, had driven on the trail with the XIT's, worked in the stockyards of Chicago, left there between suns, returned to the range in Texas, and had eventually gone to southern Arizona. All good Texas cowboys in trouble at home seemed to head that way. He threw in with Alvord and company.[3]

Then, on September 9, 1899, two men boarded the westbound passenger train at Cochise, a little station west of Willcox, and forced the crew to uncouple the express car and run it a mile

[1] Dane Coolidge, *Fighting Men of the West*, 170–74; C. L. Sonnichsen, in *Billy King's Tombstone* (Caldwell, Idaho, 1942), 68 ff., has a readable account of Alvord. E. L. Chalfant to J. E. H., as cited, says "he was a damned renegade, a hard one, and plenty tough."

Willcox started as a town in 1879 when the grading crews were working on the railroad dump. The Southern Pacific built through in 1880. Trail herds began coming in for shipment, from the White Mountains on the north down into Mexico to the south. Alvord was hired as constable apparently in 1898. Harry Parks to J. E. H., February 27, 1945.

[2] Downing is dressed up for reading, and perhaps history, in Sonnichsen, *Billy King's Tombstone*, 76; Walters, *Tombstone's Yesterdays*, 190 ff.; Coolidge, *Fighting Men of the West*, 174 ff., says that Downing served as night watchman and levied on the prostitutes in that ancient and dishonorable fashion that still flourishes.

[3] Bob Beverly to J. E. H., February 24, 1945. See Beverly's book, *Hobo of the Rangeland* (Lovington, New Mexico, n. d.), for something more of Burt's experiences.

303

farther toward the pass through the Dragoons. They blew the safe, took its gold and paper contents—estimated at fantastic figures—and coolly rode off into the stimulating Arizona night. Next day a posse took their trail and followed them toward Willcox but soon lost their tracks.

Sheriff Scott White came tearing in from Tombstone, and John W. Thacker, detective for Wells Fargo, showed up. Downing had been on duty that night, and Alvord and the others had splendid alibis. Downing and Stiles joined White's pursuing party. Alvord took up the search, and officers and posses jumped into their saddles and loped off in all directions hell-bent after the thieves. The trails were elusive, and the clues seemed groundless.[4]

But the officers nursed their suspicion of Alvord and his newly prosperous associates, and kept plugging away on "the perfect holdup." It had been planned by Alvord and the others for months. Downing had furnished the horses. They had pried into Soto Brothers' store and stolen the powder. Matt Burts and Billy Stiles had robbed the train, had delivered the loot to Alvord, and had then rushed into town to join the posses. Horse tracks toward Willcox were not unusual. Small wonder they were not caught![5]

Then they planned to rob the southbound train from Benson to Nogales. They would take it at Fairbank, a lively little stopping place because of the mail, express, and passengers handled there for Tombstone. The one to be avoided, however, was Jeff Milton's run for Wells Fargo. After each trip to Guaymas, Jeff laid over at Nogales a day. The outlaws knew it. They would hold up the train the day he was off, but to be absolutely sure of the schedule, they hit upon a ruse.

Billy Stiles went down to tell Jeff that he had a "mining man" who wanted to look at some of his claims out in the Quijotoas.

[4] *Arizona Daily Star*, September 12, 1899.

[5] The newspapers at the time reported three robbers, while other stories say that there were four. Walters, *Tombstone's Yesterdays*, 190–93; Sonnichsen, *Billy King's Tombstone*, 78–94; Coolidge, *Fighting Men of the West*, 175–77; *Arizona Daily Star*, as cited; *Arizona Daily Citizen*, March 2, 1900; and a good article by Elizabeth Nelson Beach, in *Arizona Daily Star*, August 8, 1909.

He definitely established the day that Jeff would be free to meet his "mining man," but to make assurance doubly sure, he asked Jeff to wire him from Nogales in case of change of plans. On the appointed day Jeff picked up a wire at Imuris, Sonora, from W. F. Overton, of the express company, advising him that Messenger Jones, who would ordinarily relieve him, was sick, and that he would have to go on through. Jeff forgot about Billy.

Apparently, then, everything was in good shape. Alvord and Stiles arranged the affair but sent their confederates to do the work. Five of them—"Three-Fingered Jack" Dunlap,[6] George and Louis Owens, Bravo Juan Yoas, and Bob Brown—camped in a canyon in the Dragoons the night before and laid their final plans. After making solemn compact to kill the first man who wavered, they elected Bravo Juan as their captain, split up to avoid suspicion, and on the morning of February 15, 1900, saddled off down the long slope that reached from the rugged Dragoons to the railroad grade at Fairbank.[7]

The train came in just at dark. The Tombstone stage awaited its passengers, and the usual crowd was on hand. The band had drifted in quite casually and, now playing the part of drunken cowboys, had lined a number of bystanders up between them and the railroad tracks. As the train slowed to a standstill, Jeff was standing in the open door in his shirt sleeves. The agent was on hand to take the express. Suddenly a voice cried, "Hands up!"

"What's going on here?" Jeff asked of the agent, as he started handing out the packages.

"Just a bunch of drunk cowboys having a joke, I guess," answered the agent.

"That kind o' joke is liable to get somebody killed," said Jeff, handing out another package.

[6] Dunlap was a noted Arizona outlaw who had been captured in 1895 by Joe McKinney, undersheriff of Gila County, but later released. Joe McKinney to F. L. Lockwood, December 28, 1935.

[7] From the author's notes and a good manuscript account, "The Affair at Fairbank," by Mildred Taitt Milton; the *Tombstone Epitaph* detailing George Owens' confession at the trial, October 17, 1900; and Mrs. George F. Kitt's notes, March 18, 1935.

"Throw up your hands and come out o' there," came a command, then a shot, and Jeff's hat flew off.

He reached for his sawed-off shotgun leaning beside the door, yelling back, "If there's anything here you want, come and get it."

From behind the screen of innocent people, they opened fire with their high-powered rifles. Jeff would have jumped out and mixed it with them on the ground except that his six-shooter was on his desk back in the car. He could not shoot, for his spraying buckshot would surely kill some of the hostages as well as his foes. He had to hold his fire.

The volley cut his shirt to shreds. Several shots hit his left arm between the elbow and shoulder, spinning him around and knocking him down. The outlaws thought they had him and rushed from behind their human breastworks toward the door. Jeff raised up, threw down on them with his right hand gripping the upper stock like a six-shooter, and cut loose at the lead man. Jack Dunlap fell with eleven pellets in his body, while a stray buckshot caught Bravo Juan in the seat of the pants. And although he was captain and had entered the compact, he hightailed it at once and never stopped this side of Mexico.

"Look out for the s——o——b——, he's shooting to kill," shouted Dunlap as he fell.

The bullets had shattered Jeff's arm and cut the artery. As he felt faint, he reached up during the commotion caused by his shot and rolled the door closed. He pulled the keys to the safe from his pocket and flung them among the packages at the end of the car. He grabbed and placed his useless hand in the rung of a trunk, caught his sleeve in the cuff, ripped it back to his shoulder, and began twisting it about his arm above the wound to cut off the flow of blood spurting in his face. Then he fainted and fell between two trunks.

"I felt myself going," he said, "but I enjoyed it. I heard the most beautiful music—the most wonderful band—that I ever heard in my life. I wonder if every man does."[8]

[8] This speculation finds some support in T. E. Lawrence's *The Seven Pillars of Wisdom*, 304, as well as in Robert Service's "Afternoon Tea." The author is

His quickly improvised tourniquet and his falling between the trunks probably saved his life. The three remaining outlaws riddled the door. They circled the car and shot round after round into it to make sure he was dead. A half-mile down the track a ranchman heard the racket and rushed from his supper table to see why his horses were kicking the sides out of his barn. Jeff came to with his dog standing over him, whining and licking him in the face, and he said to himself, "Shuckin's, I've never been this drunk before."

Outside he could hear the protesting voice of Engineer Avery, as he was being forced into the car ahead of the bandits: "They're going to kill me if I don't come in; they're going to shoot me if I don't come in."

He passed out again, as Avery, followed by the bandits, climbed inside. They looked him over and started to shoot him again.

"The man's dead now," Avery pleaded. They turned to the safe, searched him for the keys, and, unable to find them and not being prepared to blow it, left empty-handed. They found Dunlap alive and conscious, as the blast had hit him in the side. They grabbed him up from the ground, lifted him on his horse, and rode away into the night. Then the train backed up to Benson, where an engine and a boxcar met them to hurry Jeff to the hospital at Tucson, where Doctor H. W. Fenner was waiting to operate upon the arm.[9]

Many years before, Jeff's warm friend, Dr. George A. Goodfellow, serving his youthful apprenticeship in Tombstone—and hence experienced in treating gunshot wounds—had said, "Jeff, sometime you are going to get shot all to pieces in your business. When you do, don't let anybody operate until I get there. I'll save you."

But Doctor Goodfellow had left Tombstone and become a renowned surgeon in San Francisco. He read the news in the

grateful to Tom T. Main, April 28, 1938, for these suggestions.

[9] Account of the attempted robbery is found in *The Oasis*, February 17, 1900; files of Duane Bird, Nogales; and *Arizona Daily Citizen*, February 16, 1900. E. F. Williams, writing in the *Brewery Gulch Gazette*, September 28, 1934, says that others were involved but does not identify them.

papers next morning and wired the S. P. agent at Tucson that he was coming. The agent wired back that the operation had already been performed. Jeff regretted it the rest of his life, as he was confident that Goodfellow would have saved his arm.

After nearly three hours under chloroform at St. Mary's in Tucson, Jeff came to that night, "starving to death for water." St. Mary's was a small hospital then, and a Mexican boy instead of a nurse was on duty at night. Jeff called for a drink, and the boy said he had orders not to give him any water.

"Listen, here," reasoned Jeff, "if you don't bring me some water, when I get up from here, I'm going to kill you." The boy brought a pitcher at a trot. Jeff drank it all, called for another, and finished three pitchers before getting enough. Then he turned over and slept for eight hours without waking. But he did not rest well, and when Frank King came by to visit, he told him to get his gun from his bag and put it under the pillow. "I'll feel better with it there," he explained.[10]

Of course the nurse saw it, and with the authoritative air that marks good nurses, advised, "You can't keep that thing there."

"Well, if I can't, I'll go to some other hospital," he retorted.

Dr. Fenner tied the bone with wire, and the wound would not heal. So he sent Jeff to the Southern Pacific Hospital at San Francisco. Dr. Goodfellow, mindful of professional ethics and sensitive at not being called at first, still did not come to see him. He lay there for nearly eight months. Dr. Gardner, the chief surgeon, twitted him about his gun.

"You're not afraid of these girls?" he laughed.

"Not exactly afraid of them, but I'm going to keep my six-shooter, certain. And if I had not kept it," he continued, "they'd a-killed me, shore."

At length his arm was stinking and his left leg swollen the size of his body, and Gardner came, visited casually in the bedside fashion of the old-time doctor, and asked, "Have you ever made your will, Milton?"

"Why, no, Doc," said Jeff with surprise, "haven't anything to will anybody."

[10] Frank M. King, Wranglin' the Past, 250.

The surgeon suggested he must have a lot of little things he would like to leave to his friends. "Everyone has some arrangements to make," he continued. "A short time ago I made my will. Got everything straightened up. Something every man should do."

Jeff was bored with the silly suggestions until the surgeon added, "We've decided to take your arm off at the shoulder day after tomorrow. It won't be dangerous but you will be in the hospital quite a long time."

Jeff raised up, rang his bell, and to the uniformed girl who bobbed up in the doorway firmly said, "Bring me my bill."

"What's that for?" Gardner asked, with interest.

"I'm paying my bill and getting out of here, today! That talk of wills doesn't sound good to me."

"You can't do that," said Gardner, jumping up. "Think of the reputation of this hospital."

"I'm thinking about my arm," Jeff replied. "I'm quitting this place today, and anybody who tries to stop me will be carried out feet first. Nurse, get that bill and call a carriage."

He paid the bill, sat up, and got dressed. Then he shoved his gun in his waistband, and with Joe Leggett's help, staggered out to the carriage. He was driven to the Lane Hospital, where Dr. Goodfellow practiced.

Goodfellow ordered a glass of whiskey for him, which sounded like science to Jeff, at once probed the wound, and pulled out the remaining fragments of bone tied with piano wire. He dug the corruption from the swollen member with his hand while Milton grew sick and depressed.

"Why, Jeff," he soothed, "we'll both be down at Zincan's in three weeks having a champagne supper." And they were.

When Jeff left the hospital for Nogales, Goodfellow fitted him with a brace to support his arm, but he threw it out the train window the first night. A short stub of bone stuck out from his shoulder, and his limp arm, several inches too short, now swung with a tightly clenched fist. Goodfellow said that he would never use it again.

But Jeff, always resourceful in treatment of trouble, had his own ideas. He filled a buckskin bag with bird shot, tied it around his wrist to pull on his arm, and let it swing loosely against the fingers of his hand. The bag of bullets continually beat against his hand in keeping with his stride, and at every beat he consciously tried to grasp it with his fingers. In time they began to flex. Eventually they were as supple as ever, although on account of the missing bone he never recovered the free use of his arm.

Meanwhile the outlaws were dispersed. Bravo Juan Yoas, who had caught a buckshot in his hip and had quit the fray in spite of the compact to kill whoever weakened, headed in a hurry up the San Pedro into Mexico. Across the line he stopped at the ranch of an old Texan, Uncle Billy Plasters. Jeff knew him in Grimes County, Texas, and had his help when he was tried at Abilene.

When, years later, a friend asked him why he left such a fertile region as central Texas to settle in the Arizona desert, he said he was bothered too much with lawsuits.

"Uncle Bill," the friend observed, "it would seem to me that for a man of your means a few lawsuits wouldn't bother much."

"Well, you see," came the measured answer, "all those suits were entitled '*The State of Texas* vs *William Plasters.*' "[11]

Into Bill Plasters' ranch rode Bravo Juan on a "give-out horse." Plasters took him in and made him welcome until he happened to observe that he had just helped kill Jeff Milton.

"Why, you so-and-so," swore Uncle Bill, as he reached for his gun, "if you killed Jeff, I'll just kill you." But Bravo Juan limbered up his stiff leg and got away again toward Cananea. When he stopped there to get his wound dressed, the Mexican officers took him and gave him up to Sheriff Scott White at Tombstone.

After the abortive holdup, Brown and the Owens boys, supporting Jack Dunlap in his saddle, rode north by east into Walnut Gulch, between Tombstone and the Dragoons. Scott White gathered a posse and took off on their trail. At Buckshot Springs

[11] Tom T. Main to Hervey Chesley, April 28, 1938. Plasters lost one eye when cracked with a bull-whip while serving in the Mexican War. He was direct in action. He crossed the line into a hostile county in pursuit of a Texas thief, shot him, and was convicted. Houston White to Hervey Chesley. *Texas Appeals Reports*, VI, *State* v. *Plasters*, for one of his lawsuits.

they found "Three-Fingered Jack" where his partners had left him to die.

He had begged his companions not to leave him, but when they did, he swore he would spill the beans if the officers found him. They knew he would die and so had ridden off and left him. But, although one kidney was shot to pieces, he was still alive. Scott White brought him to Tombstone where he lived for several days, and made good his threat and gave the bunch away, implicating Matt Burts and confirming the suspicion that Alvord, Stiles, and Downing were back of the robberies.

After he confessed, the officers swept over into Sulphur Springs Valley to take the Owens boys at their ranch. They picked up Bob Brown. They went on to Willcox and put Downing, Stiles, Burts, and Alvord under arrest. These bad men, unaware of Dunlap's confession, surrendered peaceably, blandly professing their innocence, and were lodged in jail at Tombstone. When called before Justice of the Peace A. T. Schuster for their examining trial, Tombstone's noted criminal lawyer, Allen R. English, represented them. To their great surprise, they were denied bond and thrown back in prison.[12]

On March 2, 1900, Alvord and Downing were taken before the United States Commissioner and charged with the federal offense of obstructing the mail. Then Stiles turned state's evidence to admit that he and Burts had committed the Cochise robbery, and that Alvord and Downing had helped to plan it.[13]

Then Billy Stiles, released through confession, perhaps suffered a qualm of conscience. He walked in to visit with the jailer, George Bravin, at noon, April 8, 1900, when the courthouse was empty. He asked to talk to Alvord alone. Bravin brought him out. They talked awhile, and when Bravin started back to the cell with Alvord, Stiles drew his gun and asked for the keys. Bravin resisted, and in the scuffle Stiles shot him in the leg, took the keys, and opened the jail doors. The prisoners, like average men

[12] *Arizona Daily Citizen*, February 19, 21, and 22, 1900. George Kuhns to J. E. H.; July 2, 1945.

[13] *Arizona Daily Citizen*, March 2, 1900; Mrs. Rosa Schuster to Hervey Chesley and J. E. H., March 8, 1938. Also comment by Frank King in *Western Livestock Journal*.

everywhere, accepted freedom when it came gratis. They fogged out of their cells, while Alvord and Bravo Juan broke for the front and armed themselves with Winchesters and six-shooters. But Downing and the Owens boys refused to leave, and Bravin called to a friendly prisoner to slam the gate.[14]

Alvord, Stiles, and Yoas trotted down Frémont Street and stole two horses at John Escapule's place near town. They seemed to be gone for good. In June, *The Metropolitan Star*, published in Tucson, printed an interview with them, quoting Stiles as saying they would not leave the Territory until they were good and ready, and that although they had written Sheriff White, they had not heard from him, perhaps because of their "lack of foresight in not enclosing return postage." Alvord, as usual, protested his innocence, adding, "If I knew I could get a trial and not have to lay in jail for five or six months, I would be willing to come in."[15]

Then the Arizona Rangers were organized on the pattern of the Texas force, and Burton C. Mossman came down from the Hashknives, at Holbrook, to serve as their captain. He was intent on capturing the noted Mexican bandit, Augustin Chacon, at large from the Arizona jails. He got in touch with Alvord and Stiles extending his influence toward clemency, and arranged a meeting in the Mexican mountains below Naco, where they were to beguile Chacon into camp. The scheme worked, and he returned Chacon to be hanged by Sheriff Jim Parks, at Solomonville. Then again Alvord and Stiles were lodged in the Tombstone jail.[16]

After varied adventures elsewhere, Jeff had drifted back into

[14] *Arizona Daily Star*, August 8, 1909; Walters, *Tombstone's Yesterdays*, 194–95; Sonnichsen, *Billy King's Tombstone*, 89–91; Coolidge, *Fighting Men of the West*, 181; *Tombstone Epitaph*, April 8, 1900.

[15] As reprinted in the *Tombstone Epitaph*, June 12, 1900. Scott White, born in La Grange, Texas, in 1856, was educated at the University of Virginia, came to Arizona in 1881, and became a member of the Territorial Legislature in 1887. *Tombstone Daily Prospector*, March 12, 1887.

[16] Burton C. Mossman to J. E. H., August 6, 1937, and February 25, 1945; Jim Parks to J. E. H. and Hervey Chesley, February 27, 1945; undated clipping, *Bisbee Review*, Milton Papers; Coolidge, as cited, 266–81.

Tombstone and was playing cards at a saloon on the late afternoon of December 15, 1903, while Alvord and Stiles, along with forty-nine other unhappily crowded inmates, were still in the county jail. Someone ran down the street, yelling, "Jail break! Jail break!"

Jeff jumped up and ran for the jail. Inside he bumped into Billy King, a bartender and low-lifer of Tombstone, for whom he had the utmost contempt. King had a gun in his hand. Jeff threw down on him and told him to hand it over. He did, stammering, "Why, why, Jeff, I was going to help you catch them."

" 'Twa'n't nothin' to that," said Jeff, later. "He was just building up his case, as he had taken a quart of whiskey down to them to get their nerve up for the break."

The prisoners had dug a hole through the side of the building, cut a "suggan" into a rope, and dropped by it to the ground. Then Alvord, Stiles, and three others had mounted horses left saddled for them near Boot Hill Graveyard. Night and rough terrain insured their escape into near-by Mexico.[17]

Jeff, despite his crippled arm, took off in fury on their trail. With a horse and mule from Colin Cameron's outfit and authority for "any San Rafael horses or mules" he wanted, and with general letters in aid from Colonel Kosterlitzky and the secretary of state of Sonora, he headed after them into Mexico. Both Alvord and Stiles heard the news and threatened to kill him on sight.[18]

"I'll just beat them to it," he mused.

E. L. Chalfant, express messenger on Jeff's old run, heard somebody knock on the door of his car at Fairbank one night as he carried the Fort Huachuca pay roll. When he opened, in crawled Jeff with a six-shooter, sawed-off shotgun, a box of buckshot shells, and a bottle of whiskey.

"I'm going to take a little trip with you," he explained. "Tonight's the night."

17 Hal Kerr to J. E. H., March 6, 1944.
18 Colin Cameron, January 26, 1904; Emilio Kosterlitzky, Febrero 11 de 1904; Fran'co Munoz, Enero 13 de 1904, in the Milton Papers. A reward of $1,000 was offered for their capture, February 1, 1904. *Tombstone Epitaph*, February 10, 1904.

"What-a you mean?" asked Chalfant.

"Alvord and Stiles are going to hold up the train," he answered. Chalfant got nervous, but Jeff was cool as a cucumber. As they approached Huachuca Siding, they heard the engine go "Toot, toot, toot!"

"There they are," said Jeff, gaily. "When they come up and demand that you open the door, do so and step on out. There will be three or four of them, and when they come in, I'll kill all the bastards at one shot."

Instead, it was an old farmer who had flagged the train to catch a ride, and whom the conductor gave an awful cursing for scaring the crew to death. But Alvord and Stiles circled away around Jeff.

Del Lewis, a 240-pound, six-foot-five-inch giant of a Mormon from St. Davids, and measurably a good man, was now sheriff of Cochise. He, too, set himself the job of catching them. Meanwhile, they held up a bullion train in Mexico and captured a bar of gold—some $8,000 worth in one chunk, and divided the spoils by sawing it in two. Then Hal Kerr, deputy at Douglas, got a call from Lewis to enlist help and ride to Nigger Head Gap, in the Nigger Head Mountains of Mexico, while Lewis posted himself at another pass, as Alvord and Stiles were expected to come through one or the other that night.

On the night of February 17, 1904, they came through the pass guarded by Lewis and Ranger Brooks. The officers opened fire with rifle and shotgun, and wounded and captured Alvord with his gold, which he carried in a morral from the horn of his saddle. Stiles got away.

They brought Alvord into Tombstone. He was already under sentence for two years to the penitentiary at Yuma—tolerant treatment for a designing criminal murdering cowboys with impunity because of constituted authority, perpetrator of two notorious train robberies, and two more under design at the time of the Fairbank affair.[19]

Jeff had one personal encounter with Alvord that amused him greatly. Once Alvord, thinking him still in California, had

[19] *Tombstone Epitaph*, February 18 and 24, 1904; Hal Kerr, as cited.

dropped into Tucson with Charlie Hood, smuggler of Chinamen, and another outlaw friend, and noised it about right sharply that he was on the warpath. Jeff happened to arrive that day from the west, and stopped to visit in Kirt Hart's gun shop.

"Good Lord, Jeff, you in town?" Hart exclaimed with concern. "Burt Alvord, Charlie Hood, and that bunch ain't been away from here a half an hour. He just came and got his six-shooter. I cleaned it up for him, and he was looking for you to kill you."

"The hell he was," said Jeff.

"Yeah!"

"Say, Kirt, there are two or three of 'em running together, ain't they?"

"Yes."

"Well, give me that shotgun over there," Jeff said, pointing to the gun. "Wrap it up. I won't need it going down the street. Got my six-shooter. But I'll take it down where I'm going—to the Kelton Hotel."

He went on to the hotel to join W. S. Sturgis, a cowman friend, Cap Kelton, his old *compadre* of the Customs Service, and several other congenial souls. Someone in the bar suggested a game of cards for the drinks, and a drummer joined—as drummers were willing then. Jeff sat to watch the door, and leaned the shotgun against the wall behind him.

"What're you doing that for, Jeff?" asked Kelton.

"Well, Alvord's been a-huntin' me to kill me, I understand. There's three of them, and I'd just as soon have it there, where I can use it on 'em."

Everybody sat down to the game. In a moment the swinging doors flew back with a bang against the walls and Burt Alvord came striding in. Jeff reached for the shotgun and straightened up. At that instant Alvord saw him, turned a little white under his swarthy skin, and whirled to run.

"Stop, or I'll kill you," Jeff commanded. "One more step, and I'll kill you!"

Alvord stopped dead in his tracks, crying, "My God, don't kill me!"

"Well, back up there," snapped Jeff. "What's the matter with you."

And as Alvord came back, Jeff advancing to meet him, Sturgis yelled, "Why don't you kill him, Jeff? He's been hunting you to kill you."

Then Cap Kelton popped up, his Southern blood in commendable commotion, yelling, "Kill the son-of-a-bitch, Jeff! Kill him!"

"Why, I hate like the devil to kill a man," Jeff grinned, "unless he's got a six-shooter on, or something."

He felt for Alvord's gun in his waistband, but it was not there. He figured it was in his boot, under his breeches leg, but he did not search him, thinking "maybe he'd go after it," and the bother would be over. At this moment, Doc Donovan, an officer, walked in, saw what was up, and joined in the harmony.

"Jeff, why don't you kill the so-and-so. He's been telling down the street that he was looking for you; going to run you out of town or kill you on sight."

"I don't believe I'll shoot him," Jeff rejoined. "I'll take him over and let Mr. Buehman shoot him. Then we'll have the picture of a brave man."

He reached up with his sound, right hand, grabbed Alvord by the ear, spun him around, kicked him through the swinging doors, and marched him over to Buehman's, with Donovan trailing along to witness the "shooting." The picture was made. Then, with Jeff's positive warning that if he ever crossed his trail again it would be a shooting of a different sort, Burt Alvord—one of the worst of the Arizona gunmen—parted company with Arizona for good.

"He had murdered a bunch of men, and I should have killed him," Jeff would say in retrospect. "But you just hate to shoot a man when he's hollerin'!"[20]

William Larkin Stiles, as another of "Arizona's famous bandits" had been hopefully named, was at last killed in Nevada in

[20] Both Dane Coolidge, in *Fighting Men of the West*, and C. L. Sonnichsen, in *Billy King's Tombstone*, give chapters on Burt Alvord and his adventures.

January, 1908, where, after wide wanderings, he was serving as a deputy sheriff under the name of William Larkin.[21]

Bob Brown, Matt Burts, and the Owens brothers went to the pen. Bill Downing was accommodatingly killed a few years. later in Willcox. Bravo Juan Yoas died on the Amazon, and Burt Alvord, after a time in Brazil, died of fever in the Barbados in 1910, still with a pocket full of gold in his possession.

For a while these widespread connections had flowered into splendid outlaw enterprise. Jeff Milton's courageous, one-handed use of a sawed-off shotgun, and the resulting bitter and dying confession of "Three-Fingered Jack" at Tombstone, broke it up. Jeff was saddened that his old friend Scarborough, his own peer at the point of a gun, had been killed in April, 1900,[22] while charging five desperate men above him in the crags of the Chiricahuas. In mellow years he observed, "I think I am a pretty lucky man to be here. My old friends are all gone—every damned one of them."

Yet there still hangs a sort of mistaken aura, compounded of design and daring, around the heads of the Western outlaws. The rough and liberal territory of Arizona seemed a perfect place to practice the trade except for one thing—it eventually ran into the stout resolution of honest and brave men, who, too, were good with guns.

[21] Hal Kerr, as cited; *Arizona Daily Star*, August 8, 1909.

[22] Walter Birchfield was with him in this fight. Scarborough was shot down. Birchfield went for help. At last he was taken to the hospital at Deming and died there, April 5, 1900. Walter Birchfield to J. E. H., November 2, 1939; *El Paso Times*, April 5, 1900; *El Paso Herald*, April 5 and 28, 1900.

Prospector's Luck

It was natural for Jeff Milton to feel the powerful lure that takes hold of men and turns them into prospectors. For years the arid Southwest—actually giving so little, while promising so much, to imaginative men—had been his home.

For years men with horny hands and hearts of hope had torn at the hard and torrid earth of southern Arizona. In camp and in town, talk turned to the wealth that folks of faith just knew was there. The Old Gila Diggings, the ancient mines of Ajo, the strikes at Tombstone, and the fabled wealth of Plancha de la Plata, stirred the memories of poor but hopeful prospectors. And now, in Milton's time, the necessary enterprise to exploit whole mountains of copper, beyond the reach of the individual, was furnished by that ingenious aggregation of capital called the corporation.

And so in casting about for something that a man without money and only one good arm could do, Jeff thought of the mines he had poked into in desert and mountain. There were many prospects which he had found and on which he had filed. In the late eighteen nineties he, Luke Smith, and George Kuhns had just missed wealth by inches far south in the Sierra Madres.

They struck out with George on a stocking-legged, bald-faced horse called Tiger, which Jeff had taken from Bronco Bill, Luke on Nigger, and Jeff on a sorrel named Flaxie. Their two gray pack mules trailed faithfully behind from Nogales to John Slaughter's ranch, where they turned south into the Sierra Madre. Over the divide from the Tigre Mine, not far from the Yaqui River, was a ledge of silver an old Mormon had showed Jeff on an earlier trip. The three had decided to prospect it.

They worked like beavers on the ledge and threw up a pile of ore. When they ran out of food, they fell back on the mountains, full of deer and turkey. They killed the birds in quantity, sliced the breasts, salted and peppered them well, "jerked" them like beef, and toiled for weeks on nothing but meat. Both Smith and Kuhns were miners, and Smith estimated their tellurium ore was worth $2,700 a ton. Each knew it was fabulously rich. Jeff took a sample at last and rode for the Tigre to get it assayed.

He made himself known to King and Jones, the operators of the mine.

"You are not Jeff Milton who used to be chief of police at El Paso?" one exclaimed.

When he admitted he was, Jones recalled that Jeff had lent him a hundred dollars when he and his wife were stranded there at the Pierson Hotel. And King reminded him of the time Jeff had kept him out of jail at Juárez, where he had been held with a shipment of goods under suspicion as a smuggler.

So they joyfully took him in, gave him a bath and shave, and let him admire the piano they had brought in for Mrs. Jones—packed in on the backs of mules through those precipitous mountains—no mean feat in the history of music, even if it has escaped the notice of the *maestros*.

They gave him all the supplies he could carry and ran a test of his samples. It showed between seven and eight dollars of pay to the ton. Jeff was so disappointed that he tied his provisions on his saddle and rode back that night and got Smith and Kuhns out of bed. They packed their tools and camp equippage and pulled out by day—cursing, a little incomprehensibly, their rotten luck.

In time a man named McNiell took up the claim. He reported that none of the ore on their dump ran less than $2,000 to the ton. It was very heavy, and Jones and King simply had not known how to assay it. In reminiscence, Jeff would tell how they slaved for so long on nothing but jerky and then walked off and left a fortune lying on the ground.

"Well, I just had to laugh," he would say. "We was rich and didn't know it."[1]

Again and again his prankish and impulsive nature cost him

1 George Kuhns to J. E. H., July 2, 1945, as well as Milton notes.

money, and once, he liked to tell, three chilipitin peppers cost him a fortune. He carried a silver cap-box in his watch pocket, similar to the snuffboxes now collected as antiques. It was a relic of the days of percussion-cap guns and just the right size for a month's supply of that tiny, wild, Southwestern pepper pod that is the quintessence of canned fire. Three or four of the pods, slightly larger than a match head, will season a pot of beans. Jeff was fond of peppery food and carried his chilipitins with him.[2]

When a Boston mining man showed up at Nogales in search of prospects, Jeff told him of a good one to which the superintendent of bridges, on the railroad to Guaymas, had directed him. The man was interested when Jeff priced the properties at $20,000, and asked to see the claim. From Nogales they took the train south through Sonora, got off at Llano, and spent the night.

The next morning at breakfast Jeff, as usual, slipped his cap-box from his watch pocket and crumbled a chilipitin over his eggs.

"Mr. Milton, what's that?" inquired the mining man with the commendable curiosity of the scientific mind and that perfect willingness to ask questions that marks the tenderfoot.

"Water coolers," said Jeff.

"Do they really make water cool?" pressed the tenderfoot.

"Quite cool," answered Jeff, as he worked the fragments into his eggs.

"Where do you get them?"

"Grow wild."

"Isn't that remarkable," observed the mining man, "that nature, here in this terrible desert, produces something that actually makes water cool."

"Quite remarkable," said Jeff, busy with his bacon and eggs.

When breakfast was over, he engaged horses, made up an outfit, and packed into the mountains. He reached a water hole on a hot afternoon, pointed to the mine on a hill above, and told his prospective buyer that here they would camp. He threw off the pack while the tenderfoot took a tin cup and went to the hole

[2] Chilipitin or *Capsicum baccatum* is common in the Southwest. See Ellen D. Schultz, *Texas Wild Flowers* (Chicago, 1928), 325.

for a drink of water. But he came back saying, "I believe I'll try some of those water coolers. How do you use them?"

"Just chew 'em and drink," said Jeff, fishing out his cap-case.

"How many should I take?" asked the adventurer in that brave new world.

"Three or four are quite ample," said Jeff, enjoying the joke.

The man went back to the hole while Jeff hobbled the horses out on grass, and then came back to the camp site, and said, "If you are ready, we'll go up and examine the vein."

"Not on your life," growled the man with hot eyes and hotter mouth. "I wouldn't look at a mine with anybody who would treat me like that."

Jeff was never a man to argue, placate, or cajole, and seeing the fat was really in the fire, he quietly said, "Very well, sir." He went and caught up the horses, and quietly, and very coolly in spite of the desert heat, they made the return trip to Llano and caught the train for Nogales.

"And those three chilipitins cost me $20,000," Jeff would laugh in later years, "for that claim was a good one, and he'd a-bought it, certain."

As it was, he never did sell it, for, in keeping with the time and his temperament, he just walked off and left it, as fun, if not fortune, was then beckoning from every direction.

While Jeff was prospecting and hunting outlaws, William C. Greene was driving his great venture in Cananea Copper to success. And Greene, with genuine affection for Jeff, tried to take him in and make him wealthy, too.

321

When Jeff first knew him, Greene and Jim Burnett were running a butcher shop at Tombstone and prospecting on the side. Greene had come to Arizona in 1877, to Tombstone to work as a miner during the boom, and used to stop at Jeff's customs camp at the site of Hereford as he prospected in and out of Mexico. Then he married and settled in the San Pedro Valley near by.

Charleston, a mining and smelting town below Tombstone, on the San Pedro, was a tough place that came to be presided over by Justice of the Peace Jim Burnett. He was noted for legality, if not justice, and in his own style.

He fined Jack Schwartz $1,000 for killing a man, and he pulled a cowman off his horse and fined him twenty steers then and there for being drunk, making, it is claimed, $22,000 out of the office in two years.[3]

Meanwhile, Greene had built a dam on the San Pedro. Burnett resented his appropriation of the waters, somebody blew the dam up, and Greene's little girl, Helen, along with a playmate fell into a hole left by the flood and were drowned. Greene suspected Burnett, and in rage hunted him up on the streets of Tombstone, walked up to him, and shot him down, saying, "The Lord giveth and the Lord taketh away."[4]

Greene wired Jeff at Nogales and he came by train, bringing Colonel Harlow, a lawyer, with him. Greene's bond was set at $20,000, which was made, as old lady Warnekros, friend of Burnett and hotel proprietress, went charging up and down Tombstone's streets, six-shooter in hand, swearing she would kill him on sight.

Since Greene thought he might be shot at the trial, Jeff sat behind him in the courtroom. He was acquitted, "more on account" of his colorful, dominant personality, one Arizona historian wrote, "than on account of the jury's belief that Burnett had really blown up the dam."

It has been freely stated that the jury and officials friendly

[3] See *The Arizona Citizen*, August 23, 1893; McClintock, *Arizona*, II, 487–88; Frank C. Lockwood, *Pioneer Days in Arizona* (New York, 1932), 266–67.
[4] This was Milton's recollection. McClintock, *Arizona*, II, 603 ff., says Greene shot him, remarking, "Vengeance is mine, I will repay, saith the Lord." Anyway Burnett was "plumb" dead. *Arizona Star*, July 9, 1897.

to Greene were given good jobs at Cananea in later years, for "Bill Greene never forgot a friend." Jeff thought he hired all the officials there. "I know," he continued, "that he hired Scott White, who was sheriff, at $12,000 a year, and I guess he had an expense account of $20,000." But this generosity came with the growth of Cananea Copper.

For twenty years Greene had dreamed of a fortune from mining in Mexico. By 1898 he had acquired options on the properties at Cananea, Sonora, and the next year promoted the Cobre Grande Copper Company. From here on, there is debate about his ethics but none whatever about his drive. He was a dominant man. As a minor, dissatisfied stockholder in the first company, he took forcible possession late in 1899. He pushed his claims through a Mexican court with influence, got the properties transferred to the Cananea Consolidated Copper Company, which was his own, and then really "went to town."

In spite of strong opposition, he built a railroad from his mines to Naco, and Cananea became a teeming town of twenty thousand people in five years. Trouble brewed as his ventures spread. He hired personal bodyguards and gunmen, spent his money lavishly, bought a splendid house in the capital of Hermosillo for entertainment of public officials, became a close friend of President Díaz, and wielded influence in Mexico where it counted. He fought his battles in the courts, ostentatiously breezed into New York, and willingly locked horns with the moneyed interests there.

Among Jeff's old friends whom he hired was Allen Bernard, to serve as his go-between with the Mexican officials. Jeff recalls seeing Bernard "gamble off a thousand dollars at a throw and put it down as expenses." Any and everything went, for Greene had the spirit of an inveterate gambler, and Greene now had the money.

Then he began buying land along the San Pedro, apparently wanting only that range and all that joined it. He told his agents to buy out his old friends, paying their price. Jim Wolf priced his place at a fancy figure, and then spent the rest of his life regretting that he had not doubled it, because Greene had urged his

323

buyer to treat Jim well. By 1904 he claimed six million acres of ranch land, much of which was in Mexico. His chuck wagons were stocked with cases of champagne, and the way his waddies choused his stock was a caution.

When he started to pay high wages to his Mexican miners, it is said that Díaz stopped him—reminding him that great disparity between wages at Cananea and income in the country meant desertion of the farms.

Cananea began pouring out fortunes in copper, and Bill Greene, the Tombstone butcher, was flying high. He was sharp, however, and knew that trouble was in the offing. He gathered gun-fighters on his pay roll, and kept after Jeff to join him, telling him all he had to do was just go to Cananea "and hang around."

"What'll you pay?" asked Jeff.

"Pay you?" said Bill. "Why I'll just write a note to my treasurer and let you name it." And he meant it.

Jeff declined. He would help his friends anywhere and at any time. But he had never hired out as a fighter—a professional gunman—and he never would. Greene urged him to take three thousand shares in Cananea Copper at $3.00 a share, and offered to carry him for the investment. But Jeff abhorred obligation to any man, and turned it down. The stock soon went to $37.50[5]

After Jeff left the hospital, Greene again offered employment. But the business did not look good to him, and besides, he was thinking of Texas. The Lucas discovery of oil had fired adventurous capital to seek black gold along the Gulf Coast. W. S. Sturgis, of Tucson, and W. S. Tevis, "the California land and cattle king," agreed to put up some money.

So Jeff pulled out for Texas. What took him back was the Beaumont boom and the boyhood memory of a natural-gas jet northeast of Navasota, where he used to go with parties on

[5] Greene was a man of such fantastic ventures that it is difficult to find a conservative account of Cananea. Dane Coolidge, *Fighting Men of the West*, gives a chapter to him. McClintock, *Arizona*, II, 603–605; *Tucson Citizen*, July 13, 1907; *Prose and Poetry of the Cattle Industry* (Kansas City, Mo., 1904), I, 621–26; John Cameron to J. E. H., as cited.

picnics, punch a hole in the middle of a tin pan, turn it over the "gas spring," mud up around the edges, set fire to the gas spewing out through the hole, and cook meals over the improvised burner for novelty. Jeff reasoned there ought to be oil where there was gas.

He went first to Beaumont, walked in on an auction of leases, and bid one in. An anxious buyer who had missed the bid rushed up and offered him a profit of $4,500. He took it even before he had paid for the purchase. It was too good a start in the "oil business."

Twelve miles west of Huntsville in the vicinity of the old "gas spring," he blocked six thousand acres in leases with the help of Edward Lee Spell, a local man, and prepared to sink a test. Early in March a news dispatch from Bryan reported that "J. D. Milton, an oil man from California," had started a boom by leasing and buying land in Burleson County. "He found seventeen old wells on his property where oil prospecting had been done several years before in a crude way," the account continued.

When he passed through Tucson in April, the paper there noted that "Captain J. D. Milton, the Wells, Fargo & Co. express messenger and noted gun fighter" was en route to his properties in Texas, "where oil has just been struck at eighty feet in large quantities." Certainly oil laid a powerful stimulus on the venturesome nature of men and even skidded the news clear out of line.

Jeff hired two California drillers named Henry and Dave Griminger. Henry took charge of the crew, while Dave, a powerful man, dressed the tools. Dave weighed 190 pounds and seemed to be all body. Though he stood five feet, ten and one-half inches high, he had a leg length of only twenty-nine inches and could flip a six-hundred-pound bit off the ground, across his thigh, on to the drilling floor. When a Walker County Negro, the local strong man, backed up to a five-hundred-pound bale of cotton and skidded it into a wagon, Griminger put him to shame by taking the hooks, picking it up, and pitching it in.

Edgar Spell, who took much interest in the venture, appreciated, too, the quality of the native whiskey, and found a moonshiner to supply them. Whenever Jeff's jug was empty, he left it in a hollow stump near the lease, and invariably the next morning it would be full of powerful meadow dew.

And so with Beaumont booming, leases blocked, location made, a California driller manhandling bits to the wonderment of the countryside, and their naturally ebullient spirits bolstered by the jug in the tree stump, there was really room in Texas for optimism.

In fact, too much! Somebody came by with the oil fever and the frenzied finance to match, and offered Jeff $50,000 profit on his leases. Instead of selling, however, he felt obligated to discuss the offer with his backers, and the opportunity passed. The Grimingers got to work on the lease in August, 1901.

It turned out to be an old story in the highly technical and dearly expensive search for oil. There were mistakes and mismanagement, disappointing delays, local chicanery, and at last the scarcity of funds that has stopped so many wildcat bits short of the "bottom of the hole."

Henry Griminger's log of the well shows that they drove pipe on March 25, 1902. But the driving through heavy blue clay was hard, and, he recorded, the pipe "Dove[d] together Can't drive no more." They had drilled only 820 feet. At the end of the month they were shut down, "waiting for orders." It was the end of the story for the "J. D. Milton Oil and Development Company" No. 1.[6] With his rewards for stopping the Fairbank robbery—at such cost to himself—completely gone, along with the advances by Sturgis and Tevis, Jeff walked off and left the lease.

He had an old friend at Nogales named Bill Cranz, who had been drunk on mescal for years. Cranz and a Mexican, José G. Moraga, of Ensenada, California, owned a gold mine in Lower California that had played out. Jeff had met Moraga, who was

[6] Milton notes; D. A. Griminger to J. E. H., November 18, 1945; MSS, "Log, Well No. 1, J. D. Milton Oil and Development Company"; "Time Book" kept by H. W. Griminger, foreman, Macedonia, Texas, 1901–1902; Warranty Deed, Edgar Spell to J. D. Milton, Deed Records, Vol. XIX, 206, Walker County; *Tucson Citizen*, June 24, 1901; contemporary clippings, Milton files; and *The Oasis*, August 24, 1901.

now interested in prospecting for oil on the peninsula. Moraga had written for Jeff to come and see him. He already had friends in California, among them a lovely lady named Alba Bennett, sister-in-law of Lucky Baldwin—the famous, wealthy San Francisco and Yukon man. It was easy to go and talk with Moraga, for California was attractive then.

Milton found Moraga an imaginative and courageous man with a great zest for life, whose friends were likewise willing to get rich in oil. And Moraga's story launched their venture. He knew an old coastal captain plying between San Francisco and Mazatlán, who had told him that just off the coast of Baja California, near San Gregorio's Bay, he once had sailed for six miles through a lake of oil.

It was a challenging tale that started them on their quest. Three prominent Mexicans in Guaymas, and Tevis, of the great Victoria Land and Cattle outfit, took stock in the company that Moraga formed. Jeff traded some of his Texas stock, put in a little cash, and he and Moraga left for Lower California to prospect together.

It is a barren, tough, and torrid land. Jeff found the natives "the poorest but the finest people in the world." He was tremendously impressed with the apparent relationship between poverty imposed by the rigid discipline of nature and the sterling character of its simple people.

"It hadn't rained enough in sixteen years to wet a man in a white shirt," he recalled. Cattle were living off the branches of the mesquite. On the trip down, he visited long, over good drinks, with the captain of the little steamer, the *Curaçao*.[7] He, a veteran of the West Coast, told Jeff that they would have a rainy year. The Japan Current had shifted north, he observed, which always brought rain to Lower California.

So when Jeff began mingling with the natives and the talk turned to the drought, as it always does in arid lands, he knowingly looked at the brassy skies and confidently prophesied that the year 1903 would be a rainy one. He had studied the stars, he said in impious delight, and he knew.

[7] Pronounced "Ku-ray-sow'o."

327

The only mode of travel there was by mule. He and Moraga
rode for weeks. Besides the search for oil, he became interested
in phosphates. He conceived the idea that Lower California, similar in climate and terrain to Chile, might hold this treasure, too.
At the University of Arizona, at Tucson, he had discussed the
minerals with Professor William P. Blake, had learned how to an-
alyze them, and went prepared to find the stuff and to know
when he found it. And so it turned into an engaging pursuit with
a congenial companion in a rough and primitive land.

Jeff, too, at last found oil in the Pacific and traced it to its
source. They bought some land from the Gil Flores estate and
picked a location for their drilling test about halfway down the
west coast near San Juanico Bay. They returned to California,
and Jeff wrote Dave and Henry Griminger, who came at once.
Dave, with the strength of a grizzly and the loyalty that goes
with honest labor, would always do to take along.

In fact, he was too good a hand at times. Once when Jeff was
stopping at the Hollenbeck Hotel in Los Angeles, he saw his first
Smith and Wesson six-shooter and told Dave he was going out
to buy one.

"No, Cap, don't do that," said Dave. "There's a nigger police
man here that is pretty sassy. I'll just bring you his gun in the
morning."

Next morning Jeff was pulling on his clothes when in walked
Dave and pitched a policeman's badge and six-shooter on the
bed. Jeff "just had to laugh. But," he said, "I had my Smith and
Wesson."

In June, 1903, Jeff, Moraga, and the Grimingers assembled
their equipment, supplies, harness, and wagons at San Pedro,
and loaded them on a vessel bound for Guaymas. Opposite San
Juanico Bay they set their stuff off on a lighter and ran it into the
beach. They bought a string of bronc and midget mules, broke
them to work, and snaked their equipment to their location, five
miles inland at a little fresh-water lake, six or eight miles west
of the village of Purísima.

Then, in keeping with the changing Japan Current, if not in
the course of the stars, it began to rain. It almost washed that

328

rugged land away. Jeff's reputation as a seer was made. The toads, those anachronistic curiosities of the desert, came out of the hard and hot recesses of the earth in grotesque but dignified swarms. A man could not lay his hand on level ground without putting it down on one. As soon as the toads left, mice swarmed over the country in millions. Dave Griminger put some barley in the bottom of a five-gallon can, inclined a board to the top, and left it overnight. The can was teeming with mice the next morning.

Grass sprang up to cover the barren earth. The native cattle that had been as poor as rawhide strings, that had lived all their lives on cactus, without water, with atrophied bladders hardly larger than a man's thumb, grew fat as butter. Their tallow turned as yellow, and Jeff thought they were "the finest beef" that he ever ate.

He never found a region more fascinating. It appeared to be the most desolate in the world. Yet they drew on the Pacific for lobsters and luscious fish, and an Indian rode with them in their boat to catch all the giant turtles they could eat. Upon seeing one near the beach, he would dive from their boat to catch it by the tail, and, using it as a rudder, steer the surprised reptile right out on land as he scrambled to get away.

It is claimed that turtle furnishes a connoisseur with every type of edible flesh. Jeff found it delicious. He delighted in doing the cooking, especially in camp, and he found that the best way of "fixing them" was on the lower shell. The legs were left attached after the upper shell and the inedible portions had been cut away. Then the lower, soft shell was placed directly on the coals. The heat caused it to curl. Pepper, salt, and tomato sauce were applied to the exposed meat, broiling, too, in the heat. When it was done to a turn, the cupped shell held the pure juice of the meat—"the finest soup in the world."

Figs and dates were grown by irrigation in the canyons, dried in the open air, and packed and sewed in rawhide bags for home use and sometimes export. In his wanderings Jeff met an aristocratic old settler with four to five thousand gallons of wine fifty years old; another with fifty hogsheads of tequila that had likewise aged for half a century. There was no market. All they could do was to keep the stuff until it wasted away with age, which, too, is suggestive of the observation of the sages that wasting with age is tragic.

Once a month the prospectors took the ancient coastal mule trail south to Magdalena Bay, where the *Curaçao* put in on its monthly rounds, and got the mail from California. Alba Bennett remembered Jeff with letters and literature. So, with lobsters and fish from the Pacific, fruits from the canyon of Comondu, ducks from their near-by lake, quail, sheep, and venison from the mountains, and rare old wines and liquors from the cellars of generous people grateful for the breaking of sixteen years of drought—with all this plus *Fifty Songs of Love* and Browning's *Sonnets from the Portuguese* sent by Alba—it didn't matter a whole lot to Jeff whether they struck oil or not.

Dave Griminger recalls that Jeff would sit by the lake as the drilling went on—unable to work with both hands—and kill messes of ducks with his six-shooter. One day he came in and said, "Dave, this damned old gun don't shoot straight. Instead of shooting their eyes out, it shoots their bills off."

He worked on the sights awhile, Griminger recalled, until it shot "straight" again and he could easily shoot a bird's eye out at thirty feet.[8]

But while the Grimingers were drilling and Bill Cranz, who had joined them, was soaking up mescal, Jeff and Moraga were riding. They covered the coastal trail that Fierro Blanco has described so well in *The Journey of the Flame*, the life story of a redheaded Mexican centenarian whose Irish father had dropped from a passing ship.

Milton read the story in his old age and found it a "lovely book." He recalled meeting some redheaded Mexicans named Smith at the tip of the peninsula, descendants, they claimed, of a ship-wrecked English sailor who had leisurely drifted north toward California, "marrying in every village," and leaving a host of redheaded progeny along *The Journey of the Flame*. No wonder "there will always be an England" and a British Empire.

8 D. A. Griminger to J. E. H., as cited.

330

Across the peninsula east of their drilling location was the town of Mulege. At times Jeff and Moraga rode over the tortuous divide and dropped down on that side. On the way they stopped one night at a ranch where the owner took them in for supper and served them bull meat, after the custom of that rigorous land.[9] Moraga, with Castilian grace, turned to Milton and said, "Jeff, isn't this very delicious meat?"

And Jeff, unaware that anyone there knew English, blurted with Anglo-Saxon frankness, "It's so goddamned tough I can't chew it."

The next night they camped over the range eighteen miles away, and shortly after they had stopped, a *mozo*, or servant, from the ranch showed up on a hard-ridden mule with the hind-quarters of "the fattest calf you ever saw," said Jeff, "and a note of apology for the tough bull beef the ranchman had fed us the night before." Jeff was humiliated half to death.

At Mulege they rented rooms from a Mexican woman, as hotels were unknown. When Moraga got into a game of coon-can with their landlady, Jeff suggested that whoever lost should give a two-day dance. They fell upon the idea with relish. Moraga lost, the plans were made, and the good news spread. "They saddled their jackasses from up to two hundred miles away," according to Jeff, "and came for the dance."

Jeff had brought a can of "Allen's Foot-Ease" powder to use when hiking and kept it on the dresser in his room. During the dance the guests had full run of the house, and when it was over, he found that the fair señoritas had used all his "Foot-Ease" for face powder, and it seemed to do just as well at that.

Wherever he went, Jeff became noted as a doctor. Everyone on the frontier had a chance to turn his hand to medicine and surgery; and Jeff, with a genuine passion for patching folks up, got more than his share. Dr. Goodfellow had fitted him up with a kit of drugs that he might need, At Mulege he treated a girl about to die with a terrible abscess, simply lancing it. But the natives began to call him *"El Medico,"* and send for him in

---

[9] Fierro Blanco notes that bull meat, with the full flavor of maturity, was considered the only suitable food for real men in Lower California.

emergencies. Sometimes he rode two hundred miles to attend a person in distress.

Once it was a boy who had detonated a blasting cap and mangled his hand. Jeff had to amputate his shattered fingers. He whetted up his pocket knife—"just as good as anything when sharp"—deadened the hand with cocaine, and went to work.

"Doctor, can I smoke a cigarette," the boy asked.

"You shore can," soothed Jeff. And so he lay and smoked, feeling as big as a man, as Jeff unjointed all his fingers and sewed the skin together over the wound.

One day when Milton rode into Purísima, a runner came up to urge him to hurry to a man who was very ill. He took his kit of drugs off his saddle and walked to the place. Anxious womenfolk met him in the front room. One showed him to the back where her husband lay, and then excused herself with thoughtful Latin propriety while Jeff sat down and talked to the patient. The man was very sick, insisted he could not get well, and begged Jeff to give him something to end his misery.

"No, I can't do that," said Jeff. But he sat and talked awhile, and, seeing that the man was in terrible distress and beyond recovery, asked the lady for a glass of water. She brought it and again retired. He took a drug from his kit, stirred a heavy dose into the glass, set it on a table by the bed, and rose to go, saying, "Don't drink that. If you do, it'll kill you, certain."

In the outer room he met the solicitous wife, who asked, "How is he?"

"Very bad," Milton replied. "I don't think he'll live till morning."

Back at camp the Grimingers were pounding down the hole, while Bill Cranz, following the custom of years, was hitting the bottle until Jeff rebuked him, saying, "Bill, why don't you sober up?"

"Do you think I could stand it?" asked Bill, gravely but not soberly.

"Why you can't quit," taunted Jeff.

"I've done quit!" replied Cranz.

And quit he had. But he fell desperately ill with a urinary

infection, abscessed between the legs, went out of his head, and for two weeks tossed in his bed unable to sleep. Jeff saw he was bound to die unless something was done. Again he sharpened his knife, performed another operation, drew off the pus, and poulticed his patient thoroughly with brown sugar and turpentine soap. And Cranz lay and slept for twelve hours without moving.

Cranz was related to United States Senator George C. Perkins of California, and, through the Senator's interest and influence, an old-timer in the oil business named Joe Irwin, of the Union Oil Company, was sent down to look over their properties and pass on their prospects. Irwin, who liked the country but not their particular location, was there at the time and likewise fell desperately sick. Jeff decided that he had to get them back to the States.

The *Curaçao* was about due to touch at Magdalena Bay, far to the south, on its regular run back up the coast. Jeff sent a runner down the trail to have a small boat sent after them. One was brought by two sailors. Jeff and the crew packed Cranz to the beach on a litter and prepared to take him and Irwin out. The seas were running so high that one of the sailors quit and walked into Purísima.

Milton managed to load the sick men, although he would have lost the other sailor except for his lucky pitch of a line. Then he took the rudder himself—he had sailed in Florida as a boy—and they beat their way down the coast. When they came to enter Magdalena Bay, the surf was flying. The sailor said there were two *puertocitos*—two little doors or ports—pointing into the churning surf. Jeff could see nothing but the splash of waves, but he headed for the spot. Everyone, at times, is dependent on others and much in life must be taken on faith. Instead of crashing, as he expected, they rode through the surf to peaceful water inside, where they could hear the *Curaçao* whistling down the bay. They got there just in time.

He carried the men to California. There a surgeon on call examined Cranz and exclaimed, "What doctor performed this operation?"

Bill pointed at Jeff.

"Where'd you get your training?" he asked. "That's as good as anybody could have done."

"I got my education riding a-straddle of a mule," Jeff laughed.

Jeff returned to Lower California. The drillers struck a strong flow of soda water at one thousand feet, which they used to irrigate a little garden, and enjoyed roasting ears on Christmas Day of 1903. At twelve hundred feet the bit dropped into a cavity two hundred feet deep, where they lost the flow, and they drilled for two weeks before the water boiled out again, full of volcanic ash.

While hunting minerals, Jeff once stopped seventy-five miles up the coast at the jacal of a Mexican ranchero, whence he scouted the surrounding country for several days. The region was alive with game, but the Mexican's family was starving for meat. They were so poor they had no guns. Jeff took off a day to lay them in a supply of antelope and deer, which they "jerked."

He discovered a deposit of phosphate on the west coast near Comondu. His analyses showed it to be very rich, but he kept the location to himself, planning to return and develop it in the future. Meanwhile, the biting of the bit in the hard malpais was bringing him nothing, and at last he was definitely broke. In spite of the appeal of that land of arid rock and gracious people, he had to leave.

The powerful Griminger boys got down about eighteen hundred feet, when they ran out of sand line and the promoters ran out of patience about the same time. Thus another wildcat venture passed into that comfortable oblivion that covers lost fortune and failure.[10]

The zest of the search still possessed Milton, however, and he related another story about oil to Dr. H. K. Chenoweth, a friend in Nogales. Once, while in the Customs Service, scouting south to the Gulf of California, he picked up an Indian from Central America who told him a tale of life in Tabasco, in the tropics. In that land of swamps and rivers, with zopilotes for scavengers and iguanas and monkeys for food, he said, was a

[10] D. A. Griminger, as cited, and the voluminous Milton recollections.

334

"spring" in the swamps that poured heavy oil out on the surface of the water, which the Indians gathered to seal and waterproof their boats.

Chenoweth and others were fascinated with the story. Advancing mechanization of American life, with fabulous fortunes being made in oil, fired many a man with ambition to get at least a little greasy. Chenoweth and a wealthy Mexican at Magdalena, Sonora, put up the money for a prospecting trip.

Jeff went by way of El Paso, where he called his friend, Dr. Jessup, and told him what he had in mind.

"Why, you're crazy if you go," exclaimed Jessup, telling him that yellow fever was raging in lower Mexico.

"I know it," he agreed, "but I'm going."

"Well, if you must go, don't do any drinking at all," Jessup warned.

"I'll think about it," promised Jeff.

He took a Parker shotgun, a .30-.30 Winchester, a slicker, several hundred rounds of ammunition, and of course his old Colt .45. He always believed in being prepared.

He went by rail to Mexico City, where he stopped to see his friend of Pullman days, Dr. Bray, who, too, warned against the lower country, telling him that he "would never come back."

"I don't care," said Jeff. "I'm going."

"Then if you must go," Bray suggested, "don't drink any water unless you have poured some brandy into it." Now that sounded like real medical advice, and Jeff determined to follow it. Then, fortified with optimism and plenty of brandy, he left for Vera Cruz.

From there he took a boat to Coatzacoalcos, which he found in the throes of yellow fever. He stopped at a German-kept hotel, where another American was down with the fever. He bought all the brandy the landlord had, and for ten days treated the sick man himself, giving him enough Epsom salts to kill a cow and building him back on brandy until he was well. "Really and truly it was a pity," Jeff recalled, "to see the carts going through full of dead people. And the buzzards were just having a picnic."

Among the letters which Jeff carried from bankers in Mexico

City and Vera Cruz was one to Santiago Carter, a prominent man at San Juan Bautista. Since he planned to take off on his search from there, he caught another boat to the mouth of the Grijalva River and up it to the capital of Tabasco.

The iguanas, or giant lizards, tied in the stalls at the market place to be butchered did not bother him much, but the buzzards, sitting in somber gravity outside his window and cleaning up carrion as the protected scavengers of the place, did. But he was there on business, not for speculation on buzzards, and he found the house of Santiago, or Jim, Carter, and sent his letter in by a boy. A man rushed out and grabbed him in his arms. It was such a surprise that Jeff started to hit him.

Carter exclaimed, as he stepped back to look him over, "Why, Jeff, don't you know me!"

And Jeff did, for Jim Carter—which was an assumed name— had been a friend in Company B in the early eighties in the Ranger service in Texas.[11] He had killed a man near Laredo, and Jeff had given him a horse and helped him escape. He had drifted to the tropics of Tabasco, had married a Spanish woman, and now was the "king bee" of San Juan Bautista, the very man who could and would do everything that Milton needed.

When an Indian came down the Grijalva in a long dugout, Carter got him to take Jeff to the Indian town of San Juan de Estancia Vieja, with a letter to its Indian governor—a prolific breeder said to have a hundred children, and rich, too, in land. Yet, despite his potency and power, he "went around in his shirttail and a pair of *guaraches.*" They passed through the region where the brother of President Díaz had been killed by the Indians, and where, in retribution, Díaz had killed off nearly all its able-bodied men. In one Indian town of about two hundred women, Jeff did not see a male over eight years old. And where there were a few men, they were "stall-fed and cared for" as though they were genuinely important.

After a trip through streams and swamps, Jeff gave Carter's

[11] Milton never divulged his real name or the circumstances surrounding his trouble. At one time Carter wrote a column for a Mexico City paper called "Tabasco Sauce."

letter to the Indian governor at San Juan, who assigned him an open hut where he could sleep on the floor. During the night he awoke to feel something shoving him over in bed. He reached for his flashlight, the first he ever had, turned it on, and found an old hog sleeping beside him. He poked her out and went back to sleep.

San Juan was near his "oil spring." The governor furnished him a guide and some horses. They rode awhile, waded for two or three miles through a swamp up to their knees, and came to where a number of poles, stuck in the muck, extended above the water. The Indian indicated that this was the place. Jeff got out his cans for his samples. The guide churned a pole up and down in the mud and pulled it out, and the oil flowed after it. Jeff began skimming it up. When it had dissipated on the surface, they churned the muck and drew another pole, and Jeff left with a generous supply as evidence.

On the way out he stopped at a place on the Coatzacoalcos River where a Captain Stout detailed a servant and sent him monkey hunting in the jungle. It was genuine sport to shoot monkeys, Stout maintained, and besides they were good for food. They found plenty of monkeys, and Jeff was charmed by their antics. His *mozo* rushed up, pointing to the chattering swarms, shouting, "*Mate los! Mate los!*—Kill them! Kill them!"

But Jeff could not find it in his heart to shoot. Instead, he stood and watched the drove until it disappeared, and then he and the puzzled Mexican returned to Stout's.

"I'd just as soon of killed a man," he recalled. "In fact, a little rather!"

Back at Nogales he reported to his financial backers and showed his samples. Nothing came of it, for this search for oil— especially in a foreign land—called for heavy outlays of capital and real technical skill, as well as venturesome spirit. Jeff had the spirit, but that was not enough.

Then he went into Mexico to inspect a stand of timber for Bill Cranz, prospective buyer and developer. He went by train to Guaymas, to Las Mochias by boat, by stage to Álamos, and from there back into the Sierra Madres by team and buckboard.

He took a Mexican driver and a *mozo* outrunner, who trotted along afoot and whipped up the team.

Their horses balked in the middle of the Yaqui River. The *mozo* packed the Mexican to the bank on his back, but told Jeff he would have to wade if he wanted out.

"Nothing doing," snorted Jeff, opposed to such unjust racial discrimination. "Back up here, and I will ride you out."

The *mozo* objected and returned to the bank. Jeff had a bed and their chuck in the buckboard. He dug into the box for a lunch, and settled down to enjoy himself while the hungry Mexicans watched from the bank. After half an hour the servant waded back and again urged him to walk out.

"No, I'll just stay here until tomorrow," said Jeff, still munching his lunch. So the Mexican backed up to the buckboard at last, and Jeff mounted.

"I took him by both ears," he said, in describing the ride, "and told him I'd drown him, shore, if he dropped me. He didn't drop me."

He finally got the team out and inspected the timber, in beautiful, game-infested country. But in order to get it out, he found, the developers would have to drop the logs from a mesa one thousand to fifteen hundred feet into the river, and float them out, "and they'd be nothing but kindling then." Therefore, he returned and reported that it was a lovely country but unlikely business.

He told his friends about his phosphates, and a banker at Nogales showed considerable interest, called him into the bank, spread a map on the table, and said, "Jeff, can you point out the place? Are you sure you know where it is?"

"Certain!" said Jeff. The banker handed him a pencil and asked him to put it on the spot. As he started to do so, a warning impulse moved him just as the point went down. He avoided the proper place and put it about seventy-five miles up the coast, where he had killed the supply of game for the poor but hospitable ranchman.

Weeks passed as he pursued his other hopeful but fruitless enterprises. One day a letter came from the old Mexican rancher, addressed to him, his "very dear friend," and asking why he had not written him where the minerals were, so that he might have piloted his visiting friends to them. Jeff saw that the banker surreptitiously had sent an expedition to take his phosphates, and he headed for the bank, corralled the official in the back room, and asked if he had anyone who could read Spanish. Of course he did, and he called the clerk in. Jeff handed him the letter and told him to read it in English. The banker grew a little pale, and Jeff read him the riot act for being a double-crosser, and he did it in vigorous literary style. Another confidence had a similar ending.

It seemed to be enough to make a cynic out of a saint. Thereafter he kept the location and the talk of phosphates strictly to himself, and those of Lower California have never been found or mined.

Time and age never tarnished the recollections of that stark and torrid land that gave him so much in happiness but nothing whatever of fortune. It is not so bad to try for substance and fairly fail; the only sordid part of the story was shaken confidence coming from base betrayal. But that was perversely human and not elemental. After all, the real riches of that land of shimmering horizons and brilliant celestial stars were for the spiritual souls who could possess them. Poor prospector's luck was but a passing worry.

22

Mounted Chinese Inspector

In April, 1904, Jeff settled down in a steady job as "Chinese agent for the United States in a Foreign Country." It was unique work, and it, too, turned into a lot of fun.

Exclusion of Chinese from the United States had long been in effect.[1] But Mexico was open territory to them. They flocked there from the Orient, dribbled north through Sonora, and were smuggled across the Arizona line, at a price, by renegades who made a regular racket of the business.

The Immigration Service had developed no system to resist them, as the Border Patrol had not been organized. The smugglers were often desperate and always designing men who could be stopped only by an officer of sense and sand. Sam Webb, in charge of the customs office at Nogales, saw the need of a line rider, and thought of Milton. He was the best six-shooter shot in the country and had the reputation of being afraid of nothing on earth. He loved to range alone across the arid lands, and he knew them like a wild cow knows her range. It occurred to Webb that he was the man for the place, even if he did have but one good arm. Webb sounded him out, and Jeff showed some interest.

Webb then got in touch with Sturgis, Governor Brodie, and other of Jeff's friends, and in April, 1904, the appointment came through from President Theodore Roosevelt. Apparently there has been no other job just like it, for, as Harry Saxon, old-time sheriff of Nogales said, "It was just created for him."

He was his own boss, choosing his location, and, according

[1] Restrictions, given a broad status in the Burlingame Treaty in 1868, were restated and amplified in .the Restriction and Exclusion Acts of 1882. Mary Roberts Coolidge, *Chinese Immigration* (New York, 1909), 148, 160, 183, 240, 302. For law of 1904, see the *United States Code*, Chapter 7, Title 8, and for a case at law in exclusion, 130 U. S., 581.

to the official records, working "entirely upon his own initiative and responsibility." He was nominally under the inspector in charge of immigration at Tucson as well as the immigration office for the Southwestern District at San Antonio, but directly under the commissioner general of immigration, then of the Department of Commerce and Labor, at Washington. Such an independent connection, coupled with his spirit, assured a measure of unpopularity in the bureaucratic hierarchy.[2]

The object of the Chinese smuggler was to get the illicit immigrant across the line at some safe and distant point, direct him into friendly hands on this side, and collect the ransom for his own trouble. Usually it was collected in advance. Then, if anything went wrong, he could leave the luckless Chinese to fate, escape with the fee, and return to the relative obscurity of a decent occupation on this side, or the indifferent public reception of buccaneering pursuits on the other.

There was no attempt to regulate immigration except for Chinamen. The principal routes of entry naturally avoided the courses of conventional travel. Smuggling followed the tortuous trails, too rough for ordinary travel, across the desert lands. The worst of these came up by way of Altar to Sonoita, and across the desert to Wellton or Gila Bend. Another followed the mule trails out of Cananea, down the San Pedro Valley, and frazzled out to friendly destinations in Huachuca, Fairbank, and Tombstone, or the cellars of other Chinese merchants and menial laborers as far north as Globe.

Sometimes this human contraband paid its own freight; sometimes it was financed by wealthy relatives or friends of the aliens already established here; and often, according to Milton, it was engineered, planned, and paid for by the "Six Companies"[3] of San Francisco, whose far-reaching records and influence

[2] The character of this unique job was explained by Milton, and is verified by ferreting the files of the department at El Paso.

[3] Mary Roberts Coolidge, in her study of *Chinese Immigration,* seems to disparage the notion that these six great enterprises—well financed and powerful combinations of joint business and fraternal interests, to which most American Chinese belonged—were engaged in support of smuggling. Jeff Milton was convinced of the contrary. For a discussion of these Six Companies, see *Chinese Immigration,* 401–404.

touched the gentle if alien sympathies and the hard-working lives of all Southwestern Chinese.

But the chicanery connected with getting Chinamen across the line was predominantly the work of bold and bad white buccaneers. There was big money in the trade, and when money gets big, even though illicit, it tests the faith of good men and provokes the cupidity of bad. Hence the Immigration Service, conceived for the legitimate protection of the country, was touched and tainted, too.

But some men devoted to the high art of independent living care little for good money, and harbor a complete repugnance for bad. Jeff Milton was such a man. He was not only independent of the local political powers by virtue of vigorous nature, but likewise by official channels, and he and George Webb—brother of Sam—already in the Immigration Service, were giving the smugglers and their official henchmen a lot of trouble.

Once while Jeff was working for Wells Fargo, he and Sam Webb had stopped some smuggling in the service, simply because he had no use for corruption, official or unofficial. Again, upon a return trip from Guaymas, he saw Chinamen and a Mexican hiding in a ravine as he left the express office.

Jeff, a powerful man, rushed in and gathered the Chinamen by their queues, and with four pigtails in hand, piloted them to the immigration office. He and George Webb, inspector in charge of immigration at Tucson, gathered evidence on a crooked inspector, and got him indicted for smuggling. Feeling in the service was tense, and Jeff, fearing an attempt might be made on Webb's life, kept his weather eye open.

One night while tension was at its height, the indicted inspector walked into his home and picked up a shotgun, saying he was "going to kill a skunk." A shot was heard a little later, and when they went to investigate, they found he had killed himself.

George Webb, one of Jeff's dearest friends, had been brought up near Phoenix in a poor family. He told Jeff that as a boy he had hunted wild camels on the desert—apparently survivors and offspring of the government stock introduced in the late fifties—and had jerked their meat and sold it in Phoenix for beef. He was

a real frontiersman with a hand like a ham, who could burst a line of beer bottles with his six-shooter from across the street as fast as he could pull the trigger.

"He didn't have as much education as I had," Jeff would observe, "and I didn't have a damned bit. But he was a very true man and wa'n't afraid of nothing on earth."

Once while riding alone, he came upon three smugglers in Josephine Canyon, in the Santa Rita Mountains north of Nogales. They made a break. He came in and told Jeff that "they got away," but "from the looks of things" Jeff figured how far they got. Later he passed through the canyon himself, and at intervals of about three hundred yards were three skeletons.

At first he and Webb thought it wise that Jeff take station at Altar, Sonora, on the old trail from Mexico. But as that would throw him a long way from the smuggling at Nogales, and completely out of touch with that which followed the San Pedro, he settled in Nogales and again took up the old ride to the west that he had learned so well in the Customs Service.

The operations of Billy Stiles and Charlie Hood, who had been smuggling through Sonoita for a long time, ended abruptly when Milton again started riding the line.[4]

[4] Tom Childs to J. E. H. and Hervey Chesley, March 4, 1945; John Cameron to the same, March 5, 1945.

A Nogales constable had been nosing into Hood's and Stiles's smuggling before Jeff entered the service. They discovered his interest. "But instead of walking over there and killing them, as he ought to have done," Jeff remarked, he got scared and left Nogales for good. As he left, he divulged, to Jeff, his discovery of a dug well in Ephraim Canyon just west of Nogales, where Hood and his band had killed and thrown sixteen Chinamen—after collecting one hundred dollars each for smuggling them into the United States.

Jeff would recall this incident with the regretful remark that "I started to kill old Charlie two or three times." But Hood never started a fight, and somebody else finally performed the commendable deed down at Guaymas.

Saponaris, the Corsican, was another notorious smuggler who made his headquarters around Nogales. John Cameron, veteran of the desert, says that he admitted that he never smuggled Chinamen unless he tied them. Once one escaped when he started to kill them, he confided, and turned him in. Then, with the wisdom that comes with years, he admitted "he tied them all before he killed them."[5]

Another smugglers' trick that saved them trouble of ultimate delivery was that of taking their coolies into the desert and leaving them to certain death from thirst. Jeff and his friend Rube Daniels—lean but powerful desert rat, Papago squaw man, and a prospector rich in the sound metal of personal loyalty—once rescued three Chinamen trying to get in by way of the Pinacate Range. Yet Charlie Foster, seasoned desert man, told Jeff in later years that he successfully piloted several hundred Chinamen across the desert.

Around Nogales, Jeff got wind that Saponaris was crossing several Chinamen west of town one night, and rode out with a Mexican immigration officer named Gonzales, whom Webb had hired. When the Corsican and his coolies came by the graveyard, Jeff called upon him to halt. All broke to run. Jeff tapped one of the Chinamen over the head with his shotgun, gathered up the others, and yelled at Gonzales to catch Saponaris.

[5] John Cameron to J. E. H. and Hervey Chesley, March 5, 1945.

344

Then he took the Chinese in, locked them up, and went out to meet Gonzales, who, he found, had let the smuggler get away, and who now advised Jeff not to say anything about it. Jeff jerked his badge off and took his six-shooter, saying, "I'll attend to that right now," and set off to report to Webb, who immediately "let the gentleman go."[6]

Billy Stiles, Arizona's mercurial outlaw, bobbed up again. On February 23, 1907, Jeff's nephew, Jim Gamble, in the Customs Service, wrote from Lochiel that Billy Olds, one-time Arizona Ranger, had given him the latest news from Stiles:

"Bill Olds told me the day I left Nogales to tell you to keep a look out for Bill Stiles as he has been up in this country & made the talk that he only wanted to get a chance to get a shot at you then he was going to leave the country   so keep your eyes open for him."[7]

In spite of the fact that Stiles was supposed to be one of the worst of Arizona's current bad men, he was not about to tie into Milton but decided "to leave the country" without that coveted shot, and soon after met a bullet intended for him, as has been noted.

When Jeff got report that a boatload of aliens was putting into the Gulf Coast, he took Johnnie Wakefield along for the outing, the Papago, Juan the Coyote, as guide, and scouted along the Sonoran coast, south, until they bumped into the Seri Indians, opposite their home on the island of Tiburon.

Since the Chinese traffic seemed worse to the west, Jeff moved to the Sonoita country to break up the smuggling following the ancient trail beat by Father Kino. He set up camp at the belegended lake of Quitobaquito, renewed his affections for the taciturn Papagoes, and cut for sign up and down the line. Sometimes he took the smuggled Chinese; sometimes the desert got them. It was not a gentle land.

Once after he had walked for miles packing a famished alien

---

[6] There is some dispute whether Saponaris was Greek, Italian, or Corsican. Some thought he got the drop on Milton and disarmed him, but this report was erroneous. E. K. Cumming to J. E. H., February 1, 1945.

[7] J. B. Gamble to Jeff D. Milton, February 23, 1907, in files of the author.

out of the desert on his horse instead of leaving him to die of. thirst, a friend inquired why in the world he had done it.

"We're supposed to deport Chinamen," he answered, "and you can't deport a dead 'un."

And so time passed, with Jeff patrolling the desert. To begin with, in May, 1904, he was paid seven dollars a day. By November, 1905, he was being paid five dollars a day with three dollars and a half for subsistence and expenses, which represented a slight raise. He always had to equip and feed himself and furnish and care for his horses.

He was still officially stationed "at large" after being in the service for four years, although actually he was camped at Quito-baquito, on the border south of Ajo. He had thrown a permanent damper on smuggling through that section. But when nobody was getting caught or killed—when nothing was happening—his letters to headquarters showed it. He knew nothing whatever of "padding reports," and he never adorned the dispatch when he did have something to tell. Writing, too, was work, and what was the use of reporting to his superiors if there was nothing to say?

But bureaucracy thrives on reports, and when F. W. Berkshire, in charge of the district at San Antonio, did not get them, he reached the conclusion that Milton "was not accomplishing anything," and he recommended to the inspector in charge of the Tucson district, George W. Webb, that he be moved to another station.[8]

Webb agreed that it would be better to move him farther east—to the Ventana ranch—and his transfer was ordered by Berkshire, February 18, 1908.[9] Six months later Berkshire was still dissatisfied. Jeff's reports were rarely received, and when they were, they were two months old. Surely, Berkshire curiously commented, Jeff's "whole efforts would not have been given

[8] The outline of Jeff's service up to this time has been traced through the records of the Office of Immigration, El Paso, Texas. See L. O. Murray to J. D. M., May 1, 1904, and November 16, 1905; F. W. Berkshire to George W. Webb, February 6, 1908; and J. D. M. report, July 2, 1907. File No. 5005-81.

[9] Webb to Berkshire, February 10, 1908; Berkshire in return, February 18, 1908. Immigration Files, El Paso.

to preventing violations of the laws in the section of the country where he has been located."[10] Prevention of smuggling obviously was not enough. The bureaucratic mind is bent on making a show. Berkshire concluded by recommending that he be reduced to the status of an "incapacitated employee."

In May, 1909, Jeff asked for a transfer to the San Diego district, in California. He reviewed the fact that he had spent five years in the Arizona desert, "with no station at which I can stop for any length of time, traveling incessantly from the vicinity of Nogales to near Yuma, Arizona." He was not only growing tired of it, he intimated, but the burden of keeping "four horses or mules in order to transport from point to point myself and outfit, consisting of not only feed and water for myself and horses, but also bedding and cooking utensils . . . the cost of which is but partially covered by the present allowance," was entirely too much. Berkshire referred the matter back to the inspector in charge, now John J. Murphy, at Tucson. Jeff had suspected Murphy's intentions and had cussed him out. Murphy now contended that Jeff had never caught any Chinamen and that his transfer would "make room for some person who would have the good of the service at heart rather than merely being an employe waiting for his salary each month."[11] When it came to decision, however, Berkshire relented, and, in his letters to Washington, admitted that the job in the desert was one that "few officers would be willing to accept," and the work was "in the nature of a preventative."[12]

Although the Chinese and Japanese were making a lot of trouble on the lower California border, and although his transfer was further recommended by his friend Webb, he was sent to Hereford, Arizona, instead. There he was to patrol the San Pedro Valley, which, as Murphy described, was a "hitherto unguarded,

[10] F. W. Berkshire to Commissioner General of Immigration, January 23, 1909. File No. 5005-81.

[11] J. D. Milton to Commissioner General of Immigration, May 18, 1909; Berkshire to Inspector in Charge, Tucson, May 24, 1909; John J. Murphy to Supervising Inspector [Berkshire], May 27, 1909. Unless otherwise noted, the following correspondence can be found in Immigration Files, El Paso.

[12] Berkshire to Commissioner General, May 31, 1909.

... direct route through a fertile country from Cananea, Mexico, the headquarters of Chinese smugglers in Sonora, Mexico, into interior points in this Territory." He was moved in June; his station made permanent July 9, 1909.[13]

He took up his new post, caught four Chinamen at once, and reported that others had been seen passing the San Rafael ranch and through the Huachucas.[14] His most notable work in the Immigration Service took place in this section.

During this period Jeff pulled a prank that brought an investigation from Washington. Nogales was celebrating a holiday, and somebody bet him that he could not ride into M. M. Conn's Palace Saloon. Conn entered into the fun, and Jeff rode right through the swinging doors just to show them that his horse would go anywhere, but he rode out faster still when the floor threatened to cave into the basement beneath.[15] He had proved his point.

Dave Cresswell—an immigration inspector "who didn't like me," said Jeff, "and I didn't think too much of him"—reported the affair to Washington. When the investigator came, Jeff told him the story and suggested he canvass the town to see whether he had been either offensive or malicious. The federal man did, firing his ardor with a few drinks of Johnnie Jund's fine mescal to set the pace in the investigation. When his inquiry was complete, he told Jeff good-bye, saying, "Milt, I'd have given a hundred dollars to have been with you. We'd have sure had a good time."

When he got back and reported, they fired the complainant by wire from Washington. After all there were imaginative and decent men in the service.

In April, 1910, Jeff was transferred from Hereford to Fairbank because the railroads from Nogales and Naco, and the

13 Harry H. Weddle to Commissioner General, June 14, 1909; Murphy to Supervising Inspector, July 6, 1909; approval, July 9, 1909.

14 F. W. Berkshire to Commissioner General, July 21, 1909; J. D. Milton to Berkshire, October 7, 1909; and Milton notes.

15 Conn's saloon was located at the wedge, at the site of the Western Union, in Nogales. Some thought that it occurred in Gates's saloon, but Jeff says it was Conn's. Harry W. Kelsey and E. L. Chalfant to J. E. H., February 1, 1945.

wagon roads and trails down the San Pedro, came to a focus there, and because of the further fact, according to the supervising inspector, that it had "one of the largest Chinese ranches in Arizona, and in the past has been the harboring place of Chinese illegally in the United States."[16]

He caught sixteen aliens the second night, and was actively engaged along the border from Nogales east until he was ordered to Ajo. In 1913, his status was changed, in keeping with the growth of the service, from "Chinese Inspector" to that of "Immigrant Inspector." His work continued with his usual efficiency at catching smugglers, and his usual dereliction in reporting.

Alfred A. Burnett, inspector in charge, recommended a raise in his pay to $1,740 in 1913 under the firm conviction that "an officer's compensation should bear some relation to his services. . . . The number of his friends in this Territory is practically limited only by the population," Burnett continued; "experience has demonstrated that he possesses the happy faculty of enlisting the aid of his friends in the enforcement of our laws. . . . His unique reputation is in itself of value to this service."[17]

And so it was obvious that his work was at last meeting with the enthusiastic approval of practical and patriotic men with a sense of humor, of the sort of men who have distinguished the federal services of the country.

The smugglers turned to piloting their would-be immigrants to the line and directing them by trails to the Chinese farms near Fairbank, and to merchants, restaurant owners, and laundrymen at Tombstone, Globe, and elsewhere. Every Chinaman's house in Tombstone had a cellar, where aliens were hidden as they came by convenient stages from Cananea to Huachuca, Fairbank, and Charleston, and then scattered to friendly refuge and a period of labor to pay the ransom of entry. By rail, they went west to California, eventually armed with their "chock gee," a forged or transferred certificate of residence.

For a while the government paid a reward of five dollars for

[16] Charles T. Connell to Supervising Inspector, March 29, 1910, and order of April 8, 1910.

[17] Alfred E. Burnett to Supervising Inspector, May 28, 1913.

349

information leading to their apprehension. And, as Burnett indicated, Jeff had friends from John Slaughter's, at San Bernardino, to rugged John Cameron's, in the desert beyond Ajo, discovering, reporting, and capturing Chinamen, Japs, and Hindus for him, and holding them until he could get there.

Jim Parker, warm cowman friend in the Huachuca country, wanted to join the Chinese Masons so that he could keep Jeff posted, but Jeff advised against the fraternal and obviously helpful connection, while Kelly Hogg, the railroad agent at Luis Springs, notified him of many a passing Chinaman.

Jeff caught them by the dozens. The unhappy but unprovocative prisoners were then taken before the immigration commissioner for a hearing, and, if their credentials were found defective, they were deported. A. J. Milliken, long in charge of the office at Nogales, recalls that many who wanted to return to China came in from Mexico when proscription started there, and were "deported" at United States expense, as they desired, to their native home.

Milton's methods in capturing aliens were peculiarly his own. At Webb's suggestion he once crossed the desert from Quitobaquito to Yuma on a summer trip. The heat was intense. By the time he reached Yuma, his horses could hardly walk, and they stood for days cooling their feet in a *ciénega*, or marsh, along the Colorado River.

Milton relieved the inspector there and locked up a lot of Yuma's Chinese businessmen because they did not have proper certificates. Then he took to checking the trains, with authority to break the seals and search the boxcars when he suspected contraband. This was slow and bothersome for him and railroads alike. One day, as he passed a hardware store, he noticed a bee smoker in the window, and walked in and bought it. He loaded the smoker with tobacco seasoned with sulphur and cayenne pepper, and when the next freight train stopped at Yuma, he traveled its length puffing the smoke from the gadget into the cracks beneath the doors. Then he turned and walked back, listening at each car. When at last he heard sneezing and coughing in one, he broke the seal—although the billing was still short of destination—and took out a "whole bunch of Chinamen." After that he smoked them out with ease.

But the best territory for hunting Chinamen continued to be the San Pedro Valley. Once when he wanted to search a cave across the river, finding it inconvenient to cross because the river was on a rise, he drew a bead with his rifle, shattered some dirt loose from the roof of the cave, and a "bunch of Chinamen" poured out of its darkness. He gathered them where he found them and sent them to Tucson. Once he raided a Chinese temple, or "synagogue" as he called it, near Fairbank and not only got the worshipers but their vestments besides. And there is the amusing story of his "wounded" Chinaman at his camp near Fairbank.

Milton lived in a little rented house near the San Pedro River. One bright moonlight night just before he started to bed, a sudden intuition or impulse hit him, and he said to himself, "I'll just go down to the river and catch a Chinaman." And without further ado, he picked up his six-shooter, walked down to the river, and squatted in the brush by the bank. "And I hadn't been there five minutes," he related, "when I heard one coming." He rose to stop him.

"*¿Quién es?*—Who is it?" whispered the Chinaman, in Spanish.

And Jeff, thinking how funny it was, whispered back, "*Un amigo*—A friend." "*¿Donde vá*—Where are you going?*"

"Globie!" said the Chink.

"*Bueno*, Globie," said Jeff, and motioned for him to follow. He led the way to his house, went in at the back, the Chinaman following, and closed the door.

"Me very hungry," the Chinaman confided, seeing that Jeff was a white man. Jeff went into the next room to get his flashlight, intending to take the captive over to Fairbank, where a legitimate Chinaman ran the restaurant, and get him something to eat. When he got back, his captive was gone. Milton ran out the back door, saw him going around the corner of an outhouse a few steps away, and shot a couple of times straight into the air.

The Chinaman went down in a heap and started to scream.

351

When Jeff got to him, he had one leg and arm stuck up in the air while the others were drawn across his abdomen like a winged hawk. He was in downright agony, swore he was shot through the stomach, and would not be reassured until Jeff got him to Tucson, where a doctor saved him two days later.

Southwest of Fairbank, against the base of the Huachuca Range, Milton frequently checked on Chinamen out at Fort Huachuca. Sam Kee, a wealthy Chinaman, ran a restaurant there. When Jeff dropped in, Sam assured him there was nothing irregular about the place. But Jeff, in apparently casual but sharp-eyed inspection, noticed a loose board in the floor, caught it with his fingers, and lifted it up. Two long gray objects stretched across the opening.

"What's that, Sam," said Jeff, peering in the half-light, "water mains?"

"Yes, Mr. Milton, water mains! Water mains!" Kee answered quickly, while Jeff slipped off his badge and poked them with its pin, and, he recalled with a hearty laugh, "The water mains shore moved—the legs of Sam Kee's nephew, who had just been smuggled in from Mexico.

Kee hogged Jeff to let him go "You like'm good time," soothed Kee. "I give $3,000; you take'm; go to Mexico, and have'm good time." Jeff left the money with Kee but took his nephew.

Some time later a lawyer friend at Tucson inquired, "Why weren't you here as a witness against that Chinaman?"

"Why, I never was called," said Jeff.

"They turned him loose," said his friend.

Jeff was hot for years, as he knew full well "the evidence" that turned the trick. There was really money on the wrong side of the Immigration Service.

When at Fairbank, Jeff ate at times at Wong's Chinese restaurant. One day Wong served him some tainted meat, and Jeff rounded him up and dressed him down, telling him at last to take it back and bring him something fit to eat.

Wong was mad and spluttering. "Some day you die right quick. You won't know what killed you."

Jeff just "had to laugh" while Wong brought him some better food. But that night he thought of the possible significance of the remark by the man who was fixing his food, and he hurried back to the restaurant.

"Wong, let me tell *you* something," he said, gripping him with a deadly eye. "The first time I come in here, eat, and get a bellyache—sick in any way—I'm going to kill you." "And I meant it, too," he emphasized in recountal. And a few days later Wong, who had weighed his words, left Fairbank for parts unknown, while Jeff had to go back to his own cooking. And yet at another time he walked into a Chinese restaurant where a patron, upon refusing to pay for his dinner, had got into a fight with the owner. Other white men were joining to help him until Jeff pulled his six-shooter and quieted the fracas by shouting, "The next man that touches him—I'm going to shoot him. Give him his money; he's got a right to his property." And he got it.

So it went, with variations, for years. Jeff caught hundreds of aliens—mostly Chinese, but he never caught one who put up a fight. Berkshire was won wholeheartedly to his services; George J. Harris, another and later supervising inspector, likewise became his warm friend, and even Commissioner Anthony Caminetti came down from Washington to see him.[18]

Berkshire traveled with Caminetti to Arizona, and, with Burnett, arranged to meet Jeff at Huachuca Siding. Jeff put a couple of quarts of "Old Jordan" in a morral, hung it on the horn of his saddle, and met them at the train. Caminetti looked him over severely when they met, as Jeff gaily said, "Mr. Caminetti, you look tired. I believe a drink of whiskey will do you good."

Berkshire wildly waved his disapproval from behind the Commissioner, while Caminetti seemed to rear back on his dewclaws and exclaim, "Whiskey?"

"Yes, sir," said Jeff, as both Burnett and Berkshire continued to wigwag warnings.

[18] Caminetti, the first native-born Californian to be elected to Congress, was United States commissioner of immigration from 1913 to 1921. He died November 17, 1923. *Biographical Directory of the American Congress*, 780.

"You mean to tell me, sir, that you drink whiskey and work for the government?"

"I take a drink of whiskey whenever I dern please if I can get it. I have a bottle . . . "

"Do you mean to tell me that you've got whiskey with you?" Caminetti broke in.

"Just wait a minute, and I will show you," said Jeff, going out, bringing in the morral, and calling to Gene Larrieu, agent at the Siding, "Gene, bring us some glasses and some sugar." Then turning to the Commissioner in his most gracious manner, he said, "Would you like a little sugar, Mr. Caminetti?"

"Yes," the Commissioner answered, relaxing from his official dignity, "I'll take a little toddy."

"Mr. Berkshire needs one," Jeff continued, gleefully. "I can tell he'll take a drink by looking at him."

Gene brought the glasses, Berkshire got off his high horse and had one, and Caminetti—being from Washington—of course "took two." And so they had a genial visit—called a "tour of inspection" in the official records.

They found that Jeff was not only a daring officer but a delightful host, and went back to report that the Immigration Service was decidedly better. Berkshire was so completely won over that instead of recommending Jeff's demotion, he voluntarily approved a voucher for his "traveling and other expenses" while, with them, "making a general investigation in connection with the enforcement of the Chinese Exclusion Laws."[19]

When Caminetti stepped on the train to leave, he told Jeff that he was going to send him to the world's fair, to be held in San Francisco soon, to represent the Immigration Service. And for Jeff, still holding a modest job in the ranks, it was genuine if long-delayed recognition of eleven years of eternally and alone laughing at death on the desert.

He made the trip with George Webb, and although neither was a kid, they took the town in—which is something in San Francisco. As a memento, Jeff brought back a six-shooter that he took from a thug who tried to hold him up. The department

[19] F. W. Berkshire to Jeff D. Milton, June 11, 1915.

could have sent more important and officious but no sturdier or more dependable men.

The Six Companies knew they were there. They knew that these two fighting men stood as their strongest barriers to the smuggling of Celestials along the Mexican border. Ambitious and illicit power has three ancient ways of perverting men to its uses. They provided entertainment of sparkling champagne and luscious women, and although some of the force were there, "handsome Jeff" turned them down. Then they offered him their bribes. An agent who took him to dinner proposed that if he wished to turn to ranching, they would acquire and deed him the historic Warner ranch in Southern California. All he had to do in turn was to wink his black and burning eye and let their Chinese coolies cross.

Now Jeff's worldly possessions consisted, as Alfred Burnett had reported, of his arms and camp equipment, a spring wagon, a team, and two of the best saddle horses in southern Arizona. But that, with humor and character, was quite enough. He paid his own way, he contemptuously turned their "fixers" down, and told them what to expect on his side of the American border. Thus he justified the choice of Caminetti and the faith that a free country, if it is to survive, must finally be able to repose in its public servants.

He came back from the world's fair happy and broke, a solid and sober man of fifty-four, on the portly side of life, but with the straight and noble carriage that comes with strength and pride, still fired by the unappeased zest for life that blesses men of strong blood and healthy appetites. He laid off his store-bought clothes, put on the duckin' garb of a workingman, and walked out of his rented adobe shack to patrol the border, in gallant poverty, if need be, but for the unsullied honor and protection of the United States.

His dun horses, Dan and Montie, and his dogs, Rex and Rowdy, were delighted to see him. He stepped into the stirrup, settled himself comfortably in his Navasota saddle, and, alone, headed for the line. San Francisco, with all her women, wine, and wiles could never compete with this.

23

Settling Down

Lt should not be thought that Milton settled down without a struggle. Responsibility never curbed his irrepressible spirit. The almost insurmountable barriers to sedate and settled life were his environment and his temperament. Time would slightly soften but not materially alter either.

There seemed no end to his escapades and exploits. Many took place at Nogales. With rare mescal from Johnnie Jund's, the best food from Cazabon's café, and high-hearted company from everywhere, things were just bound to happen. Yet the ribald humor of the place was set back when a tinhorn gambler ran amuck at Conn's saloon. He had struck a lucky streak, won several thousand dollars, acquired a fair-weather girl, and was riding high. In a few days his luck changed, he was broke, and his girl was gone. With misplaced humor, led by "Cowboy" Johnson, the crowd at Conn's went to hurrahing him. Like most extreme familiarity, which Jeff disliked and deplored, it was carried too far.

The tinhorn got up from lunch, stuck his gun against Johnson's head and pulled the trigger, killed Conn in passing, and as he went by the table where George Spindles, a cowman, sat, threw down on him. Spindles dodged, and the bullet caught a Mexican on the other side of the table right between the eyes. He walked out at the door and shot himself, and four men were "deader'n hell in a minute" over a little banter. Personal affairs then and there were properly considered private, and it was poor taste to talk unless the talker was ready to fight. Jeff was decidedly a man of taste.

When he was passing through Benson one day, an officious deputy noticed him at the station, walked up to him and said, "You've got a gun on!"

"Yes, sir," said Jeff, "I have."

"Let me have it," commanded the deputy, and before he could bat an eye, he had it barrel first in the belly.

"Back out of here," said Jeff. "There are some ladies, and we don't want to disturb them."

The deputy backed out with alacrity. Jeff kicked him off the sidewalk, and he broke and ran, obviously headed for help. In a few minutes Billy Bennett and Rye Miles rounded the corner with Winchesters and stopped short. "Oh, was that you, Jeff?" they laughed, while one turned to the deputy and remarked, "You're lucky he didn't break it over your head."

Eventually the news got back to the immigration office at Nogales, where the Chief Inspector said, "Why didn't you report that row you had at Benson?"

"I had no row," said Jeff, a little hotly. "I kicked a fellow off the sidewalk but no row to it." There was a distinct difference. A "row" in the West implied real disagreement.

Harry Saxon, who was elected sheriff at Nogales in 1906 with Jeff's hearty support, says that Jeff did have a row with Charlie Fowler, a rather noted fighter whom Saxon succeeded as sheriff. Apparently Fowler had said that Jeff was a liar about some forgotten subject. On the day that Fowler was leaving office, Jeff was intent on killing him. Every little while he walked into the Arcade Saloon, called Fowler up, and demanded that he come downtown and get killed like a man. Jeff was saying that "he ought to have killed the so-and-so long ago," and that he wanted to do it now while he was still sheriff. Finally he phoned Fowler that if he did not come out and fight, he was going to come up and shoot him in the sheriff's office.

Saxon, who said it would have made an awful mess, was doing his best to prevent it. Unable to do anything with Jeff, he went to the sheriff's office and opened the door, and there sat Fowler with a sawed-off, double-barreled shotgun trained on the opening. He told him where Jeff was, and Fowler disappeared until he got in a better humor.[1] Times have changed. And

[1] Harry Saxon to J. E. H., February 28, 1945. Santa Cruz County was created on March 15, 1899, and the first election was held in 1900, when the county had 4,545 people. *Nogales Herald*, February 7, 1942.

while everybody is not intent on shooting the sheriff, it is still kind of rash away out West to call a gentleman a liar.

Then there was the incident with Dave Black, alleged saloon loafer, Chinese Mason, and Chinese smuggler. Black, in his business, had it in for Jeff. One day Jeff came in from his ride to find that Dr. Purdy had kept a man at his house all day to warn him against coming to town. Black was waiting for him with a shotgun "and going to kill him on sight." Jeff took off his belt, slipped his six-shooter out of his holster into his waistband, and really went to town. When Black saw him coming, he hid his gun, and the incident passed.

On February 27, 1907, Black appealed to President Theodore Roosevelt by letter to relieve the country of Milton, who had "shot up the town of Nogales, some," who had "threatened to murder citizens, and more than once shoved a gun with the hammer back against unarmed and quiet people." The President referred the complaint to the Commissioner General of Immigration, who called on George Webb for a report.

Webb told how Jeff's hot pursuit of Black in his illicit designs had led to the enmity back in 1904, and that "Black being a man with a record as a gun fighter, was induced while under the influence of liquor by his confederates to pick a row with Milton," with the hope that Milton would get killed and thus be taken out of their way. He had picked the row. Jeff had cursed him out, and Black had lacked the nerve "to go for his gun." Bad blood had been brewing since.

Shortly after this, Webb continued, while he and Milton were eating at Cazabon's, friends had warned that Black was again threatening him. After ordering their meal, Webb went off as peacemaker. He found Black, bitter, profane, and obdurate—Milton was a so-and-so, and "he proposed to kill him on sight." Webb came back and reported, and Jeff, hotter than a pistol barrel, went off to settle the matter. He walked to where Black stood at the bar, dropped his "crippled left arm on Black's shoulder," whirled him around with his right, and told him to draw his gun. Black wilted and stayed away from Nogales until Jeff moved to Quitobaquito.

Then he returned, Webb reported, to complain to the President[2] and to continue his crooked work. Eventually he committed suicide.

Complete individual responsibility, however, tends to breed restraint. Usually a simple word of warning to the wise was sufficient. Jeff's nephew, Jim Gamble, of the Customs Service, had fallen in love with the daughter of Old Kundy, Cameron's foreman on the San Rafael ranch. Kundy had killed a man in Texas and come west on account of the climate. It mattered not to him whether Gamble was descended from Gouverneur Morris; none of this high-brow stuff for him. He disapproved the match and threatened to kill Gamble if he caught him on the place. Jeff heard of his talk, and although Jim was almost as old as he, he saddled his horse and rode over to the San Rafael.

"Listen here, old stud," he said after corralling Kundy, "you've been making a lot of talk. If anything happens to that boy—just anything—I'm coming down here and kill you if it's the last act of my life, and I'll kill you—certain!"

There seemed a positive futility in paternal objections, anyway. Kundy reconsidered, and Gamble got the girl.

Down at Cananea about this time Bill Greene was having trouble. A regular riot of humanity swarmed in his mines of a day and fought, five and six deep, to reach their drinks at Frank Proctor's seventy-five-foot bar of a night. John Cameron, veteran of the works in its earliest stages, recalls that every night thugs hammered "from one to three" drunks to death in the streets, usually with rocks, and robbed them. The Americans went in bunches for safety. Then Kosterlitzky and his *rurales* came and cleaned the place up in short order to where a drunk, even if he had money, could "sleep it off" in the streets with perfect impunity.

But there was gross racial disparity at the mines. Of 5,300 on the pay roll when Cameron was there, 80 per cent were Americans instead of Mexicans, and the cause of this was in part the

[2] Dave Black to Theodore Roosevelt, February 27, 1907; George W. Webb to Commissioner General of Immigration, March 25, 1907; copies in Milton Papers.

359

JEFF MILTON

Díaz edict—Americans were paid eight pesos or four dollars in gold, while the Mexicans were paid three and four pesos. It was bad business which could not be offset by Greene's hiring of every American outlaw and gun-fighter who drifted in.

In 1906, Bill Greene's swarming hordes rose in wrath and struck. Just before the strike, Frank Proctor came to Jeff in Nogales and asked him if he wanted to make five hundred dollars real easy.

"Shore," said Jeff.

"Bill Greene wants fifty thousand dollars and wants it bad—right now. When can you start?"

"In fifteen minutes," said Jeff—"just as soon as I can go and saddle a horse."

He saddled up but decided to wait until night. Proctor brought the money to his room in an old tow sack and threw it down on his bed. Jeff tied it on his saddle and after dark set out on a good horse, at a lively gait. He changed mounts at one of Greene's haciendas on the way and rode into Cananea about day. When the strike came, Jeff had returned to his job.

Greene mounted his expensive automobile—then the wonder of their world—and showed his own mettle. He drove into the middle of the rioters and harangued the mad mass while standing in the open seat. But to no avail. The fighting started and raged about the town.

Tom Rynning, pretentious and voluble captain of the Arizona Rangers, raised a force of fighters around Bisbee and blew into Mexico by way of Naco. In his immodest book called *Gun Notches,* he says he co-operated with Kosterlitzky, whose *rurales* came riding from the west. But Jeff said it was a horse of a different color. The Cossack Colonel ran him out for illegal entry into Mexico and quelled the riot himself, although Greene's cowboys and Texas gun-fighters had done pretty well before he got there.[3]

Then *"El Pando"*—"The Swayback"—as the Mexicans called the proud old Colonel, summoned the strikers, who were now

[3] Thomas H. Rynning, *Gun Notches* (New York, 1931), 306–307; for Milton's story, notes of March 1, 1945; Beery, *Westerners Brand Book,* 100.

360

intent on running all Americans out, and read the riot act to them. They could either work, be drafted into the army, or be killed. They decided to work. He is said to have marched twenty-two of the leaders off to the railroad at Imuris, but they were all lost to *ley del fuga* before they got there. "They got away, but just a little way."[4]

On another occasion, as John Cameron recalls, the Colonel received a call from Governor Torres, of Sonora, for recruits for the Mexican Army. At that time the policy of a *felón* army—one of criminal prisoners—was practiced in Mexico. At Arizpe Kosterlitzky rounded up some criminals, handcuffed them together, and marched them off to Hermosillo with a message to Governor Torres: "I am sending you twenty-five brave and patriotic men," he reported. "If you will kindly return my handcuffs, I'll send you twenty-five more."[5]

The Revolution was at hand, and those who had ridden the wave with Díaz were destined to be caught in the backwash. But "Old Bill," to Jeff—"Colonel W. C. Greene" to his sycophantic followers—did not live to witness the worst. He died early in August, 1911, following injuries in a runaway accident, although his enterprises survived both the Revolution and himself.[6]

Kosterlitzky lived through its bitterness. By overwhelming numbers, Madero's men encompassed him and Colonel Reyes at Nogales. Reyes was killed, and the *rurales* surrendered. Kosterlitzky refused. He marched his loyalist troops across the line into Nogales, Arizona, March 13, 1913, under a flag of truce, stacked his guns, and was placed in a detention camp, at last to be moved to San Diego Bay. On account of his eminent services in Mexico, official amnesty had already cleared his record here.

And at San Diego, in old age, he became attached to the Department of Justice of the United States. E. L. Chalfant, who visited him there, was told that this remarkable old warrior,

[4] John Cameron to J. E. H., January 29, 1945; E. L. Chalfant to J. E. H., February 1, 1945.
[5] Cameron, as cited.
[6] *Arizona Daily Star*, August 5, 1911; *Tombstone Epitaph*, of the sixth.

writing and speaking five languages, was "the most valuable man" the office had.

He has been damned by the sentimental for his ruthless discipline of his *rurales* and his summary disposal of evildoers, but there are those who hold that this was what his country needed. Jeff's admiration for him knew no bounds: "I'd like to say I never saw a man I'd trust farther than Emilio Koster-litzky," he summed up, which was saying a lot.[7]

At the same time some two hundred Chinese crossed the line into Nogales, but the immigration officers rounded them up and moved them back.[8] Jeff missed the trouble there, but he was in Douglas when Red López took the twin Mexican town of Agua Prieta. Governor Richard Sloan happened to be there, too. As with all revolutions, there was a lot of careless shooting, some of which hit close to Jeff and his friend Guy Welch, while they were walking over to see the excitement. Meanwhile, about twenty-five cowpunchers in town were "getting organized" at the saloons and willing to fight on either side in any revolution, just so they were fighting for their rights.

Jeff knew that the careless bullets kicking up the sovereign If arid Arizona dust were an affront to proper national pride, and he struck a trot to Governor Sloan, holed up in the best Douglas hotel.

"Governor, if you'll say the word, I'll organize a force and take Agua Prieta in thirty minutes."

"Get out of here!" yelled the Governor, horror stricken at the very idea. "I know *you*, Jeff. *You* get out of here!" And Jeff got out to join his cowpuncher confederates in regretting the lack of imagination in high places. But the way they whipped Mexico around the bars that night almost redeemed the national honor.

Later, at Nogales, Jeff was approached by some of his friends who asked him to join the American Protective Association.

[7] Cameron, as cited; Chalfant, as cited; James H. McClintock, *Arizona*, II, 605; *Arizona Daily Star*, October 24, 1909; "The First Battle of Nogales," letter by Mrs. Ada Jones, March 14, 1913; and a mass of Milton notes set down by the author. Noah Beery, Jr., in his sketch, says he spoke nine languages "fluently." He died March 2, 1928. *Westerners Brand Book*, 101.

[8] Mrs. Ada Jones, as cited.

"For the protection of the United States? By Jacks, shore," said Jeff.

When the local election approached, its true color, "anti-Catholic and all that rot," said Jeff, came out. He was busily speaking his open mind on the virtues of a friend who was running for sheriff when a committee of three from the "A. P. A." called on him at Brickwood's saloon, invited him out at the back, and told him he must support another ticket—"our man."

"Why, he's a damned scoundrel," Jeff retorted. They insisted that since Jeff was a member, he had no choice. He angrily told them he would expose the entire racket. They reminded him of its secrecy and threatened him if he should.

"Now, I will tell *you* so-and-so's something," he said, looking them over. "If anybody monkeys with me, there'll be plenty of buzzard meat around here—for certain." Then he gave a list of the membership to Allen T. Bird, suggested he publish it in *The Oasis,* and noised it generally about Nogales what sort of an outfit the American Protective Association really was. And so it, too, faded out on the desert air in the face of the firm conviction that the only genuine protection of freedom was the uninhibited, unorganized impulses of individual men of honor.

Other incidents occurred at Nogales illustrative of Jeff's character. George Webb heard of a refugee Yaqui Indian who had crossed the line west of Nogales ahead of Mexican officers, and passed the word on to Jeff, who cut for sign, picked up the trail, and caught the Yaqui. The Indian had been fighting against the Mexicans, had been shot through the foot and leg, and had crossed into Arizona to evade capture.

"When we got ready to deport one then," Jeff recalled, "we didn't go through a lot of bother—we just deported him. I took him back to Nogales. The Mexicans were waiting for him at the line."

"They'll kill me," the Yaqui told him.

"We'll see if they do," said Jeff, backing off from the line and backtracking to a point west of town. When they were out of sight, Jeff said, "I put him across and told him to drag it, and believe me, he drug it." Back in town Jeff innocently sauntered down to the port of entry, and the Mexican officials inquired when he was going to deport the Indian.

"Why, I've already deported him."

"We've been here all the time and didn't see him."

"You didn't?" Jeff answered, with feigned surprise. "I took him down to the line and he walked right across."

Some time later Webb asked, "Milt, did you ever put that Indian across?"

"Shore, he walked right across," Jeff answered his superior. "But," he would smile, "I was afraid to tell him where; afraid he'd fire me if I did. But do you think I was going to put that old Indian across to be murdered?—No, not me."

On another occasion Jeff ran into old John Short'nin' Bread, an Apache scout from Fort Huachuca. He did not know the Indian then and had him covered as he came up the mountain. When Jeff passed him later, near Huachuca Siding, he had a bottle of whiskey, and with another Indian man and a squaw was headed for the Whetstones. They camped that night out on a ridge, ánd when Jeff saw him a little later, he asked old Short'nin' Bread, "What you been doing?"

"Killing buck; kill heap big buck." And then Jeff learned that he really had killed a buck, "the heap big buck" who was with him. But that was small bother in southern Arizona, for by that time the Americans had subdued and civilized the Indians, and Jeff "went on" about his own business.

And part of "his business" by personal preference was with the barbarians of his own race. Jeff Kidder, gunman and Arizona Ranger, a fine shot and a bear for trouble, seemed to have been among them.

"The trouble with Jeff Kidder," Milton judiciously appraised, "was that he wanted to be a bad man and didn't know how." The Rangers got the name of being overbearing—so much so in fact that they were finally disbanded. Some of them, like Billy Olds and Jeff Kidder, were always in trouble. Milton and Kidder sat down to dinner together once at Cazabon's restaurant, and in the course of the meal Kidder got to cursing. Jeff told him to "dry up," as some women and children were present.

Kidder jumped up, drew his gun, and threw down on Jeff. He was consciously putting on a show, and glanced about to see what effect his play had made.

"I could have killed him then, dead easy," Jeff explained, "but I didn't want to do it there." In all his life he had quieted a lot but he had never raised a racket in front of a woman. He would not here. He rose up slowly, his good arm raised, index finger pointing at Kidder.

"Better put that gun up," he quietly advised. "Then we'll go outside, old hoss, and if you're wantin' a fight, you're goin' to get one, certain." Kidder shoved his gun into his holster, and they walked outside. Milton said he never talked so mean to a man in his life as he did to Kidder, trying to get him to fight. He flung every insult that his hot Southern tongue could muster, hoping he would draw on equal terms. But Kidder threw his hands up and kept them up and ignominiously "just got up and drug it."

"I wanted to kill him the worst way," Milton observed, "but you just can't kill a man like that."

Kidder wound up at Naco in 1907, where he got drunk, killed three Mexicans, and died in the fight himself. Some considered him the fastest hand with a gun in the whole country, and there has been controversy concerning the way he died.[9] Anyway his final effort was a decided success.

Although Jeff left Nogales and spent the last active years of his life in the Tombstone country, he went back when word came from A. J. Milliken, a young friend of his in charge of the immigration office, that Johnnie Brickwood, son of the noted saloon owner and a sort of a fighter, was threatening to kill him. Brickwood had been let out of the border service and apparently held Milliken responsible.

Jeff went to Nogales and told Milliken that he ought to have killed old man Brickwood long ago, as he needed it, and that now, if Milliken would just say the word, he would go and tend to the matter with Johnnie. Milliken, deeply appreciative of his

[9] John Cameron, as cited; J. J. Lowe to J. E. H., February 1, 1945; Frank Hamer to J. E. H.; and Ryning's Gun Notches, 286.

good intentions, thought it improper to suggest that Johnnie be killed. But word got around to Johnnie, and he was bothered no more with him.[10]

Out on the desert to the west, a warm friend of Milton's—John Campbell Greenway, that genius in the production of copper—took hold of the ancient mines of Ajo, and the mantle of lethargy and obsolescence that had stymied operations there for generations was cast aside by his management and drive.

He was born of distinguished Southern stock in Alabama, educated for mining at Andover and Yale, took his degree and went to work as a helper at the furnaces of Carnegie Steel at $1.32 a day, joined the Rough Riders in San Antonio and served in the Spanish-American War, returned to iron and steel and worked in the great Mesaba Range, in Michigan, and in 1913 became manager of the Calumet and Arizona at Bisbee. He built the big smelter at Douglas, acquired the giant deposits of copper at Ajo, laid a railroad in from Gila Bend, and opened operations there in 1915.[11]

Beneath the touch of his dynamic enterprise, Ajo sprang from a desert village on the farther edge of the torrid Papago land into a town of prominence. And toward it, out of Mexico by way of the old desert trail from Altar to Sonoita, flowed the traffic in aliens. When those in the Immigration Service thought of the desert, they thought of Jeff, although Berkshire had once turned down the suggestion that he be sent there because of his value at Fairbank.

On November 1, 1915, Jeff requested the station, "as my personal business is in that country," he wrote, "and it would be to my interest to be there." He did not want to quit the service, he assured Berkshire, but characteristically added: "You will please consider this personal or official, just as it suits you." Berkshire approved late in December, and Jeff crossed the desert "through almost continuous rain, snow and flood conditions" by buggy and team, getting to Ajo January 25, 1916.[12]

[10] Mrs. J. D. Milton to J. E. H., March 1, 1944; A. J. Milliken to J. E. H., November 19, 1945.

[11] See James H. McClintock, *Arizona*, III, 48–50.

It is interesting to observe that at last Jeff felt he had some "personal business." And he did, though of a nebulous nature. He had poked into prospective mines all over the desert. Greenway's venture gave him hope that he might make a little money and settle down. Besides, Greenway had work for him to do that fit in with his knowledge of the desert and his scouting for aliens.

When he got to Ajo, Greenway told him he planned to extend his railroad south and ship his ore by the way of St. George's Bay and the Gulf of California.

"Jeff, you know all that country and all the mines," Greenway proposed. "I am going to put surveyors in there next month, dig wells, and have everything ready to go. You go down, buy those mines, and draw on the bank here for your money."

The surveys were run and wells were dug, while Jeff made the trip and investigated the claims. But Greenway was back in New York, and although he had orders to buy, he showed his usual conservative nature with other men's money, saying to himself, "Something might happen."

Upon his return Jeff met Greenway at Ajo, who asked, "How many mines did you buy?"

"Not a one," Jeff replied. "Are you going to build the railroad?"

"No," Greenway admitted. "We were both just looking the wrong way." Jeff always suspected that the Southern Pacific, which naturally had no desire to see the ocean traffic tap southern Arizona so directly, had something to do with the abandonment of the plan.

Greenway insisted that Milton take enough stock in the New Cornelia, on credit, to make him independent and wealthy. But he was independent already, and he wanted obligation to no man. So he refused and went back to catching Chinamen.

In September, 1916, however, Burnett, the supervising inspector in Arizona, while recognizing the importance of watching the Altar route, recommended Jeff's return to the San Pedro

<hr>

12 A. E. Burnett to Supervising Inspector, September 7, 1915; Berkshire to Burnett, September 20, 1915; Milton to Berkshire, November 1, 1915; approval, December 21, 1915; Milton to Supervising Inspector, January 25, 1916.

Valley because he was "the very best available man for the Fair-bank station." His superiors agreed, and Jeff was back at his old stand, October 21, 1916, coming in by team.[13]

By the spring of 1918, however, Burnett had decided that the smuggling of Chinese through the San Pedro basin had prac-tically ceased, and since the Customs Service was stationing a man at Indian Oasis, in the Papago country, sixty-five miles southwest of Tucson, near the border and "on one of the principal routes of travel from Altar," Jeff was sent down there.

He made the trip in a Model T Ford stripped down for desert use. But the exposure of the San Pedro was immediately discovered by the smugglers, and the service shot him back to Fairbank, October 1, 1919. Meanwhile, however, he had fallen in love.

Early in that year while he was still stationed in the desert, the most powerful influence that was ever brought to bear upon his life since he had left his mother's home came into his hot and hard world—that land of shimmering space and sun—in search of health. Mildred Taitt, a sprightly witted school teacher of Gouverneur, New York, had come to Tucson for a rest cure and was casually taking courses at the University of Arizona.

Zest for life is essentially a matter of spirit instead of health, and when the winter holidays came, this frail wisp of a little lady with eager mind, insatiable love of nature, and deeply religious

[13] Burnett to Supervising Inspector, September 2, 1916; ordered, September 14, 1916; report, October 31, 1916.

spirit went to Indian Oasis to visit with her friends, the Wilsons, in charge of the Presbyterian Mission among the Papagoes.

There, on January 4, 1919, she met this fabulous character who fogged in from among the organ-pipe cactus in a stripped-down Ford, covered with dust and the glamour of daring deeds. But the story of that trip to the desert is best told in her own words, in a letter of January 8, 1919, back to her folks at home.

"You know I had been expecting at some time to get a trip to the Wilson's on the Papago reservation. On the thirtieth Mr. Wilson called and asked if I could start early next morning. He was in town on business, and the Simkins would be out Wednesday or Thursday at the latest and would bring me back. Of course I was delighted. Monday had been cold and rainy with snow on the mountains. Tuesday dawned cold, windy, but clear.

". . . Finally about eleven thirty we were off with twenty-five pounds of dynamite riding on our running board.

"We began climbing as soon as we left town for we had to cross several ranges, the pass of one being six hundred feet above Tucson. We followed the Ajo (Aho) road for sixty-eight miles, stopping now and then to blaze away at a coyote—their skins being at the present rather valuable. The minister always drives with his heavy cavalry carbine—a Krag—at his left hand.

"Before the days of autos for the poor it used to be a two day trip to the Oasis with a night camping out. Now it can be done in from three to four hours with a light load. As the little Ford bobbed around on and off the road it made me think of something of familiar past experiences that I couldn't quite place. Have had the feeling before on some of my auto rides out here. Suddenly it came to me—the jumping and sliding of a drop of water spilled on a hot stove top. That is just the way we traveled and every where we went the dynamite went too. We would dash down into an arroyo—across and up, straddle a rut, run off the road for a few feet to avoid a rough spot and back on the road again. And yet the roads are not so bad. The arroyos (dry stream beds) have no bridges, but otherwise the going is not unlike bad country roads back home, for when a spot gets too bad there is the limitless unfenced desert on which to detour, and no crops to harm. . . .

"We passed many interesting peaks named from some peculiarity as Cats Back, Hippopotamus, Elf's Head, etc. One of the dominating peaks is Baboquiveri. We can see it from Tucson and I have viewed all aspects now except from above. It is a peak of the Fresnele range and the name means "straight up and down and small around the waist." We went through Robles' Pass and past one of the Robles Ranches, names you may recall in Western stories you have read, saw "The mountain with a white belt," the Coyotes, a rugged range, Comobabi, and others I can't recall. Then we climbed a rough hill and started down another with the Oasis spread out before us. To the right, the row of government buildings—the farmer's home, the school with dwelling attached, the Indian office, the Clerk's house, and the Doctor's. Beyond these the little Presbyterian Church. To the right, the Indian village, and on a hill rising like a volcanic cone from the surrounding mesa, the store. The hill is fenced with barbed wire around the base, and the store is thick walled, and is one of the places menaced by the Villistas a few years ago.

"There is another store about ten miles away at Topawa. On the reservation of 2,700,000 acres are forty Indian villages. Many of them are some distance from water—two to eight miles—and most of that used is toted in clay ollas on the heads of the squaws.

"Mrs. Wilson and her mother gave me a warm welcome and I felt at home at once. . . . We were just getting up from a fine home cooked supper when we saw the lights of a car approaching—two deputy sheriffs and a driver—hungry and cold. The sheriff and a deputy had gone out several days before after some cattle rustlers. Had not returned and people were getting worried so these men had been hunting them and came in search of food and a night's rest. One of the men was an "Old Timer" and all were interesting with their gentle voices and fierce display of cartridge belts and guns. . . .

"Mrs. Wilson and I went sight seeing New Year's morning. . . . We had an early dinner and then Mr. Wilson and I started for San Miguel (Migill) twenty-five miles south and two miles from

Old Mexico. A few miles from town (?) we passed through the most marvellous growth of giant cacti I have seen, and I doubt if there is one to excel it— Thousands of them, tall and straight as telephone posts, or with arms spread like a cross, or reaching toward heaven, or most fantastic of all twisting down toward earth like elephant's trunks.

"At San Miguel . . . I met Chief Sam Cochara and his small boys, and admired his winter's supply of meat draped over the outside of his house to dry. . . .

"On our way back we stopped at Vamori, another village, and I met "Jim Blain" a husky buck with a white haired patriarch of a father. All are great hand-shakers. We drove on through the sunset over Comolick (thin mountain) and saw the stars come out getting home to a good supper at seven. At Vamori the Indians till the fields in common.

"The evening passed in pleasant conversation, and the decision was reached that the Simkins would arrive on Thursday.

"Thursday morning Mr. Wilson took us to call on Mrs. Jose (Hosay) one of the staunch church going Indians of the community. . . .

"In the afternoon, Mrs. W. and I walked out to the store for a bit of gossip with Mr. Power, and then down the hill to call on Mrs. Neblina—a pretty Mexican woman with two small children. Here I aired a little of my Spanish to the delight of all concerned. After that we went to a little Yaqui settlement—Mexican Indians who have moved across the border, but are not wards of the reservation. Their houses, instead of being made of adobe, are made of ocotilla (okatiya) stems, and the ribs of the giant cactus. These are driven in the ground, and laced together by twine or binding wire and give the effect of a bamboo screen—a well ventilated house. . . .

"A call on Mrs. Morris, the doctor's wife, a fine supper, music on the little organ which can be folded up like a suitcase, a little chat and Thursday passed with no Simkins. . . .

"On Saturday—a beautiful day—it was decided the Simkins would come that afternoon and go back Sunday. Saturday is the weekly mail day so I joined the crowd at the store—met Indians,

371

Mexicans, government people, and a number of dogs. One much resembled Pirate and belongs to the Bachelor of the place—Jefferson Davis Milton, born in Florida during the Civil War times, a Texas ranger at fifteen, a Wells Fargo man in the early days of the S. P.; at present an Immigration Inspector, who has been in many a gun fight, and broken a few laws himself. Well, the old tales of the lone female in the gold camps are no exaggeration I am sure, for his world was mine from the moment we met to the huge delight of the bystanders and to my own gain in rides, gifts of game, etc. for the rest of my stay.

"Sunday morning after a call from Mr. Milton, Mrs. Wilson and I started out to make a call or two on the Indians. There was to be no church as Mr. W. was away. You will note the Simkins had not arrived. Mr. M. would have taken me in, but I couldn't quite see sixty-eight miles of his ardor so compromised on a short drive for the afternoon.

"When Mrs. W. and I returned we found some of the Indians had not understood about the services and were on their way, so the church was opened, swept, a fire built, the bell rung, the organ carried over, and services begun. The meeting was of the nature of a prayer meeting. The Indians like to sing, and sing in English, but pray in Papago. They brought their luncheons and had another service in the afternoon.

"Monday morning I made some calls and walked over to the Yaqui village and bought some eggs from Dolores—carrying the transaction to a successful finish in Spanish. Then rode with Mr. Milton. It is really quite thrilling to fly about the country in a car that mounts two guns.

"Took a nice long walk in the afternoon, insects buzzing like mid-summer. When I got back some government people called and then Jefferson Davis Milton dashed up to leave some quail and evening again. I'm not telling so much about the evening visits. . . .

"Tuesday morning I called at the government school, and climbed to the store, also did another little hill. No ride as the owner of the red "cockroach" and the white dog, spent the morning wrestling with the aforesaid.

372

"Mr. Wilson returned just before dinner and in the afternoon took me back to town, meeting the Simkins on the way. Having no dynamite on the running board made the trip more enjoyable."[14]

Mildred Taitt went back to her studies at Tucson, but her memories hovered about Indian Oasis and that vigorous "Desert Chesterfield," as Greenway called him, who courted, as he lived, through his prowess with his guns. It is idle to imagine what might have been had the Simkins arrived to take her back on time. She would have missed Jeff at the store, and it is hardly to be supposed that he would have been chasing Chinamen on the university campus. Fate flips the scales of human destiny with a deft but unobtrusive finger.

Once each month he journeyed to the immigration office at Tucson to report, and there is no complaint from this period that his reports were not made on time. Instead of quail he now brought mints, having found that Mildred enjoyed them. Always generous to provide, he scorned the usual small packages and brought them in five-pound lots. In just less than six months she succumbed to his tempestuous wooing against the advice of her doctors, who thought she might not live.

"I'll take care of that," said Jeff. "I'm a pretty good doctor myself."

They were married on June 30, 1919, at Tucson, and scooted back to Indian Oasis in the "red cockroach" of a car, finding the sixty-eight miles short for his ardor indeed. She was frail as a reed and forty, weighing about ninety pounds; he was over two hundred pounds of vigorous flesh and nervous energy at fifty-seven. The friends of each wagged their heads in concern, while a Tucson lady, hearing of the marriage, exclaimed in horror, "How did that sweet Miss Taitt come to marry that terrible man!"

And down on the great Boquillas ranch along the San Pedro, Henry Street cursed loud and long as he complained, "It can't last! Just wait till she sees old Jeff get mad."

14 Mildred Taitt to Mrs. James Otis Sheldon, January 8, 1919. Mildred Taitt was born February 21, 1879, in Gouverneur, New York. Her father, George P. Taitt, was a Union officer and merchant; her mother was Lucretia Maria Barnes.

On the peaceful drive to Indian Oasis in the car "mounting two guns," Jeff was considering the imminent sacrifice he must manfully make to meet his new obligation in life. At last he soberly said, "I'll have to give up chewing." And he did.

His wife may have been wondering a little about the tales told of this "terrible man" who had "been in many a gun fight and broken a few laws," too. When they topped the hill looking down on Indian Oasis and the bachelor's camp which was to be their home, he observed, a little wistfully, "I guess my birds will be glad to see me back."

"Your birds?" she spoke inquiringly. "I didn't know you had any birds."

"Oh, my wild birds," he explained. "I bake a pan of bread for them every day I'm home."

"And then I knew," she later confessed, "that I hadn't married such a wild man."

The news met with vigorous reaction back in Florida. There the loss of a father, a palatial home, and a fortune was still blamed on the North and still rankled in the hearts of Jeff's people. The thought of a Milton's marrying a Yankee Republican was simply too much for words, but his sister Louise, who had married Louis Gamble—a descendant of the Morrises of Revolutionary fame—took her sister-in-law's side. After all, Mildred Taitt's home town of Gouverneur had been named for one of the Morrises and she reassured the others, "You know there *are* good Republicans."

When Jeff returned to Tucson to make his monthly report, one of his friends inquired, "Well Jeff, how do you like married life?"

"None of your damned business!" snapped Jeff.

Back at home he mentioned the man's impertinence to Mrs. Milton, saying, "Don't you think I did just right, wife?"

"No, Jeff, I don't think you did," she had to tell him, and he began to wonder a little about the subtle nature of women. When he next met Judge Edwin Jones, a dear and old-time friend at Tucson, the Judge said, "Jeff, I'm sure glad to hear it. You were getting to be a very dangerous man—a *very* dangerous man. But

374

this will settle you down." And in later years he recalled the comment with gratitude, "for as long as I was a single buck," he admitted at eighty, "I didn't give a damn whether school kept or not."

Mrs. Milton, with rare sense of humor, got great fun out of his closest friends from the fact that he, such a rabid Southerner, had married a Yankee Republican.

"You know, I hope to live to see Jeff split the Democratic ticket," she would chide. She hardly suspected that she would, although in later years she saw him do it with vigorous vengeance. It was serious business, however, instead of a joking matter with Henry Street.

Jeff had first known of Street when he was punching cows for the Millett ranch, a hard-fighting outfit in the Fort Griffin country, in the seventies. He had met him at Conteracio, New Mexico. Later, Street had been foreman of the Spurs, near Luna, where he had killed a man, and then he had come to the Diamond A's for the Victoria Land and Cattle Company. When the great Bakersfield outfit bought the San Pedro country from the Greene Cattle Company—a range reaching from near Benson to the Mexican line—H. E. Jastro, the manager, announced that Henry K. Street was to run the ranch. Back of Jastro, of course, was W. S. Tevis, who had backed Jeff in his oil venture in Texas.

Street was a little man of fiery temper, with tiny feet trimly encased in boots, of which he was inordinately proud. He was from Tennessee, had been married three times, and lugged a four-poster bed about as a sort of tangible tie to the gentle land of his birth. Some suspected he had been a member of Sam Bass's band, and Jeff, always in guarded defense of a friend, admitted that he had probably done some fighting for the Milletts. Street named his first boy "Hi," for Hi Millett, and this noted family from Texas kept in touch with him, although he was far away in Arizona. He would get on a drunk when Jastro, the general manager, came to the ranch, refuse to talk to him, and otherwise treat him with disdain. But he was a cowman who handled the Boquillas empire—"the Wagon Rods"—with discipline and skill and made them money.

"I never saw a place go to pieces so fast in my life as when Henry died," Jeff observed, "and he was a very wa'm friend of mine."[15]

They were often together when Jeff was stationed at Fairbank, in the Boquillas range. Street, who always wore a gun, showed up one day with a prisoner, whom he had taken for killing a Wagon Rod beef. As Jeff looked on, Street gave the man such a terrible cursing that he began to cry.

"I just had to kill that beef," he blubbered. "My mother was sick and had to have something to eat."

"Well, you so-and-so," said Street, "kill another one, but be damned sure to hang the hide on the fence."

In the fall of 1919, Jeff was sent back to Fairbank, and on his ride dropped by Street's as usual to see him. As usual Street urged him to spend the night.

"Can't do it," Jeff replied. "Got to get back to my wife."

"Oh, Jeff," he complained, in jealous anguish, "why did you do it?"

Jeff's dog Doc was jealous, too, although Jeff called him to his knee, pointed at his wife, and said, "We now belong to her." Doc looked at Jeff a little reproachfully but accepted the inevitable and shared his loyalty with philosophical resignation, but as much is not to be expected of a man. Henry Street scuffed his boots in nervous impatience, for he was the warmly human sort who could forgive a cow thief but just could not get over the fact that Jeff was a married man.

Meanwhile, Jeff, doing his best to break Mrs. Milton into the ways of the West, impressed her with the cardinal courtesies of the land. "Wife," he seriously admonished, "you *must* shake hands with people and *don't* ask where they're from." In spite of her frailty, she wrestled with the meals with his efficient help, for he loved to cook. One day they had company and entirely on her own she proudly prepared some creamed cabbage.

Now we of the Deep South believe in boiling our cabbage in

[15] The Milletts had "the largest cattle ranch in North Texas," with 40,000 cattle, in 1879. *Fort Griffin Echo*, June 21, 1879; and for recollections of Street, Montague Stevens to J. E. H., February 27, 1945; *Tucson Citizen*, April 24, 1912.

bacon rind for half a day. What if it does wilt like a worn-out dishrag and smell up the place—for that is the way we like it. So when Mrs. Milton served crisp and quick-cooked cabbage smothered in cream sauce, Jeff was sure something had happened, but being genuine gentlemen, he and the company politely ate it. After the visitors were gone, he turned to her and said, "Wife, you shore played hell with that cabbage!"

At last the boss of the Boquillas screwed up his courage and brought his wife to visit. Mrs. Milton rushed to serve refreshments, and Street, used to whiskey and mescal when visiting Jeff, told about it afterwards: "And what 'o you think she gave us to drink? Tea! Dammit! Tea!"

Jefferson Davis Milton obviously at last had settled down, and his friends were shocked to see his handsome head bowed in grace at every meal. What they had never realized was the reverent nature of the soul behind those burning eyes that spurred his character into pace with his courage. "I never sat down to a meal in my life, on the desert or anywhere else," he once modestly explained, "without consciously offering thanks for what I had." And when they became audible little prayers, they, never stereotyped, came right out to fit the occasion in a sort of a conversational partnership with God.

It is a glorious thing to see a completely fearless man with a gun in hand stand up to death in battle. It is a sobering experience to hear his humble soul commune with his God. Coffee was never cooled and bread was never broken at the simple Milton board until his good gun hand came down on the table to encompass the frail little fingers of another hand that sought it, and he had bowed his head to talk it over with God. And now he realized, apologetically, that he had not provided for age, as he admitted once in his benediction: "Well, wife, we have our ideals, and we have each other."

They found that quite sufficient as they clung with all the vigor of life to both.

24

When the Trail Plays Out

Jeff Milton was left in station at Indian Oasis on the Papago Reservation until the fall of 1919. Mrs. Milton was far from well, but he carried her to the desert, spread her bed upon the ground, lifted her out of the car to the pallet, and fed her on hot biscuits, broiled quail, and the other campfire delicacies of which he was master. He bought her a gun, taught her to shoot, and nursed her back to health.

In December, soon after his transfer back to Fairbank, mysterious orders came for him quietly to report in New York for service in a frigid land. He left his wife with friends in Tucson, mounted the train, and rode into New York, where an agent picked him up and carried him to George W. Webb, who was already on hand and who urged that they get a-going.

"I ain't going anywhere," he answered, "until I get plenty of tobacco and some clothes." He bought enough tobacco for a crew, and then Webb rushed him off to Ellis Island, where he saw the nature of his next assignment: helping to guard Emma Goldman, Alexander Bergman, and 247 more alien radicals who were so sure that revolutionary Russia was the promised land that the vigorous federal policy then prevailing was being invoked to get them there.

They were loaded on an old tub built at Cork called the *Buford,* and with a guard of fifty soldiers and three old-timers from the border service shipped for Russia. Never before had a boatload of aliens been deported by the department. The *Buford* pulled away before day, December 21, 1919, to miss the demonstration of New Yorkers bent on protesting their free delivery from "the slavery" of the States. They took the northern route and immediately ran into stormy seas.[1]

[1] *The Boston Globe,* December 22, 1919. Emma Goldman eventually re-

378

Old Emma and two pretty Russian girls had cabins on the upper deck without objecting to the class distinction, but the mill run of the Reds were democratically piled in the hold. The engines broke down, the boat drifted about, and Jeff fretted to be back with his wife on the desert. Finally he began keeping a journal filled with observations on the ship and the weather but mainly with his concern for her. He found the north star out of place, for they had gone "plumb above it," and after many days on stormy seas, he wrote that he "would give a thousand dollars to see a jack rabbit."

It was a long and slow trip. Off the coast of England a cruiser dropped into their wake to follow them in. They put in at Kiel and passed through the Baltic, close by the mainland of Sweden, as he noted in his journal:

"15th(January)3am Good morning wife. I am up now looking after the Reds. Cold oh my, and storm on down below decks the thunder of the icy water sounds like big guns, and big slabs of ice hitting the old tub—who was it had the big hammer Thor I believe was the Gent and still the miles reel on takeing me away from the onely human on Earth that I care for. . . . I have no desire to see any of Europe alone but do want to be with you. We are haveing long nights now. Dark at 4—and Day break at 8' We are now in the middle of the great mine fields of the Baltic and the old German who is pilot is some uneasy, but what's the dif if we go down will have plenty of company."[2]

He had bought a new pistol and two hundred rounds of ammunition, confiding to his wife that he expected "some trouble" in unloading. "Maybe not Hope not anyway I have made up my mind all ok that no mans life shall keep me away from you if it comes to mine or his." As Russia refused to let them land, the "Soviet Ark," as the ship had been dubbed, put in at Hango, Finland, January 16, 1920, where the White Finnish Guard met the boat, received the cargo, and locked the Reds in cattle cars for the last stage of their pilgrimage to the promised land.

turned to Canada, wrote a book, *My Disillusionment in Russia* (New York, 1923), and died in May, 1940. A. P. notice of May 14, 1940.

 [2] J. D. Milton, MS "Journal," n. p., entry of date.

Jeff considered the White Guards the finest specimens of manhood he had ever seen and approved their businesslike manner. As Emma was being marched up the ramp into a cattle car with the others while Jeff and a Finnish guard sat on the car above, she stopped halfway and began to orate—orations are always in order with the American Reds. But a White Guard poked her in the rear with his bayonet and said something that sounded like "Getsky!" to Jeff, "and believe me," he recalled with a hearty laugh, "She gotsky."

And then happily, on January 19, he entered his daily note to Mrs. Milton:

"Dear girl   just think   I am now on return trip home   that means you   The boat just pulled out   4520 miles to N Y   about 2600 more to you   Stop at Antwerp   then Washington   I wish both places were off the map. one thing singular I do not feel the cold here—also the sun rises describes a small ¼ circle and goes out of sight.   the north star is all wrong being straight over head."

The *Buford* tied up again at Kiel where, he wrote, he had "done something I never did before. I hired a man to steal 2 loaves of Bread to give a Kid as the poor Devil's mouth was watering . . . but such is life [he added] I guess we will never miss the Dollar."

At Brussels he got into a lace shop on Sunday and bought a few pieces for his wife, wishing however that he had a million dollars so he could load the boat for her.

"The people over here [he wrote] are in better shape than they are at home   better dressed and seem to have more money— just think 5 men for Dinner   Beef potatoes vegetables soup— cakes—coffee and 5 Beers—$1.90   one bone and ninety cents— and then we talk of the poor Belgians   The buildings here are all well built and every one you see seems well off   not one beger so far   no Bums at all"

The *Buford* took the southern route back while Jeff walked the decks by day, read when he could, and fretted for Arizona and his "Millie." In his diary, still addressed to her, he recorded finishing another "daily letter to you that I imagine I mail to you—make believe you know and drop it in the sea so the waves can read and sob. When it is finished and dropped in the Deep letter box I retire"

The deathless devotion of Sir William Wallace, of which he had read in the woods of Florida, and the eternal passion that spoke to him from the sonnets of Browning as he covered the desert ranges of Lower California on a mule, had not been lost on him. In love as in war he went the limit of his ardent soul.

At last he was back in the United States, stopping off long enough at El Paso to tend to a little business and confide to Will Burges that the trip had broken his heart—"didn't get to finish it a-tall." To Burges' obvious question he replied that he had "hoped to kill some of them and never got a chance." Mushy-headed appeasement with enemies of his land was not for him. No wonder the daily news of his late years kept him in a stew.

He continued in the government service with frequent trips to the desert, where his skill, endurance, and intimate knowledge of growth and terrain made him the best companion available. In fact, for years his help had been frequently sought. Zane Grey got him into his *Desert Gold*, and when Carl Lumholtz made his observant trip to the deserts in 1909 and 1910, resulting in his informative study, *New Trails in Mexico*, he sought Milton as guide. Jeff turned the proposition down as he had had enough of guiding on the so-called Hornaday Expedition to the Pinacates, detailed in W. T. Hornaday's book, *Camp-Fires on Desert and Lava*.

Hornaday, the professional naturalist of New York, was invited on a trip to the desert in 1907 by D. T. MacDougal, director of the Department of Botanical Research, the Carnegie Institution, at the Desert Botanical Laboratory near Tucson. John M. Phillips, iron manufacturer and sportsman of Pittsburg, went along and financed the party, as Jeff understood. Godfrey Sykes, zestful English adventurer then with the Desert Laboratory, was the other principal member of the "expedition."[3]

[3] Hornaday's book, while readable, makes some extravagant claims about the country's being unknown. He speaks of their discovery of craters, peaks, passes, and so on. Jeff, Rube Daniels, and others had known the country intimately for years—Jeff since the late eighties.

381

When they reached Sonoita, Jeff supplied an extra wagon, helped rustle additional horses, and took off to go with them as he knew the volcanic range they wished to hunt and explore. Dr. David Trembly MacDougal irritated him from the start because he took the attitude that Jeff was a hired hand, when in truth he went in accommodation. When they reached the Sonoita River and found no grass, Jeff suggested they turn back to San Domingo and camp, since hay could be had there.

MacDougal ordered camp on the river anyway, and to keep their horses from going hungry, Jeff took them back that night himself. Even Hornaday, while publicly devoted to animals as a naturalist, thought little of leaving the horses without feed, and openly poked fun at Jeff because of the gentle care that he gave his dogs, Rex and Rowdy, while in the desert.

Under Jeff's guidance, Hornaday and MacDougal "discovered" and named the craters, mountains, and peaks for themselves and party—features of the country that he and Rube Daniel had known for years. The "explorers" tore up a little cairn of stones that Jeff, Rube and Joe Meeks had built long before, to build another and encase a can with a notation of their pioneer mastery of Pinacate Peak, November 20, 1907, in commemoration of "The Hornaday Expedition."[4]

Sykes, with genuine scientific bent, was everywhere. Bareheaded and sunburnt, he tirelessly climbed peaks, packing aneroid and plane table to determine elevations and plot the area. He scorned a mule, went everywhere afoot, and showed up missing one night for supper. Jeff was getting uneasy when at last he returned at one o'clock in the morning, having decided, in the afternoon, to walk to the Gulf of California and test his aneroid at sea level. His pedometer showed a round trip of forty-three miles.[5]

At last the party straggled back with fine specimens of desert

[4] All of which is detailed at great length, with splendid pictures and some interesting observations on desert growth and life, in Hornaday's handsomely printed *Camp-Fires on Desert and Lava* (New York, 1908).

[5] This remarkably versatile man, associated with the Desert Laboratory at Tucson for years, has written his autobiography—a charming story called *A Westerly Trend* (Tucson, 1945).

antelope and Pinacate mountain sheep, while Jeff and Phillips
came out together with a pack outfit. Jeff had made the trip at his
own expense and some irritation, and it was all the guiding he
wished.

Whatever his experience with people, however, the desert
never ceased to interest him. He could kill a mountain sheep, a
deer, or an antelope any time he needed meat, and there were
quail "by the million." He once saw a convocation of quail near
Indian Oasis that covered a mountainside in thousands. He saw
the same with hawks. He recalled a plague that hit the desert
jack rabbits about 1906 and killed most of them off—at times
there were five or six dead beneath a single bush. He never destroyed a thing in camp—not a crumb a wren could eat nor a bone
a coyote could gnaw. In the desert he learned the genuine economy of nature—nothing wasted and nothing lost. Everything
with him had a right to live.

Antelope lived there without water for months and deer and
even cattle likewise, on the frightful fruit of the cholla. He
laughed with and at the wild jackasses except when their pierc-
ing screams at night told that a mountain lion had caught one.
He watched with awe as a big old mountain ram butted the base
of a tough saguaro into pulp. It was hard going, but he backed

off from the giant cactus and hit it full drive, like a real man, and although he bounced off like a rubber ball, he tore it up so that his band could fill on its watery pulp to quench their thirst.

When in timber, in the mountains, Jeff found that porcupines were mighty good eating when a man was really hungry—"rich, like pork." On the Plains he had eaten prairie dogs—and a coyote while in the Ranger service, but he never relished him. Yet in life he found him to be a most interesting and amusing friend and was outraged that the government should sponsor the killing of any form of wild life: "If I was running the government, I'd make it a hundred-dollar fine to kill a coyote," he savagely observed.

On one desert scout, he and a man named Theiss, likewise in the government service, observed a coyote eating his meal while they were stopped for dinner. Jeff investigated and found it the carcass of a man but did not tell Theiss until they had resumed their ride.

"We must go back and report," the excited Theiss exclaimed.

"Hell no," said Jeff, "we won't do that. If we go back every time we see something to report, we'll never get anywhere. He's already dead and we couldn't help him anyway."

Among the bothers of the desert the Hualapai tigers of the Sonoita country were something to be remembered. In reality, he recalled, they are "chinches—flying bedbugs. It's a funny thing about them. When they stick their bill into you about a quarter of an inch, you don't feel it a-tall. But when they pull it out, step back, and go on about their business, boy, you sure know it." Once a party of his camped at some abandoned dobes in that region and rolled out their beds in the houses. When he observed that he would sleep outside "where the tigers won't get me," they all laughed at the idea of tigers, but they did not know the Hualapai tigers. That night they found them out.

While he had killed a number of grizzlies in his time, he at last joined the Papagoes in rejecting bear as food. The last bear he killed, a big old fellow in the mountains below John Slaughter's ranch, made a lasting impression on him. He and a party scouting for outlaws rode right up on him, and without dismounting Jeff pulled his saddle gun, threw it down in his right hand,

and aimed to shoot the bear in the eye. His horse moved just as he pressed the trigger, and the bullet went low, breaking the bear's jaw. The animal reared straight up, dropped his paws across his chest like human hands and with sagging, broken jaw, reproachfully looked him in the eye as if saying, "What for?"

His next shot broke the bear's neck, but the experience cured him for good. "I wouldn't kill another bear for nothing. Just as soon kill a man—in fact, a little rather."

Once as he and two friends rode in the Santa Ritas through a lot of balanced rocks, he kept trying to get them to stop and help him tilt some of them off and watch them roll down the mountain. They laughed at him and kept a-riding. When he topped a divide ahead of them, with timber and thickets below, he rushed back and said, "A couple of bears ran into that thicket down there. We'll roll some rocks and scare them out."

They piled off their horses and heaved at the boulders with a ready will. Jeff was having a mighty good time watching them crash down the canyon when "I'll be damned," he said, "if two bears *didn't* run out."

It is a rather general practice in the Southwest for riders to stop and kill every rattlesnake they see. Milton refused to kill them and to the wonderment of others kept them from doing so. When he and a man named Williams once camped in the desert near La Lesna after dark and rustled around for wood, he reached down and touched a big one nearly six feet long, thinking it was a stick. Williams rushed up saying, "Good God, Milt, let's kill him."

"Nothin' doing," he said firmly. "We won't do anything like that, certain."

"Why not," Williams asked. "Let's kill him."

"I won't hear to it," Jeff fussed.

"Why?"

"He could have killed me, dead easy, but he didn't. No use to kill him. Let him go on about his business."

Jeff rarely rode the desert at night, for there the snakes came out in the cool of evening and he feared his horse might be bitten. Once he and a ranchman friend, Mariano Jaques, were camped against a bluff in the Big Ajos. The Mexican was sitting against the bluff when Jeff drew his gun and apparently aimed it squarely at him.

"My God, Militone, don't kill me," he pleaded. Jeff, ordering him not to move, shot an instant later and Mariano turned to see a large, writhing, headless rattlesnake that had crawled from under the bluff right at his side. Jeff knew that if he warned the man of the snake, he would instinctively put his hands down to push himself up, slap one on the snake, and surely be bitten. The safest thing for him was to shoot the reptile's head off. Several times rattlesnakes crawled into bed with him, but he was never bitten, and in appreciation he always rolled them off his suggans and let them "go on about their business."

When on the Hornaday expedition he kept the camp rustler, Tex, from killing one, it apparently rankled in Tex's memory. For later, at Tucson, Tex raised a row, bowed up like a fighting shoat, and invited him into the back room of the saloon. They went back in a hurry and closed the door, "where I explained it to him right," mused Jeff, "and when we came out, we was wa'm pussenal friends."

To him, the desert growth was a long and intriguing study within itself. The time of ripening of the saguaro and organ-pipe fruit was a time of festival among the Indians. They gathered the luscious stuff, ate it fresh, dried it for future use, or made it into a strong alcoholic drink. Mesquite beans made good food when ground into meal on their metates.

There is almost nothing in the way of growth along the upper Gulf of California except the *chamisa del sal.* A wide belt of barren sand intervenes between the coast and the approaches to the Pinacate—a word meaning "broken arrow" to the Indians, "black bug" to the Spanish. The greasewood, called *hediondilla* or *gobernadora* by the Mexicans, sets in on the slopes. Just south of the Pinacates was the heaviest growth Milton ever observed, though that along the trail on the eastern side of the Quijotoas is heavy and pungently attractive.

Since horses' backs scalded badly in the terrific heat of the desert, Jeff used a brew of broiled greasewood leaves, a strong astringent, to wash and toughen them. It is a widely distributed growth, but the Mexicans used to come a long way for that below the Pinacates, which they brewed for fevers, diarrhea, snake bite, wounds, infections—in fact, for whatever ailed them.[6]

Along the washes is the desert broom, a bushy shrub from one foot to ten feet high, trimmed up by nature like an ornamental shrub of hothouse origin and tipped with a mass of tiny yellow blooms in hairlike—almost gossamer—form.

When Jeff came to the desert first in 1887, there was grama grass for game and a mount of horses everywhere, but now a spear of grass is hard to find. Turpentine weed, missing then, grows everywhere instead.

Scarlet mallow brightens the trails across the desert after a rain, and the "evening star," a lovely flesh-tinted flower opens on the Pinacate desert with the cool stimulus of night. The Mexicans call it the "good-woman flower" because its leaves pull off when touched by clothing and "stick to a man like a good woman."[7] Then Mexican children gathered the rubbery effusions from the stems of the guayule, and chewed it in place of *chicle*. Mesquite, palo verde, and ironwood were widely distributed.

On the left of the trail as Jeff came north from Sonoita was the marvelous stand of organ-pipe cactus that has since been made into a national monument. On the right was the magic range of mountains known as the Big Ajos—always dark, cool, and inviting from the west before the broiling sun passed the meridian; copperish white, hot, and repellent in roughest confusion as they frowned in the glare of midafternoon. Always, just as the sun settles beyond the burning sands of the Tule desert, they blaze like fire for one brief moment above the darkening desert—a range of vivid flaming glory. Small wonder men were claimed, body and soul, by the awful nature of the desert.

In the Big Ajos, Jeff used to gather his chilipitins—such as cost him the sale of the mine—for the seasoning of his eggs, meat,

6 Nacho Quiroz, as cited; Lumholtz, *New Trails in Mexico*, gives much attention to desert growth. In later years it has been called the creosote bush—*Carilla tridentata. Range Plant Handbook*, U. S. Department of Agriculture, B 67.
7 Mrs. J. D. Milton, "Days and Nights among the Craters," *Ajo Copper News*, August 10, 1933.

and beans. There the jojoba grew, laden with oily beans, to fatten the big mule deer. The Papagoes gathered them, too, and pounded out the oil for use on their hair. Milton declared they "are pretty good eating for man and the finest deer feed in the world." At least one man tried to get them into commercial trade.

M. G. Levy, propelled by the restless enterprise that characterizes his race, had crossed the desert and started a store at Ajo. Jeff had met him in 1884 at San Marcial, New Mexico. He had burned out there. When Jeff next saw him, he had a store at Nogales. But after a fire there, he moved to the desert west of Quitovac. And he burned out there. Then he set up at Ajo; and Jeff, while scouting the border, left a trunk and some valued mementos with him, and he burned down there, trunk and all. He moved next to Clarkston, at the edge of Ajo, but the fire-fighting facilities were poor, and flames destroyed his place there. "Old Levy sure had bad luck," Jeff recalled in sympathy.

Anyway, the enterprising Levy, between fires, conceived the idea that if the oil of the jojoba bean was good for Papago hair, it ought to be good for other races addicted to vaseline-tinted scalps. He bought all the beans he could induce the Indians to gather. Jeff saw him with a house full, but the market never developed. They must have grown stale on his hands unless, unfortunately, he lost them in a fire, too.[8]

Jeff made friends with the desert people and greatly admired the Papagoes, never presuming for a moment that his way of life was better for them. He enjoyed their lore, approved their integrity, treated them right, and went on about his business.

Once he camped and staked his mule near the Baboquivaris. During the night he heard something stirring. He raised on his elbow, picked up his double-barreled shotgun, and watched two Indians come up through the darkness—right up to his mule. He threw down on them as he thought to himself, "Whenever you untie that rope, you'll be out of luck."

They proved to be two old Papagoes, drunker than lords, who

---

[8] Lumholtz observed that Levy thought they would become a great cattle feed. *New Trails in Mexico*, 81. *Range Plant Handbook*, B 148.

recognized their danger just in time and instead of taking the mule staggered into his camp. A few days later he met the son of one, who said, "Militone, you come pretty near killing the old man one night. If you had, I sure would have laughed. He didn't get home for three days." Now it was physically impossible for anybody with a sense of humor to get out of patience with people like that.

Milton served as judge and jury at times in Indian disputes. Once a Papago complained that another had stolen six head of his cattle, "and sure enough we found this other fellow with the cattle," Jeff recalled. "I told him he had stolen them, which he readily admitted. I told him he would have to give them back, but must also give up two more head of cattle for every one he had stolen. He did, and everyone was satisfied without it costing the government a cent."

Again Jeff is said to have settled a case in which a Papago was charged with murder by levying on the defendant for forty head of cattle, which he delivered to the widow, who probably felt well repaid. And in telling how it turned out, he simply reasoned, "Why haul him all the way to Tucson, have a long jury trial, and have the man sent to the pen? It would have cost the county and government a lot of money, and while he was locked up, the widow and his own family might be starving."[9]

Jeff Milton got along well in Papago land. Only once by the record was there a ripple in his relations with the Indians. As he celebrated Christmas at Rube Daniel's ranch on the desert, one time, a bunch of drunk Papagoes were there, "and while Rube and I wa'n't drunk," he recalled, "we wa'n't exactly sober." Rube had married a Papago.

During the season of good-will he heard an awful commotion up on a little knoll near the house, ran out to investigate, and saw that a couple of Papagoes had got Rube down. One had a big knife out, and they were about to kill him. If he had had his rifle, he would have shot them off, but fearful of hitting the wrong man with his six-shooter at that distance, he yelled at Rube to hold on and ran for the fray. He tapped the one on top across the

9 Mrs. Edith Kitt, in *The Arizona Star*, August 16, 1936.

head with his gun and toppled him off, cocked his six-shooter, and threw down to kill the one with the knife.

"For some reason, maybe God," he felt, "I changed my mind just as I went to shoot and pulled off as I pressed the trigger. The bullet just went through his arm and burnt a streak across his belly, and you ought to have seen him run—a rabbit wa'n't in it."

Another Papago, Juan Segundo, came running out with a rifle, and Jeff threw down on him, saying, "Give me that"; and he, overawed by the incomprehensible compulsion of legal authority on simple minds, as well as in keeping with good common sense, did, observing, "What the government says, I do."

Rube's father, who was on hand visiting his son and who had been trying to sleep, got up and stormed, "I'm getting out of this country. Damned if I'm going to stay where they are always fighting."

"Mr. Daniels, it is quiet here," Jeff reassured him, "no trouble! The Indians are not killing anybody." The old man was hardly soothed, so Jeff stayed at the ranch while Rube took him to the railroad, though Rube worried lest his dusky married relations come back and murder Jeff.

"Don't think they'll bother me," said Jeff. "Never did have any trouble with them." And he did not then.

In age he spoke of his life among the Papagoes with genuine appreciation: "I don't believe any man was more fearless than the Papago Indian. I lived with them for years and for me I think they were the best friends I ever had."[10]

On the desert, too, Jeff came to be known as a doctor. Willing improvisation stood him in stead of science. He rode into Sonoita once to find everybody suffering with sore eyes. He treated them generously with a bottle of horse medicine from his pack, "and in a few days they were all cured."

When he saw a set of dental tools in a window in Tucson, he said to himself, "By Jacks, that's just what I need," and went in and bought them. The forceps served for pliers and the drills

[10] The Papago name for Jeff was *Samoick Noffe*—"Soft Arm"—because of the missing bone in his left arm. Tom Childs to J. E. H., March 4, 1945.

"were mighty handy to bore holes through leather with," and besides he "began practicing dentistry" down in the desert.

Once at Sonoita, Theiss, the New Yorker, got down in agony with a bad tooth. But he had to suffer, as the nearest dentist was at Gila Bend. When he saw Jeff working on his gear with the dental tools, he wanted to know what he was doing with them.

"Used to practice dentistry before I did this," said Jeff airily.

"Yet I'm doing all this suffering, and you wouldn't help me," the man complained.

"I'll help you in the morning," Jeff answered.

The next morning he gave the patient "three or four drinks to brace him up a little bit" and then took him out to a forked mesquite. He stepped astraddle his chest to hold him down, pushed his head back in the crotch with his left hand, grabbed the offending tooth with the dental pliers, and pulled with all his might and main—and Milton was a powerful man. The tooth refused to budge. Although Theiss yelled that he was breaking his neck, he bore down on him that much tighter and still pulled, but without avail until he recalled seeing a dentist twist his forceps. Then he twisted his. Theiss staggered up complaining that his neck was broken, while Doctor Milton proudly displayed the extracted tooth and "part of the jawbone." Thereafter, he said, "I practiced dentistry quite a bit, but finally quit; afraid I'd get into trouble over it."

In the border service and out, Jeff was recognized as the man who knew and could cope with the desert. For all those who wanted to venture into that weird land of seemingly archaic and anachronistic growth, he was a focal figure. He knew just what to do and he did it with evident relish. Yet a sort of malignancy broods over it for those who fear to face the rigors of a relentless nature.

Jeff had a pack mule which he thought was as wise an animal as a man ever owned. He was on the trail south of Ajo one night when a bottle of whiskey slipped out of his pack. The mule, following behind as well-bred mules were wont to do, felt it slip, and immediately stopped. Jeff did not see it in the dark and had an awful time getting her away from the spot. She knew something had fallen out and that he had not got down to replace it. At last he got her started and continued on his trip.

Upon his return with a Mexican companion about two weeks later, he came to the place where his mule had stopped. There in the middle of the trail, unbroken where it had fallen, right end up, was his bottle of whiskey. The impact of the fall had shot the cork out of the bottle. A number of riders had passed the spot, but everyone, fearing poison or a trap, had turned out and ridden around it. Jeff got off and picked it up, and although evaporation had materially lowered its level, it smelled all right.

He asked his companion if he wanted a drink. Of course he did, for everybody out there was thirsty. Jeff watched him for a while as they rode along, and, seeing no signs of his being poisoned, tried it out on himself. It was all right. The wary eye of suspicious men had kept his liquor safe until his return.

From a pack outfit Jeff turned to a spring wagon especially made for his use and pulled by a team of light mules, while his saddle horse followed behind. He never lost a horse in all his years on the desert, although a few mustangs were running wild southwest of Sonoita to tempt his own horse to sacrifice security for freedom.

A thoroughbred race horse named Brownie was one of his prize mounts. Brownie had been run on the track at El Paso, but he combined a little perversity with a lot of speed and would go to pitching when he ought to have been running. Hal Kerr had bought him and given him to Jeff, who ran him a time or two but kept him for use on the desert. Jeff always carried a little barley or corn in wagon and pack for his horses—"even if only a cupful—enough to let them know I was taking care of them." So Brownie was trained to follow the wagon. Upon reaching the border, Jeff would camp his wagon, saddle his horse, pack his mules, and take off on his long patrol.

Once in the mustang country south of Ajo, Brownie, while following the wagon, got wind of a bunch of wild horses and took after them.

"Good-bye, Brownie," Jeff thought to himself. About five miles farther, he met Brownie coming back and realized that when a horse gives up the wild bunch for a man, animal affection is compounded with noble nature.

Jeff bought Old Dan, his famous quarter horse, at Pecos, Texas. He ran him at Fairbank and Nogales and once at Tombstone with Pink Murray in the saddle. Pink was about half-drunk and instead of holding him, as Jeff had directed, foolishly hit him with his quirt, and he beat everything so badly that Jeff could never match him in another race. He, too, was a splendid saddle horse that "could knock off five miles an hour all day long at a running walk"; and as for speed, Jeff contended, "he was the fastest horse for a quarter I ever saw—bar nothing. I wish to hell I had him now," he said in 1945. "I'd be a rich man."

Montie was a light dun and another marvelous mount. He, too, was a quarter horse with plenty of bottom to stand the roughest country and the hardest riding. But he soon learned that Jeff was sympathetic and resorted to ruses. If lying in the corral when Jeff came to get him, instead of jumping up, he would just lie still and begin to groan. When Jeff lifted his head up for the bits, he would groan all the louder and continue to do so until his master turned to walk off, reins in hand, saying, "Come on, fello'!" Then Montie would rise in disgust and follow him for whatever joint adventures the San Pedro had to offer.

He had other notable horses. Flaxie, given him by Cameron, Reb used in the Customs Service, the big brown from Henry Street, the iron grey from Kosterlitzky, and many another. Supercilious people would say that he held them in sentimental regard. "I've owned some wonderful horses in my time," he observed, "that had just as much sense as I did. If they didn't go to Heaven, then I don't care to go there." Sentimental perhaps, but close association with noble nature has never bred superciliousness in men. It does cultivate appreciation.

Next to his horses, he held his dogs in dearest regard. After having his special wagon made at Los Angeles, he got a bird dog, Rex, and a fighting bull called Rowdy. They could not follow him far on the desert, for the heat burned their feet up. So he hauled them. A jack rabbit was always hanging from his wagon bed, and every night in camp he cooked one for them. Once he

393

camped his wagon near the border, put plenty of meat out, tied two buckets of water to the wagon wheels where they could not turn them over, and said, "You boys stay here until I get back."

As he disappeared in the distance with pack mules following, he could still see them sitting on the wagon seat, watching him go. A week later, after a big circle, he came back from another direction, and there, on the wagon seat, sat the two dogs, looking off longingly in the direction that he had gone. For a hundred yards in every direction about the wagon the ground was torn up where they had been fighting with coyotes to keep them away from their feed.

Rowdy was seasoned in the ways of the world. When Jeff got Rex as a pup, Rowdy watched over him with paternal benevolence as he grew up. Rowdy, a real fighter, would not jump on a little dog, but many a time, Jeff would tell with pride, he had seen Rowdy shoulder his way into a racket where a big bully was abusing a timid dog and say, "Listen here, Cap, jump on a real man."

Jeff had contempt for anybody that abused any animal, and anybody who touched his dogs was knocking at the morgue. When age had brought retirement at Tombstone and news of poisoning of neighborhood dogs reached Jeff, he beat a hot trail to the home of the offending person, called him out on the gallery, and gave him the latest word from the sunny side of the Episcopal Church.

"Listen here, Cap, if my dog dies, I'm coming over here and kill you just as shore as hell." And immediately there was a noticeable improvement in the health of Tombstone's dogs.

Jeff's and Rowdy's most notable escapade took place in Benson, where a gambler and owner of a "fancy place" out on the edge was the proud possessor of a fighting bulldog that "had et up everything in town." Jeff and Rowdy had got off the train and were walking down the street with civilized restraint when they met the other two, and the canine bully of Benson bowed his back at Rowdy.

"Hey, Cap," Jeff warned, "better watch your dog or there'll be a fight."

"Looks like plenty of room 'round here for a dog fight," the other replied sourly. It was never in Jeff's nature to keep people from getting what they wanted.

"If that is the way you feel about it, all right," he rejoined, as he leaned over and patted Rowdy on the back, saying, "See that dog!" And Rowdy "shore saw him."

They went together, the gambler's dog grabbed for Rowdy's leg, but he, knowing that trick, slid it under him, caught the bull by the back of the neck, flopped him over, and grabbed his throat to kill him—as he had done many coyotes before. The gambler ran up to kick Rowdy, but there was the flash of cold blue steel in the morning sun as he drew back his foot. Jeff's .45 was poking in his ribs while his warning voice clipped the air like a knife. "I'll cut you in two if you do. I think there is plenty of room for a man fight."

"Don't hurt me," the gambler cried. "He's killing my dog! That is a fine dog—cost me $180."

"That's your business," Jeff retorted hotly. "I tried to keep you from having a dog fight, but you wanted it. There is still plenty of room here for a man fight."

But the Benson bad man did not want one, and as it was obvious that Rowdy was killing the other dog, Jeff slapped him and told him to "get back." Rowdy turned the dog loose. The gambler gathered him in his arms and struck off down the street, while the delighted bystanders, tired of seeing the town dogs chewed up, took Jeff and Rowdy into the nearest saloon—and it was never a grueling grind to get into one at Benson—and treated them both to champagne, although Rowdy refused to drink that early in the morning.

Soon after Jeff's marriage, however, his nephew Jim Gamble got word to Mrs. Milton, "If you want to keep Jeff out of trouble, you'd better get rid of that bulldog." Jeff's only regret with them came when he gave Rex, "a very peculiar dog," away. Rex loved him but would have nothing to do with anybody else. While down on the Mexican line below the Huachucas, he decided to give him to Gamble. When Gamble started off, Jeff pointed at him and said, "That's your boss, Rex; go with him." Rex started

JEFF MILTON

off and looked back inquiringly while he repeated, "Go with Jim." Rex followed Gamble home. A few weeks later Jeff was there and stopped to talk with Rex—as he liked to do with every dog he met—but Rex would not let him touch him, nor would he have a thing to do with Rowdy, although Rowdy had raised him from a pup. He stayed with Gamble for several months, then came in one night, kissed his hand, trotted out, and was never heard of again.

"Guess I broke his heart," grieved Jeff. "I've regretted it ever since."

But to get back to the border and the business of aliens, Jeff had, in 1917, supplemented his movements with a stripped-down car and on the Sonoran deserts those old cars were something of a problem, too. A. J. Milliken tells how Jeff was stranded on the border once with a dry differential and no grease within a hundred miles. He had to do something or die. As he pondered his problem, his eye fell on the side of bacon among his supplies—he always had plenty of bacon in camp—and he built a fire, rendered the bacon out in his skillet, poured the lard in for lubrication, and went fogging off across the desert towards grease and civilization.[11]

Jeff had the car when he married and found that he could make his patrol with ease and once in a while dash off to the Huachuca Mountains for a short visit with his old friend, Gustave Peterson. Just as increased speed enables some to do more work, it enabled Jeff to ride faster toward adventure. When he was stopped on the road near Fairbank by two men who started to hold him up, he was so amused that he just laughed in their faces. "I'll tell y'u what y'u do, by Jacks. Just drive down this road and ask the first person y'u meet how safe it would be to hold up Jeff Milton."

When he turned his stripped-down Ford over, the neighbors gathered him and his equipment up, and one gently broke the news to his wife by appearing at the door and simply saying, "Mrs. Milton, here's Jeff's gun." But when Grover C. Wilmoth, director of the immigration district, wrote from El Paso to sug-

[11] A. J. Milliken to J. E. H., November 18, 1945.

gest that he submit a report on his injuries for disability conces-sions, he declined with thanks because he was not driving on "official duty."[12]

Now, after his official tour of duty, he could drive over the hills to Tombstone, take a toddy or two, and pass a pleasant hour with his friends. One of his best, Captain Harry Wheeler, late of the Arizona Rangers and sheriff of Cochise, could always count on his help. Wheeler was a real officer, "not afraid of noth-ing on earth except his wife," who was quite jealous of her hand-some husband. Once when he showed up with his head band-aged, Jeff inquired about his trouble. Wheeler explained that his wife had hit him over the head with a chair. When he came to, he was lying on the kitchen floor, he explained, with his wife stroking his brow and sobbing over him.

"Oh, that's all right, honey," Wheeler consoled. "You didn't hurt me," whereupon she grabbed the chair and charged him again, screaming, "Then you so-and-so, I will," and Wheeler had beat a strategic retreat to get patched up and to plan with Jeff the capture of men who would do no worse than shoot them. Then Wheeler went off to the World War and Guy Welch was acting sheriff when Jeff drove in at noon, November 3, 1917, and met Spike Springer running down the street shouting that T. R. Brandt, the banker, had just been killed.[13] He reported that the robber had fled out of town across the greasewood hills afoot, toward Gleeson.

Jeff had left his Winchester out of the scabbard and was armed only with a .38 automatic pistol. He raced down to Guy Welch's, who had no rifle handy, either, but they took off to-gether and about two miles out they got within a hundred yards of the fleeing man and Jeff jumped out with his .38. When the

[12] J. D. Milton to District Director, July 23, 1927, File No. 5005-81, Immi-gration Office, El Paso.
[13] Brandt, Jeff's old friend at San Simon, had sold out his mercantile business and now ran the bank at Tombstone. The robber, a simple-witted Austrian named Fred Koch, had walked in with a .41 army model and demanded the money. Brandt walked into the vault, ostensibly to get it, came out with a double-barreled shotgun, but instead of cutting Koch in two, pulled off the gun into the ceiling. Koch shot him and ran. Brandt lived for about three weeks. See *Tomb-stone Epitaph*, November 4, 1917.

fugitive failed to halt at his call, he shot and wounded him in the arm. Then the man, a foreigner named Fred Koch, threw his gun away and came up to them. Brandt was a very popular man, and when a lot of the enraged townspeople got there, they begged Jeff to kill him and then threatened to lynch him.

Although Jeff had been warmly attached to Brandt for many years, he put his foot down hard: "Nuthin' doin'."

They carried Koch to jail, got the story from Brandt, who died a lingering death to Jeff's tearful distress, and tried Koch at Tombstone before Brandt had died. An amusing incident marked the procedure. The town was well posted on Jeff's marksmanship, and when he was asked on the stand if he were "shooting to kill," and he admitted he was, the crowded courtroom considered it such a good joke that it boomed with laughter. Koch was sentenced to death, but Governor George W. P. Hunt—"Old Pin-Head" Hunt, as Arizona irreverently called and Jeff considered him—remitted the sentence, and Koch was lodged in an asylum.[14]

When Jeff married, he was still scooting about the desert in this "red cockroach" of a car; and he and his bride planned to go to the Huachucas—where Gustave Peterson, after his discharge from the army at Fort Huachuca in the eighties, had filed on a bold spring on the sunny slope that looked down into Mexico—and spend their honeymoon at a smaller spring that trickled from the mountainside a short way down from Pete's camp. But a heavy rain fell that day, and they went to the desert instead, although they always called the place "Honeymoon Spring." After three months on the desert, they moved to Fairbank, to which Jeff had been reassigned, where he gave a Mormon fifty dollars to move out of the best rentable house in town. Then they got in the car, circled the Huachucas to the south side, and churned their way up the slope to Pete's ranch.

He was the "little bitty," gentle man whom Jeff had rescued from the Fort Griffin bully in the late seventies, and whose bond he had made when Cameron had him arrested for trespassing

14 *Tombstone Epitaph*, as cited; Mrs. Jeff D. Milton to J. E. H., December 17, 1938; and Dr. Frank C. Lockwood, in the *Epitaph*, March 22, 1945.

and hauled to court in Tucson. Although he had once served as scout for Custer, he was as mild as an old saddle horse. He worked at his and Jeff's claim up on the mountain, irrigated a garden from his spring, and puffed his pipe in the genial sunshine of Arizona and age with perfect contentment as his chickens and cats kept him company. Mrs. Milton liked him at once. He got Jeff to shoot a chicken's head off and cooked the fowl with macaroni according to his own recipe, while his chickens and cats took their liberties in the house with obvious familiarity in spite of his fussing.

"Children! Children!" he scolded, and then turned to Mrs. Milton in apology. "I never saw them act up so. I never let them in the house."

When the Miltons got up to leave, he followed them to the car and confided to her, as they said good-bye, "I was afraid Jeff had married a high-brow; but you'll do."

The following spring, after Jeff's return from escorting Emma home, Colonel C. H. Hilton, who had commanded the army detail on the Buford, was to join Jeff in Tucson for a trip to the desert to look at some mines. Jeff, with car packed, was at the station to meet him when the agent walked out and handed him a telegram advising him that Peterson had been murdered. When Hilton stepped off the train, Jeff, after their greeting, handed him the message. He read it and handed it back, saying, "Jeff, I know you well enough to know that you want to go."

"Colonel, I do, for certain," he replied.

They ate dinner, Hilton caught the next train for San Francisco, and Jeff took off posthaste for the ranch in the Huachucas. But so many people had already been there that they had fouled the trails and he could not pick up the trace. Whoever committed the crime had chopped little "Pete" in the head with his meat cleaver and shot him with his own rifle from behind. He had been missed and the entire place searched before he was found in a shed back of his cabin, where the killers had tromped him into a small packing box and thrown a piece of tarp over it. His little trunk had been rifled of his Liberty Bonds, but undisturbed beneath a piece of newspaper spread in the bottom of it was his

399

last will and testament to "Jeff Milton, my old friend." And so for them this stark little cabin, on the wild but beautiful slopes of an Arizona range, became "Sylvania," pathetically suggestive, except to him and his wife, of the rich, broad, and generous estate far away in Florida that nurtured him at birth.

Meanwhile, he had to labor to live, and his work went on with the Immigration Service, his active mobility extended through the use of cars. Yet on the desert cars are potentially dangerous, and one of the closest calls he ever had was in September, 1930, while patrolling the border with a young member of the service, Nick Collaer. They started from Tucson in a new car to cut for sign the length of the line from Sonoita to a "point south of Tinajas Altas," hunting evidence of illegal entry of aliens. They made it without trouble through Quitobaquito to Cerro Colorado, where Jeff showed that remarkable memory and sense of location that stood him in good stead. Collaer has recorded the incident:

"As we drove up on the long volcanic-ash slope leading to the crater, we stopped the car (lest we get stuck), and Jeff looked around as he always did—sorta 'soaking in' a view that he loves."

Then he said as he pointed, "Nick, right over there was where I knocked a nice fat antelope in 1907 when I was down here with Dr. Hornaday. We had been eating ham and bacon, and I wanted some fresh meat. He ran from right over there and I knocked him down right about there."

Collaer recalls that they were out in the open at the time with no immediate, distinguishing landmarks. The shot had been made just twenty-three years before. Then Milton shifted his position a little, saying, "Yes, I was standing right about here," and at that moment he leaned over and picked up a .45-.70 rifle shell, adding, "Yes, here is the shell. I still have that rifle at home; it's one of the best guns I've ever owned." Time and again he showed this uncanny sense of exact location.[15]

From there he and Collaer continued on their scout and decided to follow the so-called "Abelardo Rodríquez Military

[15] Nick Collaer to Mrs. Jeff D. Milton, March 8, 1947.

Highway" through to the Colorado River. They made it fine for a while and then got stuck in the shifting sands from the Gulf.

They deflated their tires to increase the traction and still they could not get out. They threw most of their provisions and equipment away and chopped off the car doors to cut down the weight, spread their beds on the ground to drive on, and struggled for two torrid days and moonlight nights to get out, gaining a few feet at a time with Jeff at the wheel and Nick, a powerful man, virtually lifting their car on to the tarps from the rear. As their water was fast giving out, they rested during the worst heat of day and took counsel in the shade of a mesquite. They would make one more attempt and, failing, they would filter the water from the radiator, Jeff would stay behind so as not to burden the younger man, and Collaer would take a canteen and try to cross the burning sands, that had claimed so many sturdy lives, to water and help on the Colorado.

With their brand-new car stripped of every expendable fixture, supplies and equipment thrown away, bed tarps beneath the tires, Jeff at the wheel, and Nick to push it off and grab on if they got a-going, they braced for their last attempt, rolled off the tarps into the sand, maintained their precarious start, and at last made it to firmer footing on the dreary road toward San Luis.

As they approached the waters of the Colorado, they thought, a little gravely, Collaer has noted, of "the twenty-nine wrecked passenger-carrying automobiles . . . seen along the road . . . and the number of graves with articles of clothing and shoes of men, women, and children near."[16]

Jeff was then just short of sixty-nine. He had first ridden those desert trails on a dependable horse forty-three years before. This new hazard they had just met was symbolic of change but suggestive of the fact that when it comes to coping with nature, a good horse is still a convenience and comfort. Jeff's connection with the Immigration Service came to an end soon afterward, for the work that he had pursued so long was now taken over by the Border Patrol. He had been a Mounted Chinese Inspector and

[16] Collaer, as cited.

a line rider for the service since May 1, 1904, and had long been eligible for retirement.

Before he had reached sixty-five, George J. Harris, assistant commissioner of immigration, in discussing retirement between that age and seventy, had made this comment: "He is simply a wonder when it comes to physical endurance, activity and value to the Service. All his life he has been an outdoor man, a Texas Ranger, Sheriff, Chief of Police, Customs officer, etc., a fearless, active, resourceful man with a host of friends ever ready to give him information or otherwise assist him. He is invaluable to this service and barring unforeseen accidents or illnesses, is likely to continue so right up to the maximum age of 70."[17]

When he reached seventy, he was going so strong that his official superiors recommended the extension of his service for another two years. And he was still an invaluable officer when the "Economy Act" of 1932 dropped him from the service on June 30, although he was granted an annuity of $100 a month upon which to live the balance of his days.[18]

His friend, Grover C. Wilmoth, in charge of the office at El Paso, regretfully wrote: "Your friends have come to regard you as an institution rather than an individual. No other immigration officer has your value in cultivating for the Service the good will and friendship we must have for effective enforcement of the law."[19]

His station had been transferred from Fairbank to Tombstone in 1931 because there was "no jail at Fairbank" and because he was still hauling in aliens with a generous will. Now at last he was out. But the chief inspector of the Border Patrol in Arizona, Earl Fallis, reported his capture of an alien three years later and commended his helpful advice based on intimate knowledge of that rough and ragged terrain which the Border Patrol—now under his friend Carson Morrow—still watches with eagle eyes. But at last, after seventy-one years of restless, fearless living, his own wild trails had frazzled out.

[17] George W. Harris to W. W. Husband, April 11, 1925, File No. 5005-81.
[18] Correspondence in Immigration Office, El Paso, File No. 5005-81.
[19] *Ibid.*

25

Back to the Dust of the Desert

After 1931 the Miltons made their home across the street from the Episcopal church, a few blocks east of the Boot Hill Graveyard, on the gravelly northern slope of the crumbling town of Tombstone. Jeff had seen it first in 1884 after riding across from New Mexico, when its mines were prosperous and it was really booming. He found it full of toughs whom he held in contempt—who wanted to be bad men "but just didn't know how." "Of course they would murder you," but compared to the fighting cowmen he had mixed it with in Texas, its late and champion gunman "Wyatt Earp was nothing but a scrub." He thought so little of its character then that he returned to the Río Grande.

In spite of the bravado of its slogan, "the town too tough to die," the village was now in decadence. He had known a lot of men who thought the same thing, "deader 'n hell" long ago. The bravest men he had ever known—and he placed Scarborough, Slaughter, and Webb at the head of his list—were all quiet men with "no blow-hard about them." Fortunately, however, climate is beyond the pretense of the boomers, and "progress" and charm are not synonymous. Tombstone was a good place for a man in years to drink the invigorating air of early morning and take his ease in the genial sun of afternoon.

Mrs. Milton tended her garden of desert growth and fruitful fig and peach trees while Jeff pottered about the place, keeping his camp equipment and his blacksmith tools in perfect order at his little barn. His stovewood was stacked beyond the weather on one side, not a splinter out of place. On the other, his Dutch ovens, coffeepot, and frying pans, clean and precise, seemed expectantly to await a sudden dash back to the desert. His rasp, horseshoe hammer, and other farrier's tools lay in order in his tool chest, but Old Dan, his dun quarter horse, was long since gone.

At the near end of his workbench back of a couple of battered canteens covered with tow sacks and ever full of water, always stood a bottle of liquor—whiskey, tequila, or mescal—never quite full. An inverted glass beside it had so long and daily drained its mellow or biting drops, as the case may have been, into the receptive grain of the workbench as to rot out a sizable and significant circle. Behind the loose swinging doors of his car-shed, this was a private bar. Gentlemen of his day did not drink before ladies. In deference to Mrs. Milton, he took his toddy at the barn.

At the other end of the workbench was a battered but loaded Springfield rifle, with extra ammunition tied to the stock in a small sack. "Never know when you'll need it; it'll cut a man in two at a mile." Twelve-gauge buckshot, .45 cartridges and .30-.30 shells in buckskin bags and nickel salt sacks were stuck at convenient points all over the place. His specially made Colt .45 lay on a bed-stand beside him at night until the very end; another rode in an old holster strapped to the post of the steering wheel of his open car whenever he drove off to camp, to visit, or even to get the mail, for a gallant gentleman "never knows when he will need one." The visitor browsing among the Milton mementos and books might kick another from under a Navajo rug, and he would always find the loaded gun that Jeff had taken off the Frisco thug stuck handily in a lovely Papago basket.

The Miltons made frequent overnight trips to the ranch, but little work was done on the mine, and the range was too small for cattle. Jeff's various claims on the desert were given away to friends, although he was still sure some were "very rich," and in between times he dreamed of going back to Lower California to claim his phosphate discovery there.

Mainly, however, the last fifteen years of his life presented the delightful idyl of a poor but contented man with a cultured and devoted wife. Even for men of restless action, nature has wisely provided a period at the end for peaceful meditation. And while it is inspiring to see a bold spirit fare fearlessly in his prime, it is comfortably conducive to poise to see him face decrepitude with courage, mirth, and grace.

For those whose trails took them by the Milton home in

Tombstone, and their little cottage later in Tucson, there was the unforgettably warm welcome, the genuine and eager interest in their visitors' affairs, and the persistent memory of his compelling personality. As Mrs. Milton, in pure and precise English, pursued her anxious inquiry about the caller's family, health, and fortune, Jeff chose a pipe from the collection of a dozen and more clustered about his tobacco bowl reposing in the middle of a large Papago basket, always at hand on a low table, puffed it to a fiery start, and tolerantly rocked in his great chair until her questions were done. Then with feigned severity followed by a hearty laugh, he "ordered" her off to the kitchen to "fix something to eat"—something was always being fixed for callers to eat at the Miltons'.

Then the expectant visitor turned to the master of the rocking chair, who pointed a few terse questions on his own, indulged some vivid comment on the state of the nation and the world, and rocked through a few more peaceful puffs on the pipe. Then, following the timid suggestion of a question or the brash probing of a boldly inquisitive mind, depending on the nature of the visitor, no matter the cue—men, horses, mules, mines, birds, or beasts —the charming stories began to flow. He removed his corncob pipe, his choice from a collection that ranged from briar to meerschaum, usually lifted his crippled arm to take it, thus leaving his good strong hand free for emphasis, and almost invariably started with a happy backward toss of his noble head as he observed, "Well, I just had to laugh—" and laugh he would. His conversation never took a long and tedious narrative or expository trail through a wilderness of speculation or fact, but danced about in the sunlight and shade of human emotion, mostly in the sunshine, like a fantasy of Peter Pan. His stories were not suggestive or brutal. Unless he was pressed into a particular line, or giving vent to righteous wrath on the course of public affairs or world war, his tales always turned to something mirthful and nobody was long with Jeff until he, too, "just had to laugh."

He was no doddering old man babbling in his chimney corner, but at eighty-five years of age was a master storyteller. Characterization of birds, animals, reptiles, and people, with genuine

405

gusto, pantomime, and deep feeling pounded out with his fist on the well-polished arm of his chair, poured out of the rich recesses of his experience to delight, to astound, and at times to move to tears. He never simply told a story, but from gusty laughter to moving pathos, and through high emotion burning in black, expressive eyes, he lived it. Shades of the lovable warrior Cyrano de Bergerac—what an actor he would have been!

Hence it is with a feeling of futility that an ordinary biographer attempts even to suggest the gay and gentle, blithe but dynamic, delightful but dangerous nature of this man. After all, heroic tales were meant for telling. To hear his stories of the flight of Charlie Trentham, his remorse over killing his last bear, his levity over the loss of fortune through three little peppers, his pride in the battles of Rowdy, his affection for intelligent horses, and his escapades with the zestful Sedberry, was almost to run the gamut of human emotion and to realize that their reduction to print falls just short of sacrilege.

They were so sweeping and absorbing that his most critical listeners, his educated and accomplished wife and his "wa'm pussenal friend," professor of English and historian, Dr. Frank C. Lockwood of the University of Arizona, would not believe he was as ungrammatical as my recorded conversations proved he was. They protested his actual words in print as being an injustice to the man, and at last I realize that they were right. My recordings proved the grammar, but they proved a lie. In print, his words are often flagrantly ungrammatical. But in life, boldly pouring from his ready tongue, they were vital and earthy idiom, always softened by the Negro dialect of his boyhood, right out of the soil of the Old South. Grammar, no more than anything else, ever got in his way. Human emotion bubbled and boiled up in his stories until healthy danger grew strangely seductive, until even death wore a face of mirth, until—until we all "just had to laugh."

His skill with his guns and his reputation as a fighting man were known far and wide. He had met the worst in the wide West and not a one excelled him. People naturally curious came to see him and stayed to marvel that a man who had lived so long and close to violence, had looked so often into the face of death, and had been shot up so much himself, bore not a boorish mark from conflict and battle. When really aroused, his temper was terrible to behold, and while he held a vigorous contempt for low and common natures, he never harbored a trace of malice for those fighting men with whom he had battled and bled. In this generous breadth of genuine bravery, he was a revelation to all who knew him.

Young fighting men who called to say good-bye as they marched off to war felt their spirits lifted by his own gay challenge to battle, and unknowingly left him despondent because he was not going to die with them. Frequent letters yet filtering through the mail to his widow confess in groping words that "Jeff gave me something." And that "something" their awkward words nobly seek to suggest was a revived faith in righteous conflict, in the invincible spirit of the individual, and in the inviolable nature of the human soul.

Although old age is generally conceded to be a time for reminiscence, he never got over the feeling that it was bad taste to talk about himself. He did not allude to his fights, and he did not tell of the men he had killed. "When I die, I hope they have something better to say about me," he observed, as his wife concluded reading the epitaph of another pioneer, "than to tell how many men I've killed." For that matter we never knew. But he did tell, frequently and apologetically, of the many he "ought to have killed," who would not fight when he faced them, usually adding, in extenuation of his sins of omission, "Well, you just can't kill a man like that."

Enough has been told of his marksmanship to indicate its merit. Until the end he could handle a .45 six-shooter with consummate skill. At eighty-three, as a modest statement of fact, he told young Jack Holliday, as he hefted Jack's gun and answered his eager questions, that he could easily hit the door knob at the other end of the Holliday living room, and as for distance, well, that handsome room is long enough. Fortunately for Mrs. Holliday and the door, he did not demonstrate, though Jack, Jr., would have been decidedly happier if he had.

He was extremely restless, but never nervous in danger. He was the agent of a proud and mighty land; he was always armed with the escutcheon of high honor. Not a pang of conscience ever plagued him. With a clean code, a sense of justice tempered with fairness, and a mind quick in appraisal, he positively knew that right had always ridden close at his side. When a dangerous and designing man had passed completely beyond the pale, "it's not a bit of bother in the world. If a man needs killing, either kill him or be a cur." He firmly believed that "a real man" would never temporize if his cause were just. Hamlet's indecision was not for him. As in his clashes with Selman and Hardin, "settle your troubles at once and go on about your business." "Dunlap? Dunlap?" he mused aloud over a name in the news. "I've known somebody by the name of Dunlap. Oh yes," he added without emotion, "I had to kill him."

He would sometimes tell of the men he had trailed and tried to catch; he rarely carried the narrative to the point of capture. The art of withholding was innate modesty in part, and in part due to the fact that the most fun in life comes before the end, and he was always more concerned with mirth than with death. His wife, upon discovering a faded and hitherto unnoticed bullet scar beneath his jaw, naturally inquired, "Jeff, who shot you there?"

"A man who is not alive," he explained tersely.

Dr. Lockwood, zestful and gentlemanly companion of his last days, listened to his tale of long, hard, and dangerous trailing of an outlaw in the wildest part of the Mogollons until at last the story just trailed off with the trailing.

"What happened to him, Jeff?" Dr. Lockwood inquired, with that anxiety of factual minds to possess it all.

"Why," he replied, "he's still there."[1]

These stories of his serious fights have been gathered from other sources, but as a device in verification were read back to him for his denial of erroneous detail, in a historical process of negative corroboration. While fully aware of my ultimate design, he wanted no book in his time. He deplored pretense and error. He confirmed by silence or denial.[2]

It should not be assumed that all of his adventures are even suggested here. Testimonials were for others. There was the time he would have been stabbed to death at El Paso except that his badge deflected the knife. There was the mark of the Mexican's bowie knife in his left palm, made when "I grabbed the blade of his knife in my bare hand and with the other I pulled my six-shooter and shot him," as related by his banker brother-in-law, James O. Sheldon of Gouverneur. There is Columbus Giragi's story of the four men who died while attempting to waylay him, though when the biographer probed for detail, he lightly tossed it off as being "away back yonder," and then conscious of verification by indirection, vigorously asserted " 'twa'nt nothing to it, a-tall." Now, as a matter of fact, he positively meant that it was either unworthy of mention since "anybody could o' done it," or he meant the report was erroneous. Why elaborate anything so personally obvious?

There is Dave Griminger's story of the fighter who shot at him in New Mexico and then died with "four death shots," in the forehead, the mouth, the neck, and the chest, before he could fall. And there was the shot he apparently got from ambush south of Ajo, his own quick shot at the flash, and the eternal silence of the desert night in return, an incident which he always dismissed as just "an accident." He told his companion to get off his horse and smell of the hole in his side, as he knew there was "no use to bother" if his bowels were punctured. After he did, saying, "All I can smell is good clean blood," Jeff staunched the outward flow with cigarette papers, rode nine miles that night into Ajo, and carried the bullet the rest of his days.

The native Mexicans looked upon him with affectionate awe, explaining his alertness by saying, "He has eyes in the back of his head," while Francisco Bedoya emphasized his uncanny way with death and danger by explaining: "*El tiene mas vidas de un*

1 Frank C. Lockwood to J. E. H., December 14, 1942.

2 His close friend Frank King contends that, despite his letting the Bronco Bill episode stand as written, Scarborough was not immediately in camp at the time of the fight, and that Jeff had it out alone with Bronco and Johnson.

Almost inadvertently Jeff added a few details to this, the Fairbank, and M'Rose incidents after they were written out of other contemporary sources.

409

gato—He has more lives than a cat."[3] An old Mexican, passing him on the streets of Socorro for the first time in fifty years, suddenly stopped and said, "Militone! Militone!"

"How did you know me?" Jeff marveled.

"*Los ojos,*" he answered. "The eyes."

No one, from John Wesley Hardin, looking through them into eternity at El Paso, down to his youthful friends, either vicariously facing danger through them or entranced by their impish mirth, ever forgot his eyes, dark and deep like those of a doe deer. They were the sort, as the naturalist Hudson observed, that predominate in nature and, as he thought, "most vividly exhibit the raging emotions within" as an element of defense.[4] Hudson would have been fascinated by his eyes.

He firmly believed in the balance of nature, remarking, a little remorsefully after shooting a butcher bird at Indian Oasis for killing a nest of baby mockingbirds, "I guess I oughtn't to o' done it. That's the way God made him." Although he had spent much of his life in public service, he had no faith in government nostrums. He observed that grass stayed good and the springs did not dry up, that there was no need of terraces and dams on range lands in Arizona until the government had "co-operated" in killing off the wild life—coyotes, badgers, ground squirrels, and rats—as their burrows once drank up and retained the "run-off" water.

He had spent as much as three months "alone on the Frontier in early days without speaking to anyone but was not lonely at all."[5] The creatures of the desert were company enough for him. He could never tolerate abuse of them. In the early days, he rebuked a man for tantalizing a pet Gila monster at Fairbank, who persisted, however, until the reptile bit him. He was dead in five minutes, not from poison of course, but from heart failure induced by pure fright. No need grieving for the fool; it was just a case of cause and effect.

Much has been made in Western fact and fiction of the men

[3] W. H. Brady to Hervey Chesley and J. E. H., March 7, 1938.

[4] W. H. Hudson, *Idle Days in Patagonia* (New York, 1923), 179 ff.

[5] J. D. Milton, MS "Journal," January 23, 1920.

who were "fastest on the draw." And while, with his own exception of John Wesley Hardin, Jeff was possibly the quickest and the best, it is a matter of historical record that he never killed a man who had not first shot at him or his associates.

He modestly admitted that he had never known the feeling of fear, except for ghosts and graves when he was a boy. "I never did get excited in battle. It was just business." And as for his sheer bravery being commendable, "by Jacks, it was nothing. Anybody could o' done it."

"Jeff," his wife once inquired, "didn't you ever have a feeling of fear when you went into a fight?"

"Yes, wife," he admitted in modification. "I was afraid of what I might have to do to the other fellow. But after he had taken a couple of shots at me, I got over it." And so when the Immigration Service named a Coast Guard cutter in his honor in 1936, the Commissioner, D. W. MacCormack, could quote him with proper pride as the ideal of the frontier service: "I never killed a man who didn't need killing; I never shot an animal except for meat."[6]

His devotion to his friends was as generous and true as the expansive sweep of the stars. Whether weak or strong, timid or bold, they were always men of honor to him. Their pursuits, religion, and prejudices were strictly their own business; their troubles essentially his own. From the outlawed Trentham to John C. Greenway, "the greatest man Arizona has produced, bar none," they were the bravest and the best "for certain." He was strictly subjective and never brooked their critical appraisal. "To hell with" this coldly objective view of the world, this critical logic of history; "real men" of his time tolerantly took their friends short of perfection and personally practiced good neighborliness with those who rubbed their elbows, rather than on the distant masses of mankind.

He was comforted in sensitive age by recurrent expressions of gratitude for past bravely generous favors, as in the case of a young man who called to tell him of the happy fruition of his "shotgun wedding," at which, years before, Jeff had unobtru-

6 News release by MacCormack, August 10, 1936, File No. 5005-81.

411

sively officiated. His fondness for good food and dress bespoke his cultivated tastes, and his gracious way with people and Southern gallantry with ladies was a gentle cloak that he wore until the end. When, in 1938, the state of Arizona bestowed the first and only commission of its kind upon him, a colonelcy in the Arizona Militia, he was genuinely appreciative. Yet he never grew stiff or stuffy, always preferring the familiar address of his friends: "Just call me Jeff."

His tastes were aristocratic and never common. He wanted his friends close around him; he preferred those he did not like on another planet. He fussed himself almost to fury when friends were dilatory in coming. "I wish I had told Earl Fallis to come over to see us," he remarked, after a long-distance call to the Border Patrol at Tucson, "but dammit, he ought to have sense enough to come anyway."

He could never quite get over the idea that with all our time-saving devices there was less time for gracious living than long ago. "Call Dogie Wright, wife! Why don't he and Carson come to see me?" he would storm in his last days, though perhaps they were then a hundred miles and more away on the Sonoran desert, grappling with the problems that he had loved to tackle so long ago. He could not recall that his friends had ever had to wait for him. "What, with all these cars and they still don't have time to visit?" he would snort to his patient wife. "By Jacks, what's the world a-coming to?"

It was eight hundred miles of weary driving from my ranch to his last home, yet when one of my periodic trips was deferred by an unforeseeable twist of the weather, he dictated an impatient letter, closing, "Dam the history; I want to see *you*."

In his last years, Mrs. Milton read aloud to him, and he relived the stirring story of his boyhood, the adventures of Wallace and Bruce in *The Scottish Chiefs*. But he preferred his articles short and his books devoid of villains and rapid action, full of quiet and simple folks. Hudson's *Green Mansions* was a "lovely story but just too tragic," while Gladys Carroll's account of Maine farm life, *As the Earth Turns*, was to his liking, and Elizabeth

Goudge's story of an English cathedral town, *A City of Bells*, was a great book to him.

He never believed in being caught unprepared. His larder was always stocked for a siege, ammunition was in reserve, and pipes were all over the place. He was generous to the point of embarrassing his friends, but never wasteful. Hence he never threw a pipe away, though he frequently discarded one for fear his wife, who did not complain, might find it growing too strong. On trips to the ranch and the desert, it was not unusual for him to reach under an apparently random bush and pull out an old pipe, that had been dissipating some of its power with age, and put it back to work.

When aroused to wrath, his language was as hot as a desert blast, though his gentle wife found his profanity a "sort of an inverted prayer." And so he prayed right powerfully when things went wrong, and after every trip to the desert with the Border Patrol or other friends, his wife observed that he "had to prune down on his language." "But wife, these boys were perfect gentlemen," he was wont to reassure. "I never heard a swear word on the whole trip—no, not a damned one."

His deep and gallant attachment to his wife was touching, and he grew restless as a caged bear if she were long from his sight. He delighted to prepare his special dishes and always cooked their breakfast. Sometimes when she hurriedly joined him at the table and raised her head from grace to look out the window, there traced with his finger in the condensed moisture on the pane was his morning message: "Milly, Dear"; or "Wife, I love you."

His only grudge was harbored for fifteen years against a Tombstone woman who had spoken slightingly of his wife. He grew violent whenever he thought of it, swearing that if she were drowning and he were the only one in the world to save her, he would not even put out his little finger. When the woman died, he took his wife to the funeral but stopped outside with most of the menfolks. Formal funerals made him sad anyway. Inside there were no mourners, and the few attendants seated themselves at the rear. Just as the services began, Mrs. Milton heard

413

his step in the aisle and without turning made room for him in the pew. But Jeff, hat in hand, walked down to the front seat usually reserved for mourners, never took his eyes off the coffin, and after the stark service said in benediction, "Poor old lady; it was just too pitiful."

While independent of churches, he liked all preachers because he found them "such decent fellows." His individualistic style extended even to his blessings. With head held high at the breakfast table, he thanked the Lord for rest and friends and food, "and especially for my dear and beautiful wife"; and if by chance at the end he had overlooked a guest by name, he reopened negotiations and added a codicil in his behalf. After being smitten by the sublime significance of the Colorado River, he suggested that "if there's anything to this transmigration of souls stuff," he wanted to be an eagle and fly in and out of the Grand Canyon.

In a way he ought to have been a physician. He was always critical of the profession; he was always prescribing himself. He examined Joe Brazil, a Boquillas cowpuncher down with arthritis, and passed his friendly diagnosis: "By Jacks, I can cure you, Joe. Cure you or kill you one."

"Let's go, I'm ready," came the brave response, and with an Indian remedy he had learned in Mexico, built on a base of mescal, Joe was "cured in six weeks."

As for himself, he was a powerful physical man scornful of aid, while his endurance of pain was next to heroic. Daily, for years, he suffered agonies with his feet, induced by hardening of the arteries, while damning the prescriptions that did not relieve him as the malady moved apace.

His wife would explain to his friends, "Jeff's a better hand at prescribing for the other person than for taking medicine himself," which usually provoked his quick response, "The reason I've lived so long is because I've let the other fellow take the medicine. When a man gets as old as I am, he can't feel like a four-year-old in a rye patch."

As his infirmity grew, they moved to Tucson; and there, after an excruciating period that never quite incapacitated him, he died May 7, 1947, exactly eighty-five years and six months after his birth. He was survived by his widow and "his children"—all the birds and animals of the desert.

His vigorous line had come straight down from bold and "merrie Britain." From statesmen to poets, they were distinguished there. From statesmen to warriors, they were distinguished here. But with his own land loose in lawlessness, and torn by the dissensions of class conflict and war, he could not face the future with the philosophical resignation of his great blind forebear who believed that "They also serve who only stand and wait." Incapacity was not for him. Instead, in the terse if untutored terms of the American frontier, he added his own mite to the heritage of a bold, if not modern, Britain: "When I get too old to pull a trigger and lay a man down, then I'm ready to go." He was an able warrior until the last.

He never forgot that he was born and bred an aristocratic gentleman. No definite purpose, pattern, or design ever held him to routine work or financial gain. Understandably, fortune never smiled for him, and he came to the end poor in goods but proudly independent.

The call of honor and high adventure carried him through a vivid and colorful career that has few equals for fantastic deed and peerless daring in all our history. In the lush woods of Florida, on the Staked Plains of Texas, in the cool crags of the Rockies, and on the shimmering sands of the desert, Jeff Davis Milton was simply Sir William Wallace on a cow horse.

The hostile growth of the Arizona desert, resisting drought and death with seemingly indomitable fortitude, had cast its lacy and lovely shade for him for sixty years. And when his tempestuous life gave way to death, his frail widow carried his ashes back to where the stark saguaros reverently lift their arms in silent but suppliant dignity to the God of the bright and eternal skies.

His spirit will be at home in the awesome bosom of the desert, dancing in delight with her wildest storms, rejoicing in vivid color when that stern but honest earth bursts into bloom. While far away, across that land of vast space and brilliant sunshine,

415

challenging still to bold adventure, beckon his beloved Big Ajos, crimson glory in the setting sun—a proper monument to his sturdy nature and his flaming soul.

So long as free people burnish the bright badge of courage, cherish the traditions of genuine chivalry, and revere the memory of honorable men, so long they should not forget him.

Index

417

418

a clerk, 93; as deputy at Murphyville, 97; to N. M., 102; shot, 113;
files on claim, 114; returns to Florida,
115; cost of Patterson trial, 115; held
up, 143; marksmanship, 153; mescal
smuggler, 173; smallpox, 176; the
saddlemaker, 184; trouble with
Hamilton, 188; firing, 196; trouble
with porter, 198; chief of police,
213 ff.; and Selman, 218; and Hardin,
228 ff., 245; in Juárez, 240; with
Wells Fargo, 252 ff.; at Nogales, 258;
in jail at Nogales, 259; at Nayarit,
261 ff.; after Black Jack, 271 ff.;
Stein's Pass holdup, 281 ff.; after
Bronco Bill, 290; Fairbank holdup,
305 ff.; will, 309; trouble with Alvord, 314; mine claims, 320 ff.; oil
prospecting, 324 ff.; Oil and Development Co., 326; practices medicine,
331 ff.; catching Chinamen, 342 ff.;
horses, 355; and Greenway, 367;
meets Mildred Taitt, 372; courtship,
372 ff.; marriage, 373; birds, 374;
grace, 377; and the reds, 378 ff.;
diary, 379; letters, 380; in Belgium,
380; sense of location, 400; last
years, 403 ff.; death, 415
Milton, Mrs. Jeff D. (Mildred Taitt):
viii, 281 n., 305 n., 368, 374, 377, 378
Milton, John (poet): 4
Milton, Governor John: 3–4; marriage,
5; death, 5
Milton, John (brother): 7
Milton, Homer Virgil: 4
Mitchell County, Tex.: 27; organized,
48
M'Rose, Martin: 228 ff.; death, 241
M'Rose, Beula: 242
Mobeetie, Tex.: 18
Mount Blanco: 18
Mount Fra Cristoval: 140
Monument Draw, Tex.: 232–33
Monument Springs, N. M.: 35
Mountain lions: 155
Mountain sheep: 383
Mogollon Mountains: 103–104
Monahan's Wells, Tex.: 57
Monte: 99
Money, dutiable: 269
Monkeys, hunting: 337
Montezuma Hotel (Nogales): 270
Moore, Bill: 152, 185, 187

Moore, W. C.: 122
Moraga, José G.: 326
Morgan (well-driller): 148
Morley, Wm. Raymond: 255
Mormon Battalion: 154
Morrison, Allen: 15, 21
Morrow, Carson: 284 n., 402
Mossman, B. C.: 125, 312
Mothersill, Phillip: 139
Mule deer: 388
Mule: skinners, 43; pack, 391
Mulege, Mex.: 331
Murphee, Sam: 55
Murphy, Dan (Daniel): 93; sketch of,
96 n.
Murphy, Helen: viii
Murphy, John: viii
Murphyville, Tex.: 93
Murray, Pink: 393
Muskgrave, George: 268
Musquiz, Camp: 84
Musquiz Canyon: 64
Musquiz, Manuel: 64
Mustangs: nature, 16; desert, 391
Mustang Springs, Tex.: 57

Nasworthy, John: wagon yard, 37
Nature, economy of: 383
Navasota, Tex.: 14, 15, 54
Navajo Springs, Ariz.: 138
Nayarit, Mex.: 261
Negroes: 6, 9, 36, 204; troops, 62; at
Fort Davis, 95
Nevill, Bob: 34
Nevill, C. L.: 61, 63; nature, 76–77;
as sheriff, 95–96
Newman, Jim: 266
New Mexico Fair: 143
Nigger Annie: 199
Nigger Head Gap, Mex.: 314
Nigger Joe: 193
Night guard: 140
Nimitz Hotel (San Angelo, Tex.): 36
Nimmo, Rufe: 216
Nip and Tuck Saloon (Colorado
City): 45
Noble, J. S.: 196
North Canyon: 114, 131
Northern, John: 229
Nogal Canyon: 117
Nogales, Ariz.: 255 ff.; holdup, 268

Oasis, The: 254, 259, 363

425

Oberwetter, Oscar: 29
Oden, B. A.: 229 n.
Oglesby, Capt. T. L.: 69
Oil: 327; prospecting, 324; spring, 337; venture in Lower California, 328 ff.
Olds, Billy: 345
One-Lunger's Club: 224
Oro Blanco, Ariz.: 155, 255
Ortega, Cipriano: 156
Orsay, Henry: 23
Ossenberg shirt: 8
Oury, W. S.: 147; death, 166
Outlaws: 60, 129; captured, 128; "High Fives," 271; fight at Deer Creek, 272; horses, 273; nature, 288; Santag and Evans, 175
Overton, William F.: 254, 305
Owens, Commodore: 144
Owens, George: 305
Owens, Louis: 305

Pace, T. P.: 81
Padgett saddle: 29
Pajarito Mountains: 270
Palace Hotel (Tucson): 151
Palo Pinto: 54
Panguingui: 153
Pankey, Rube: 117 n.
Papagoes: 369, 384; Indians, 149, 154; squaw man, 152, land, 157; morals, 179; trial, 181; reservation, 370, 378; church, 372; Jeff's friends, 388; name for Milton, 390 n.
Parham, Young: 110
Parker, Daisy: 5 n.
Parker, Frank W.: 290
Parker, Jim: 171, 350
Parks, Harry: 303 n.
Parks, Jim: 278 n., 312
Parramore, D. D.: 267 n., 266
Parlor car: 195
Parlor Saloon (El Paso): 244
Paso del Norte Hotel (El Paso): 211
Patagonia Mountains: 176
Patterson, Charlie: 210
Patterson, W. P.: 49–50; character, 52
Paugh, Old Man: 39
Paul, Bob: 152
Payne, Floyd: 234
Peak, June: 27
Pecos River: 59
Pecos County, Tex.: 60 n.
Pecos, Tex.: 65; character, 67

Peña Colorado, Tex.: 84, 86
Perkins, George C.: 333
Peterson, Gustave: 20, 396; death, 398 ff.
Petmecky's gun shop: 29
Phillips, John M.: 381
Phosphates: 328; discovery, 334
Piano, packed: 319
Piety: 185
Pima County, Ariz.: 151, 195
Pinacate Mountains: 383, 386
Pipkin, Red: 299
Pistol: 29–30
Pittman, Park: 211
Plancha de la Plata: 318
Plaster, Bill: 172, 310
Plaza, Upper: 110, 164
Poker: 82, 185
Politics: frontier, 195; El Paso, 210
Potter, Tuck: 268
Powell, Gage, and Gano (surveyors): 85
Prairie dogs: 42, 384
Practical jokes: 120
Preacher, frontier: 19, 276
Presbyterian mission: 369
Presidio County, Tex.: 60 n., 94
Presidio del Norte, Mex.: 82
Presidio, Tex.: 83 n.
Prize fight, frontier: 224
Proctor, Frank: 359
Prospecting: 318 ff.; in Tabasco, 334 ff.
Profanity: 413
Pruitt, P. H.: 73
Puertocito, N. M.: 292
Pullman work: 197 ff.
Pumpelly, Raphael: 158 n.
Pyne, Carl: 288 n.

Quail: 383
Queen, Vic: 232
Queléle (Papago): 179
Quemado, N. M.: 119
Quijotoa: mining camp, 180; Mountains, 386
Quiroz, Nacho: 157 n.
Quitobaquito: Lake, 157; Jeff's camp, 345

Rabbit stew: 42
Radicals deported: 378
Raht, C. G.: 65 n.
Railroads: Texas and Pacific, 42;

426

Southern Pacific, 43; effect, 43; character of crews, 44; construction, 65; reach the Pecos, 66; changes wrought, 67; proposed by Greenway, 366
Railston, Cole: 125 n.
Rainey, Tom: 137 n.
Ramsdell, C. W.: 10 n.
Ranching, in N. M.: 104–105
Randolph, Epes: 294
Rangers: reunion, *viii*; 22, 23, 132, 167; in camp, 25–26; country, 26; prayer, 28; equipment, 29; guns, 30; rations, 31; mail, 31; love letters, 32; to San Angelo, 37; inspection, 39; trouble at Colorado City, 50; at Colorado City, 53; at Graham, 53; Company E, 63; Company B, 66; scouting, 68; in court, 69; escorts, 77; sickness, 80; trial at Abilene, 89; Jeff quits, 93
Ranger Lake: 35
Rattlesnake: 298, 385; oil for rheumatism, 202
Rawhide: 73; buckets, 158
Reconstruction: 8
Redondo, Jesús: 161
Redondo's Well, Ariz.: 162
Reed, Billy: 149, 187
Reed, Jim: 119
Reed, S. B.: 275
Reed, S. G.: 43 n.
Reed, Scott: 125 n.
Remuda: 16
Reynolds, Mrs. Tom: 255 n.
Rice, Lee: 50 n.
Riggs, Lee A.: 147 n.
Riggs' ranch: 293
Río Grande River: 60; surveying, 84–85
Roberts, Bill: 49, 70, 79
Roberts, Capt. D. W.: 43, 52, 56
Roberts, Ed: 269
Roberts, Governor O. M.: 60
Roberts, W. H.: 28 n.
Robinson, Corporal Charlie: 51, 66
Robinson, Stud: 42, 89
Robles' Well, Ariz.: 159
Robson, Frank: 270
Rockefellow, J. A.: 171 n.
Rogers, Kim Ki: 138
Rogers and Daley (Bar N Cross ranch): 139
Rook, Dave: 277

Rook's Well: 281, 283, 280
Rooney, Nigger Annie: 222
Roosevelt, Theodore: 340, 358
Roskruge, George J.: 151
Ross, Bob: 213
Ross, Edmund G.: 123, 143
Rurales: 281
Russell, Bill: 82, 36
Russell, Charlie: 114, 122, 144, 132
"Russell's Army": 123
Ryan, Con: 244
Ryan, Fatty: 281
Rynning, Tom: 360

Saddlemaker: 184
Saponaris (smuggler): 344
Sage-Brush Bill: 288
Saint, Joe. E.: 137
Saloons, troubles: 67
Salt Flats, Tex.: 60
Salt deposits (Gulf): 157
San Angelo, Tex.: 27; jurisdiction, 65
San Antonio Pass: 270
San Bernardino Grant: 169
San Carlos, Ariz.: 295
Sanderson, Tex.: 68
San Domingo, Mex.: 382
San Francisco River: 104
San Gregorio Bay: 327
San Juanico Bay: 328
San Juan Bautista, Mex.: 336
San Marcial, N. M.: 102, 116, 136, 142
San Mateo Mountains: 103
San Pedro Valley: 322, 350
San Rafael: Grant, 169; de Valle, 169 n.; ranch, 359
Santa Cruz: 148; County, Ariz., 357 n.
Santo Domingo, Sonora, Mex.: 156
Santa Fe Railway: 103; robbery, 291
Santa Helena Canyon: 85
Santa Rita Mountains: 343
San Simon Cattle Co.: 266
San Xavier, Ariz.: 149, 155
San Xavier Hotel (Tucson): 148
"Sammie Behind the Gun": 272
Sasabe, Sonora, Mex.: 165
Satterwhite, Judge: 183
Saxon, Harry: 340, 357
Sawed Horn Cattle Company: 15
Scarborough, George: 19–20, 233, 294, 284, 317, 403
Schaefer, Joe: 273
Schmitt, Martin F.: 155 n.

INDEX

Sykes, Godfrey: 381
Sylvania: plantation, 6; ranch, 400

Taitt, George P.: 373n.
Taitt, Mildred: see Mrs. Jeff D. Milton
Tally brand: 140
T. and P.: see Texas and Pacific Railway
Tank dump: 272
Tankersley, Mrs. Frank: 36
Tarantula: 175
Target practice: 126
Taylor, John J.: 211
Taylor-Sutton feud: 227
Teepe City, Tex.: 18
Tellurium: 319
Tevis, W. S. ("Cap"): 281, 324, 375
Texas and Pacific Railway: 41, 205; building road, 42–43, 57, 58
Texas State Historical Association: ix
Thacker, Eugene: 294
Thacker, John W.: 304
Thirst, deaths from: 159ff.
Thomas, Blub: 39
Thomas, Beverly, G.: 211
Thompson, Albert W.: 280n.
Thorp, Jack: 288n.
Tigre Mine: 318–19
Timber prospecting: 337
Tinajas Altas: 159, 400
Toddy, Old Jordan: 353
Tombstone, Ariz.: 12, 45; stage, 305; bank robbery, 397; trial, 311, 403
Tornillo: 143
Townsend, E. E.: 83n.
Tough towns: 41
Toyah Springs, Tex.: 67
Trans-Pecos: 58
Trentham, Charlie: 38, 50, 81, 83, 89, 132
Tubac, Ariz.: 155, 176
Tucson, Ariz.: 147; nature, 149; life, 178, 182
Tule Desert: 158
Tule Viejo, Ariz.: 161
Tumacacori, Ariz.: 155
Turkeys, jerky: 319
Turpentine weed: 387
Twitchell, R. E.: 137n.
Turtles: 329
Twohig, John: 77
Tyson, Capt.: 61

Union Oil Co.: 333
Upshur and Stevens: see Stevens and Upshur

Vandale, Earl: *viii*; library, 229n.
Verdugo, Manuel: 182
Vega Blanca ranch: 125
Ventana ranch: 346
Victorio (Apache chief): 123
Victoria Land and Cattle Co.: 327, 375
Virgin, John: 103, 114
Vinegaroon: 68, 69–70
VVN ranch: 229

Wabash Cattle Company: 144
Wagon Rod ranch: 375
Wakefield, Johnnie: 345
Walker, Dan: 118, 143
Walker, J. D.: 233
Wallace, George E.: 210
Wallace, Sir William: on a cowhorse, 415
Waller, John: 73n.
Walnut Gulch: 310
Walters, Bronco Bill: *vii*; death, 301
Walters, Lorenzo: 268n.
Warderman, Bill: 281
Wandlous, George: 123
Ware, Dick: 24, 28, 32, 48, 57, 252
Warner, Opie L.: 175n.
Warner ranch: 355
Weadock, Jack: 181n.
Weatherford, Tex.: 54
Webb, George: 342, 346, 358, 378, 403
Webb, Sam: 340
Webb, Walter Prescott: 24n.
Weem's store (at Separ, N. M.): 271
Weiler, Tillie: 215
Welch, Guy: 362, 397
Wells, desert: 158–59; digging, 106
Wells, Fargo & Co.: 252n., 301ff.
Wells, Ranger: 50
Werner, Jim: 27
Whalen, J. P.: 284n.
Wheeler, Harry: 397
Wheeler, Judge T. B.: 89
White Mountains: 137, 265, 291
White, Houston: 310
White, Owen P.: 214n.
White, Scott: 278, 304, 310, 312n.
Wickersham, D. W.: 273
Wigwam Saloon (El Paso): 249
Wilcox, Nick: 185

JEFF MILTON: A Good Man with a Gun

HAS BEEN SET ON THE LINOTYPE

IN THE CALEDONIA TYPE FACE

DESIGNED BY W. A. DWIGGINS

UNIVERSITY OF OKLAHOMA PRESS

NORMAN